CHAMBERS
An imprint of Chambers Harrap Publishers Ltd
7 Hopetoun Crescent
Edinburgh, EH7 4AY

First published by Chambers Harrap Publishers Ltd 2003

A CIP catalogue record for this book is available from the British Library.

ISBN 0550 10066 0

Designed and typeset by Chambers Harrap Publishers Ltd, Edinburgh
Printed and bound in Malaysia

Contents

Contributors

Project Editor
Hazel Norris

Editor
Rosalind Fergusson

Publishing Manager
Patrick White

Editorial Assistance
Eleanor Holme

Prepress
Marina Karapanovic

*The editors would like to acknowledge with
thanks the assistance and advice of the following:*

Briar Hill Lower School, Northampton
Hatherleigh Community Primary School,
Hatherleigh, Devon
Ide First School, Ide, Exeter
Woodlands Junior School, Tonbridge, Kent

*The editors would also like to acknowledge the use of
material in the Spelling Rules by George W. Davidson*

Preface

Chambers School Spelling has been designed for use by students aged 10-14, but will also be useful for both younger and older pupils. The book was compiled to address the requirements for spelling of the National Curriculum in England and Wales, and the Curriculum and Assessment in Scotland National Guidelines.

The aim of the book is to provide a quick reference for finding correct spellings as and when needed, and also to give guidance to help users permanently improve their spelling. Thousands of words are covered, from short and simple words for younger pupils to longer, more challenging words for older students.

For quick reference, a selection of 200 commonly misspelt words of varying difficulty is given in the Worst Words Hit List, each with a fun mnemonic or helpful hint to help the user remember the correct spelling. These words are also highlighted in blue in the main text, with the note given in an eye-catching box. Notes are also supplied at words that are often confused in their spelling or usage, such as *board* and *bored*, to help the user pick the right word.

Of particular benefit to students are the panels, which provide interesting information on specific spelling topics such as prefixes and letter patterns. These have been specially written to support classroom teaching of spelling, and to encourage active participation by pupils. Additional tips throughout the text cover strategies for learning spellings at school and at home, whilst supplementary material, such as a list of spelling rules, aids in building a firm base for the consolidation of students' spelling skills.

An invaluable addition to the Chambers School range, *Chambers School Spelling* will help pupils of all ages to spell with confidence. We hope that it generates interest in, and understanding of, the importance of good spelling, and that it will help students develop spelling skills which will be invaluable both in their studies and in the future.

How to use this Book

This spelling book helps you to spell words correctly. If you know which word you want to write, but do not know how it is spelt, then you can look it up in this book. It will not tell you what the words mean – for that you should use a dictionary, such as *Chambers School Dictionary*. But it will help you to find and use the right spelling, and help you to remember how to spell it again the next time.

Finding a Word

You might wonder how, if you do not know how to spell a word, you can find it to look it up! The answer is to think about the first two letters of the word, as these are often easy to guess. In the blue bar at the top of each page, the first two letters of the first word on the page and the first two letters of the last word on the page are given. This shows you the series of words that appear in alphabetical order on that page. So, for example, if you want to find the word *necessary*, you should look for the page which begins:

na-	227	**ne-**

Sometimes a word starts with a silent letter and so it is more difficult to find it using the first two letters. In this case, a key is given at the start of the letter and repeated at the bottom of each page, reminding you that you might have to look elsewhere. So if the word you are looking for sounds as if it starts with 'N', it suggests you could look instead under 'GN', 'KN', 'PN' or 'MN' for the word.

Inflections and Hyphens

Inflections for words in this book are only given if they do not change in the expected way, if they are complicated or unusual, or if you might be unsure how to form them. Information on inflections is given in the panel on p.179 and in the Spelling Rules section. Some nouns in this book have more than one plural, and if both forms are common, then both are given.

Sometimes it is possible to spell a word with or without a hyphen, or write it either as one word or two. In this book the most common form of a word is shown, as this is the one you should use in your own writing. This does not necessarily mean that any spellings you might see elsewhere are wrong.

Really Difficult Words

If it is an especially difficult word to spell, it may be given at the front of the book, in the Worst Words Hit List. Each word in this list has a helpful hint how to remember the spelling in future, so that the next time you want to use it you might not have to look it up again. These hints are also repeated in boxes in the main part of the book, and the difficult word is highlighted in blue:

necessary

> ❶ One collar and two sleeves are necessary on a shirt.

Words which are Easy to Confuse

Lots of people have trouble remembering which is the correct way to spell words which sound alike. For example, does a bride walk down the *isle* or the *aisle*? If a word is easy to confuse with another one, it is often highlighted in blue and there is a box next to it with a warning symbol. The box reminds you that it is easily confused, and gives an example sentence which shows the correct sense of the word:

aisle

> 🔥 Do not confuse with **isle** *the aisle of the church*

Spelling Focus Panels and Spelling Tips

There are Spelling Focus panels throughout the book which explain how spelling works, and which help you understand some particularly important topics. They also suggest fun games and exercises for you to try. Similarly, Spelling Tips suggest ways of learning tricky spellings at school and at home.

Supplements

At the back of this book you will find other information to help you. The Appendix: Quick Reference section has useful lists, for example days of the week, numbers and countries. The Glossary of Spelling Terms explains some spelling-related terms you might come across in this book or at school. And there are Spelling Rules for you to refer to if you are stuck on a tricky point, or want to learn more.

List of Spelling Focus Panels

List of Spelling Tips

Worst Words Hit List

There are some words that most people find difficult to spell. Here are 200 of the really tricky ones, with a tip to help you remember them. Sometimes we have split the word up to show another word hiding inside, and sometimes the word is broken down into syllables – these words are easy to spell if you say them slowly in your head. For some words we remind you of a spelling rule, and for many others we suggest mnemonics – rhymes or guides. Use these tips to improve your spelling for good!

abbreviation
An **abb**reviation is the **b**eginning **b**it of a word.

accelerator
A **c**ar-**c**razy **ele**phant pressed the **accele**rator to the floor.

accessible
Remember, **I** am always accessible.

accidentally
He acci**dent**ally shot a **c**lose **c**omrade and **ally**.

accommodation
Good a**cc**o**mm**odation has **c**omfortable **c**hairs and **m**odern **m**achines.

achieve
Ach**ie**ve follows the rule: **i** before **e**, except after **c**.

across
There's only one sea [one **c**] to get a**c**ross.

address
Letters are **d**irectly **d**elivered, **s**afe and **s**ound.

aerial
With this **a**erial **e**veryone **r**eceives **i**mportant **a**nnouncements **l**ive.

aeroplane
All **e**ngines **r**unning **OK** before take-off.

almond
An **al**mond has an o**val** shape.

although
Although there is only one **l**…

argument
Chew over an ar**gum**ent!

assassination
Word within word: **ass-ass**-i-**nation**

asthma
Asthma may be caused by sensitivity to household mites.

autumn
Autumn ends in November.

bachelor
Word within word: b-**ache**-lor

battalion
A batt**alion** includes two **t**'s and a **lion**.

beautiful
Big elephants **a**re **u**sually **beau**tiful.

beginning
We **n**eed a **n**ew begin**n**ing.

believe
Don't be**lie**ve a **lie**.

biscuit
The bis**cuit** was **c**ut **u**p **i**nto **t**iny pieces.

broccoli
Bro**cc**oli may **c**ause **c**ramp **o**r **l**ight **i**ndigestion.

business
Work **busi**ly at your **busi**ness.

calendar
A cal**e**ndar shows the **end** of the ye**ar**.

ceiling
The **cei**ling **c**overs **e**verything **i**nside.

cemetery
Word within word: ce-**meter**-y

changeable
Word within word: **change-able**

chaos
Cyclones, **h**urricanes **a**nd **o**ther storms cause **chaos**.

character
Charlie **a**cts **ter**ribly – what a **character**!

column
At the end of each colum**n** is an **n**.

committee
Many **m**eetings **t**ake **t**ime – everyone's exhausted!

competition
Word within word: com-**pet**-ition

conscience
Word within word: con-**science**

consensus
Word breakdown: con-sen-sus

continuous
Word breakdown: con-tin-u-ous

correspondence
She **correc**ts **corre**spon**den**ce in the **den**.

definitely
Word within word: de-**finite**-ly

deliberate
It was a de**liberate** attempt to **liberate** the captives.

description
Word within word: de-**script**-ion

desperate
In des**per**ate **per**il!

diarrhoea
Diarrhoea? **R**un **r**apidly **h**ome **o**r **e**lse – **a**wful!

disappear
Remember – a single **s** and a pair of **p**'s.

disappoint
Remember – a single **s** and a pair of **p**'s.

doubt
It's right to **be** in doub**t**.

draughty
An **u**npleasant **g**ale **h**owled **t**hrough the **draught**y building.

eccentric
He's as **ec**centric as a **c**razy **c**amel.

eczema
Even **c**lever **z**ebras **may** have **eczema**.

embarrass
I went **r**eally **r**ed and **s**miled **s**hyly.

embodiment
Word within word: embo-**dime**-nt

environment
Word within word: env-**iron**-ment

exaggerate
A br**agger** will always ex**agger**ate.

exceed
There's no **exc**use to **exc**eed that sp**ee**d.

excellent
Word within word: ex-**cell**-ent

exhaust
Don't ex**haust** yourself **hau**ling **st**ones.

experience
Word breakdown: ex-per-i-ence

explanation
Word breakdown: ex-plan-a-tion

fascinate
Science fa**sci**nates me.

February
Feb**r**uary is so cold you go '**Brrr**!'

fierce
Fighting **i**s **e**specially **fie**rce.

foreign
Bef**or**e **I** g**o** **n**orth to **foreign** lands…

forty
Forty **for**gets the **u**.

friend
Share your **fri**es with your **frie**nd.

fulfil
Remember – both **full** and **fill** drop extra **l**'s.

gauge
To **gauge** is to **get** **a** **u**seful **g**eneral **e**stimate.

genuine
Word breakdown: gen-u-ine

ghastly
Go **h**ome **a**nd **s**tay **t**here, little **y**ob!

ghost
Gasp with **h**orror when you see a **gh**ost!

gorgeous
Word within word: **gorge**-ous

government
Governments gover**n**.

grammar
Grand**ma** is good at gram**mar**.

guarantee
Get up and rant about the guarantee.

guard
The guard has a gun.

guilty
You [u] and I are guilty.

haemorrhage
Haemorrhage – an emergency often requiring rapid hospital attention.

height
Height – everyone is guessing how tall.

humorous
Word breakdown: hu-mor-ous

hygiene
You get ill unless you follow the rules of hygiene.

illiterate
Word breakdown: il-lit-er-ate

immediately
Word within word: im-**media**-tely

independent
Word within word: in-**depend**-ent

indispensable
Only the most **able** people are indispens**able**.

innocent
In no century have more innocent people died.

innocuous
Innocuous ingredients are found in no curry.

inoculate
Can you **ino**culate a rh**ino** in **cul**ottes?

instalment
An inst**alment** is **a** little pay**ment**.

interrupt
It's really rude to interrupt.

irresistible
Word within word: ir-**resist**-ible

jealous
I'm not **jealous** of your lousy **jea**ns!

jewellery
A jew**eller** is a s**eller** of jew**eller**y.

jodhpurs
Remember the hidden **h** for **h**orse.

knowledge
Word within word: **know-ledge**

laughter
Loud **a**nd **u**ncontrolled **g**iggling **h**as **t**urned into **laught**er.

leisure
It's our **lei**sure time, so **l**et's **e**njoy **it**!

leopard
Leo pardoned the **leopard** for eating his sister.

liaise
You need two eyes [two **i**'s] to lia**i**se properly.

lieutenant
The **lieut**enant will **lie ut**terly still.

liquorice
Is water **liqu**id **or ice**?

listening
Word within word: **listen**-ing

maintenance
The **main ten**t is where the d**ance** is held.

manageable
Word within word: **man-age-able**

manoeuvre
Manoeuvre the **canoe u**p **v**iolent **r**apids.

marriage
Can you get **marri**ed at any **age**?

martyr
Word within word: m-**arty**-r

mayonnaise
Word breakdown: may-on-naise

medicine
I see [**c**] **I** n**e**ed some med**icine**.

millennium
A mil**lenn**ium is a lot **l**onger than **n**inety-**n**ine years.

miniature
Word breakdown: min-i-a-ture

miscellaneous
Word breakdown: mis-cell-a-ne-ous

mischief
Causing **h**avoc **is** excellent **f**un!

misspell
Don't **miss** an **s** out of **miss**pell.

mortgage
We took out a **mortgage** on the **mort**ar for the **garage**.

moustache
Your **moustache** looks like a **mou**se with **st**omach **ache**!

naive
Naive people are **a**wfully **i**nexperienced.

necessary
One **c**ollar and two **s**leeves are ne**c**e**ss**ary on a shirt.

neighbour
We invited **eigh**t of **our** neigh**bour**s.

niece
My **ni**ece is **ni**ce.

noticeable
Word within word: **not-ice-able**

nuisance
This **new** **u**mbrella **is a nuisa**nce.

obscene
He will cut any **scene** he considers ob**scene**.

occasion
It's an o**cc**a**s**ion to seize [two **c**'s] an **s**.

occurrence
Crimson **c**ats and **r**ed **r**abbits are rare o**ccurr**ences.

opportunity
Pick the **p**erfect o**pportun**ity to make your **fortune**.

parallel
Word within word: par-**all**-el

parliament
Liam is a Member of Par**liam**ent.

people
People **e**njoy **o**ther **p**eople's laughter everyday.

permanent
The **man** **ent**ered the country as a per**manent** resident.

perseverance
Word breakdown: per-sev-er-ance

Pharaoh
  Pyramids **h**ouse **a**ncient **r**elics **a**nd **o**ther **h**istorical items.

phenomenon
  Word breakdown: phen-o-men-on

phlegm
  People **h**ave **phleg**m in their throats, not their **leg**s.

physical
  Practice **h**elps **y**our **s**porty **phys**ical fitness.

playwright
  A play**wright** has to spell words **right**.

pneumonia
  People **n**ever **e**xpect **u**s to get **pneu**monia.

possession
  I'm in po**ss**e**ss**ion of four **s**'s.

precede
  To pre**ced**e is to be pla**ced** ahead.

prejudice
  People **re**ject **u**nfair **dice**.

privilege
  Word within word: privi-**leg**-e

proceed
  Pro**ceed** **c**arefully, **e**xamining **e**very **d**etail.

process
  The pro**c**e**ss** needs care for suc**c**e**ss**.

professor
  Word breakdown: pro-fes-sor

pronunciation
  Word breakdown: pro-nun-ci-a-tion

publicly
  He was public**l**y **c**leared of all blame.

pyjamas
  Put **y**our **py**jamas on.

questionnaire
  There are **n**o **n**ew questions in this questio**nn**aire.

queue
  There are two **u**gly **e**lves in the q**ue**ue.

receipt
  I want a recei**pt** for the cash **I p**aid them.

receive
Receive follows the rule: **i** before **e**, except after **c**.

recommend
I re**comm**end **co**oked **m**arshmallows.

refrigerator
There's a **fr**ightened **tiger** in the re**friger**ator.

reign
Rulers **e**verywhere **ign**ore their subjects.

relief
Relief follows the rule: **i** before **e**, except after **c**.

remember
Word breakdown: re-mem-ber

repetition
A parrot is a **pet** that loves re**pet**ition.

reservoir
The **reservoir** provides a **reserve of i**cy **r**ainwater.

restaurant
My **aunt rant**s about this rest**aurant**.

rhyme
Remember **h**ow **y**ou begin to **rhy**me.

rhythm
Rhythm **h**elps **y**ou **t**o **h**ear **m**usic.

righteous
Each **of us** is right**eous**.

satellite
Tell me what a sat**ell**ite is.

Saturday
You are [**u r**] happy on Satur**day**.

sausage
Sausages **a**re **u**sually **s**picy.

scissors
She **c**ut **i**t **s**nipping **s**wiftly – **o**uch!

secretary
Can your **secret**ary keep a **secret**?

seize
To **s**eize is to **s**natch **e**agerly **in**.

separate
To se**par**ate things is to keep them a**par**t.

sergeant
Word within word: **serge-ant**

shriek
I tried to shriek.

siege
Stuck inside, everyone got excited.

silhouette
The silent house was in silhouette.

sincerely
Word within word: **since-rely**

skilful
Remember – both skill and full drop extra l's.

spaghetti
You can't hide the elephant's two trunks in spaghetti.

sphinx
Some pyramids have a sphinx.

strength
Stretches never gain them height.

subtle
There's a silent unexpected b to learn in subtle.

succeed
Two c's and two e's will help you succeed.

success
Can cats use sixth sense for success?

supersede
Semi-detached houses will supersede all others.

surprise
You are [u r] in for a surprise – I'm giving you a rise!

technique
What's your technique for choosing nice questions?

temperature
Don't lose your temper at high temperatures.

tomorrow
Tomatoes ripen in rows.

truly
Answer truly – are you [r u] lying?

unfortunately
Tuna tastes especially lovely.

unwieldy
Something that's unwieldy isn't easily lifted.

vacuum
How does one see to use [one **c** two **u**'s] a va**cuu**m cleaner at night?

valuable
Unusual **a**ntiques are often val**ua**ble.

vehicle
I get **hic**cups when I'm in a ve**hic**le.

verruca
Barefoot **r**unning **r**ound **u**nder **c**over = ve**rruc**a!

villain
A **villa**in **wi**ll **c**ause **pain**.

Wednesday
Word breakdown: Wed-nes-day

weight
We **w**eigh **e**verything **i**n **g**rams **h**ere **t**oday.

weird
It's w**ei**rd that it's spelt **ei**.

wholly
Was the **holly wholly** destroyed?

women
Why **o**ld **m**en **e**njoy **n**agging!

wrath
We're **r**eally **a**ngry.

yacht
Yes, **a**ll **c**raft **h**ave **t**riangular sails.

yield
An **i**rate **e**lk will never y**ie**ld.

zoological
A **zoo** is the **logical** place to find animals.

a
aardvark
aback
abacus
  abacuses
abandon
  abandoned
  abandoning
abandonment
abase
  abased
  abasing
abasement
abashed
abate
  abated
  abating
abatement
abattoir
abbess
  abbesses
abbey
  abbeys
abbot
abbreviate
  abbreviated
  abbreviating
abbreviation

---

❶ An **ab**breviation is the **b**eginning **b**it of a word.

---

abdicate
  abdicated

abdicating
abdication
abdomen
abdominal
abduct
abduction
abductor
aberrant
aberration
abet
  abetted
  abetting
abeyance
abhor
  abhorred
  abhorring
abhorrence
abhorrent
abhorrently
abide
  abided, abode
  abiding
abiding
ability
  abilities
abject
abjection
abjectly
ablative
ablaze
able
  abler
  ablest
able-bodied

ablutions
ably
abnormal
abnormality
  abnormalities
abnormally
aboard

💣* Do not confuse with **abroad** *aboard the ship • All aboard!*

---

abode
abolish
abolition
abolitionism
abolitionist
abominable
abominably
abominate
  abominated
  abominating
abomination
Aboriginal
Aborigine
abort
abortion
abortionist
abortive
abound
about
about-face
about-turn
above
above board

abracadabra
abrasion
abrasive
abrasively
abrasiveness
abreast
abridge
 abridged
 abridging
abridgement,
 abridgment
abroad

✷ Do not confuse
with **aboard** *He goes
abroad on holiday •
There's a rumour
abroad*

abrupt
abruptly
abruptness
abscess
 abscesses
abscond
absconder
abseil
 abseiled
 abseiling
absence
absent
absentee
absenteeism
absently
absent-minded
absent-mindedly
absent-mindedness
absinthe
absolute
absolutely
absolution
absolutism
absolutist

absolve
 absolved
 absolving
absorb
absorbed
absorbency
 absorbencies
absorbent
absorbing
absorption
abstain
 abstained
 abstaining
abstainer
abstemious
abstemiously
abstention
abstinence
abstinent
abstract
abstracted
abstractedly
abstraction
abstruse
absurd
absurdity
 absurdities
abundance
abundant
abundantly
abuse
 abused
 abusing
abusive
abusively
abusiveness
abut
 abutted
 abutting
abuzz
abysmal
abysmally

abyss
 abysses
abyssal
acacia
academic
academically
academy
 academies
accede
 acceded
 acceding
accelerate
 accelerated
 accelerating
acceleration
accelerator

❶ A **car**-**c**razy
elephant pressed the
accelerator to the
floor.

accent
accentuate
 accentuated
 accentuating
accentuation
accept

✷ Do not confuse
with **except** *to accept a
gift • to accept his
decision*

acceptability
acceptable
acceptably
acceptance
access

✷ Do not confuse
with **excess** *access to
the motorway • He has
access to his children •
to access information
on a computer*

accessibility
accessible

❶ Remember, **I** am always accessible.

accessibly
accession
accessory
 accessories
accident
accidental
accidentally

❶ He accident**ally** shot a close comrade and **ally**.

accident-prone
acclaim
 acclaimed
 acclaiming
acclaimed
acclamation
acclimatization,
 acclimatisation
acclimatize,
 acclimatise
 acclimatized,
 acclimatised
 acclimatizing,
 acclimatising
accolade
accommodate
 accommodated
 accommodating
accommodation

❶ Good accommodation has comfortable chairs and modern machines.

accompaniment
accompanist
accompany

accompanies
accompanied
accompanying
accomplice
accomplish
accomplishable
accomplished
accomplishment
accord
accordance
according
accordingly
accordion
accordionist
accost
account
accountability
accountable
accountant
accredit
 accredited
 accrediting
accreditation
accredited
accrual
accrue
 accrued
 accruing
accumulate
 accumulated
 accumulating
accumulation
accumulator
accuracy
accurate
accurately
accursed
accusation
accusative
accuse
 accused
 accusing

accuser
accusingly
accustom
 accustomed
 accustoming
accustomed
ace
acellular
acerbic
acerbity
acetate
acetic

☛* Do not confuse with **ascetic** *Vinegar contains acetic acid*

acetone
acetylene
ache
 ached
 aching
achievable
achieve
 achieved
 achieving

❶ Achi**eve** follows the rule: **i** before **e**, except after **c**.

achievement
achiever
achy
acid
acidic
acidify
 acidifies
 acidified
 acidifying
acidity
acidly
acknowledge
 acknowledged
 acknowledging

acknowledgement,
  acknowledgment
acne
acorn
acoustic
acoustically
acoustics
acquaint
acquaintance
acquaintanceship
acquainted
acquiesce
  acquiesced
  acquiescing
acquiescence
acquiescent
acquire
  acquired
  acquiring
acquisition
acquisitive
acquit
  acquitted
  acquitting
acquittal
acre
acreage
acrid
acridly
acrimonious
acrimoniously
acrimony
acrobat
acrobatic
acrobatically
acrobatics
acronym
acropolis
across

❶ There's only one sea
[one **c**] to get a**c**ross.

acrostic
acrylic
act
acting
action
actionable
action-packed
activate
  activated
  activating
activation
active
actively
activism
activist
activity
  activities
actor
actress
  actresses
actual
actuality
actually
actuarial
actuary
  actuaries
acuity
acumen
acupressure
acupuncture
acupuncturist
acute
acutely
acuteness
ad

✎* Do not confuse
with **add** *an ad in the
paper*

adage
adagio
  adagios

adamant
adamantly
Adam's apple
adapt
adaptability
adaptable
adaptation
adapter

✎* Do not confuse
with **adaptor** *the
adapter of a play for TV*

adaptor

✎* Do not confuse
with **adapter** *an
adaptor for an electrical
plug*

add

✎* Do not confuse
with **ad** *to add two
numbers*

addendum
  addenda
adder
addict
addicted
addiction
addictive
addition

✎* Do not confuse
with **edition** *the
addition of the numbers
• an addition to the
family*

additional
additionally
additive
addle
  addled
  addling
add-on

address
addresses

❶ Letters are **d**irectly **d**elivered, **s**afe and **s**ound.

addressee
adenoidal
adenoids
adept
adeptly
adequacy
adequate
adequately
adhere
adhered
adhering
adherence
adherent
adhesion
adhesive
ad hoc
adieu
adieus, adieux
ad infinitum
adjacent
adjectival
adjectivally
adjective
adjoin
adjoined
adjoining
adjoining
adjourn
adjourned
adjournment
adjudicate
adjudicated
adjudicating
adjudication
adjudicator
adjunct

adjust
adjustable
adjustment
ad-lib
ad-libbed
ad-libbing
admin
administer
administered
administering
administrate
administrated
administrating
administration
administrative
administratively
administrator
admirable
admirably
admiral
admiralty
admiration
admire
admired
admiring
admirer
admiring
admiringly
admissibility
admissible
admissibly
admission
admit
admitted
admitting
admittance
admittedly
admonish
admonishing
admonishingly
admonition
admonitory

ad nauseam
ado
adobe
adolescence
adolescent
adopt
adopted
adoption
adoptive
adorable
adorably
adoration
adore
adored
adoring
adorer
adoring
adoringly
adorn
adornment
adrenal
adrenaline
adrift
adroit
adroitly
adroitness
adulation
adulatory
adult
adulterate
adulterated
adulterating
adulteration
adulterer
adulteress
adulteresses
adulterous
adulterously
adultery
advance
advanced
advancing

advanced
advancement
advantage
advantageous
advantageously
advent
adventure
adventurer
adventurous
adventurously
adverb
adverbial
adverbially
adversarial
adversary
adversaries
adverse

♦* Do not confuse with **averse** *in adverse circumstances*

adversely
adversity
adversities
advert
advertise
advertised
advertising
advertisement
advertiser
advertising
advice

♦* Do not confuse with **advise** *She gave him good advice* Remember that **ice** is a noun.

advisability
advisable
advise
advised
advising

♦* Do not confuse with **advice** *to advise him to go*

advised
advisedly
adviser
advisory
advocaat
advocacy
advocate
advocated
advocating
aeon, eon
aerate
aerated
aerating
aeration
aerial

ⓘ With this **a**erial everyone **r**eceives **i**mportant **a**nnouncements **l**ive.

aerially
aerobatics
aerobic
aerobics
aerodrome
aerodynamic
aerodynamically
aerodynamics
aeronaut
aeronautics
aeroplane

ⓘ **A**ll engines **r**unning **OK** before take-off.

aerosol
aesthete
aesthetic
aesthetically
afar

affability
affable
affably
affair
affect

♦* Do not confuse with **effect** *Will her nervousness affect her playing?*

affectation
affected
affectedly
affection
affectionate
affectionately
affective
affidavit
affiliate
affiliated
affiliating
affiliation
affinity
affinities
affirm
affirmation
affirmative
affix
afflict
affliction
affluence
affluent

♦* Do not confuse with **effluent** *the affluent society*

afford
affordable
afforest
afforestation
affray
affront
aficionado

aficionados
afield
afloat
afoot
aforementioned
aforesaid
afraid
afresh
aft
after
afterbirth
after-effect
afterlife
aftermath
afternoon
aftershave
aftertaste
afterthought
afterwards
again
against
agape
agar
agate
age
 aged
 ageing, aging
aged
ageism
ageist
ageless
agency
 agencies
agenda
agent
age-old
aggrandize,
 aggrandise
 aggrandized,
 aggrandised
 aggrandizing,
 aggrandising

aggrandizement,
 aggrandisement
aggravate
 aggravated
 aggravating
aggravating
aggravatingly
aggravation
aggregate
aggression
aggressive
aggressively
aggressiveness
aggressor
aggrieved
aggro
aghast
agile
agilely
agility
aging
 another spelling of
 ageing
agitate
 agitated
 agitating
agitated
agitatedly
agitation
agitator
agnostic
agnosticism
ago
agog
agonies
agonize, agonise
 agonized, agonised
 agonizing, agonising
agonized, agonised
agonizing,
 agonising
agonizingly,

agonisingly
agony
 agonies
agoraphobia
agoraphobic
agrarian
agree
 agreed
 agreeing
agreeable
agreeably
agreement
agricultural
agriculturally
agriculture
aground
ahead
aid

🖋* Do not confuse
with **aide** *aid for the
poor • come to their aid*

aide

🖋* Do not confuse
with **aid** *the president's
aide*

AIDS, Aids
aikido
ail
 ailed
 ailing

🖋* Do not confuse
with **ale** *What ails her?*

aileron
ailing
ailment
aim
 aimed
 aiming
aimless
aimlessly

air
aired
airing

● * Do not confuse
with **heir** *fresh air*

airbag
airbase
airbed
airborne
airbrush
 airbrushes
air-conditioned
air-conditioner
air-conditioning
aircraft
air-drop
 air-dropped
 air-dropping
aired
airfield
air force
air-gun
airily
airing
airless
airlift
airline
airlock
airmail
airport
air-raid
airship
airsick
airspace
airstream
airstrip
airtight
airway
airy
 airier
 airiest

aisle

● * Do not confuse
with **isle** *the aisle of the
church*

ajar
akimbo
akin
à la carte
alacrity
à la mode
alarm
alarmed
alarming
alarmingly
alarmist
alas
albatross
 albatrosses
albeit
albino
 albinos
album
alchemist
alchemy
alcohol
alcoholic
alcoholism
alcove
al dente
alder
alderman
 aldermen
ale

● * Do not confuse
with **ail** *two pints of ale*

alert
alertly
alertness
alfalfa
alfresco

algae
algebra
algebraic
alias
 aliases
alibi
 alibis
alien
alienate
 alienated
 alienating
alienation
alight
 alighted
 alighting
align
alignment
alike
alimentary
alimony
alive
alkali
 alkalis
alkaline
all
Allah
allay
 allayed
 allaying

● * Do not confuse
with **alley** *to allay his
fears*

allegation
allege
 alleged
 alleging
alleged
allegedly
allegiance
allegorical
allegorically

allegory
  allegories
allegro
  allegros
alleluia
all-embracing
allergic
allergy
  allergies
alleviate
  alleviated
  alleviating
alleviation
alley
  alleys

❥* Do not confuse
with **allay** *a bowling
alley • He ran down the
alley*

alliance
allied
allies
alligator
alliterate

❥* Do not confuse
with **illiterate** *Sand,
sea and sun alliterate*

alliteration
alliterative
allocate
  allocated
  allocating
allocation
allopathic
allot
  allotted
  allotting

❥* Do not confuse
with **a lot** *allot some
time for homework*

allotment
all-out
allow
  allowed
  allowing

❥* Do not confuse
allowed with **aloud** *she
was allowed to go out*

allowable
allowance
alloy
all-purpose
all right
all-round
all-rounder
allspice
all-time
allude
  alluded
  alluding

❥* Do not confuse
with **elude** *She did not
allude to the matter*

allure
  allured
  alluring
alluring
alluringly
allusion

❥* Do not confuse
with **delusion** or
illusion *She made no
allusion to the matter*

allusive
allusively
alluvial
alluvium
  alluvia
ally
  allies

allied
allying
almanac
almighty
almond

ⓘ An **al**mond has an
oval shape.

almost
alms
alms-house
aloe
aloft
alone
along
alongside
aloof
aloofness
a lot

❥* Do not confuse
with **allot** *a lot of people*

aloud

❥* Do not confuse
with **allowed** *he read
aloud to the class*

alp
alpha
alphabet
alphabetical,
  alphabetic
alphabetically
alphabetize,
  alphabetise
  alphabetized,
  alphabetised
  alphabetizing,
  alphabetising
alphanumeric
alphanumerical
alphanumerically
alpine

already
alright

🔷* It is best to spell this as two words **all right**. Some people consider the spelling **alright** to be incorrect.

alsatian
also
altar

🔷* Do not confuse with **alter** *the priest at the altar*

alter
altered
altering

🔷* Do not confuse with **altar** *to alter your plans • to alter a dress*

alterable
alteration

🔷* Do not confuse with **altercation** *an alteration to my plans • an alteration to my dress*

altercation

🔷* Do not confuse with **alteration** *The altercation ended in a fight*

alter ego
alternate
alternated
alternating
alternately

🔷* Do not confuse with **alternatively** *alternately hot and cold*

alternative
alternatively

🔷* Do not confuse with **alternately** *You could go by bus, or alternatively you could go by train*

alternator
although

🛈 Although there is only one l…

altimeter
altitude
alto
 altos
altogether
altruism
altruist
altruistic
altruistically
aluminium
alumnus
 alumni
alveolus
 alveoli
always
Alzheimer's disease
am
amalgam
amalgamate
 amalgamated
 amalgamating
amalgamation
amaretti
amaretto
amass
amateur

🔷* Do not confuse with **amateurish** *an amateur golf player*

amateurish

🔷* Do not confuse with **amateur** *an amateurish attempt at building a shed*

amateurishly
amaze
 amazed
 amazing
amazement
amazing
amazingly
ambassador
ambassadress
 ambassadresses
amber
ambidexterity
ambidextrous
ambience
ambient
ambiguity
 ambiguities
ambiguous
ambiguously
ambition
ambitious
ambitiously
ambivalence
ambivalent
ambivalently
amble
 ambled
 ambling
ambrosia
ambulance
ambush
 ambushes
ameliorate
 ameliorated
 ameliorating
amelioration

amen
amenable
amend

●* Do not confuse
with **emend** *to amend
the law*

amendment
amenity
 amenities
amethyst
amiable

●* Do not confuse
with **amicable** *an
amiable young man*

amiably
amicable

●* Do not confuse
with **amiable** *on
amicable terms • an
amicable separation*

amicably
amid, amidst
amiss
ammonia
ammonite
ammunition
amnesia
amnesiac
amnesty
 amnesties
amoeba
 amoebas, amoebae
amok, amuck
among, amongst
amoral

●* Do not confuse
with **immoral** *an
amoral person doesn't
know right from wrong*

amorality

amorous
amorously
amorousness
amount
amp
amperage
ampere, ampère
ampersand
amphetamine
amphibian
amphibious
amphitheatre
ample
amplification
amplifier
amplify
 amplifies
 amplified
 amplifying
amplitude
amply
amputate
 amputated
 amputating
amputation
amputee
amuck
 another spelling of
 amok
amulet
amuse
 amused
 amusing
amused
amusedly
amusing
amusingly
amusement
an
anabolic steroids
anachronism
anachronistic

anachronistically
anaconda
anaemia
anaemic
anaerobic
anaesthesia
anaesthetic
anaesthetist
anaesthetize,
 anaesthetise
 anaesthetized,
 anaesthetised
 anaesthetizing,
 anaesthetising
anagram
anal
analgesic
analogous
analogy
 analogies
analysable
analyse
 analysed
 analysing
analysis
 analyses
analyst
analytic
analytical
analytically
anarchic
anarchical
anarchist
anarchistic
anarchy
anathema
anatomical
anatomically
anatomist
anatomy
ancestor
ancestral

ancestry
anchor
 anchored
 anchoring
anchorage
anchorman
 anchormen
anchorwoman
 anchorwomen
anchovy
 anchovies
ancient
and
andante
androgynous
android
anecdotal
anecdote
anemone
aneurysm, aneurism
anew
angel

✦* Do not confuse
with **angle** *an angel
from heaven • Be an
angel and help me*

angelic
angelically
anger
 angered
 angering
angina
angle
 angled
 angling

✦* Do not confuse
with **angel** *an angle of
90° • a new angle on the
story • to angle the
camera • to angle for a
job*

angler
Anglican
anglicism
anglicize, anglicise
 anglicized,
 anglicised
 anglicizing,
 anglicising
angling
anglophile,
 Anglophile
anglophone,
 Anglophone
Anglo-Saxon
angora
angrily
angry
 angrier
 angriest
angst
anguish
anguished
angular
angularity
animal
animate
 animated
 animating
animated
animatedly
animation
animator
animosity
aniseed
ankle
anklet
annals

✦* Do not confuse
with **annuals** *The
Annals of the Parish •
in the annals of crime*

annex, annexe
 annexes

✦* The spelling
annexe is only used for
the noun *build an
annexe to the house • to
annex a country*

annexation
annihilate
 annihilated
 annihilating
annihilation
anniversary
 anniversaries
annotate
 annotated
 annotating
annotation
announce
 announced
 announcing
announcement
announcer
annoy
 annoyed
 annoying
annoyance
annoyed
annoying
annoyingly
annual
 annuals

✦* Do not confuse
annuals with **annals**
Christmas annuals

annually
annuity
 annuities
annul
 annulled
 annulling

annulment
anodyne
anoint
anomalous
anomaly
 anomalies
anon
anonymity
anonymous
anonymously
anorak
anorexia (nervosa)
anorexic
another
answer
 answered
 answering
answerable
ant

🌢* Do not confuse
with **aunt** *An ant has
six legs*

antacid
antagonise
another spelling of
 antagonize
antagonism
antagonist
antagonistic
antagonistically
antagonize,
 antagonise
 antagonized,
 antagonised
 antagonizing,
 antagonising
anteater
antecedent
antechamber
antedate
 antedated

antedating
antelope
antenatal
antenna
 antennae, antennas
anteroom
anthem
ant-hill
anthology
 anthologies
anthracite
anthrax
anthropological
anthropologist
anthropology
anti-aircraft
antibiotic
antibody
 antibodies
anticipate
 anticipated
 anticipating
anticipation
anticipatory
anticlimactic
anticlimax
 anticlimaxes
anticlockwise
antics
anticyclone
antidepressant
antidote
antifreeze
antihero
 antiheroes
antihistamine
antimatter
antioxidant
antipasto
 antipasti, antipastos
antipathy
antiperspirant

antipodean
antipodes
antiquarian
antiquated

🌢* Do not confuse
with **antique**
antiquated ideas

antique

🌢* Do not confuse
with **antiquated** *an
antique table • a
valuable antique*

antiquity
 antiquities
anti-Semitic
anti-Semitism
antiseptic
antisocial
antithesis
 antitheses
antler
antonym
anus
 anuses
anvil
anxiety
 anxieties
anxious
any
anybody
anyhow
anyone
anything
anyway
anywhere
aorta
apart
apartheid
apartment
apathetic
apathetically

SPELLING  *focus*

Apostrophes

The *apostrophe* is a punctuation mark (') that can cause spelling problems.

Apostrophes of omission

When you write a short form such as *I'm* (instead of *I am*) or *couldn't* (instead of *could not*), you usually put an apostrophe in the place of the missing letters and close up the space between the words. Here are some examples of these short forms, which are called *contractions*:

is or has → 's: **he's, here's**   are → 're: **we're, you're**
have → 've: **I've, you've**   will or shall → 'll: **you'll, he'll**
had or would → 'd: **you'd, it'd**   not → n't: **isn't, haven't**

There are two exceptions, *shan't* (*shall not*) and *won't* (*will not*), which both change slightly in other ways as well.

Be careful with the **n't** ending – remember that the apostrophe replaces the **o** of *not*. Also watch out for the **'ve** ending, especially in *could've*, *should've* and *would've* – do not write *of* instead of **'ve**. Remember that **'ve** represents *have*.

Can you put the apostrophe in the correct place in these contractions?

wheres _____	were _____	theyve _____	well _____
shed _____	dont _____	cant _____	mustnt _____

Here are some full forms. Can you write the correct contraction next to each?

what is _____	they are _____	I have _____
you will _____	it had _____	he would _____
was not _____	should not _____	

Apostrophes are used in a similar way in words like *ma'am* (short for *madam*), *o'clock* (short for *of the clock*), and *'tis* (short for *it is*), and in phrases like *rock 'n' roll* or *pick 'n' mix*.

Some contractions are homophones, for example *they're* and *their*, *you're* and *your*, and *who's* and *whose*. Make sure you know the difference.

you're: you are   **who's: who is** or **who has**
your: belonging to you   **whose: belonging to which person**

Apostrophes continued

Apostrophes of possession

The possessive apostrophe shows who or what has or does something, or how long something takes.

- You use **'s** after a singular noun, as in *the dog's tail*, *Friday's newspaper*, *a full day's work*, and *the bus's wheels*.

- You also use **'s** after a plural noun that does not end in **s**, as in *children's books*, *people's favourites* and *women's rights*.

- If something belongs to someone, the apostrophe comes after the owner's name, as in *Jack's bike*, *Lisa's book*, and *Rover's lead*.

- You use an apostrophe alone after plural nouns ending in **s**, as in *the dogs' leads*, *my parents' fault*, *a boys' school*, and *in two hours' time*.

- You also sometimes use an apostrophe alone after names or other words ending in **s**, as in *Archimedes' principle*, *for goodness' sake*, and *Mrs Jones' cakes*. Using the apostrophe alone in this way is becoming more common as it is easier to say, although in the past you would always have added **'s** (*Charles Dickens's novels*).

Remember that words like *hers*, *ours*, *yours* and *theirs* do not have apostrophes, even though they show possession.

It's and its

Many people have trouble deciding when to use **it's** and when to use **its**. Remember:

It's: it is or **it has**   **Its: belonging to it**

Remember that it is only if you could substitute **it is** or **it has** in the sentence that you should use an apostrophe. Fill in the gaps in the following passage with the correct form, **its** or **it's**:

I have a sick parrot. _____ been off _____ food for days, and now _____ started pulling out _____ feathers with _____ beak. I bought some new toys for _____ cage, but _____ no better. I guess _____ time to call the vet!

Can you make up any sentences which use both **it's** and **its**?

apathy
ape
 aped
 aping
aperitif
 aperitifs
aperture
apex
 apexes, apices
aphid
aphrodisiac
apiary
 apiaries
apices
apiece
aplomb
apocalypse
apocalyptic
apocryphal
apologetic
apologetically
apologize,
 apologise
 apologized,
 apologised
 apologizing,
 apologising
apology
 apologies
apoplectic
apoplexy
apostle
apostrophe
apothecary
 apothecaries
apotheosis
 apotheoses
appal
 appalled
 appalling
apparatus
 apparatuses

apparel
apparent
apparently
apparition
appeal
 appealed
 appealing
appear
 appeared
 appearing
appearance
appease
 appeased
 appeasing
appeasement
appendage
appendectomy
appendicitis
appendix
 appendixes,
 appendices
appertain
 appertained
 appertaining
appetiser
 another spelling of
 appetizer
appetising
 another spelling of
 appetizing
appetite
appetizer, appetiser
appetizing,
 appetising
applaud
applause
apple
appliance
applicable
applicant
application
applicator

appliqué
apply
 applies
 applied
 applying
appoint
appointee
appointment
apportion
 apportioned
 apportioning
apposite
appositeness
apposition
appraisal
appraise
 appraised
 appraising
appraiser
appreciable
appreciably
appreciate
 appreciated
 appreciating
appreciation
appreciative
apprehend
apprehension
apprehensive
apprehensively
apprentice
apprenticeship
apprise
 apprised
 apprising
approach
 approaches
approachable
approbation
appropriate
 appropriated
 appropriating

appropriately
appropriateness
appropriation
approval
approve
 approved
 approving
approvingly
approximate
 approximated
 approximating
approximately
approximation
après-ski
apricot
apron
apropos of
apse
apt
aptitude
aptly
aptness
aqualung
aquamarine
aquaplane
aquarium
 aquaria, aquariums
aquatic
aqueduct
arabesque
arable
arachnid
arbiter
arbitrarily
arbitrariness
arbitrary
arbitrate
 arbitrated
 arbitrating
arbitration
arbitrator
arboreal

arboretum
 arboreta
arbour
arc

> 💧* Do not confuse
> with **ark** *the arc of a*
> *circle* Remember that
> an arc is a **c**urve.

arcade
arcane
arch
 arches
archaeological
archaeologist
archaeology
archaic
archaically
archaism
archangel
archbishop
archdeacon
archduchess
archduke
arched
arch-enemy
archer
archery
archetypal
archetype
archipelago
 archipelagos,
 archipelagoes
architect
architectural
architecturally
architecture
archives
archivist
archway
arc-lamp,
 arc-light

arctic
ardent
ardently
ardour
arduous
arduousness
are

> 💧* Do not confuse
> with **our** *they are going*
> *out* • *the flowers are*
> *blue*

area
arena
aren't
areola
 areolae
arguable
arguably
argue
 argued
 arguing
argument

> ❶ Chew over an
> arg**u**ment!

argumentative
argumentatively
aria
arid
aridity
arise
 arose
 arisen
 arising
aristocracy
aristocrat
aristocratic
aristocratically
arithmetic
arithmetical
arithmetically
arithmetician

ark

💧* Do not confuse
with **arc** *Noah's ark*

arm
armada
armadillo
 armadillos
armageddon
armaments
armband
armchair
armed
armful
armies
armistice
armorial
armour
armoured
armoury
 armouries
armpit
army
 armies
aroma
aromatherapist
aromatherapy
aromatic
arose
around
arousal
arouse
 aroused
 arousing
arpeggio
 arpeggios
arrange
 arranged
 arranging
arrangement
array
 arrayed

 arraying
arrears
arrest
arresting
arrival
arrive
 arrived
 arriving
arrogance
arrogant
arrogantly
arrow
arrowroot
arsenal
arsenic
arson
arsonist
art
artefact, artifact
arterial
artery
 arteries
artful
artfully
arthritic
arthritis
arthropod
artichoke
article
articulate
 articulated
 articulating
articulately
articulation
artifact
 another spelling of
 artefact
artifice
artificial
artificiality
artificially
artillery

artisan
artist

💧* Do not confuse
with **artiste** *a portrait
artist • songs recorded
by different artists*

artiste

💧* Do not confuse
with **artist** *a circus
artiste*

artistic
artistically
artistry
artless
artwork
arty
 artier
 artiest
as
asbestos
ascend
**ascendancy,
 ascendency**
**ascendant,
 ascendent**
ascension
ascent

💧* Do not confuse
with **assent** *the ascent
of the mountain*
Remember that ascent
involves **c**limbing.

ascertain
 ascertained
 ascertaining
ascertainable
ascetic

💧* Do not confuse
with **acetic** *Monks
lead ascetic lives*

ascetically
asceticism
ascribable
ascribe
  ascribed
  ascribing
asexual
ash
  ashes
ashamed
ashamedly
ashen
ashes
ashore
ashtray
aside
asinine
ask
askance
askew
asleep
asp
asparagus
aspartame
aspect
aspen
asperity
aspersion
asphalt
asphyxia
asphyxiate
  asphyxiated
  asphyxiating
asphyxiation
aspic
aspidistra
aspirant
aspirate
  aspirated
  aspirating
aspiration
aspire

aspired
aspiring
aspirin
aspiring
ass
  asses
assail
  assailed
  assailing
assailant
assassin
assassinate
  assassinated
  assassinating
assassination

> ❶ Word within word:
> **ass-ass-i-nation**

assault
assemblage
assemble
  assembled
  assembling
assembly
  assemblies
assent

> ◆* Do not confuse
> with **ascent** *The
> Queen gave her assent
> to the new Bill*

assert
assertion
assertive
assertively
assertiveness
assess
assessment
assessor
asset
assiduity
assiduous
assiduousness

assign
assignation
assignment
assimilable
assimilate
  assimilated
  assimilating
assimilation
assist
assistance
assistant
assizes
associate
  associated
  associating
association
assonance
assorted
assortment
assuage
  assuaged
  assuaging
assume
  assumed
  assuming
assumed
assumption
assurance
assure
  assured
  assuring
assured
assuredly
aster
asterisk
astern
asteroid
asthma

> ❶ **Asthma** may be
> caused by sensitivity to
> household mites.

asthmatic
asthmatically
astonish
astonishing
astonishment
astound
astounded
astounding
astoundingly
astral
astray
astride
astringency
astringent
astrologer
astrological
astrologically
astrology

> ◉* Do not confuse
> with **astronomy**
> *Astrology deals with
> the signs of the zodiac*

astronaut
astronomer
astronomical
astronomically
astronomy

> ◉* Do not confuse
> with **astrology** *He is
> studying physics and
> astronomy*

astrophysicist
astrophysics
astute
astutely
astuteness
asunder
asylum
asymmetric
at
ate

atheism
atheist
atheistic
athlete
athletic
athletically
athletics
atlas
  atlases
atmosphere
atmospheric
atmospherically
atmospherics
atoll
atom
atomic
atomize, atomise
  atomized, atomised
  atomizing,
  atomising
atomizer, atomiser
atone
  atoned
  atoning
atonement
atrium
  atria, atriums
atrocious
atrociousness
atrocity
  atrocities
atrophy
  atrophies
  atrophied
  atrophying
attach
attaché
attaché-case
attached
attachment
attack
attacker

attain
  attained
  attaining
attainable
attainment
attempt
attend
attendance
attendant
attention
attentive
attentively
attentiveness
attenuate
attenuation
attest
attestation
attic
attire
  attired
  attiring
attitude
attorney
  attorneys
attract
attraction
attractive
attractively
attractiveness
attributable
attribute
  attributed
  attributing
attribution
attributive
attrition
attune
  attuned
  attuning
aubergine
auburn
auction

auctioned
auctioning
auctioneer
audacious
audacity
audibility
audible
audibly
audience
audio
audiotypist
audiovisual
audit
audited
auditing
audition
auditor
auditorium
auditoria,
auditoriums
auditory
au fait
augment
augmentation
augmentative
au gratin
augur
augured
auguring
august
auk
aunt

🖊* Do not confuse with **ant** *She visited her aunt in London* Remember a**unt** and **unc**le.

auntie
au pair
aura
auras

aural

🖊* Do not confuse with **oral** *The music exam includes an aural test* Remember that a**ural**, a**udible**, and a**udio** have to do with hearing.

aurally
aurora
auroras
aurora borealis
auspices
auspicious
austere
austerely
austerity
authentic
authentically
authenticate
authenticated
authenticating
authentication
authenticity
author
authorisation
another spelling of **authorization**
authorise
another spelling of **authorize**
authoritarian
authoritative
authority
authorities
authorization,
authorisation
authorize, authorise
authorized,
authorised
authorizing,

authorising
autism
autistic
autobiographer
autobiographical
autobiography
autobiographies
autocracy
autocracies
autocrat
autocratic
autocue
autograph
automate
automated
automating
automatic
automatically
automation
automaton
automata,
automatons
automobile
automotive
autonomous
autonomy
autopilot
autopsy
autopsies
auto-reverse
autoteller
autumn

🄸 Autumn ends in November.

autumnal
auxiliary
auxiliaries
avail
availed
availing
availability

available
avalanche
avant-garde
avarice
avaricious
avenge
 avenged
 avenging
avenger
avenue
aver
 averred
 averring
average
 averaged
 averaging
averse

✎* Do not confuse
with **adverse** *I'm not
averse to work*

aversion
avert
aviary
 aviaries
aviation
aviator
avid
avocado
 avocados
avocet
avoid

avoidable
avoidably
avoidance
avoirdupois
avow
avowal
avowed
avowedly
await
 awaited
 awaiting
awake
 awoke
 awoken
 awaking
awaken
 awakened
 awakening
award
aware
awareness
awash
away
awe
awe-inspiring
awesome
awestruck
awful
awfully
awfulness
awhile

awkward
awkwardly
awkwardness
awl
awning
awoke
awoken
awry
axe
 pl axes
 axed
 axing

✎* Do not confuse
axes with **axis** *axes for
chopping wood*

axiom
axiomatic
axis
 axes

✎* Do not confuse
with **axes**, the plural of
axe *turning on an axis*

axle
ayatollah
aye

✎* Do not confuse
with **eye** *Aye, aye,
captain!*

azalea
azure

B

babble
 babbled
 babbling
babe
baboon
baby
 babies
 babied
 babying
babyhood
babyish
babysit
 babysat
 babysitting
**babysitter,
 baby-sitter**
bachelor

ⓘ Word within word:
b-**ache**-lor

bachelorhood
bacillus
 bacilli
back
backache
backbench
backbencher
backbiting
backbone
backbreaking
backcloth
backcomb
backdate
 backdated

 backdating
backdrop
backer
backfire
 backfired
 backfiring
backgammon
background
backhand
backhanded
backing
backlash
backlog
backpack
backpacker
backpacking
back-pedal
 back-pedalled
 back-pedalling
backside
backslide
 backslid
 backsliding
backspace
 backspaced
 backspacing
backstage
backstroke
backtrack
backup
backward
backwards
backwater
bacon

bacteria
bacterial
bacteriologist
bacteriology
bacterium
 bacteria
bad
 worse
 worst

💧* Do not confuse
with **bade** *a bad boy* •
bad for your health

bade

💧* Do not confuse
with **bad** *They bade me
wait* • *He bade her
farewell*

badge
badger
 badgered
 badgering
badly
 worse
 worst
badminton
bad-tempered
baffle
 baffled
 baffling
bag
 bagged
 bagging
bagel

baggage
bagged
bagginess
bagging
baggy
 baggier
 baggiest
bagpipes
baguette
bail
 bailed
 bailing

✎* Do not confuse
with **bale** *released on
bail* • *bail him out of
prison* • *the bail was
knocked off the wicket*
You can use **bail** or
bale for **bail out** of an
aircraft or **bail out**
water.

bailiff
bain-marie
bairn
bait
 baited
 baiting

✎* Do not confuse
baited with **bated** *He
baited his line*

baize
bake
 baked
 baking
baker
bakery
 bakeries
balaclava
balalaika
balance
 balanced

 balancing
balcony
 balconies
bald
baldness
bale

✎* Do not confuse
with **bail** *a bale of
cotton* You can use
bale or **bail** for **bale
out** of an aircraft or
bale out water.

baleful
balefully
balk, baulk
ball

✎* Do not confuse
with **bawl** *a ball of wool*
• *a tennis ball* • *dance
with him at the ball*

ballad
ballast
ball-bearings
ballcock
ballerina
ballet

✎* Do not confuse
with **ballot** *a ballet
dancer*

balletic
ballistic
balloon
 ballooned
 ballooning
ballot
 balloted
 balloting

✎* Do not confuse
with **ballet** *vote in a
secret ballot*

ballpark
ballpoint
ballroom
balm
balmy
 balmier
 balmiest
balsam
balsawood
balti
balustrade
bamboo
bamboozle
 bamboozled
 bamboozling
ban
 pl bans
 banned
 banning

✎* Do not confuse
bans with **banns** *bans
on smoking and
drinking*

banal
banality
 banalities
banana
band
bandage
 bandaged
 bandaging
bandana
bandeau
 bandeaux
bandit
bandstand
bandwagon
bandy
 bandies
 bandied
 bandying

bandy-legged
bane
bang
banger
banging
bangle
banish
banishment
banister
banjo
 banjos, banjoes
bank
banker
banknote
bankrupt
bankruptcy
 bankruptcies
banner
banns

✎* Do not confuse
with **bans** *marriage
banns*

banoffee pie
banquet
 banqueted
 banqueting
banshee
bantam
banter
 bantered
 bantering
baptise
 another spelling of
 baptize
baptism
baptismal
Baptist
baptize, baptise
 baptized, baptised
 baptizing, baptising
bar

barred
barring
barb
barbarian
barbaric
barbarically
barbarism
barbarity
 barbarities
barbecue
 barbecued
 barbecuing
barbed
barber
barbershop
barbican
barbiturate
bard
bare
 bared
 baring

✎* Do not confuse
with **bear** *bare legs • to
bare one's teeth*

bareback
barefaced
barefoot
barely
bareness
bargain
 bargained
 bargaining
barge
 barged
 barging
bargepole
baritone
barium
bark
barley
barmaid

barman
 barmen
bar mitzvah
barmy
barn
barnacle
barnyard
barometer
baron

✎* Do not confuse
with **barren** *He has the
title of baron*

baroness
 baronesses
baronet
baronetcy
baronial
baroque
barracks
barracuda
barrage
barre
barred
barrel
barren

✎* Do not confuse
with **baron** *barren
fields • a barren woman*

barrenness
barricade
 barricaded
 barricading
barrier
barring
barrister
barrow
bartender
barter
 bartered
 bartering
basalt

base
based
basing

🖋* Do not confuse
with **bass** *the base of
the lamp* • *use the office
as a base* • *run to first
base* • *to base an
argument on facts*

baseball
baseless
baseline
basement
bash
bashes
bashful
bashfully
basic
basically
basil
basilica
basilisk
basin
basis
bases
bask
basket
basketball
bas-relief
bass
basses, bass

🖋* Do not confuse
with **base** *a bass guitar*
• *the bass clef* • *the
basses in the choir* • *The
fisherman caught
several bass* The plural
bass is only used for
the fish.

bassist
bassoon

baste
basted
basting
bastion
bat
batted
batting
batch
batches
bated

🖋* Do not confuse
with **baited** *with bated
breath*

bath
bathed
bathing

🖋* Do not confuse
with **bathe** *to bath the
baby*

bathe
bathed
bathing

🖋* Do not confuse
with **bath** *to bathe in
the sea* • *to bathe a
wound*

bather
bathos
bathrobe
bathroom
bathtub
batik
batman
baton

🖋* Do not confuse
with **batten** *a
conductor's baton*

batsman
batsmen
batswoman

batswomen
battalion

ⓘ A batta**lion**
includes two **t**'s and a
lion.

batted
batten
battened
battening

🖋* Do not confuse
with **baton** *The joiner
put up a batten* • *Batten
down the hatches!*

batter
battered
battering
battering-ram
battery
batteries
batting
battle
battled
battling
battle-axe
battledress
battlefield
battlement
battleship
batty
bauble
baulk
another spelling of
balk
bauxite
bawl

🖋* Do not confuse
with **ball** *The child
began to bawl*

bay
bayed

baying
bayonet
bayoneted
bayoneting
bazaar, bazar

💣* Do not confuse
with **bizarre** *an
Eastern bazaar • a
church bazaar*

bazooka
be
am, is, are
was, were
been
being

💣* Do not confuse
with **bee** *to be helpful*

beach
beaches

💣* Do not confuse
with **beech** *a sandy
beach*

beachcomber
beachcombing
beacon
bead
beady
beagle
beak
beaker
beam
beamed
beaming
bean

💣* Do not confuse
with **been** *a French
bean*

beansprout
beanshoot
beanstalk

bear
bore
borne
bearing

💣* Do not confuse
with **bare** *a brown bear
• I can't bear the noise •
to bear the strain • to
bear children*

bearable
beard
bearded
bearer
bearing
bearskin
beast
beastliness
beastly
beastlier
beastliest
beat
beat
beaten

💣* Do not confuse
with **beet** *to beat time •
He beat her at tennis
yesterday • the
policeman's beat*

beatific
beatify
beatified
beatifying
beatitude
beatnik
beau
beaux, beaus

💣* Do not confuse
with **bow** *Her latest
beau is very handsome*

beauteous

beautician
beautiful

ℹ **B**ig **e**lephants **a**re
usually **beau**tiful.

beautifully
beautify
beautifies
beautified
beautifying
beauty
beauties
beaver
beavered
beavering
becalmed
became
because
beck
beckon
beckoned
beckoning
become
became
become
becoming
becoming
bed
bedded
bedding
bedazzle
bedazzled
bedazzling
bedbug
bedclothes
bedding
bedeck
bedevil
bedevilled
bedevilling
bedevilment
bedlam

bedpan
bedraggled
bedridden
bedrock
bedroom
bedsit
bedsitter
bedspread
bedstead
bed-wetting
bee

💧* Do not confuse
with **be** *a honey bee*

beech
beeches

💧* Do not confuse
with **beach** *a beech tree*

beef
beefburger
beefeater
beefy
beefier
beefiest
beehive
beekeeper
beeline
been

💧* Do not confuse
with **bean** or **being** *he
has been • they have
been*

beep
beeped
beeping
beeper
beer

💧* Do not confuse
with **bier** *a drink of
beer*

beeswax
beet

💧* Do not confuse
with **beat** *sugar beet*

beetle
beetroot
befall
befell
befallen
befalling
befit
befitted
befitting
befittingly
before
beforehand
befriend
befuddle
befuddled
befuddling
beg
begged
begging
began

💧* Do not confuse
with **begun** *It began to
rain*

beget
begot
begotten
begetting
beggar
beggared
beggaring
beggarly
begged
begging
begin
began
begun

beginning
beginning

ℹ️ We need a new
beginning.

begonia
begot
begotten
begrudge
begrudged
begrudging
beguile
beguiled
beguiling
begun

💧* Do not confuse
with **began** *It has
begun to rain • The
game was begun again*

behalf
behave
behaved
behaving
behaviour
behavioural
behead
behest
behind
behold
beheld
beholding
beholden
beholder
beige
being

💧* Do not confuse
with **been** *He is being
funny • a human being*

bejewelled
belabour
belaboured

belabouring
belated
belatedly
belch
belches
beleaguer
beleaguered
beleaguering
belfry
belfries
belie
belied
belying
belief
beliefs

💧* Do not confuse
with **believe** *her belief
in God • It's beyond
belief!*

believable
believe
believed
believing

❶ Don't be**lie**ve a **lie**.

💧* Do not confuse
with **belief** *to believe in
God*

believer
Belisha beacon
belittle
belittled
belittling
belittlement
bell

💧* Do not confuse
with **belle** *ring the bell •
a church bell*

belladonna
bell-bottoms
bell-boy

belle

💧* Do not confuse
with **bell** *the belle of the
ball*

belligerence
belligerent
bellow

💧* Do not confuse
with **below** *Bulls
bellow*

bellows
bell-ringer
belly
bellyache
belly-dance
belly-danced
belly-dancing
belly-dancer
belly-dancing
belly-flop
bellyful
belong
belongings
beloved
below

💧* Do not confuse
with **bellow** *below the
surface*

belt
beluga
belying
bemoan
bemoaned
bemoaning
bemuse
bemused
bemusing
bench
benches
benchmark

bend
bent
bending
bendy
beneath
benediction
benedictory
benefactor
benefice
beneficial
beneficially
beneficiary
beneficiaries
benefit
benefited
benefiting
benevolence
benevolent
benevolently
benign
benignly
bent
bequeath
bequest
berate
berated
berating
bereaved
bereavement
bereft
beret

💧* Do not confuse
with **berry** or **bury** *She
wore a blue beret*

bergamot
berry
berries

💧* Do not confuse
with **beret** or **bury** *a
holly berry*

berserk

berth

> ♦* Do not confuse
> with **birth** *a berth on a*
> *ship*

beryl
beseech
 beseeched, besought
 beseeching
beseechingly
beset
 beset
 besetting
beside

> ♦* Do not confuse
> with **besides** *standing*
> *beside the tree*

besides

> ♦* Do not confuse
> with **beside** *I have*
> *other friends, besides*
> *him*

besiege
 besieged
 besieging
besmirch
besotted
besought
bespoke
best
bestir
 bestirred
 bestirring
bestow
bestowal
bestseller
bestselling
bet
 bet, betted
 betting
beta

bête noire
 bêtes noires
betray
 betrayed
 betraying
betrayal
betroth
betrothal
betrothed
better
 bettered
 bettering
betterment
betting
between
bevel
 bevelled
 bevelling
beverage
bevy
 bevies
bewail
 bewailed
 bewailing
beware
bewilder
 bewildered
 bewildering
bewilderment
bewitch
beyond
bhangra
biannual
biannually
bias
 pl biases
 biased, biassed
 biasing, biassing
bib
Bible, bible
biblical, Biblical
bibliographer

bibliographic
bibliographical
bibliography
 bibliographies
bibliophile
bicarbonate
bicentenary
 bicentenaries
bicentennial
biceps
bicker
 bickered
 bickering
bicycle
bid
 bade, bid
 bidden, bid
 bidding
biddable
bidder
bide
 bided, bode
 biding
bidet
biennial
biennially
bier

> ♦* Do not confuse
> with **beer** *a funeral bier*

bifocal
bifocals
bifurcate
big
 bigger
 biggest
bigamist
bigamous
bigamy
bigger
biggest
bighead

big-headed
bight

🔹* Do not confuse
with **bite** or **byte** *A
bight is a small bay*

bigot
bigoted
bigotry
bigwig
bike
biker
bikini
 bikinis
bilateral
bilaterally
bilberry
 bilberries
bile
bilge
bilingual
bilingualism
bilious
bill
billboard
billet
 billeted
 billeting
billiards
billion
billionaire
billionairess
 billionairesses
billionth
billow
billowy
billycan
billy-goat
bimbo
bin
 binned
 binning

binary
bind
 bound
 binding
binder
binding
bindweed
binge
 binged
 bingeing, binging
bingo
binned
binning
binoculars
biochemical
biochemistry
biodegradable
biographer
biographical
biography
 biographies
biological
biologically
biologist
biology
bionic
biopsy
 biopsies
biplane
birch
 birches
bird
birdie
birdwatcher
birdwatching
Biro®
 Biros
birth

🔹* Do not confuse
with **berth** *the birth of
her child*

birthday
birthmark
birthplace
birthright
biscuit

ℹ️ The bis**cuit** was **c**ut
up **i**nto **t**iny pieces.

bisect
bisexual
bishop
bishopric
bison
bistro
 bistros
bit
bitch
 bitches
bitchiness
bitchy
 bitchier
 bitchiest
bite
 bit
 bitten

🔹* Do not confuse
with **bight** or **byte** *Did
the dog bite you?*

bitmap
 bitmapped
 bitmapping
bitten
bitter
bitterly
bittern
bitterness
bittersweet
bitty
bitumen
bivouac
 bivouacked
 bivouacking

bi-weekly
bizarre

> ☀* Do not confuse
> with **bazaar** *clowns*
> *wearing bizarre*
> *costumes* • *We met in*
> *bizarre circumstances*

blab
 blabbed
 blabbing
blabber
black
blackball
blackberry
 blackberries
blackbird
blackboard
blackcurrant
blacken
 blackened
 blackening
blackhead
blackjack
blackleg
blacklist
blackmail
 blackmailed
 blackmailing
blackmailer
blackness
blackout
black-pudding
blacksmith
bladder
bladderwrack
blade
blame
 blamed
 blaming
blameless
blameworthy

blanch
blancmange
bland
blank
blanket
 blanketed
 blanketing
blare
 blared
 blaring
blarney
blasé
blaspheme
 blasphemed
 blaspheming
blasphemer
blasphemous
blasphemy
 blasphemies
blast
blast-off
blatant
blaze
 blazed
 blazing
blazer
blazon
 blazoned
 blazoning
bleach
 bleaches
bleak
bleakly
bleakness
blearily
bleary
bleat
 bleated
 bleating
bleed
 bled
 bleeding

bleep
 bleeped
 bleeping
bleeper
blemish
 blemishes
blend
blender
bless
 blessed
 blessing
blessed
blessing
blether
 blethered
 blethering
blew

> ☀* Do not confuse
> with **blue** *She blew the*
> *whistle*

blight
blind
blindfold
blinding
blindness
blink
blinkered
blinkers
blip
bliss
blissful
blissfully
blister
 blistered
 blistering
blithe
blithely
blitz
 blitzes
blizzard
bloated

bloater
blob
bloc

♠* Do not confuse with **block** *nations of the Eastern bloc*

block

♠* Do not confuse with **bloc** *a block of wood • a block of flats • to block a pipe*

blockade
 blockaded
 blockading
blockage
blockbuster
blockhead
bloke
blond

♠* Do not confuse with **blonde** *blond hair*

blonde

♠* Do not confuse with **blond** *She's a blonde*

blood
bloodbath
bloodcurdling
bloodhound
bloodshed
bloodshot
bloodstained
bloodsucking
bloodthirsty
bloody
 bloodier
 bloodiest
bloom
 bloomed
 blooming

bloomers
blossom
 blossomed
 blossoming
blot
 blotted
 blotting
blotch
 blotches
blotched
blotchy
blotter
blotting paper
blouse
blow
 blew
 blown
 blowing
blow-by-blow
blow-dry
 blow-dries
 blow-dried
 blow-drying
blower
blowhole
blowlamp
blowtorch
 blowtorches
blowy
blubber
 blubbered
 blubbering
bludgeon
 bludgeoned
 bludgeoning
blue

♠* Do not confuse with **blew** *a blue sky*

bluebell
blueberry
 blueberries

bluebird
bluebottle
blue-chip
blue-collar
bluegrass
blueprint
blues
bluff
blunder
 blundered
 blundering
blunt
blur
 blurred
 blurring
blurb
blurt
blush
 blushes
bluster
 blustered
 blustering
boa
boa constrictor
boar

♠* Do not confuse with **boor** or **bore** *a wild boar*

board

♠* Do not confuse with **bored** *a board of directors • a wooden board • to board a ship*

boarder
boarding
boarding card
boarding house
boarding pass
 boarding passes
boarding-school
boardroom

boast

●* Do not confuse with **boost** *to boast about your results*

boastful
boastfully
boat
boater
boathook
boathouse
boating
boatswain, bosun
bob
 bobbed
 bobbing
bobbin
bobsleigh
bobtail
bode
 boded
 boding
bodge
 bodged
 bodging
bodice
bodily
body
 bodies
body-building
bodyguard
bodywork
boffin
bog
 bogged
 bogging
bogey
 bogeys
boggle
 boggled
 boggling
boggy

bogus
bohemian
boil
 boiled
 boiling
boiler
boisterous
bold
boldly
bolero
 boleros
bollard
bolshie, bolshy
bolster
 bolstered
 bolstering
bolt
bomb
bombard
bombardment
bombast
bombastic
bomber
bombshell
bombsite
bonanza
bond
bondage
bonding
bone
 boned
 boning
bonfire
bong
bongo
 bongos
bonhomie
bonk
bonkers
bonnet
bonny
 bonnier

bonniest
bonsai
bonus
 bonuses
bon voyage
bony
boo
 booed
 booing
booby
booby-trap
boogie
 boogied
 boogieing
book
bookable
bookcase
bookie

●* Do not confuse with **bouquet** *to bet with a bookie*

bookish
book-keeping
booklet
bookmaker
bookmark
bookseller
bookshelf
 bookshelves
bookshop
bookworm
boom
 boomed
 booming
boomerang
boon
boor

●* Do not confuse with **boar** or **bore** *an ill-mannered boor*

boorish

boost

💧* Do not confuse with **boast** *to boost his self-confidence* • *to boost her resistance to disease*

booster
boot
  booted
  booting
bootee

💧* Do not confuse with **booty** *a baby's bootee* Remember that babies wear bootees on their feet.

booth
bootleg
booty

💧* Do not confuse with **bootee** *booty from the wrecked ship*

booze
border
  bordered
  bordering
borderline
bore
  bored
  boring

💧* Do not confuse with **boar** or **boor** *He's a tiresome bore* • *to bore a hole* • *to bore the audience* • *She bore the burden*

bored

💧* Do not confuse with **board** *The audience looked bored*

boredom
boring
born

💧* Do not confuse with **borne** *He was born at midnight* • *newly born kittens*

borne

💧* Do not confuse with **born** *I couldn't have borne it any longer* • *He was borne on the shoulders of the crowd* • *She has borne four children*

borough
borrow
bosom
boss
  bosses
bossy
  bossier
  bossiest
bosun
  another spelling of
  boatswain
botanic
botanical
botanically
botanist
botany
botch
both
bother
  bothered
  bothering
bothersome
bothy
  bothies
bottle
  bottled

  bottling
bottleneck
bottom
  bottomed
  bottoming
bottomless
botulism
boudoir
bouffant
bough

💧* Do not confuse with **bow** *the bough of a tree*

bought

💧* Do not confuse with **brought** *She bought a house with her savings*

bouillon
boulder
boulevard
bounce
  bounced
  bouncing
bouncer
bouncy
  bouncier
  bounciest
bound
boundary
  boundaries
boundless
bounteous
bountiful
bounty
  bounties
bouquet

💧* Do not confuse with **bookie** *a bouquet of flowers*

bouquet garni
bourgeois
bourgeoisie
bout
boutique
bovine
bow

✒* Do not confuse
with **bough** or **beau** *to
bow one's head • tie the
ribbon in a bow*

bowels
bower
bowl
bow-legged
bowler
bowling
bowls
box
 boxes
boxer
boxing-glove
boy

✒* Do not confuse
with **buoy** *a boy and a
girl*

boycott
boyfriend
boyhood
boyish
boyishness
bra
brace
 braced
 bracing
bracelet
braces
bracing
bracken
bracket
 bracketed

 bracketing
brackish
brae

✒* Do not confuse
with **bray** *a steep brae*

brag
 bragged
 bragging
braggart
braid
braille
brain
 brained
 braining
brainchild
 brainchildren
brainless
brainstorm
brainstorming
brainteaser
brainwash
brainwashing
brainwave
brainy
 brainier
 brainiest
braise
 braised
 braising
brake
 braked
 braking

✒* Do not confuse
with **break** *the brake of
a bicycle • to brake
going round a corner*

bramble
bran
branch
 branches
brand

brandish
brand-new
brandy
 brandies
brash
brass
 brasses
brasserie

✒* Do not confuse
with **brazier** or
brassière *They ate at a
little brasserie*

brassière

✒* Do not confuse
with **brazier** or
brasserie *She bought a
new brassière*

brassily
brassy
brat
bravado
brave
 braved
 braving
bravely
bravery
bravo
bravura
brawl
brawn
brawny
 brawnier
 brawniest
bray
 brayed
 braying

✒* Do not confuse
with **brae** *the donkey
brays*

brazen

brazened
brazening
brazier

✱ Do not confuse
with **brassière** or
brasserie *a brazier of
burning coal*

Brazil nut
breach
breaches

✱ Do not confuse
with **breech** *a breach of
the peace* • *to breach
their defences*

bread

✱ Do not confuse
with **bred** *a loaf of
bread*

breaded
breadline
breadth
breadwinner
break
broke
broken
breaking

✱ Do not confuse
with **brake** *to break a
leg* • *a lunch break*

breakable
breakage
breakaway
breakdancing
breakdown
breaker
breakfast
break-in
breaking-point
breakneck
break-out

breakthrough
break-up
breakwater
breast
breastbone
breastfeed
breastfed
breastfeeding
breaststroke
breath

✱ Do not confuse
with **breathe** *a breath
of air* • *take a deep
breath*

breathalyse
breathalysed
breathalysing
Breathalyser®
breathe
breathed
breathing

✱ Do not confuse
with **breath** *to breathe
in and out*

breather
breathing
breathless
breathtaking
breathy
bred

✱ Do not confuse
with **bread** *She bred
racehorses* • *born and
bred*

breech
breeches

✱ Do not confuse
with **breach** *the breech
of a gun* • *a breech birth*

breeches

breed
bred
breeding
breeze
breezily
breezy
breezier
breeziest
breve
brevity
brew
brewer
brewery
breweries
brewing
briar, brier
bribe
bribed
bribing
bribery
bric-à-brac
brick
bricklayer
bridal

✱ Do not confuse
with **bridle** *The bridal
suite is for newly-weds*

bride
bridegroom
bridesmaid
bridge
bridged
bridging
bridle
bridled
bridling

✱ Do not confuse
with **bridal** *a horse's
bridle* • *ride along the
bridle path* • *to bridle in
anger*

Brie
brief
 briefs
briefcase
briefing
briefly
briefs
brier
 another spelling of
 briar
brigade
brigadier
brigand
bright
brighten
 brightened
 brightening
brightly
brightness
brilliance
brilliant
brilliantly
brim
 brimmed
 brimming
brimful
brimless
brimstone
brine
bring
 brought
 bringing
brink
briny
brioche
briquette
brisk
brisket
bristle
 bristled
 bristling
bristly

brittle
broach

💧* Do not confuse
with **brooch** *to broach
the subject*

broad
broadcast
 broadcast
 broadcasting
broadcaster
broaden
 broadened
 broadening
broadly
broad-minded
broadness
broadsheet
broadside
brocade
broccoli

ℹ️ Broccoli may cause
cramp or light
indigestion.

brochure
brogue
broil
 broiled
 broiling
broiler
broke
broken
broken-hearted
broker
brokerage
bromide
bronchial
bronchitic
bronchitis
bronco
 broncos
brontosaurus

bronze
bronzed
brooch
 brooches

💧* Do not confuse
with **broach** *a silver
brooch*

brood
broody
 broodier
 broodiest
brook
broom
broomstick
broth
brother
brotherhood
brother-in-law
 brothers-in-law
brotherly
brought

💧* Do not confuse
with **bought** *He
brought his dog to
school*

brouhaha
brow
browbeat
 browbeat
 browbeaten
 browbeating
brown
brownie
Brownie Guide
browning
browse
 browsed
 browsing
browser
bruise
 bruised

Look/Cover/Write/Check

Look/cover/write/check is a four-stage way of learning difficult spellings.

First you *look* at the word, then you *cover* it over and *write* it down from memory, then you uncover it to *check* that you have spelt it correctly. You can do this on your own, but it is more fun to do it with a friend. Here are some tricky words to practise with:

artificial delicious frightening desperate neighbour accommodation vegetable medicine

When you first look at the word, or if you get the spelling wrong, try to concentrate on the parts that you have problems with, or that are not spelt as they sound.

bruising
bruising
brûlé
brunch
brunches
brunette
brunt
bruschetta
bruschettas
brush
brushes
brush-off
brush-up
brushwood
brusque
brusquely
brusqueness
Brussels sprout
brutal
brutalise
another spelling of
brutalize
brutality
brutalize, brutalise
brutalized,
brutalised
brutalizing,

brutalising
brutally
brute
brutish
bubble
bubbled
bubbling
bubbly
buccaneer
buccaneering
buck
bucket
bucketed
bucketing
bucketful
bucketfuls
buckle
buckled
buckling
buckler
buckwheat
bucolic
bud
budded
budding
Buddhism
Buddhist

budding
buddleia
buddy
buddies
budge
budged
budging
budgerigar
budget
budgeted
budgeting
budgetary
budgie
buff
buffalo
buffaloes
buffer
buffered
buffering
buffered
buffet
buffeted
buffeting
buffoon
buffoonery
bug
bugged

bugging
bugbear
bug-eyed
buggy
 buggies
bugle
bugler
build
 built
 building
builder
building
build-up
built
built-up
bulb
bulbous
bulge
 bulged
 bulging
bulghar wheat
bulgy
bulimia
bulk
bulkhead
bulkily
bulky
 bulkier
 bulkiest
bull
bulldog
bulldoze
 bulldozed
 bulldozing
bulldozer
bullet
bulletin
bullet-proof
bullfight
bullfighter
bullfinch
 bullfinches

bullfrog
bullion
bullish
bullock
bull-ring
bull's-eye
bully
 bullies
 bullied
 bullying
bulrush
 bulrushes
bulwark
bum
bumbag
bumble
 bumbled
 bumbling
bumble-bee
bumf
 another spelling of
 bumph
bump
bumper
bumph, bumf
bumpkin
bumptious
bumptiousness
bumpy
 bumpier
 bumpiest
bun
bunch
 bunches
bundle
 bundled
 bundling
bung
bungalow
bungee
bungle
 bungled

 bungling
bunion
bunk
bunkbed
bunker
bunkum
bunny
 bunnies
Bunsen burner
bunting
buoy

 ●* Do not confuse
 with **boy** *a mooring
 buoy* Remember that a
 b**u**oy stays **up** **o**n the
 water.

buoyancy
buoyant
bur
 another spelling of
 burr
burble
 burbled
 burbling
burden
 burdened
 burdening
burdensome
burdock
bureau
 bureaux, bureaus
bureaucracy
 bureaucracies
bureaucrat
bureaucratic
bureau de change
burgeon
 burgeoned
 burgeoning
burger
burgh

burglar
burglary
 burglaries
burgle
 burgled
 burgling
burgundy
burial
buried
buries
burlesque
burly
 burlier
 burliest
burn
 burnt, burned
 burning
burner
burnish
burnt
burp
burr, bur
burrito
 burritos
burrow
bursar
bursary
 bursaries
burst
 burst
 bursting
bury
 buries
 buried
 burying

💣* Do not confuse
with **berry** or **beret** *to
bury the corpse*

bus
 buses
busby

busbies
bush
 bushes
bushed
bushel
bushy
 bushier
 bushiest
busier
busiest
busily
business
 businesses

❶ Work **busi**ly at your
business.

businesslike
businessman
 businessmen
businesswoman
 businesswomen
busk
busker
bust
bustle
 bustled
 bustling
bust-up
busty
busy
 busier
 busiest
busybody
 busybodies
but

💣* Do not confuse
with **butt** *nobody but
her* • *I asked him but he
didn't know*

butane
butch
butcher

butchery
butler
butt

💣* Do not confuse
with **but** *the butt of the
rifle* • *to butt in* • *The
goat may butt you*

butter
 buttered
 buttering
buttercup
butterfingers
butterfly
 butterflies
buttermilk
butterscotch
buttery
buttocks
button
 buttoned
 buttoning
buttonhole
 buttonholed
 buttonholing
buttress
 buttresses
butty
buxom
buy
 bought
 buying

💣* Do not confuse
with **by** or **bye** *to buy a
new computer*

buyer
buyout
buzz
 buzzes
buzzard
buzzer
buzzword

by

💧* Do not confuse with **buy** or **bye** *written by him • Stand by me!*

bye

💧* Do not confuse with **buy** or **by** *a bye in cricket • Bye! See you later!*

bye-bye

bye-law
another spelling of
by-law

by-election

bygone

by-law, bye-law

bypass
bypasses

by-product

bystander

byte

💧* Do not confuse with **bite** or **bight** *A byte is a measure of computer data*

byword

Cc

If the word you're looking for sounds as if it begins *ch* but you can't find it there, remember that **C** on its own can sometimes be pronounced *ch* (as in *cello* and *cellist*).

cab
cabaret
cabbage
caber
cabin
cabinet
cabinet-maker
cable
 cabled
 cabling
cacao
cache

> ✒ Do not confuse with **cash** *a cache of treasure*

cachet
cackle
 cackled
 cackling
cacophonous
cacophony
 cacophonies
cactus
 cacti, cactuses
cad
caddie

> ✒ Do not confuse with **caddy** *a golf caddie*

caddish

caddy
 caddies

> ✒ Do not confuse with **caddie** *a tea caddy*

cadence
cadenza
cadet
cadge
 cadged
 cadging
cadger
Caesarean,
 Caesarian
café
cafeteria
cafetière
caffeine
caftan, kaftan
cage
 caged
 caging
cagey, cagy
cagily
caginess
cagoule
cagy
 another spelling of
 cagey
cahoots
cairn

cajole
 cajoled
 cajoling
cake
 caked
 caking
calamine
calamity
 calamities
calciferous
calcify
 calcified
 calcified
calcium
calculable
calculate
 calculated
 calculating
calculation
calculator
calculus
calendar

> ❶ A cal**endar** shows the **end** of the year.

calf
 calves

> ✒ Do not confuse with **calve** *a cow and her calf* • *the calf of his leg*

calibrate
 calibrated
 calibrating
calibration
calibre
calico
calipers
 another spelling of
 callipers
call
caller
calligrapher
calligraphy
calling-card
callipers, calipers
callous

> ●* Do not confuse
> with **callus** *cruel and*
> *callous*

callously
callow
callus
 calluses

> ●* Do not confuse
> with **callous** *a callus on*
> *her toe*

calm
calmly
calmness
calorie
calorific
calorimeter
calvary
calve
 calved
 calving

> ●* Do not confuse
> with **calf** *When will the*
> *cow calve?*

calves

calypso
 calypsos
calyx
 calyces, calyxes
cam
camaraderie
camber
camcorder
came
camel
camellia
Camembert
cameo
 cameos
camera
camisole
camomile,
 chamomile
camouflage
 camouflaged
 camouflaging
camp
campaign
campaigner
campanology
camper
camphor
camping
campion
campsite
campus
 campuses
can
 canned, could
 canning

> ●* Do not confuse
> **canned** with **could**
> *They canned the*
> *tomatoes • She said he*
> *could go*

canal

canary
 canaries
canasta
cancan
cancel
 cancelled
 cancelling
cancellation
cancer
cancerous
candid
candidacy
candidate
candidature
candidly
candied
candle
candlelight
candlelit
candlestick
candlewick
candour
candy
 candies
candyfloss
cane
 caned
 caning
canine
caning
canister
canker
cankerous
cannabis
canned
cannelloni
cannery
 canneries
cannibal
cannibalism
cannibalistic
cannily

canning

cannon
cannoned
cannoning

●* Do not confuse with **canon** *fire a cannon in battle* • *to cannon into the wall*

cannonball

cannot

canny

canoe
canoed
canoeing

canon

●* Do not confuse with **cannon** *a deacon and a canon* • *a canon of the saints* • *sing a canon*

canonical

canonization, canonisation

canonize, canonise
canonized, canonised
canonizing, canonising

canoodle
canoodled
canoodling

can-opener

canopy
canopies

cant

●* Do not confuse with **can't** *jargon and cant* • *a cant or slope* • *The boat will cant to the left*

can't

●* Do not confuse with **cant** *I can't go* **Can't** is a short form of **cannot**.

cantankerous

cantata

canteen

canter
cantered
cantering

canticle

cantilever

canto

canton

canvas
canvases

●* Do not confuse with **canvass** *a canvas for painting* • *a canvas tent*

canvass

●* Do not confuse with **canvas** *to canvass for votes*

canvasser

canyon

cap
capped
capping

capability
capabilities

capable

capably

capacious

capaciously

capaciousness

capacitor

capacity
capacities

cape

caper
capered
capering

capercaillie, capercailzie

capillary
capillaries

capital

capitalisation
another spelling of **capitalization**

capitalise
another spelling of **capitalize**

capitalism

capitalist

capitalistic

capitalization, capitalisation

capitalize, capitalise
capitalized, capitalised
capitalizing, capitalising

capitation

capitulate
capitulated
capitulating

capitulation

capon

capped

capping

cappuccino
cappuccinos

caprice

capricious

capsicum

capsize
capsized
capsizing

capsule

captain
 captained
 captaining
captaincy
 captaincies
caption
captivate
 captivated
 captivating
captivation
captive
captivity
captor
capture
 captured
 capturing
car
carafe
 carafes
caramel
**caramelization,
 caramelisation**
**caramelize,
 caramelise**
 caramelized,
 caramelised
 caramelizing,
 caramelising
carat

> ✒* Do not confuse
> with **carrot** *18-carat
> gold*

caravan
caravanning
caraway
carbohydrate
carbolic
carbon
carbonaceous
carbonate
carbonated

carboniferous
carbuncle
**carburettor,
 carburetter**
carcass, carcase
 carcasses, carcases
carcinogen
carcinogenic
card
cardamom
cardboard
cardiac
cardigan
cardinal
cardiogram
cardiologist
cardiology
cardiovascular
care
 cared
 caring
career
 careered
 careering
carefree
careful
carefully
carefulness
careless
carelessly
carelessness
carer
caress
 caresses
caretaker
careworn
cargo
 cargoes
caribou
 caribou
caricature
 caricatured

 caricaturing
caricaturist
caries
caring
carnage
carnal
carnation
carnival
carnivore
carnivorous
carob
carol
 carolled
 carolling
caroller
carotene
carousal

> ✒* Do not confuse
> with **carousel**
> *Carousal is drinking
> and merrymaking*

carouse
 caroused
 carousing
carousel

> ✒* Do not confuse
> with **carousal** *take
> your luggage off the
> carousel at the airport*

carp
carpenter
carpentry
carpet
 carpeted
 carpeting
carpetbagger
carriage
carriageway
carried
carrier
carrion

carrot

◆* Do not confuse with **carat** *eating a raw carrot*

carry
carries
carried
carrying
carrycot
carry-on
carry-out
cart

◆* Do not confuse with **kart** *a horse and cart*

carte blanche
cartel
cart-horse
cartilage

◆* Do not confuse with **cartridge** *cartilage in the knee*

cartilaginous
cartographer
cartography
carton

◆* Do not confuse with **cartoon** *a carton of milk*

cartoon

◆* Do not confuse with **carton** *a Walt Disney cartoon*

cartoonist
cartridge

◆* Do not confuse with **cartilage** *a cartridge for a pen • a film cartridge*

cartwheel
carve
carved
carving
carvery
carveries
carving-knife
carving-knives
cascade
cascaded
cascading
case
cased
casing
casement
cash

◆* Do not confuse with **cache** *to cash a cheque • pay cash*

cashew
cashier
cashiered
cashiering
cashmere
casing
casino
casinos
cask
casket
cassava
casserole
cassette
cassock
cast
cast
casting

◆* Do not confuse with **caste** *the cast of a play • a plaster cast • to cast a glance*

castanets

castaway
caste

◆* Do not confuse with **cast** *a social caste*

caster
another spelling of
castor
caster sugar, castor sugar
castigate
castigated
castigating
castigation
cast iron
castle
cast-off
castor, caster
castor oil
castor sugar
another spelling of
caster sugar
castrate
castrated
castrating
castration
casual
casually
casualty
casualties
cat
cataclysm
cataclysmic
catacomb
catalogue
catalogued
cataloguing
catalyst
catamaran
catapult
cataract
catarrh

catastrophe
catastrophic
catastrophically
catcall
catch
pl catches
caught
catching
catch-all
catching
catchment
catch-phrase
catchword
catchy
catchier
catchiest
catechise
another spelling of
catechize
catechism
catechize, catechise
catechized,
catechised
catechizing,
catechising
categorical
categorically
categorize,
categorise
categorized,
categorised
categorizing,
categorising
category
categories
cater
catered
catering
caterer
catering
caterpillar
caterwaul

caterwauled
caterwauling
catfish
catgut
catharsis
catharses
cathartic
cathedral
catherine-wheel
catheter
cathode ray tube
catholic

> ♦* Do not confuse
> with **Catholic** *a*
> *catholic taste in*
> *literature*

Catholic

> ♦* Do not confuse
> with **catholic** *He's a*
> *Catholic* • *the Roman*
> *Catholic Church*

catkin
catnap
cat-o'-nine-tails
cattery
catteries
cattle
catty
cattier
cattiest
catwalk
caucus
caucuses
caught
cauldron
cauliflower
causal
causality
causative
cause
caused

causing
causeway
caustic
caustically
cauterize, cauterise
cauterized,
cauterised
cauterizing,
cauterising
caution
cautioned
cautioning
cautionary
cautious
cavalcade
cavalier

> ♦* Do not confuse
> with **cavalry** *Cavaliers*
> *and Roundheads* • *a*
> *cavalier attitude*

cavalry

> ♦* Do not confuse
> with **cavalier** *infantry*
> *and cavalry*

cave
caved
caving
caveat
caveman
cavemen
cavern
cavernous
cavewoman
cavewomen
caviare, caviar
caving
cavity
cavities
cavort
cavy
cavies

caw
cayenne
CD-player
CD-ROM
cease
ceased
ceasing
ceasefire
ceaseless
cedar
cede
ceded
ceding
cedilla
Ceefax®
ceilidh
ceiling

❶ The **ceiling** covers everything inside.

💣* Do not confuse with **sealing** *look up at the ceiling*

celandine
celebrate
celebrated
celebrating
celebration
celebratory
celebrity
celebrities
celeriac
celery
celestial
celibacy
celibate
cell

💣* Do not confuse with **sell** *a prison cell • a battery cell • a living cell*

cellar

💣* Do not confuse with **seller** *keep the wine in the cellar*

cellist
cello
cellos
Cellophane®
cellphone
cellular

💣* Do not confuse with **cellulose** *cellular blankets*

cellulite
celluloid
cellulose

💣* Do not confuse with **cellular** *cellulose paints*

Celsius
Celtic
cement
cemetery
cemeteries

❶ Word within word: ce-**meter**-y

cenotaph
censer

💣* Do not confuse with **censor**, **sensor** or **censure** *a censer for burning incense*

censor
censored
censoring

💣* Do not confuse with **censer**, **sensor** or **censure** *a film censor • to censor letters*

censorious
censorship
censurable
censure
censured
censuring

💣* Do not confuse with **censer** or **censor** *to censure him for bad behaviour • a vote of censure*

census
censuses
cent

💣* Do not confuse with **scent** or **sent** *a dollar and a cent*

centaur
centenarian

💣* Do not confuse with **centenary** *My great-grandmother is a centenarian*

centenary
centenaries

💣* Do not confuse with **centenarian** *the school's centenary celebrations*

centennial
centigrade
centigram, centigramme
centilitre
centimetre
centipede
central
centralisation
another spelling of **centralization**

centralise
another spelling of
  centralize
centrality
centralization,
  centralisation
centralize, centralise
  centralized,
  centralised
  centralizing,
  centralising
centrally
centrally heated
centre
centrefold
centre-forward
centre-half
centrepiece
centrifugal
centrifuge
centripetal
centurion
century
  centuries
ceramic
cereal

✱ Do not confuse
with **serial** *breakfast
cereal • cereal crops
such as wheat*

cerebral
ceremonial
ceremonially
ceremonious
ceremoniously
ceremony
  ceremonies
cerise
certain
certainly
certainty

certainties
certifiable
certificate
certify
  certifies
  certified
  certifying
certitude
cervical
cervix
  cervixes, cervices
cessation
cesspit
cesspool
chador
chafe
  chafed
  chafing

✱ Do not confuse
with **chaff** *My shoes
chafe my heels • to
chafe at the delay*

chaff

✱ Do not confuse
with **chafe** *separate the
wheat from the chaff*

chaffinch
  chaffinches
chagrin
chain
  chained
  chaining
chain mail
chainsaw
chain-smoker
chair
  chaired
  chairing
chairlift
chairman
  chairmen

chairperson
chairwoman
  chairwomen
chaise longue
  chaises longues
chalet
chalice
chalk
chalky
challenge
  challenged
  challenging
challenger
chamber
chamberlain
chambermaid
chamberpot
chameleon
chamois, shammy
  chamois, shammies

✱ The spelling
shammy is only used
for the cleaning
leather.

chamomile
another spelling of
  camomile
champ
champagne
champion
  championed
  championing
championship
chance
  chanced
  chancing
chancel
chancellor
chancer
chancery
  chanceries

Can't find your word under **CH**? Try looking under **C**

chancy
chancier
chanciest
chandelier
change
changed
changing
changeability
changeable

ⓘ Word within word:
change-able

changeless
changeling
change-over
channel
channelled
channelling
chant
chanter
chantry
chantries
chaos

ⓘ Cyclones,
hurricanes and other
storms cause **chaos**.

chaotic
chaotically
chap
chapati, chapatti
chapel
chaperone
chaperoned
chaperoning
chaplain
chaplaincy
chaplaincies
chapped
chapter
char
charred
charring

character

ⓘ **Cha**rlie acts **ter**ribly
– what a **character**!

characterisation
another spelling of
characterization
characterise
another spelling of
characterize
characteristic
characteristically
**characterization,
characterisation**
**characterize,
characterise**
characterized,
characterised
characterizing,
characterising
characterless
charade
charcoal
charge
charged
charging
chargeable
charger
chariot
charioteer
charisma
charismatic
charitable
charitably
charity
charities
charlatan
charm
charmer
charming
charmless
charred

charring
chart
charted
charting

💧* Do not confuse
charted with
chartered *They have
charted the coastline*

charter
chartered
chartering

💧* Do not confuse
chartered with
charted *We chartered a
plane*

chase
chased
chasing

💧* Do not confuse
chased with **chaste**
The dog chased the cat

chasm
chassis
chassis
chaste

💧* Do not confuse
with **chased** *the chaste
life of a nun*

chasten
chastened
chastening
chastise
chastised
chastising
chastisement
chastity
chat
chatted
chatting
château, chateau

Can't find your word under **CH**? Try looking under **C**

châteaux, chateaux

chattels

chatter
chattered
chattering

chatterbox
chatterboxes

chattily

chattiness

chatty
chattier
chattiest

chauffeur

chauvinism

chauvinist

chauvinistic

cheap

> ♦* Do not confuse
> with **cheep** *cheap*
> *prices*

cheapen
cheapened
cheapening

cheaply

cheapness

cheapskate

cheat
cheated
cheating

check

> ♦* Do not confuse
> with **cheque** *a police*
> *check on cars • a*
> *pattern of black and*
> *white checks • to check*
> *the oil • to check a sum*

checked

> ♦* Do not confuse
> with **chequered** *a dress*
> *made of checked fabric*

checkered
another spelling of
chequered

checkers
another spelling of
chequers

check-in

checklist

checkmate

checkout

checkpoint

check-up

Cheddar

cheek

cheekbone

cheekily

cheeky
cheekier
cheekiest

cheep
cheeped
cheeping

> ♦* Do not confuse
> with **cheap** *the cheep of*
> *a bird • to cheep merrily*

cheer
cheered
cheering

cheerful

cheerfully

cheerily

cheerio

cheerleader

cheerless

cheers

cheery

cheese

cheeseburger

cheesecake

cheesecloth

cheesy

cheesier
cheesiest

cheetah

chef
chefs

chemical

chemically

chemist

chemistry

chemotherapy

cheque

> ♦* Do not confuse
> with **check** *pay the bill*
> *with a cheque*

cheque book

chequered,
checkered

> ♦* Do not confuse
> with **checked** *a*
> *chequered career*

chequers, checkers

cherish

cheroot

cherry
cherries

cherub
cherubs, cherubim

chess

chessboard

chessman
chessmen

chesspiece

chest

chesterfield

chestnut

chesty

chevron

chew

chewing-gum

chewy
chewier

Can't find your word under **CH**? Try looking under **C**

chewiest
chic
chicane
chicanery
chick
chicken
chickened
chickening
chicken-feed
chickenpox
chickpea
chickweed
chicly
chicory
chide
chided
chiding
chief
chiefs
chiefly
chieftain
chiffon
chihuahua
chilblain
child
children
childbearing
childbirth
childhood
childish
childless
childlike
childminder
childproof
children
chile
another spelling of
chilli
chili
another spelling of
chilli
chill

chilli, chili, chile
chillies, chilies,
chiles

●* Do not confuse
with **chilly** *chilli*
pepper • chilli con carne

chilliness
chilling
chilly
chillier
chilliest

●* Do not confuse
with **chilli** *a chilly wind*

chime
chimed
chiming
chimney
chimneys
chimneypot
chimney-sweep
chimpanzee
chin
china
chinchilla
chink
chinless
chintz
chintzes
chintzy
chip
chipped
chipping
chipboard
chipmunk
chipolata
chiropodist
chiropody
chiropractic
chiropractor
chirp

chirpily
chirpy
chirpier
chirpiest
chirrup
chirruped
chirruping
chisel
chiselled
chiselling
chit
chit-chat
chitterlings
chivalrous
chivalry
chive
chivvy
chivvies
chivvied
chivvying
chlorinate
chlorinated
chlorinating
chlorine
chloroform
chlorophyll
chock-a-block
chock-full
chocolate
chocolatey,
  chocolaty
choice
choir
choirboy
choirgirl
choke
choked
choking
choker
cholera
cholesterol
chomp

Can't find your word under **CH**? Try looking under **C**

choose
chose
chosen
choosing

⚫* Do not confuse
choose with **chose**
Which should I choose?
• *He chose a different
one last time*

choosy
choosier
choosiest
chop
chopped
chopping
chopper
choppily
choppiness
chopping-board
choppy
choppier
choppiest
chops
chopsticks
choral
chord

⚫* Do not confuse
with **cord** *a musical
chord* • *It strikes a chord*
• *a chord joining two
points on a circle*

chore
choreograph
choreographer
choreography
chorister
chortle
chortled
chortling
chorus
choruses

chose

⚫* Do not confuse
with **choose** *He chose a
different one last time*

chosen
chough
choux pastry
chow
chowder
christen
christened
christening
christening
Christian
Christianity
chromatic
chrome
chromium
chromosome
chronic
chronically
chronicle
chronicled
chronicling
chronicler
chronological
chronologically
chronology
chronometer
chrysalis
chrysalises
chrysanthemum
chub
chubby
chubbier
chubbiest
chuck
chuckle
chuckled
chuckling
chuffed

chum
chummy
chunk
chunky
church
churches
churchgoer
churchwarden
churchyard
churlish
churlishness
churn
chute

⚫* Do not confuse
with **shoot** *a rubbish
chute* • *The child slid
down the chute*

chutney
chutneys
cicada
cider
cigar
cigarette
cinch
cinder
cinema
cinematic
cinematographer
cinematography
cinnamon
cipher
circa
circle
circled
circling
circuit
circuitous
circular
circularity
circulate
circulated

Can't find your word under **CH**? Try looking under **C**

circulating
circulation
circulatory
circumcise
circumcised
circumcising
circumcision
circumference
circumflex
circumflexes
circumnavigate
circumnavigated
circumnavigating
circumscribe
circumscribed
circumscribing
circumscription
circumspect
circumstance
circumstantial
circumstantiate
circumstantiated
circumstantiating
circumvent
circumvention
circus
circuses
cirrhosis
cirrus
cirri
cissy, sissy
cissies, sissies
cistern
citadel
citation
cite
cited
citing

♠* Do not confuse
with **sight** or **site** *to cite*
something as proof

citizen
citizenry
citizenship
citric acid
citrus fruit
city
cities
civet
civic
civics
civil
civilian
civilisation
another spelling of
civilization
civilise
another spelling of
civilize
civility
civilities
**civilization,
civilisation**
civilize, civilise
civilized, civilised
civilizing, civilising
civilly
civvies
clack
clad
cladding
claim
claimed
claiming
claimant
clairvoyance
clairvoyant
clam
clammed
clamming
clamber
clambered
clambering

clammy
clammier
clammiest
clamorous
clamour
clamoured
clamouring
clamp
clampdown
clan
clandestine
clandestinely
clang
clanger
clank
clannish
clansman
clansmen
clanswoman
clanswomen
clap
clapped
clapping
clapper
claptrap
claret
clarification
clarify
clarifies
clarified
clarifying
clarinet
clarinettist
clarion
clarity
clash
clashes
clasp
class
classes
classic
classical

classically
classicism
classicist
classics
classifiable
classification
classify
  classifies
  classified
  classifying
classless
classmate
classroom
classy
  classier
  classiest
clatter
  clattered
  clattering
clause
claustrophobia
claustrophobic
clavicle
claw
clay
clayey
clean
  cleaned
  cleaning
cleaner
cleanliness
cleanly
cleanness
cleanse
  cleansed
  cleansing
cleanser
clean-shaven
clear
  cleared
  clearing
clearance

clear-cut
clearing
clearly
clearness
clearway
cleavage
cleave
  cleaved, clove, cleft
  cleaved, cloven, cleft
  cleaving

✸ The past forms **clove**, **cleft** and **cloven** are only used for the meaning 'to divide or split' *the air was cleft by the moving wing* • *lightning had cloven the tree in two* • *his sword clove the ogre's head* • *lightning cleaved the tree in two* • *they cleaved to each other*

cleaver
clef
  clefs
cleft
clematis
clemency
clement
clementine
clench
clergy
clergyman
  clergymen
clergywoman
  clergywomen
cleric
clerical
clerk
clever
cleverly
cleverness

cliché
clichéed, cliché'd
click
client
clientele
cliff
cliffhanger
climactic

✸ Do not confuse with **climatic** *the climactic moment of the play*

climate
climatic

✸ Do not confuse with **climactic** *climatic changes such as global warming*

climax
  climaxes
climb

✸ Do not confuse with **clime** *I'm going to climb that mountain*

climbable
climb-down
climber
clime

✸ Do not confuse with **climb** *they moved to sunnier climes*

clinch
  clinches
clincher
cling
  clung
  clinging
clinger
clingfilm
clingy

clinic
clinical
clinically
clinician
clink
clip
 clipped
 clipping
clipboard
clipper
clippers
clique
cliquey
cloak
cloakroom
clobber
 clobbered
 clobbering
cloche
clock
clockwatcher
clockwise
clockwork
clod
clodhopper
clodhopping
clog
 clogged
 clogging
cloister
cloistered
clone
 cloned
 cloning
clonk
close
 closed
 closing
closely
closeness
closet
 closeted

closeting
close-up
closure
clot
 clotted
 clotting
cloth
 cloths

 💣* Do not confuse
 cloths with **clothes**
 *tablecloths • Use one of
 these cloths for cleaning
 the floor*

clothe
 clothed
 clothing
clothes

 💣* Do not confuse
 with **cloths** *bedclothes
 • children's clothes*

clothing
clotted
clotting
cloud
cloudburst
cloudless
cloudy
 cloudier
 cloudiest
clout
 clouted
 clouting
clove
cloven
cloven-hoofed
clover
clown
clownish
cloy
 cloyed
 cloying

club
 clubbed
 clubbing
clubhouse
cluck
clue
clueless
clump
clumsily
clumsiness
clumsy
 clumsier
 clumsiest
clung
cluster
 clustered
 clustering
clutch
 clutches
clutter
 cluttered
 cluttering
coach
 coaches
coagulant
coagulate
 coagulated
 coagulating
coagulation
coal

 💣* Do not confuse
 with **kohl** *put some
 coal on the fire*

coalesce
 coalesced
 coalescing
coalescence
coalface
coalfield
coalition
coalmine

coarse

> •* Do not confuse with **course** *coarse sand • a coarse sense of humour*

coarsely
coarsen
  coarsened
  coarsening
coarseness
coast
coastal
coaster
coastguard
coastline
coat
  coated
  coating
coat hanger
co-author
coax
cob
cobalt
cobble
  cobbled
  cobbling
cobbler
cobblestone
cobra
cobweb
cocaine
coccyx
  coccyxes, coccyges
cochineal
cochlea
  cochleae
cock
cockade
cockatoo
cockerel
cocker spaniel

cockfighting
cockily
cockle
cockleshell
cockney
  cockneys
cockpit
cockroach
  cockroaches
cockscomb
cocksure
cocktail
cocky
  cockier
  cockiest
cocoa
coconut
cocoon
  cocooned
  cocooning
cod
coda
coddle
  coddled
  coddling
code
  coded
  coding
codeine
codger
codification
codify
  codifies
  codified
  codifying
co-driver
codswallop
coeducation
coeducational
coefficient
coerce
  coerced

  coercing
coercion
coercive
coexist
coexistence
coexistent
coffee
coffer
coffin
cog
cogency
cogent
cogitate
  cogitated
  cogitating
cogitation
cogitative
cognac
cognate
cognition
cognitive
cogwheel
cohabit
  cohabited
  cohabiting
cohabitation
cohere
  cohered
  cohering
coherence
coherent
cohesion
cohesive
cohort
coiffure
coil
  coiled
  coiling
coin
  coined
  coining
coinage

coincide
  coincided
  coinciding
coincidence
coincidental
coincidentally
coitus
coke
cola
colander
cold
cold-blooded
cold-hearted
coldly
coldness
coleslaw
colic
colicky
coliseum
collaborate
  collaborated
  collaborating
collaboration
collaborative
collaboratively
collaborator
collage

♦* Do not confuse
with **college** *a collage
of pictures cut from
magazines*

collagen
collapse
  collapsed
  collapsing
collapsible
collar
  collared
  collaring
collarbone
collarless

collate
  collated
  collating
collateral
collation
collator
colleague
collect
collectable
collected
collection
collective
collectively
collector
college

♦* Do not confuse
with **collage** *study at
college*

collegiate
collide
  collided
  colliding
collie
collier
colliery
  collieries
collision
collocate
  collocated
  collocating
collocation
colloquial
colloquialism
colloquially
colloquy
  colloquies
collusion
collusive
collywobbles
cologne
colon

colonel

♦* Do not confuse
with **kernel** *an army
colonel*

colonial
colonialism
colonialist
colonially
colonic
colonisation
  another spelling of
  colonization
colonise
  another spelling of
  colonize
colonist
colonization,
  colonisation
colonize, colonise
  colonized, colonised
  colonizing,
  colonising
colonnade
colony
  colonies
colorant, colourant
coloration,
  colouration
colossal
colossus
  colossi, colossuses
colostomy
colour
  coloured
  colouring
colourant
  another spelling of
  colorant
colouration
  another spelling of
  coloration

colour-blind
colourful
colourfully
colouring
colourless
colt
coltish
columbine
column

❶ At the end of each column is an **n**.

columnist
coma

✴ Do not confuse with **comma** *The patient is in a coma*

comatose
comb
combat
 combated
 combating
combatant
combative
combination
combine
 combined
 combining
combine harvester
combustible
combustion
come
 came
 come
 coming
comeback
comedian
comedienne
comedown
comedy
 comedies
comeliness

comely
comet
come-uppance
comfort
comfortable
comfortably
comforter
comfrey
comic
comical
comically
coming
comma

✴ Do not confuse with **coma** *a comma or a full stop*

command
commandant
commandeer
 commandeered
 commandeering
commander
commandment
commando
 commandos
commemorate
 commemorated
 commemorating
commemoration
commemorative
commence
 commenced
 commencing
commencement
commend
commendable
commendation
commensurate
comment
commentary
 commentaries

commentate
 commentated
 commentating
commentator
commerce
commercial
commercialisation
 another spelling of
 commercialization
commercialise
 another spelling of
 commercialize
commercialism
commercialization,
 commercialisation
commercialize,
 commercialise
 commercialized,
 commercialised
 commercializing,
 commercialising
commercially
commiserate
 commiserated
 commiserating
commiseration
commissariat
commission
 commissioned
 commissioning
commissionaire

✴ Do not confuse with **commissioner** *the hotel's new commissionaire*

commissioner

✴ Do not confuse with **commissionaire** *the Canadian High Commissioner*

commit

committed
committing
commitment
committal
committed
committee

> **ⓘ** Many meetings take time – everyone's exhausted!

commode
commodious
commodity
  commodities
commodore
common
commoner
commonplace
Commonwealth
commotion
communal
communally
commune
  communed
  communing
communicable
communicate
  communicated
  communicating
communication
communicative
communion
communiqué
communism
communist
community
  communities
commutable
commute
  commuted
  commuting
commuter

compact
compact disc
compactness
companion
companionable
companionably
companionship
company .
  companies
comparable
comparably
comparative
comparatively
compare
  compared
  comparing
comparison
compartment
compass
  compasses
compasses
compassion
compassionate
compassionately
compatibility
compatible
compatibly
compatriot
compel
  compelled
  compelling
compendious
compendium
  compendiums,
  compendia
compensate
  compensated
  compensating
compensation
compensatory
compère
  compèred

compèring
compete
  competed
  competing
competence
competent
competently
competition

> **ⓘ** Word within word:
> com-**pet**-ition

competitive
competitor
compilation
compile
  compiled
  compiling
compiler
complacency,
  complacence
complacent
complain
  complained
  complaining
complainant
complaint
complement

> **☙** Do not confuse
> with **compliment** *the*
> *complement of an angle*
> *• a full complement •*
> *The flavours*
> *complement each other*
> Remember that a
> **comple**ment
> **comple**tes something.

complementary

> **☙** Do not confuse
> with **complimentary**
> *complementary angles*
> *• a complementary*
> *amount*

complete
completed
completing
completely
completeness
completion
complex
complexes
complexion
complexity
complexities
compliance
compliant
complicate
complicated
complicating
complication
complicity
complicities
compliment

🖐* Do not confuse
with **complement** *pay
her a compliment* •
*Please accept this with
our compliments* •
*compliment him on his
work* Remember that
you comp**li**ment
something you **li**ke.

complimentary

🖐* Do not confuse
with **complementary** *a
complimentary remark*
• *a complimentary
ticket*

comply
complies
complied
complying
component
compose

composed
composing
composer
composite
composition
compos mentis
compost
composure
compound
comprehend
comprehensibility
comprehensible
comprehension
comprehensive
comprehensively
comprehensiveness
compress
compression
compressor
comprise
comprised
comprising
compromise
compromised
compromising
compulsion
compulsive
compulsively
compulsorily
compulsory
compunction
computation
compute
computed
computing
computer
**computerization,
computerisation**
**computerize,
computerise**
computerized,
computerised

computerizing,
computerising
comrade
comradeship
con
conned
conning
concave
concavity
conceal
concealed
concealing
concealment
concede
conceded
conceding
conceit
conceited
conceitedly
conceivable
conceivably
conceive
conceived
conceiving
concentrate
concentrated
concentrating
concentration
concentric
concept
conception
conceptual
**conceptualize,
conceptualise**
conceptualized,
conceptualised
conceptualizing,
conceptualising
conceptually
concern
concerned
concernedly

SPELLING *focus*   Compound Words

A *compound word* is made up of two or more whole words joined together:

bathroom   football   grasshopper   database
somewhere   downstairs   breakthrough   nevertheless

It may help you to remember the spelling of these words if you break them
down into their separate parts, especially when there is a silent letter in the
compound word, such as the **p** in *cupboard*.

Can you join these ten words together in pairs to make five compound
words?

tea	ball	hold	hand	shine
sun	eye	bag	pot	house

Meaning

Compound words are often nouns. A compound word does not necessarily
have the same meaning as the two words used separately. For example, a
raven is a black bird, but it is not a *blackbird*. Look at the One Word or Two?
section of the Spelling Rules on p.402 and use it to make up sentences
showing the difference between compound words and their separate parts:

Everyone **brought me a cake and I ate** *every one*.
Nobody **was charged with murder because** *no body* **was found.**

Words do not usually change their spelling when they are joined together,
although there are some exceptions which you can learn about in section 7
of the Spelling Rules on p.397.

Hyphens

The parts of a compound word are sometimes linked by a hyphen, as in
hold-up or *absent-minded*. Many compound words can be spelt with or
without a hyphen. For example, you can write *baby-sitter* or *babysitter*.
Some hyphenated compounds can also be written as two separate words:
dining-room or *dining room*.

Connectives

Connectives are words used to link or extend sentences. Many connectives
are compound words: *however, meanwhile, moreover, nevertheless,
notwithstanding, therefore, whereas*.

concernedness
concerning
concert

> ✎* Do not confuse
> with **consort** *a concert*
> *of piano music* • *The*
> *departments must act*
> *in concert*

concerted
concertina
concerto
 concertos
concession
concessionary
conch
conchiglie
conciliate
 conciliated
 conciliating
conciliation
conciliatory
concise
concisely
conciseness
conclude
 concluded
 concluding
conclusion
conclusive
conclusively
concoct
concoction
concord
concordance
concordat
concourse
concrete
concubine
concur
 concurred
 concurring

concurrence
concurrent
concurrently
concuss
concussion
condemn
 condemned
 condemning
condemnation
condemnatory
condemned
condensation
condense
 condensed
 condensing
condenser
condescend
condescending
condescension
condiment
condition
 conditioned
 conditioning
conditional
conditionally
conditioner
condolence
condom
condominium
condone
 condoned
 condoning
condor
conducive
conduct
conduction
conductor
conductress
 conductresses
conduit
cone
confection

confectioner
confectionery
confederacy
 confederacies
confederate
confederation
confer
 conferred
 conferring
conference
conferencing
conferment
confess
confessed
confession
confessional
confessor
confetti
confidant

> ✎* Do not confuse
> with **confident** *You are*
> *my trusted confidant*

confidante

> ✎* Do not confuse
> with **confident** *She*
> *was the queen's only*
> *confidante*

confide
 confided
 confiding
confidence
confident

> ✎* Do not confuse
> with **confidant** or
> **confidante** *confident of*
> *success*

confidential
confidentiality
confidentially
confidently

configuration
configure
configured
configuring
confine
confined
confining
confinement
confines
confirm
confirmation
confirmatory
confirmed
confiscate
confiscated
confiscating
confiscation
conflagration
conflate
conflation
conflict
conflicting
confluence
confluent
conform
conformation
conformist
conformity
confound
confounded
confront
confrontation
confuse
confused
confusing
confusion
confute
confuted
confuting
conga
congeal
congealed

congealing
congenial
congenially
congenital
conger eel
congested
congestion
conglomerate
conglomerated
conglomerating
conglomeration
congratulate
congratulated
congratulating
congratulations
congratulatory
congregate
congregated
congregating
congregation
Congregational
congress
congresses
congressional
congressman
congressmen
congresswoman
congresswomen
congruence
congruent
congruity
congruous
conical
conifer
coniferous
conjectural
conjecture
conjectured
conjecturing
conjoin
conjugal
conjugate

conjugated
conjugating
conjugation
conjunction
conjunctivitis
conjure
conjured
conjuring
conjuror, conjurer
conker

♦* Do not confuse
with **conquer** *a shiny
brown conker* • *a game
of conkers*

con man
connect
connectable
connected
connection
connective
connector
conned
conning
connivance
connive
connived
conniving
connoisseur
connotation
connote
connoted
connoting
conquer
conquered
conquering

♦* Do not confuse
with **conker** *to conquer
a country* • *to conquer
your fear*

conqueror
conquest

conscience

ℹ Word within word:
con-**science**

♦* Do not confuse
with **conscientious** or
conscious *a guilty
conscience*

conscientious

♦* Do not confuse
with **conscience** or
conscious *a
conscientious worker*

conscientiously
conscientiousness
conscious

♦* Do not confuse
with **conscience** or
conscientious *Is the
patient conscious now?
• a conscious decision •
conscious of his
disability*

consciously
consciousness
conscript
conscription
consecrate
  consecrated
  consecrating
consecration
consecutive
consecutively
consensus

ℹ Word breakdown:
con-sen-sus

consensual
consent
consequence
consequent

consequential
consequently
conservable
conservancy
conservation
conservationist
conservatism
conservative
conservatoire
conservatory
  conservatories
conserve
  conserved
  conserving
consider
  considered
  considering
considerable
considerably
considerate
considerately
consideration
consign
consignment
consist
consistency
  consistencies
consistent
consistently
consolable
consolation
consolatory
console
  consoled
  consoling
consolidate
  consolidated
  consolidating
consolidation
consonance
consonant
consonantal

consort

♦* Do not confuse
with **concert** *the
queen's consort • to
consort with criminals*

consortium
  consortia,
  consortiums
conspicuous
conspicuously
conspicuousness
conspiracy
  conspiracies
conspirator
conspiratorial
conspire
  conspired
  conspiring
constable
constabulary
constancy
constant
constantly
constellation
consternation
constipate
  constipated
  constipating
constipation
constituency
  constituencies
constituent
constitute
  constituted
  constituting
constitution
constitutional
constitutionally
constrain
  constrained
  constraining

constraint
constrict
constriction
construct
construction
constructive
constructively
construe
  construed
  construing
consul

🔹* Do not confuse
with **council** or
counsel *the British
consul in Paris*

consular
consulate
consult
consultancy
consultant
consultation
consultative
consumable
consume
  consumed
  consuming
consumer
consumerism
consummate
  consummated
  consummating
consummation
consumption
consumptive
contact
contactable
contagion
contagious
contain
  contained
  containing

containable
container
containment
contaminant
contaminate
  contaminated
  contaminating
contamination
contemplate
  contemplated
  contemplating
contemplation
contemplative
contemporaneous
contemporary
  contemporaries
contempt
contemptible
contemptibly
contemptuous
contemptuously
contend
contender
content
contented
contention
contentious
contentment
contents
contest
contestable
contestant
context
contextual
continence
continent
continental
contingency
  contingencies
contingent
continual
continually

continuance
continuation
continue
  continued
  continuing
continuity
continuous

🅸 Word breakdown:
con-tin-u-ous

continuously
continuum
  continuums,
  continua
contort
contortion
contortionist
contour
contraband
contrabass
  contrabasses
contraception
contraceptive
contract
contraction
contractor
contractual
contradict
contradiction
contradictory
contralto
  contraltos
contraption
contrapuntal
contrariness
contrary
contrast
contravene
  contravened
  contravening
contravention
contribute

contributed
contributing
contribution
contributor
contributory
contrite
contritely
contrition
contrivance
contrive
contrived
contriving
control
controlled
controlling
controllable
controller
controls
controversial
controversially
controversy
controversies
conundrum
conurbation
convalesce
convalesced
convalescing
convalescence
convalescent
convection
convector
convene
convened
convening
convener, convenor
convenience
convenient
conveniently
convenor
another spelling of
convener
convent

convention
conventional
conventionally
converge
converged
converging
convergence
convergent
conversant
conversation
conversational
conversationalist
conversationally
converse
conversed
conversing
conversely
conversion
convert
converter
convertible
convex
convexity
convey
conveyed
conveying
conveyance
conveyancing
conveyor belt
convict
conviction
convince
convinced
convincing
convivial
convivially
conviviality
convocation
convoluted
convoy
convoyed
convoying

convulse
convulsed
convulsing
convulsion
convulsive
convulsively
coo
cooed
cooing

✎ Do not confuse
with **coup** *Pigeons coo*

cook
cookbook
cooker
cookery
cookie
cooking
cool
cooled
cooling
coolant
cooler
coolly
coolness
coop
cooped
cooping

✎ Do not confuse
with **coup** *a chicken
coop • cooped up
indoors all day*

cooper
**co-operate,
cooperate**
co-operated,
cooperated
co-operating,
cooperating
**co-operation,
cooperation**
co-operative,

cooperative
co-operatively,
cooperatively
co-opt
co-ordinate,
coordinate
co-ordinated,
coordinated
co-ordinating,
coordinating
co-ordination,
coordination
co-ordinator,
coordinator
coot
cop
copped
copping
cope
coped
coping
copied
copier
copies
co-pilot
coping
copious
copiously
cop-out
copper
copper-bottomed
copperplate
coppice
copse
copulate
copulated
copulating
copulation
copy
copies
copied
copying

copybook
copycat
copyright
copywriter
coquette
coquettish
coracle
coral

❧* Do not confuse
with **corral** *a coral reef
• a necklace of coral*

cor anglais
cors anglais
cord

❧* Do not confuse
with **chord** *the cord of a
dressing-gown • spinal
cord • vocal cords*

cordial
cordiality
cordially
cordless
cordon
cordoned
cordoning
cordon bleu
corduroy
core
cored
coring

❧* Do not confuse
with **corps** *an apple
core • the earth's core*

corer
corespondent,
co-respondent

❧* Do not confuse
with **correspondent**
*the corespondent in a
divorce case*

corgi
corgis
coriander
cork
corkage
corker
corkscrew
cormorant
corn
cornea
corned beef
corner
cornered
cornering
cornerstone
cornet

❧* Do not confuse
with **coronet** *He plays
the cornet • an ice
cream cornet*

cornflakes
cornflour

❧* Do not confuse
with **cornflower**
*thicken the sauce with
cornflour*

cornflower

❧* Do not confuse
with **cornflour** *a
cornflower growing in
the garden*

cornice
corny
cornier
corniest
corollary
corollaries
corona
coronae, coronas
coronary

coronaries
coronation
coroner
coronet

✐* Do not confuse
with **cornet** *She placed
the coronet on her head*

corpora
corporal
corporate
corporation
corporeal
corps
corps

✐* Do not confuse
with **core** or **corpse**
*join the cadet corps •
corps de ballet*

corpse
corpses

✐* Do not confuse
with **corps** *The corpse
was buried in a grave*

corpulence
corpulent
corpus
corpora
corpuscle
corral
corralled
corralling

✐* Do not confuse
with **coral** *cattle in the
corral • to corral the
cattle*

correct
correction
corrective
correctly
correctness

corrector
correlate
correlated
correlating
correlation
correspond
correspondence

ⓘ She **correct**s
correspondence in the
den.

correspondent

✐* Do not confuse
with **corespondent** *a
letter from a regular
correspondent • a
report from our
correspondent in
Jamaica*

corresponding
corridor
corroborate
corroborated
corroborating
corroboration
corroborative
corroborator
corrode
corroded
corroding
corrosion
corrosive
corrugated
corrupt
corruptible
corruption
corset
cortège
cortex
cortices
cortical
cortisone

cosh
coshes
cosier
cosies
cosiest
cosily
cosiness
cosmetic
cosmic
cosmological
cosmologist
cosmology
cosmonaut
cosmopolitan
cosmos
cosset
cosseted
cosseting
cost
cost
costing
co-star
co-starred
co-starring
cost-effective
costliness
costly
costlier
costliest
costume
cosy
pl cosies
cosier
cosiest
cot
coterie
cottage
cottager
cotton
cottoned
cottoning
cottongrass

cottonwool
couch
 couches
cougar
cough
could
couldn't
could've
coulomb
council

> ✱ Do not confuse
> with **consul** or **counsel**
> *a member of the town*
> *council*

councillor

> ✱ Do not confuse
> with **counsellor** *a town*
> *councillor*

counsel
 counselled
 counselling

> ✱ Do not confuse
> with **consul** or **council**
> *counsel for the defence* •
> *to counsel him to stay*

counsellor

> ✱ Do not confuse
> with **councillor** *A*
> *counsellor gives help*
> *and advice*

count
countable
countdown
countenance
 countenanced
 countenancing
counter
 countered
 countering
counteract

counteractive
counterattack
counterbalance
 counterbalanced
 counterbalancing
counterfeit
 counterfeited
 counterfeiting
counterfoil
countermand
counterpane
counterpart
counterpoint
counterpoise
counter-revolution
counter-
 revolutionary
countersign
counter-signature
counter-tenor
counterweight
countess
 countesses
countless
country
 countries
countryman
 countrymen
countryside
countrywide
countrywoman
 countrywomen
county
 counties
coup

> ✱ Do not confuse
> with **coo** or **coop** *The*
> *president was killed in*
> *the coup* • *Getting the*
> *interview was quite a*
> *coup*

coup d'état
 coups d'état
couple
 coupled
 coupling
couplet
coupling
coupon
courage
courageous
courgette
courier
course
 coursed
 coursing

> ✱ Do not confuse
> with **coarse** *the course*
> *of the river* • *a course of*
> *lectures* • *in due course*
> • *tears coursed down*
> *her cheeks*

coursebook
coursework
coursing
court
courteous
courtesan
courtesy

> ✱ Do not confuse
> with **curtsy** *He*
> *behaved with politeness*
> *and courtesy*

courthouse
courtier
courtly
court-martial
 pl courts-martial
 court-martialled
 court-martialling
courtroom
courtship

courtyard
couscous
cousin
couture
couturier
cove
coven
covenant
cover
 covered
 covering
coverage
covering
coverlet
covert
cover-up
covet
 coveted
 coveting
covetous
covetousness
cow
coward
cowardice
cowardly
cowbell
cowboy
cowed
cower
 cowered
 cowering
cowgirl
cowherd
cowl
co-worker
cowpat
cowpox
cowshed
cowslip
cox
 coxes
coxless

coxcomb
coxswain
coy
coyly
coyness
coyote
coypu
 coypu, coypus
crab
crabbed
crabby
crabwise
crack
crackdown
cracker
crackers
crackle
 crackled
 crackling
crackling
cracknel
crackpot
cradle
 cradled
 cradling
cradle-snatcher
craft
craftily
craftiness
craftsman
 craftsmen
craftswoman
 craftswomen
crafty
 craftier
 craftiest
crag
craggy
cram
 crammed
 cramming
crammer

cramp
cramped
crampon
cranberry
 cranberries
crane
cranefly
 craneflies
cranial
cranium
 craniums, crania
crank
crankshaft
cranky
cranny
 crannies
crape
 another spelling of
 crêpe
crash
 crashes
crashing
crash-land
crass
crassness
crate
crater
cravat
crave
 craved
 craving
craven
crawl
crawler
crayfish
crayon
 crayoned
 crayoning
craze
crazily
crazy
 crazier

craziest
creak

❖ Do not confuse
with **creek** *the creak of
the floorboards • Some
of the stairs creak*

creaky
cream
 creamed
 creaming
creamer
creamery
creamy
 creamier
 creamiest
crease
 creased
 creasing
create
 created
 creating
creation
creative
creativity
creator
creature
crèche
credence
credentials
credibility
credible
credibly
credit
 credited
 crediting
creditable
creditably
creditor
creditworthy
credo
 credos

credulity
credulous
creed
creek

❖ Do not confuse
with **creak** *canoeing
up the creek*

creel
creep
 crept
 creeping
creeper
creepy
 creepier
 creepiest
creepy-crawly
 creepy-crawlies
cremate
 cremated
 cremating
cremation
crematorium
crème brûlée
crème caramel
crème de la crème
crème fraîche
creosote
crêpe, crepe, crape
crept
crescendo
 crescendos
crescent
cress
crest
crestfallen
cretin
crevasse

❖ Do not confuse
with **crevice** *She fell
down a crevasse in the
ice*

crevice

❖ Do not confuse
with **crevasse** *He hid
the note in a crevice in
the rock*

crew
crewcut
crib
 cribbed
 cribbing
cribbage
crick
cricket
cricketer
cried
crier
cries
crikey
crime
criminal
criminality
criminally
criminologist
criminology
crimson
cringe
 cringed
 cringing
crinkle
 crinkled
 crinkling
crinkly
crinoline
cripple
 crippled
 crippling
crisis
 crises
crisp
crispy
criss-cross

criterion
 criteria
critic
critical
critically
criticise
 another spelling of
 criticize
criticism
criticize, criticise
 criticized, criticised
 criticizing,
 criticising
critique
croak
croaky
crochet
 crocheted
 crocheting

⬥* Do not confuse
with **crotchet** *a crochet
hook • to crochet a
shawl*

crock
crockery
crocodile
crocus
 crocuses
croft
crofter
crofting
croissant
crone
crony
 cronies
crook
crooked
crookedness
croon
 crooned
 crooning

crooner
crop
 cropped
 cropping
cropper
croquet

⬥* Do not confuse
with **croquette** *a game
of croquet*

croquette

⬥* Do not confuse
with **croquet** *a potato
croquette*

cross
 crosses
crossbar
crossbow
cross-check
cross-country
cross-examine
 cross-examined
 cross-examining
cross-eyed
cross-fertilize,
 cross-fertilise
 cross-fertilized,
 cross-fertilised
 cross-fertilizing,
 cross-fertilising
crossfire
crosshatch
crossing
crossly
crossness
cross-question
 cross-questioned
 cross-questioning
cross-refer
 cross-referred
 cross-referring
cross-reference

crossroads
cross-section
cross-stitch
 cross-stitches
crosswind
crosswise
crossword
crotch
 crotches
crotchet

⬥* Do not confuse
with **crochet** *A
crotchet is a note in
music*

crotchety
crouch
croup
croupier
crow
crowbar
crowd
crowded
crown
crow's-nest
crucial
crucially
crucible
crucifix
 crucifixes
crucifixion
cruciform
crucify
 crucifies
 crucified
 crucifying
crude
crudely
crudeness
crudity
cruel
cruelly

cruelty
cruet
cruise
 cruised
 cruising
cruiser
crumb
crumble
 crumbled
 crumbling
crumbly
crumby
crumpet
crumple
 crumpled
 crumpling
crunch
crunchy
 crunchier
 crunchiest
crusade
crusader
crush
 crushes
crusher
crust
crustacean
crusty
crutch
 crutches
crux
cry
 cries
 cried
 crying
crybaby
 crybabies
cryogenics
crypt
cryptic
cryptically
cryptogram

cryptography
crystal
crystalline
crystallization,
 crystallisation
crystallize,
 crystallise
 crystallized,
 crystallised
 crystallizing,
 crystallising
cub
cubbyhole
cube
 cubed
 cubing
cubic
cubicle
Cub Scout
cuckoo
cucumber
cud
cuddle
 cuddled
 cuddling
cuddly
 cuddlier
 cuddliest
cudgel
 cudgelled
 cudgelling
cue

> ✎* Do not confuse
> with **queue** *a snooker*
> *cue • The actor missed*
> *his cue*

cuff
cufflinks
cuisine
cul-de-sac
culinary

cull
culminate
 culminated
 culminating
culmination
culottes
culpability
culpable
culpably
culprit
cult
cultivate
 cultivated
 cultivating
cultivated
cultivation
cultivator
cultural
culture
cultured
cumbersome
cumin
cumulative
cumulus
 cumuli
cunning
cup
 cupped
 cupping
cupboard
cupful
 cupfuls
Cupid
cupola
cupped
cupping
cup-tie
cur
curable
curacy
curate
curator

curb

♦* Do not confuse with **kerb** *a curb on their spending • to curb your desires*

curd
curdle
 curdled
 curdling
cure
 cured
 curing
curfew
curio
 curios
curiosity
 curiosities
curious
curiously
curl
curler
curlew
curliness
curling
curly
 curlier
 curliest
currant

♦* Do not confuse with **current** *a currant bun • blackcurrants and redcurrants*

currency
 currencies
current

♦* Do not confuse with **currant** *an electric current • swim against the current • the current year • current affairs*

curriculum
 curricula,
 curriculums
curriculum vitae
 curricula vitae
curry
 curries
 curried
 currying
curse
 cursed
 cursing
cursive
cursor
cursorily
cursory
curt
curtail
 curtailed
 curtailing
curtailment
curtain
 curtained
 curtaining
curtain-raiser
curtly
curtness
curtsy, curtsey
 curtsies, curtseys
 curtsied, curtseyed
 curtsying, curtseying

♦* Do not confuse with **courtesy** *She made a curtsy to the queen*

curvaceous
curvature
curve
 curved
 curving
curvy

cushion
 cushioned
 cushioning
cushy
cusp
custard
custodial
custodian
custody
custom
customarily
customary
customer
customs
cut
 cut
 cutting
cut-and-dried
cutaway
cutback
cute
cutely
cuteness
cuticle
cutlass
 cutlasses
cutlery
cutlet
cut-off
cut-price
cutter
cut-throat
cutting
cuttlefish
cut-up
cyanide
cybercafé
cybernetics
cyberspace
cycle
 cycled
 cycling

cyclic
cyclical
cyclist
cyclone
cyclonic
cygnet

💣* Do not confuse
with **signet** *A cygnet is
a young swan*

cylinder
cylindrical
cylindrically

cymbal

💣* Do not confuse
with **symbol** *She plays
the cymbals*

cynic
cynical
cynically
cynicism
cypress
 cypresses
cyst
cystic

cystitis
cytological
cytology
cytoplasm

czar
another spelling of
tsar

czarina
another spelling of
tsarina

Dd

dab
dabbed
dabbing
dabble
dabbled
dabbling
dabbler
dachshund
dad
daddy
daddies
daffodil
daft
dagger
dahlia
daily
dailies
daintily
daintiness
dainty
daintier
daintiest
dairy
dairies

✒* Do not confuse
with **diary** *milk from
the dairy • dairy
farming*

dais
daises
daisy
daisies
daisy-chain

daisy-wheel
dale
dalliance
dally
dallies
dallied
dallying
dam
dammed
damming

✒* Do not confuse
with **damn** *to dam a
river • The dam holds
back the water*

damage
damaged
damaging
damask
dame
dammed

✒* Do not confuse
with **damned** *We
dammed the stream*

damming

✒* Do not confuse
with **damning** *We were
damming the stream*

damn

✒* Do not confuse
with **dam** *to damn a
soul • Damn! I've
dropped it*

damnable
damnation
damned

✒* Do not confuse
with **dammed** *a
damned soul • that
damned dog*

damning

✒* Do not confuse
with **damming**
*damning evidence • a
damning report*

damp
damp-course
dampen
dampened
dampening
dampener
damper
dampness
damp-proof
damsel
damselfly
damselflies
damson
dan
dance
danced
dancing
dancer
dandelion
dandruff
dandy

dandies

danger
dangerous
dangerously
dangle
dangled
dangling
dank
dankness
dapper
dappled
dare
dared
daring
dare-devil
daring
daringly
dark
darken
darkened
darkening
darkness
darkroom
darling
darn
dart
dartboard
darter
darts
dash
dashes
dashboard
dashing
dastardly
data
databank
database
date
dated
dating
date-stamp
dative

datum
data
daub
daubed
daubing
daughter
daughter-in-law
daughters-in-law
daughterly
daunt
daunting
dawdle
dawdled
dawdling
dawdler
dawn
day
daybreak
daydream
daydreamed
daydreaming
daydreamer
Day-Glo®, **dayglo**
daylight
day-release
daytime
daze
dazed
dazing
dazzle
dazzled
dazzling
deacon
deaconess
deaconesses
deactivate
deactivated
deactivating
deactivation
dead
dead-beat
deaden

deadened
deadening
deadline
deadliness
deadlock
deadly
deadlier
deadliest
deadness
deadpan
deadweight
deaf
deafen
deafened
deafening
deafness
deal
dealt
dealing
dealer
dealings
dean
deanery
deaneries
dear

> ✷ Do not confuse
> with **deer** *a dear friend*
> • *The shoes are too dear*
> • *Thank you, dear*

dearly
dearness
dearth
death
death-bed
deathly
death-mask
death-rate
death-trap
debacle
debar
debarred

debarring
debarment
debase
debased
debasing
debasement
debatable
debate
debated
debating
debauched
debauchery
debilitate
debilitated
debilitating
debilitation
debility
debit
debited
debiting
debonair
debrief
debriefing
debris, débris
debt
debtor
debug
debugged
debugging
debunk
début, debut
debutante
decade
decadence
decadent
decaff
decaffeinate
decaffeinated
decaffeinating
decagon
decagonal
decahedral

decahedron
decamp
decant
decanter
decapitate
decapitated
decapitating
decapitation
decathlete
decathlon
decay
decayed
decaying
decease
deceased
deceit
deceitful
deceitfully
deceive
deceived
deceiving
deceiver
decelerate
decelerated
decelerating
deceleration
decency
decent
decently
decentralization,
  decentralisation
decentralize,
  decentralise
decentralized,
decentralised
decentralizing,
decentralising
deception
deceptive
deceptively
decibel
decide

decided
deciding
decidedly
decider
deciduous
decilitre
decimal
decimalization,
  decimalisation
decimalize,
  decimalise
decimalized,
decimalised
decimalizing,
decimalising
decimate
decimated
decimating
decipher
deciphered
deciphering
decipherable
decision
decisive
decisively
decisiveness
deck
deckchair
declaim
declaimed
declaiming
declamatory
declaration
declarative
declare
declared
declaring
declassification
declassify
declassifies
declassified
declassifying

declension
decline
 declined
 declining
decode
 decoded
 decoding
decoder
decommission
 decommissioned
 decommissioning
decompose
 decomposed
 decomposing
decomposition
decompress
decompression
decongestant
deconstruction
decontaminate
 decontaminated
 decontaminating
decontamination
décor, decor
decorate
 decorated
 decorating
decoration
decorative
decoratively
decorator
decorous
decorum
decoy
 decoyed
 decoying
decrease
 decreased
 decreasing
decree
 decreed
 decreeing

decrepit
decrepitude
decry
 decries
 decried
 decrying
dedicate
 dedicated
 dedicating
dedication
dedicatory
deduce
 deduced
 deducing
deducible
deduct
deductible
deduction
deductive
deed
deem
 deemed
 deeming
deep
deepen
 deepened
 deepening
deep-freeze
deep-fry
 deep-fries
 deep-fried
 deep-frying
deeply
deep-rooted
deep-seated
deep-set
deer

> ●* Do not confuse
> with **dear** *We saw a*
> *deer • a herd of deer*

deerstalker

deface
 defaced
 defacing
defacement
defamation
defamatory
defame
 defamed
 defaming
default
defaulter
defeat
 defeated
 defeating
defeatism
defeatist
defecate
 defecated
 defecating
defecation
defect
defection
defective
defector
defence
defenceless
defend
defendant
defender
defensible
defensive
defensively
defensiveness
defer
 deferred
 deferring
deference
deferential
deferentially
deferment
deferral
deferred

deferring
defiance
defiant
defiantly
deficiency
 deficiencies
deficient
deficit
defied
defies
defile
 defiled
 defiling
definable
define
 defined
 defining
definite
definitely

ℹ Word within word:
de-**finite**-ly

---

definition
definitive
definitively
deflate
 deflated
 deflating
deflation
deflationary
deflect
deflection
deflower
deforest
deforestation
deform
deformed
deformity
 deformities
defraud
defray
 defrayed

defraying
defrayal
defrock
defrost
deft
deftly
deftness
defunct
defuse
 defused
 defusing

✎❋ Do not confuse
with **diffuse** *to defuse a
bomb • to defuse a
crisis*

defy
 defies
 defied
 defying
degenerate
 degenerated
 degenerating
degeneration
degenerative
degradable
degradation
degrade
 degraded
 degrading
degree
dehumanize,
  dehumanise
 dehumanized,
  dehumanised
 dehumanizing,
  dehumanising
dehydrate
 dehydrated
 dehydrating
dehydration
de-ice

de-icer
deification
deify
 deifies
 deified
 deifying
deign
deity
 deities
déjà vu
dejected
dejection
delay
 delayed
 delaying
delectable
delectably
delectation
delegate
 delegated
 delegating
delegation
delete
 deleted
 deleting
deletion
deliberate
 deliberated
 deliberating

ℹ It was a de**liberate**
attempt to **liberate** the
captives.

---

deliberately
deliberation
delicacy
 delicacies
delicate
delicately
delicatessen
delicious
delight

delighted
delightedly
delightful
delightfully
delimit
delimited
delimiting
delimitation
delineate
delineated
delineating
delinquency
delinquent
delirious
delirium
deliver
delivered
delivering
deliverance
delivery
deliveries
dell
delta
delude
deluded
deluding
deluge
deluged
deluging
delusion

♦* Do not confuse
with **allusion** or
illusion *delusions of
grandeur*

delusive
delusory
de luxe
delve
delved
delving
demand

demarcate
demarcated
demarcating
demarcation
demean
demeaned
demeaning
demeanour
demented
dementia
demerara
demigod
demise
demist
demo
demos
demob
demobbed
demobbing
**demobilization,
demobilisation**
**demobilize,
demobilise**
demobilized,
demobilised
demobilizing,
demobilising
democracy
democracies
democrat
democratic
democratically
demographic
demography
demolish
demolition
demon
demonic
demonstrable
demonstrably
demonstrate
demonstrated

demonstrating
demonstration
demonstrative
demonstrator
**demoralization,
demoralisation**
**demoralize,
demoralise**
demoralized,
demoralised
demoralizing,
demoralising
demote
demoted
demoting
demotion
demur
demurred
demurring
demure
demurely
demureness
demurral
demystification
demystify
demystifies
demystified
demystifying
den
**denationalization,
denationalisation**
**denationalize,
denationalise**
denationalized,
denationalised
denationalizing,
denationalising
denial
denied
denier
denies
denigrate

denigrated
denigrating
denim
denizen
denominate
denominated
denominating
denomination
denominational
denominator
denotation
denote
denoted
denoting
dénouement,
denouement
denounce
denounced
denouncing
dense
densely
denseness
density
densities
dent
dental
dentist
dentistry
denture
denudation
denude
denuded
denuding
denunciation
deny
denies
denied
denying
deodorant
deodorize,
deodorise
deodorized,

deodorised
deodorizing,
deodorising
depart
department
departmental
departure
depend
dependable
dependant

> ♠* Do not confuse
> with **dependent** *Her*
> *husband and children*
> *are her dependants*

dependence,
dependency
dependent

> ♠* Do not confuse
> with **dependant** *Her*
> *husband and children*
> *are dependent on her*

depersonalize,
depersonalise
depersonalized,
depersonalised
depersonalizing,
depersonalising
depict
depiction
deplete
depleted
depleting
depletion
deplorable
deplorably
deplore
deplored
deploring
deploy
deployed
deploying

deployment
depopulate
depopulated
depopulating
deport
deportation
deportee
deportment
depose
deposed
deposing
deposit
deposited
depositing
deposition
depositor
depository
depositories
depot
depraved
depravity
deprecate
deprecated
deprecating

> ♠* Do not confuse
> with **depreciate** *to*
> *deprecate her*
> *behaviour*

deprecation
deprecatory
depreciate
depreciated
depreciating

> ♠* Do not confuse
> with **deprecate** *Cars*
> *depreciate as they get*
> *older*

depreciation
depredation
depress
depressant

depressed
depressing
depression
deprivation
deprive
 deprived
 depriving
depth
deputation
deputize, deputise
 deputized,
 deputised
 deputizing,
 deputising
deputy
 deputies
derail
 derailed
 derailing
derailment
derange
 deranged
 deranging
deranged
derangement
derby
 derbies
deregulate
deregulation
derelict
dereliction
deride
 derided
 deriding
de rigueur
derision
derisive
derisively
derisory
derivation
derivative
derive

derived
deriving
dermatitis
dermatologist
dermatology
derogatorily
derogatory
desalinate
desalination
descant
descend
descendant
descent
describe
 described
 describing
description

----
❶ Word within word:
de-**script**-ion

----

descriptive
desecrate
 desecrated
 desecrating
desecration
deselect
deselection
desensitize,
 desensitise
 desensitized,
 desensitised
 desensitizing,
 desensitising
desert

✾* Do not confuse
with **dessert** *to desert
from the army • to
desert your family • a
desert island • The
criminals got their just
deserts*

----

deserter

desertion
deserve
 deserved
 deserving
deservedly
desiccate
 desiccated
 desiccating
desiccation
design
designate
 designated
 designating
designation
designer
desirability
desirable
desirably
desire
 desired
 desiring
desirous
desist
desk
desktop
desolate
desolated
desolation
despair
 despaired
 despairing
despatch
another spelling of
 dispatch
desperado
 desperados,
 desperadoes
desperate

----
❶ In des**per**ate **per**il!

----

desperately
desperation

despicable
despicably
despise
despised
despising
despite
despondency
despondent
despot
despotic
despotically
despotism
dessert

> ☙* Do not confuse
> with **desert** *We had*
> *fruit salad for dessert*

dessertspoon
destabilize,
  destabilise
destabilized,
  destabilised
destabilizing,
  destabilising
destination
destined
destiny
destinies
destitute
destitution
destroy
destroyed
destroying
destroyer
destructible
destruction
destructive
desultorily
desultory
detach
detachable
detached

detachment
detail
detailed
detailing
detain
detained
detaining
detainee
detect
detectable
detection
detective
detector
detention
deter
deterred
deterring
detergent
deteriorate
deteriorated
deteriorating
deterioration
determinant
determination
determine
determined
determining
determiner
deterred
deterrent
deterring
detest
detestable
detestably
detestation
dethrone
dethroned
dethroning
detonate
detonated
detonating
detonation

detonator
detour
detoxicate
detoxification
detoxify
detract
detraction
detriment
detrimental
deuce
devaluation
devalue
devalued
devaluing
devastate
devastated
devastating
devastation
develop
developed
developing
developer
development
developmental
deviant
deviate
deviated
deviating
deviation
device

> ☙* Do not confuse
> with **devise** *a device*
> *for boring holes*
> Remember that **ice** is a
> noun.

devil
devilish
devilment
devilry
devious
deviousness

devise
devised
devising

♦* Do not confuse
with **device** *to devise a
plan*

devoid
devolution

♦* Do not confuse
with **evolution** *the
devolution of power
from central
government*

devolutionist
devolve
devolved
devolving
devote
devoted
devoting
devoted
devotedly
devotee
devotion
devour
devoured
devouring
devout
devoutly
devoutness
dew

♦* Do not confuse
with **due** or **Jew**
*droplets of dew on the
lawn*

dewdrop
dewy
dexterity
dexterous, dextrous
diabetes

diabetic
diabolic
diabolical
diabolically
diagnose
diagnosed
diagnosing
diagnosis
diagnoses
diagnostic
diagonal
diagonally
diagram
diagrammatic
diagrammatical
dial
dialled
dialling
dialect
dialectal
dialogue
dialysis
diamanté
diameter
diametric
diametrically
diamond
diaphragm
diarist
diarrhoea

❶ **Diarrhoea**? **R**un
rapidly **h**ome **o**r **e**lse –
awful!

diary
diaries

♦* Do not confuse
with **dairy** *make a note
in your diary*

dice
dicey
dichotomy

dichotomies
dicky
dictate
dictated
dictating
dictation
dictator
dictatorial
dictatorially
dictatorship
diction
dictionary
dictionaries
dictum
dictums, dicta
did
diddle
diddled
diddling
didgeridoo
didn't
die
died
dying

♦* Do not confuse
with **dye** *to die in battle
• She died young • He's
dying to meet you • The
die is cast*

diehard
diesel
diet
dieted
dieting
dietary
dietician
differ
differed
differing
difference
different

differential
differentiate
 differentiated
 differentiating
differentiation
differently
difficult
difficulty
 difficulties
diffidence
diffident
diffract
diffraction
diffuse
 diffused
 diffusing

💧* Do not confuse
with **defuse** *The shade
diffuses the light*

diffusion
dig
 dug
 digging
digest
digestible
digestion
digestive
digger
digging
digit
digital
dignified
dignitary
 dignitaries
dignity
digraph
digress
digression
digs
dike, dyke
dilapidated

dilapidation
dilatation
dilate
 dilated
 dilating
dilation
dilatory
dilemma
diligence
diligent
diligently
dill
dilly-dally
 dilly-dallies
 dilly-dallied
 dilly-dallying
dilute
 diluted
 diluting
dilution
dim
 dimmed
 dimming
dime
dimension
dimensional
diminish
diminuendo
 diminuendos
diminution
diminutive
dimly
dimmed
dimmer
dimming
dimness
dimple
dimpled
dimwit
din
 dinned
 dinning

dine
 dined
 dining
diner
ding
ding-dong
dinghy
 dinghies

💧* Do not confuse
with **dingy** *a sailing
dinghy*

dinginess
dingo
 dingoes, dingos
dingy

💧* Do not confuse
with **dinghy** *a dark and
dingy room*

dining room
dinky
dinner
dinosaur
dint
diocesan
diocese
diode
dioxide
dip
 dipped
 dipping
diphtheria
diphthong
diplodocus
diploma
diplomacy
diplomat
diplomatic
diplomatically
dipped
dipper
dipping

dipstick
dire
direct
direction
directive
directly
directness
director
directorship
directory
 directories
dirge
dirigible
dirk
dirndl
dirt
dirtily
dirtiness
dirty
 dirtier
 dirtiest
 dirties
 dirtied
 dirtying
disability
 disabilities
disable
 disabled
 disabling
disabled
disablement
disabuse
disadvantage
disadvantaged
disadvantageous
disaffected
disaffection
disagree
 disagreed
 disagreeing
disagreeable
disagreeably

disagreement
disallow
disappear
 disappeared
 disappearing

ⓘ Remember – a
single **s** and a pair of
p's.

disappearance
disappoint

ⓘ Remember – a
single **s** and a pair of
p's.

disappointed
disappointing
disappointment
disapprobation
disapproval
disapprove
 disapproved
 disapproving
disapproving
disapprovingly
disarm
disarmament
disarming
disarrange
 disarranged
 disarranging
disarray
disassemble
disassociate
 disassociated
 disassociating
disaster
disastrous
disastrously
disavow
disavowal
disband
disbandment

disbelief

●* Do not confuse
with **disbelieve** *He
looked at me in
disbelief*

disbelieve
 disbelieved
 disbelieving

●* Do not confuse
with **disbelief** *to
disbelieve a story*

disburse
 disbursed
 disbursing

●* Do not confuse
with **disperse** *to
disburse several million
pounds from the fund*

disbursement
disc

●* Do not confuse
with **disk** *a metal disc •
a slipped disc • a
compact disc • a disc
jockey*

discard
discern
discernible
discernibly
discerning
discernment
discharge
 discharged
 discharging
disciple
disciplinarian
disciplinary
discipline
 disciplined
 disciplining

disc jockey
 disc jockeys
disclaim
 disclaimed
 disclaiming
disclaimer
disclose
 disclosed
 disclosing
disclosure
disco
 discos
**discoloration,
 discolouration**
discolour
 discoloured
 discolouring
discolouration
 another spelling of
 discoloration
discomfiture
discomfort
disconcert
disconcerted
disconcerting
disconnect
disconnected
disconnection
disconsolate
disconsolately
discontent
discontented
discontentment
discontinue
 discontinued
 discontinuing
discord
discordant
**discothèque,
 discotheque**
discount
discourage

discouraged
 discouraging
discouragement
discouraging
discourse
 discoursed
 discoursing
discourteous
discourtesy
discover
 discovered
 discovering
discoverer
discovery
 discoveries
discredit
 discredited
 discrediting
discreditable
discreet

 ♦* Do not confuse
 with **discrete** *She
 asked us a few discreet
 questions*

discreetly
discrepancy
 discrepancies
discrete

 ♦* Do not confuse
 with **discreet**
 *separated into three
 discrete groups*

discreteness
discretion
discretionary
discriminate
 discriminated
 discriminating
discrimination
discriminatory
discursive

discus
 discuses

 ♦* Do not confuse
 with **discuss** *throwing
 the discus*

discuss

 ♦* Do not confuse
 with **discus** *to discuss a
 problem*

discussion
disdain
 disdained
 disdaining
disdainful
disdainfully
disease
diseased
disembark
disembarkation
disembodied
disembowel
 disembowelled
 disembowelling
disembowelment
disenchant
disenchanted
disenchantment
disenfranchise
disenfranchisement
disengage
 disengaged
 disengaging
disengagement
disentangle
 disentangled
 disentangling
disfavour
disfigure
 disfigured
 disfiguring
disfigurement

disgorge
disgorged
disgorging
disgrace
disgraced
disgracing
disgraceful
disgracefully
disgruntled
disguise
disguised
disguising
disgust
disgusted
disgusting
dish
dishes
disharmony
dishearten
disheartened
disheartening
dishevelled
dishevelment
dishonest
dishonesty
dishonour
dishonoured
dishonouring
dishonourable
dishonourably
dishwasher
dishy
dishier
dishiest
disillusion
disillusioned
disillusioning
disillusionment
disincentive
disinclined
disinfect
disinfectant

disinformation
disinherit
disinherited
disinheriting
disintegrate
disintegrated
disintegrating
disintegration
disinterest
disinterested
disjointed
disk

♦* Do not confuse
with disc *a computer's
hard disk* • *a floppy
disk* • *a disk drive*

disk drive
diskette
dislike
disliked
disliking
dislocate
dislocated
dislocating
dislocation
dislodge
dislodged
dislodging
disloyal
disloyally
disloyalty
dismal
dismally
dismantle
dismantled
dismantling
dismay
dismayed
dismaying
dismember
dismembered

dismembering
dismemberment
dismiss
dismissal
dismissive
dismount
disobedience
disobedient
disobey
disobeyed
disobeying
disobliging
disorder
disordered
disordering
disordered
disorderliness
disorderly
disorganized,
  disorganised
disorient
disorientate
disorientated
disorientating
disorientation
disown
disparage
disparaged
disparaging
disparagement
disparaging
disparate
disparity
disparities
dispassionate
dispassionately
dispatch, despatch
dispatches,
  despatches
dispel
dispelled
dispelling

Choosing a Strategy

There are a number of strategies you can use to help improve your spelling:

- Some words are easiest to spell by sounding out individual phonemes (*d-i-a-r-y*) or syllables (*re-spon-si-bil-i-ty*).

- Are there letter patterns or features from words which you do know how to spell which you can identify and use to help you spell a difficult word (for example **eigh** in *eight* and *neighbour*)?

- Some words can be broken down into known roots, with or without prefixes and suffixes (*tele-phone, care-ful-ly*).

- Other words contain another unrelated word (*skeleton*, *source*).

- Are there any helpful mnemonics or spelling rules which you can use?

Different words are suited to different strategies, so decide which one will be most helpful for each word. You can also work with a partner, or 'spelling buddy' – it's more fun to work with a friend and help or test each other.

---

dispensable
dispensary
 dispensaries
dispensation
dispense
 dispensed
 dispensing
dispenser
dispersal
disperse
 dispersed
 dispersing

> ✱ Do not confuse
> with **disburse** *The*
> *crowd began to disperse*

dispirit
 dispirited
 dispiriting
dispirited
dispiriting
displace
 displaced

 displacing
displacement
display
 displayed
 displaying
displease
 displeased
 displeasing
displeasure
disposable
disposal
dispose
 disposed
 disposing
disposition
dispossess
dispossession
disproportionate
disproportionately
disprove
 disproved
 disproving
disputable

disputation
dispute
 disputed
 disputing
disqualification
disqualify
 disqualifies
 disqualified
 disqualifying
disquiet
 disquieted
 disquieting
disquieting
disregard
disrepair
disreputable
disreputably
disrepute
disrespect
disrespectful
disrespectfully
disrobe
 disrobed

disrobing
disrupt
disruption
disruptive
dissatisfaction
dissatisfy
dissatisfies
dissatisfied
dissatisfying
dissect
dissection
dissemble
dissembled
dissembling
disseminate
disseminated
disseminating
dissemination
dissension
dissent
dissented
dissenting
dissenter
dissertation
disservice
dissidence
dissident
dissimilar
dissimilarity
dissimilarities
dissipate
dissipated
dissipating
dissipation
dissociate
dissociated
dissociating
dissociation
dissoluble
dissolute
dissolution
dissolve

dissolved
dissolving
dissonance
dissonant
dissuade
dissuaded
dissuading
dissuasion
distance
distanced
distancing
distant
distantly
distaste
distasteful
distastefully
distemper
distend
distension
distil
distilled
distilling
distillation
distiller
distillery
distilleries
distinct
distinction
distinctive
distinctiveness
distinctly
distinguish
distinguishable
distinguished
distinguishing
distort
distorted
distortion
distract
distracted
distracting
distraction

distraught
distress
distressed
distressing
distribute
distributed
distributing
distribution
distributor
district
distrust
distrustful
distrustfully
disturb
disturbance
disturbed
disturbing
disunite
disunited
disuniting
disunity
disuse
disused
disyllabic
ditch
ditches
dither
dithered
dithering
ditherer
ditto
ditty
ditties
diuretic
diva
divan
dive
dived
diving
dive-bomb
dive-bomber
dive-bombing

diver	**divot**	**dodo**
diverge	**divulge**	dodos, dodoes
diverged	divulged	**doe**
diverging	divulging	
divergence	**dizziness**	♦* Do not confuse
divergent	**dizzy**	with **dough** *a doe is a*
diverse	**do**	*female deer*
diversification	does, do	
diversify	did	**doer**
diversifies	done	**does**
diversified	doing	**doesn't**
diversifying	**docile**	**doff**
diversion	**docilely**	**dog**
diversity	**docility**	dogged
divert	**dock**	dogging
divest	**docker**	**dog-collar**
divide	**docket**	**dog-eared**
divided	**dockyard**	**dog-fight**
dividing	**doctor**	**dogfish**
dividend	doctored	**dogged**
dividers	doctoring	**doggedly**
divination	**doctoral**	**doggerel**
divine	**doctorate**	**dogging**
divined	**doctrinal**	**doggy**
divining	**doctrine**	doggies
diviner	**document**	**doggy-bag**
diving-board	**documentary**	**doggy-paddle**
diving-suit	documentaries	**dog-house**
divining-rod	**documentation**	**dog-leg**
divinity	**dodder**	**dogma**
divinities	doddered	**dogmatic**
divisibility	doddering	**dogmatically**
divisible	**dodderer**	**do-gooder**
division	**doddery**	**dogsbody**
divisional	**doddle**	dogsbodies
divisive	**dodecagon**	**doily, doyley**
divisiveness	**dodecahedron**	doilies, doyleys
divorce	**dodge**	**doing**
divorced	dodged	**do-it-yourself**
divorcing	dodging	**doldrums**
divorcee	**dodger**	**dole**
divorced	**dodgy**	doled
		doling

doleful
dolefully
dolefulness
doll
dollar
dollop
dolly
dollies
dolphin
dolt
domain
dome
domed
Domesday book,
Doomsday book
domestic
domestically
domesticate
domesticated
domestication
domesticity
domicile
dominance
dominant
dominate
dominated
dominating
dominating
domination
domineer
domineered
domineering
dominion
domino
dominoes, dominos
don
donned
donning
donate
donated
donating
donation

done

●* Do not confuse
with **dun** *Have you
done your homework?*

donkey
donkeys
donor
don't
doodle
doodled
doodling
doom
doomed
doomsday
Doomsday book
another spelling of
Domesday book
door
doorbell
doorman
doormen
doormat
doorstep
doorstop
doorway
dope
doped
doping
dopey
dormant
dormer window
dormice
dormitory
dormitories
dormouse
dormice
dorsal
dosage
dose
dosed
dosing

dosh
doss
dosser
dossier
dot
dotted
dotting
dotage
dote
doted
doting
doth
dotted
dotty
double
doubled
doubling
double-agent
double-barrelled
double-breasted
double-check
double-cross
double-dealing
double-decker
double-Dutch
double-edged
double entendre
double-glazed
double-glazing
double-jointed
doubles
doublet
double-take
doubly
doubt

❶ It's right to be in
doubt.

doubter
doubtful
doubtfully
doubtless

dough

♦* Do not confuse with **doe** *Bread is made from dough*

doughnut
doughty
doughy
dour
douse
 doused
 dousing

♦* Do not confuse with **dowse** *to douse the flames • to douse the car with petrol* You can use **dowse** instead of **douse** with these meanings.

dove
dovecote
dovetail
 dovetailed
 dovetailing
dowager
dowdily
dowdy
dowel
down
down-and-out
down-at-heel
downcast
downer
downfall
downgrade
 downgraded
 downgrading
downhearted
downhill
download
down-market
downpour

downright
downs
downside
downsizing
downstairs
downstream
down-to-earth
downtown
downtrodden
downturn
downward
downwards
downy
dowry
 dowries
dowse
 dowsed
 dowsing

♦* Do not confuse with **douse** *to dowse for water* You can't use **douse** instead of **dowse** with this meaning.

dowser
doyley
 another spelling of
 doily
doze
 dozed
 dozing
dozen
drab
draconian
draft

♦* Do not confuse with **draught** *a rough draft • to draft a letter*

drag
 dragged
 dragging
dragnet

dragon

♦* Do not confuse with **dragoon** *St George and the dragon*

dragonfly
 dragonflies
dragoon
 dragooned
 dragooning

♦* Do not confuse with **dragon** *the dragoon guards • Did he dragoon you into going?*

drain
 drained
 draining
drainage
draining-board
drainpipe
drake
drama
dramatic
dramatically
dramatics
dramatisation
 another spelling of
 dramatization
dramatise
 another spelling of
 dramatize
dramatis personae
dramatist
**dramatization,
 dramatisation**
**dramatize,
 dramatise**
 dramatized,
 dramatised
 dramatizing,
 dramatising

drank

♦* Do not confuse
with **drunk** *They drank
their tea*

drape
draped
draping
draper
drapery
drastic
drastically
draught

♦* Do not confuse
with **draft** *a cold
draught • draught beer
• a game of draughts*

draughtsman
draughtsmen
draughtsmanship
draughtswoman
draughtswomen
draughty
draughtier
draughtiest

❶ An unpleasant gale
howled through the
draughty building.

draw
drew
drawn
drawing
drawback
drawbridge
drawer
drawing-pin
drawl
drawn
drawstring
dread
dreaded

dreadful
dreadfully
dreadfulness
dreadlocks
dreadnought
dream
dreamed, dreamt
dreaming
dreamer
dreamily
dreamt
dreamy
dreamier
dreamiest
drearily
dreary
drearier
dreariest
dredge
dredged
dredging
dredger
dregs
drench
dress
dresses
dressage
dresser
dressing
dressing-down
dressing-gown
dressing-table
dressmaker
dressmaking
dressy
dressier
dressiest
drew
drey
dreys
dribble
dribbled

dribbling
dried
drier, dryer

♦* The spelling **dryer**
is only used for the
noun *a hand dryer •
find a drier towel*

dries
driest
drift
driftwood
drill
drily
another spelling of
dryly
drink
drank
drunk
drinking
drinkable
drink-driving
drinker
drip
dripped
dripping
drip-dry
drip-dries
drip-dried
drip-drying
dripping
drive
drove
driven
driving
drive-in
drivel
drivelled
drivelling
driven
driver
drizzle

drizzled
drizzling
drizzly
droll
dromedary
dromedaries
drone
droned
droning
drool
drooled
drooling
droop
drooped
drooping
droopy
drop
dropped
dropping
droplet
drop-out
droppings
dross
drought
drove
drover
drown
drowsily
drowsiness
drowsy
drubbing
drudge
drudged
drudging
drudgery
drug
drugged
drugging
druggist
drugstore
druid
drum

drummed
drumming
drummer
drumstick
drunk

💧* Do not confuse
with **drank** *They have
drunk their tea • Her
brother came home
drunk*

drunkard
drunken
drunkenness
dry
drier
driest
dries
dried
drying
dryad
dry-clean
dry-cleaned
dry-cleaning
dry-cleaner
dryer
another spelling of
drier
dryly, drily
dryness
dual

💧* Do not confuse
with **duel** *a dual
purpose • a dual
carriageway*

dual carriageway
duality
dub
dubbed
dubbing
dubbin
dubiety

dubious
dubiousness
duchess
duchesses
duchy
duchies
duck
duckling
duct
ductile
dud
dude
dudgeon

💧* Do not confuse
with **dungeon** *She
stormed out in high
dudgeon*

due

💧* Do not confuse
with **dew** or **Jew**
*Payment is due • go due
south • death due to
starvation*

duel

💧* Do not confuse
with **dual** *They fought
a duel*

duellist
dues
duet
duettist
duff
**duffel bag, duffle
bag**
**duffel coat, duffle
coat**
duffer
duffle bag
another spelling of
duffel bag

duffle coat
another spelling of
duffel coat
dug
dugout
duke
dukedom
dulcet
dull
dullness
dully
duly
dumb
dumbfounded
dumbly
dumbness
dumbstruck
dummy
 dummies
dump
dumpling
dumpy
dun

♦* Do not confuse
with **done** *the horse
was a golden dun
colour*

dunce
dune
dung
dungarees
dung-beetle
dungeon

♦* Do not confuse
with **dudgeon** *the
prisoners in the
dungeon*

dunk
duodecimal
duodenal
duodenum
dupe
 duped
 duping
duplicate
 duplicated
 duplicating
duplication
duplicitous
duplicity
durability
durable
durably
duration
duress
during
dusk
dusky
dust
dustbin
dustcart
duster
dustman
 dustmen
dustpan
dusty
duteous
dutiful
dutifully
duty
 duties
duty-bound
duty-free
duvet

dwarf
dwarfs, dwarves
dwell
dwelt, dwelled
dwelling
dwindle
dwindled
dwindling
dye
dyed
dyeing

♦* Do not confuse
with **die** *to dye your
hair red • covered in
blue dye • She dyed her
socks*

dying
dyke
another spelling of
dike
dynamic
dynamically
dynamics
dynamism
dynamite
dynamo
dynamos
dynastic
dynasty
dynasties
dysentery
dyslexia
dyslexic
dyspepsia
dyspeptic
dystrophy

E e

If the word you're looking for sounds as if it begins *ee* but you can't find it there, try looking under **AE** for words like *aesthetic*, and **OE** for words like *oestrogen*.

each
eager
eagerly
eagerness
eagle
eagle-eyed
ear
earache
eardrum
earful
earl
earldom
earliness
early
 earlier
 earliest
earmark
earmuffs
earn
 earned
 earning
earner
earnest
earnestly
earnings
earphones
earpiece
ear-piercing
earplugs
earring
earshot

ear-splitting
earth
earthbound
earthenware
earthling
earthly

> ● Do not confuse
> with **earthy** *in this*
> *earthly life* • *no earthly*
> *use*

earthquake
earthshattering
earthworm
earthy

> ● Do not confuse
> with **earthly** *an earthy*
> *sense of humour* •
> *These potatoes are very*
> *earthy*

earwig
ease
 eased
 easing
easel
easier
easiest
easily
easiness
east
eastbound

easterly
eastern
eastward
eastwards
easy
 easier
 easiest
easy-going
eat
 ate
 eaten
 eating
eatable
eaten
eatery
eau de cologne
eaves
eavesdrop
 eavesdropped
 eavesdropping
eavesdropper
ebb
ebony
ebullience
ebullient
eccentric

---

❶ He's as eccentric as a crazy camel.

---

eccentricity
 eccentricities

ecclesiastic
ecclesiastical
echelon
echo
 pl echoes
echoed
echoing
éclair
eclectic
eclipse
eclipsed
eclipsing

> 🔸* Do not confuse
> with **ellipse** *an eclipse
> of the sun • to eclipse his
> glory*

ecofriendly
ecological
ecologically
ecologist
ecology
e-commerce
economic
economical
economically
economics
economise
 another spelling of
 economize
economist
economize,
 economise
economized,
economised
economizing,
economising
economy
economies
ecosystem
ecotourism
ecstasy

ecstasies
ecstatic
ecstatically
ectoplasm
ecumenical
eczema

> ❶ Even clever zebras
> may have **eczema**.

eddy
 eddies
 eddied
 eddying
edelweiss
edge
 edged
 edging
edgeways
edgily
edginess
edgy
edible
edict
edification
edifice
edify
 edifies
 edified
 edifying
edit
 edited
 editing
edition

> 🔸* Do not confuse
> with **addition** *a new
> edition of his book*

editor
editorial
editorially
educate
 educated
 educating

education
educational
educationally
educationalist
educationist
educator
eel
eerie

> 🔸* Do not confuse
> with **eyrie** *an eerie
> silence • a dark eerie
> house*

eerily
eeriness
efface
 effaced
 effacing
effacement
effect

> 🔸* Do not confuse
> with **affect** *the effect of
> the drug • the new law
> comes into effect • to
> effect a change*

effective
effectively
effectiveness
effectual
effectually
effectuate
 effectuated
 effectuating
effeminacy
effeminate
effeminately
effervesce
 effervesced
 effervescing
effervescence
effervescent
efficacious

Can't find your word? Try looking under **AE** or **OE**

efficacy
efficiency
efficient
effigy
 effigies
effluent

◆* Do not confuse
with **affluent** *The
factory's effluent
polluted the river*

effort
effortless
effrontery
effusion
effusive
effusively
egalitarian
egalitarianism
egg
eggcup
egghead
eggplant
eggshell
egg timer
ego
 egos
egocentric
egoism
egoist
egoistic
egoistically
egotism
egotist
egotistic
egotistically
egret
eiderdown
eider duck
eight
eighteen
eighteenth

eighth
eighties
eightieth
eighty
 eighties
either
ejaculate
 ejaculated
 ejaculating
ejaculation
ejaculatory
eject
ejection
ejector
eke
 eked
 eking
elaborate
 elaborated
 elaborating
elaboration
élan
elapse
 elapsed
 elapsing
elastic
elasticate
 elasticated
 elasticating
elasticated
elasticity
elated
elation
elbow
elbow-grease
elbow-room
elder
elderberry
 elderberries
elderly
eldest
elect

election
electioneer
 electioneered
 electioneering
elective
elector
electoral
electorate
electric
electrical
electrically
electrician
electricity
electrification
electrify
 electrifies
 electrified
 electrifying
electrocardiogram
electro-convulsive
electrocute
 electrocuted
 electrocuting
electrocution
electrode
electrolysis
electron
electronic
electronically
electronics
electroplate
 electroplated
 electroplating
elegance
elegant
elegantly
elegiac
elegize, elegise
 elegized, elegised
 elegizing, elegising
elegy
 elegies

Can't find your word? Try looking under **AE** or **OE**

element
elemental
elementary
elephant
elephantine
elevate
 elevated
 elevating
elevated
elevation
elevator
eleven
elevenses
eleventh
elf
 elves
elfin
elfish
elicit
 elicited
 eliciting

♦* Do not confuse
with **illicit** *to elicit*
information

eligibility
eligible

♦* Do not confuse
with **illegible** *an*
eligible bachelor •
eligible for the job

eliminate
 eliminated
 eliminating
elimination
eliminator
élite, elite
elitism
elitist
elixir
Elizabethan
elk

ellipse

♦* Do not confuse
with **eclipse** *An ellipse*
is an oval shape

elliptic
elliptical
elliptically
elm
elocution
elongate
 elongated
 elongating
elongated
elongation
elope
 eloped
 eloping
eloper
elopement
eloquence
eloquent
else
elsewhere
elucidate
 elucidated
 elucidating
elude
 eluded
 eluding

♦* Do not confuse
with **allude** *He tried to*
elude his pursuers

elusive
elusiveness
elves
emaciated
emaciation
e-mail, email
 e-mailed, emailed
 e-mailing, emailing
emanate

emanated
emanating
emanation
emancipate
 emancipated
 emancipating
emancipation
embalm
embalmment
embankment
embargo
 embargoes
embark
embarkation
embarrass

❶ I went **r**eally **r**ed and
smiled **s**hyly.

embarrassed
embarrassing
embarrassment
embassy
 embassies
embed
 embedded
 embedding
embellish
embellishment
ember
embezzle
 embezzled
 embezzling
embezzlement
embezzler
embitter
 embittered
 embittering
emblazon
 emblazoned
 emblazoning
emblem
emblematic

Can't find your word? Try looking under **AE** or **OE**

embodiment

ℹ️ Word within word: embo-**dime**-nt

embody
embodies
embodied
embodying
embolden
emboldened
emboldening
embolism
emboss
embrace
embraced
embracing
embroider
embroidered
embroidering
embroidery
embroil
embroiled
embroiling
embryo
embryos
embryologist
embryonic
emend

💣* Do not confuse
with **amend** *to emend
the manuscript*

emendation
emerald
emerge
emerged
emerging
emergence
emergency
emergencies
emergent
emeritus
emery

emetic
emigrant

💣* Do not confuse
with **immigrant**
*emigrants leaving their
native land*

emigrate
emigrated
emigrating
emigration

💣* Do not confuse
with **immigration**
*emigration from
America*

eminence
eminent
eminently
emir
emirate
emissary
emissaries
emission

💣* Do not confuse
with **omission** *the
emission of gases*

emit
emitted
emitting
emote
emoted
emoting
emotion
emotional
emotionally
emotive
empathetic
**empathize,
empathise**
empathized,
empathised

empathizing,
empathising
empathy
emperor
emphasis
emphases

💣* Do not confuse
with **emphasise** or
emphasize *place great
emphasis on hygiene •
The emphasis is on the
first syllable*

**emphasize,
emphasise**
emphasized,
emphasised
emphasizing,
emphasising

💣* Do not confuse
with **emphasis** *to
emphasize its worth • to
emphasize the word
'new'*

emphatic
emphatically
empire
employ
employed
employing
employable
employee

💣* Do not confuse
with **employer** *She
sacked one of her
employees*

employer

💣* Do not confuse
with **employee** *His
employer gave him a
rise*

Can't find your word? Try looking under **AE** or **OE**

Journals

It is useful to keep a journal of your own spelling problems and solutions and have it with you in all your work – you will often encounter difficult words in subjects other than English. In your journal you can include:

• Words that you always find difficult

• New words that you want to learn

• Your favourite mnemonics or other strategies for remembering tricky spellings

• Spelling rules – and exceptions to these rules

• Common root words, prefixes and suffixes

• Groups of words containing the same letter pattern, for example **-ough** or **-ight**

• Groups of words containing different spellings of the same sound

• Key words from other subjects, such as science or geography

employment
emporium
emporiums,
emporia
empower
empowered
empowering
empress
empresses
emptiness
empty
emptier
emptiest
empties
emptied
emptying
empty-handed
emu
emus
emulate
emulated
emulating
emulation
emulsifier
emulsify

emulsifies
emulsified
emulsifying
emulsion
enable
enabled
enabling
enact
enactment
enamel
enamelled
enamelling
enamoured
encampment
encapsulate
encapsulated
encapsulating
encapsulation
encase
encased
encasing
encephalitis
enchant
enchanter
enchanting

enchantment
enchantress
enchantresses
enchilada
encircle
encircled
encircling
enclave
enclose
enclosed
enclosing
enclosure
encode
encoded
encoding
encompass
encore
encounter
encountered
encountering
encourage
encouraged
encouraging
encouragement
encroach

Can't find your word? Try looking under **AE** or **OE**

encroachment
encrust
encumber
encumbered
encumbering
encumbrance
encyclopedia,
encyclopaedia
encyclopedic,
encyclopaedic
end
endanger
endangered
endangering
endear
endeared
endearing
endearment
endeavour
endeavoured
endeavouring
endemic
ending
endive
endless
endmost
endocrine
endoscope
endoscopy
endorse
endorsed
endorsing
endorsement
endow
endowment
endurable
endurance
endure
endured
enduring
enema
enemy

enemies
energetic
energetically
energize, energise
energized, energised
energizing,
energising
energy
energies
enervate
enervated
enervating
enfold
enforce
enforced
enforcing
enforceable
enforcement
enfranchise
enfranchised
enfranchising
enfranchisement
engage
engaged
engaging
engaged
engagement
engender
engendered
engendering
engine
engineer
engineered
engineering
engineering
engorged
engrave
engraved
engraving
engraver
engross
engrossed

engulf
enhance
enhanced
enhancing
enhancement
enigma
enigmatic
enigmatically
enjoy
enjoyed
enjoying
enjoyable
enjoyment
enlarge
enlarged
enlarging
enlargement
enlighten
enlightened
enlightening
enlightenment
enlist
enliven
enlivened
enlivening
en masse
enmesh
enmity
ennoble
ennobled
ennobling
ennui
enormity
enormous
enormously
enough
enquire
another spelling of
inquire
enquirer
another spelling of
inquirer

Can't find your word? Try looking under **AE** or **OE**

enquiry
another spelling of
inquiry
enrage
enraged
enraging
enrich
enrichment
enrol
enrolled
enrolling
enrolment
en route
ensconce
ensconced
ensconcing
ensemble
enshrine
enshrined
enshrining
enshroud
ensign
enslave
enslaved
enslaving
enslavement
ensnare
ensnared
ensnaring
ensue
ensued
ensuing
en suite
ensure
ensured
ensuring

♦* Do not confuse
with **insure** *Hard work
will ensure success*

entail
entailed

entailing
entangle
entangled
entangling
entanglement
enter
entered
entering
enterprise
enterprising
enterprisingly
entertain
entertained
entertaining
entertainer
entertaining
entertainingly
entertainment
enthral
enthralled
enthralling
enthralment
enthrone
enthroned
enthroning
enthuse
enthused
enthusing
enthusiasm
enthusiast
enthusiastic
enthusiastically
entice
enticed
enticing
enticement
enticing
entire
entirely
entirety
entitle
entitled

entitling
entitlement
entity
entities
entomb
entomologist
entomology
entourage
entrails
entrance
entranced
entrancing
entrant
entrap
entrapped
entrapping
entrapment
entreat
entreated
entreating
entreaty
entreaties
entrée
entrenched
entrepreneur
entrepreneurial
entropy
entrust, intrust
entry
entries
entwine
entwined
entwining
E-number
enumerate
enumerated
enumerating
enumeration
enunciate
enunciated
enunciating
enunciation

Can't find your word? Try looking under **AE** or **OE**

envelop
enveloped
enveloping

✸ Do not confuse with **envelope** *The mist began to envelop the hills*

envelope

✸ Do not confuse with **envelop** *put the letter in the envelope*

enviable
enviably
envious
enviously
environment

❶ Word within word: env-**iron**-ment

environmental
environmentally
environmentalist
environs
envisage
envisaged
envisaging
envoy
envy
envies
envied
envying
enzyme
eon
another spelling of
aeon
epaulet, epaulette
ephemera
ephemeral
ephemerality
ephemerally
epic

epicentre
epicure
epicurean
epidemic
epidermis
epidural
epiglottis
epigram
epigrammatic
epilepsy
epileptic
epilogue
epiphany
episcopacy
episcopal
episcopalian
episode
episodic
episodically
epistle
epistolary
epitaph
epithet
epitome
epitomize,
 epitomise
epitomized,
epitomised
epitomizing,
epitomising
epoch
epochs
eponym
eponymous
equable
equably
equal
equalled
equalling
equalise
another spelling of
equalize

equaliser
another spelling of
equalizer
equality
equalize, equalise
equalized, equalised
equalizing,
equalising
equalizer, equaliser
equalled
equalling
equally
equanimity
equate
equated
equating
equation
equator
equatorial
equerry
equerries
equestrian
equidistance
equidistant
equilateral
equilibrium
equine
equinoctial
equinox
equinoxes
equip
equipped
equipping
equipage
equipment
equipoise
equitable
equitably
equity
equivalent
equivocal
equivocally

Can't find your word? Try looking under **AE** or **OE**

eq- 121 **et-**

equivocate
equivocated
equivocating
era
eradicate
eradicated
eradicating
eradication
erase
erased
erasing
eraser
erasure
ere

> ◐* Do not confuse
> with **err** *They will be*
> *home ere long*

erect
erection
erectness
ergonomic
ergonomically
ergonomics
ermine
erode
eroded
eroding
erogenous
erosion
erosive
erotic
erotically
erotica
eroticism
err

> ◐* Do not confuse
> with **ere** *to err on the*
> *side of caution*

errand
errant
erratic

erratically
erratum
errata
erroneous
erroneously
error
ersatz
erstwhile
erudite
eruditely
erudition
erupt
eruption
escalate
escalated
escalating
escalation
escalator
escapade
escape
escaped
escaping
escapism
escapist
escapologist
escapology
escarpment
eschew
escort
esoteric
espadrille
especial
especially
espionage
esplanade
espousal
espouse
espoused
espousing
espresso
espressos
esprit

espy
espies
espied
espying
Esq
Esquire
essay
essayed
essaying
essayist
essence
essential
essentially
establish
established
establishment
estate
esteem
esteemed
esteeming
esteemed
estimable
estimate
estimated
estimating
estimation
estimator
estranged
estuary
estuaries
etc
etch
etching
eternal
eternally
eternity
ethanol
ether
ethereal
ethereally
ethereality
ethical

Can't find your word? Try looking under **AE** or **OE**

ethically
ethics
ethnic
ethnically
ethnicity
ethnocentric
ethnocentricity
ethnocentrism
ethnological
ethnologist
ethnology
ethos
etiquette
etymological
etymologically
etymologist
etymology
  etymologies
eucalyptus
  eucalyptuses,
  eucalypti
eucharist
eugenic
eugenics
eulogize, eulogise
  eulogized, eulogised
  eulogizing,
  eulogising
eulogy
  eulogies
eunuch
  eunuchs
euphemism
euphemistic
euphemistically
euphonium
euphoria
euphoric
euphorically
eureka
euro
  euro, euros

Eurosceptic
euthanasia
evacuate
  evacuated
  evacuating
evacuation
evacuee
evade
  evaded
  evading
evaluate
  evaluated
  evaluating
evaluation
evangelical
evangelise
  another spelling of
  evangelize
evangelist
evangelistic
evangelize,
  evangelise
  evangelized,
  evangelised
  evangelizing,
  evangelising
evaporate
  evaporated
  evaporating
evaporation
evasion
evasive
evasively
evasiveness
eve
even
  evened
  evening
even-handed
evening
evenly
evenness

evensong
event
eventful
eventfully
eventual
eventuality
  eventualities
eventually
ever
evergreen
everlasting
evermore
every
everybody
everyday
everyone
everything
everywhere
evict
eviction
evidence
evident
evidently
evil
evildoer
evilly
evince
evocation
evocative
evocatively
evoke
  evoked
  evoking
evolution

♦* Do not confuse
with **devolution** *the
evolution of the species*
• *Darwin's theory of
evolution*

evolutionary
evolutionist

Can't find your word? Try looking under **AE** or **OE**

evolve
evolved
evolving
ewe

🖈 Do not confuse
with **yew** or **you** *a ram
and a ewe*

ewer
ex
ex's, exes
exacerbate
exacerbated
exacerbating
exacerbation
exact
exacting
exactitude
exactly
exactness
exaggerate
exaggerated
exaggerating

🛈 A br**agger** will
always ex**agger**ate.

exaggeration
exalt
exaltation
exalted
exam
examination
examine
examined
examining
examinee
examiner
example
exasperate
exasperated
exasperating
exasperation
excavate

excavated
excavating
excavation
excavator
exceed

🛈 There's no ex**cuse** to
ex**ceed** that speed.

exceedingly
excel
excelled
excelling
excellence
Excellency
Excellencies
excellent

🛈 Word within word:
ex-**cell**-ent

except

🖈 Do not confuse
with **accept** *Nobody
except John went*

excepting
exception
exceptional
exceptionally
excerpt
excess
excesses

🖈 Do not confuse
with **access** *an excess
of alcohol*

excessive
excessively
exchange
exchanged
exchanging
exchangeable
exchequer
excise
excised

excising
excision
excitable
excitably
excitation
excite
excited
exciting
excited
excitement
exciting
exclaim
exclaimed
exclaiming
exclamation
exclamatory
exclude
excluded
excluding
exclusion
exclusive
exclusively
excommunicate
excommunicated
excommunicating
excommunication
excrement
excrete
excreted
excreting
excretion
excretory
excruciating
excursion
excusable
excuse
excused
excusing
execute
executed
executing
execution

Can't find your word? Try looking under **AE** or **OE**

executioner

💣* Do not confuse with **executor** *He was put to death by the executioner*

executive
executor

💣* Do not confuse with **executioner** *the executor of her will*

exemplar
exemplary
exemplification
exemplify
 exemplifies
 exemplified
 exemplifying
exempt
exemption
exercise
 exercised
 exercising

💣* Do not confuse with **exorcise** or **exorcize** *Exercise is good for your health • spelling exercises • to exercise your dog • to exercise self-control*

exert
exertion
exeunt
exhalation
exhale
 exhaled
 exhaling
exhaust

❶ Don't ex**haust** yourself **hau**ling **st**ones.

exhausted
exhaustible
exhausting
exhaustion
exhaustive
exhibit
 exhibited
 exhibiting
exhibition
exhibitionism
exhibitionist
exhibitor
exhilarate
 exhilarated
 exhilarating
exhilaration
exhort
exhortation
exhumation
exhume
 exhumed
 exhuming
exigency
 exigencies
exigent
exile
 exiled
 exiling
exist
existence
existent
existential
existentialism
existentialist
exit
 exited
 exiting
exodus
 exoduses
exonerate
 exonerated
 exonerating

exoneration
exorbitance
exorbitant
exorcise
 another spelling of **exorcize**
exorcism
exorcist
exorcize, exorcise
 exorcized, exorcised
 exorcizing,
 exorcising

💣* Do not confuse with **exercise** *to exorcize a haunted house • to exorcize evil spirits*

exotic
exotica
exotically
expand

💣* Do not confuse with **expend** *Metals expand when heated*

expandable
expanse
expansion
expansionism
expansionist
expansive

💣* Do not confuse with **expensive** *an expansive treeless plain • a talkative and expansive person*

expansively
expat
expatriate
expect
expectancy

Can't find your word? Try looking under **AE** or **OE**

expectant
expectation
expecting
expectorant
expectorate
 expectorated
 expectorating
expedience
expediency
expedient
expedite
 expedited
 expediting
expedition
expeditious
expel
 expelled
 expelling
expend

> ✎* Do not confuse
> with **expand** *to expend*
> *energy*

expendable
expenditure
expense
expensive

> ✎* Do not confuse
> with **expansive** *an*
> *expensive pair of*
> *trainers*

expensively
experience
 experienced
 experiencing

> ❶ Word breakdown:
> ex-per-i-ence

experiment
experimental
experimentally
experimentation

expert
expertise
expiate
 expiated
 expiating
expiation
expire
 expired
 expiring
expiry
explain
 explained
 explaining
explanation

> ❶ Word breakdown:
> ex-plan-a-tion

explanatory
expletive
explicable
explicably
explicit
explicitly
explode
 exploded
 exploding
exploit
 exploited
 exploiting
exploitation
exploration
exploratory
explore
 explored
 exploring
explorer
explosion
explosive
exponent
exponential
export
exportation

exporter
expose
 exposed
 exposing
exposition
exposure
expound
express
expressible
expression
expressionless
expressive
expressively
expressly
expropriate
 expropriated
 expropriating
expropriation
expulsion
expunge
 expunged
 expunging
expurgate
 expurgated
 expurgating
exquisite
exquisitely
extant
extemporary
extempore
extemporization,
 extemporisation
extemporize,
 extemporise
 extemporized,
 extemporised
 extemporizing,
 extemporising
extend
extendable,
 extendible
extensible

Can't find your word? Try looking under **AE** or **OE**

extension
extensive
extensively
extent
extenuate
 extenuated
 extenuating
extenuation
exterior
exterminate
 exterminated
 exterminating
extermination
exterminator
external
externally
extinct
extinction
extinguish
extinguisher
extol
 extolled
 extolling
extolment
extort
extortion
extortionate
extortionately
extortionist
extra
extract
extraction
extractor
extracurricular
extradite
 extradited
 extraditing

extradition
extramarital
extramural
extraneous
extraordinarily
extraordinary
extrapolate
 extrapolated
 extrapolating
extrapolation
extrasensory
extraterrestrial
extravagance
extravagant
extravagantly
extravaganza
extravert
 another spelling of
 extrovert
extreme
extremely
extremism
extremist
extremity
 extremities
extricable
extricate
 extricated
 extricating
extrovert, extravert
extrude
 extruded
 extruding
extrusion
exuberance
exuberant
exuberantly

exude
 exuded
 exuding
exult
exultant
exultation
eye
 eyed
 eyeing

♦* Do not confuse
with **aye** *a twinkle in
his eye • keep an eye on
the baby*

eyeball
eyebrow
eye-catching
eyeful
eyeglass
 eyeglasses
eyelash
 eyelashes
eyelet
eyelid
eye-opener
eyesight
eyesore
eye-wash
eyewitness
 eyewitnesses
eyrie

♦* Do not confuse
with **eerie** *an eagle's
eyrie*

Can't find your word? Try looking under **AE** or **OE**

If you can't find the word you're looking for under **F**, it could be that it starts with a different letter. Try looking under **PH** for words like *pharmacy*, *photograph* and *physical*.

fa
fable
fabric
fabricate
 fabricated
 fabricating
fabrication
fabulous
fabulously
façade, facade
face
 faced
 facing
faceless
face-lift
face-saving
facet
faceted
facetious
facetiousness
facial
facially
facile
facilely
facilitate
 facilitated
 facilitating
facility
 facilities
facsimile
fact

faction
factional
factor
factory
 factories
factotum
factual
faculty
 faculties
fad
faddish
faddy
 faddier
 faddiest
fade
 faded
 fading
faecal
faeces
faff
fag
 fagged
faggot
fah
Fahrenheit
fail
 failed
 failing
failing
fail-safe
failure

fain
faint

> 🔸 Do not confuse with **feint** *I feel faint • a faint noise • to faint in the heat • She collapsed in a faint*

faint-hearted
faintly
faintness
fair

> 🔸 Do not confuse with **fare** *all the fun of the fair • She has fair hair • It's not fair!*

fairground
fairly
fairness
fairway
fairy
 fairies
fairyland
fait accompli
 faits accomplis
faith
faithful
faithfully
faithfulness
faithless
faithlessness

fajitas
fake
 faked
 faking
falcon
falconry
fall
 fell
 fallen
 falling
fallacious
fallacy
 fallacies
fallen
fallibility
fallible
fallopian
fallout
fallow
false
falsehood
falsely
falseness
falsetto
falsification
falsify
 falsifies
 falsified
 falsifying
falsity
falter
 faltered
 faltering
fame
famed
familiar
familiarise
 another spelling of
 familiarize
familiarity
familiarize,
 familiarise

 familiarized,
 familiarised
 familiarizing,
 familiarising
family
 families
famine
famished
famous
famously
fan
 fanned
 fanning
fanatic
fanatical
fanatically
fanaticism
fancier
fanciful
fancy
 fancies
 fancied
 fancying
fancy-free
fanfare
fang
fanlight
fantail
fantasize, fantasise
 fantasized,
 fantasised
 fantasizing,
 fantasising
fantastic
fantastically
fantasy
 fantasies
fanzine
far
 farther, further
 farthest, furthest
faraway

farce
farcical
fare
 fared
 faring

♠* Do not confuse
with **fair** *bus fare* •
good wholesome fare •
How did you fare?

farewell
far-fetched
far-flung
farm
farmer
farmhouse
farming
farmstead
farmyard
far-off
far-out
far-reaching
farrier
farrow
far-sighted
far-sightedness
farther
farthest
farthing
fascia
fascinate
 fascinated
 fascinating

❶ **Sci**ence fa**sci**nates
me.

fascinating
fascination
fascism
fascist
fashion
 fashioned
 fashioning

Can't find your word? Try looking under **PH**

fashionable
fashionably
fast
fasten
 fastened
 fastening
fastener
fast-forward
fastidious
fastidiousness
fastness
fast-track
fat
 fatter
 fattest
fatal
fatalism
fatalist
fatalistic
fatality
 fatalities
fatally
fate

🖈 Do not confuse
with **fête** *a fate worse
than death*

fated
fateful
fatefully
father
 fathered
 fathering
fatherhood
father-in-law
 fathers-in-law
fatherland
fatherless
fatherly
fathom
 fathomed
 fathoming

fathomless
fatigue
 fatigued
 fatiguing
fatness
fatten
 fattened
 fattening
fatter
fattest
fattiness
fatty
fatwa, fatwah
faucet
fault
faultless
faultlessly
faulty
faun

🖈 Do not confuse
with **fawn** *A faun is a
mythological creature*

fauna
faux pas
 faux pas
favour
 favoured
 favouring
favourable
favourably
favourite
favouritism
fawn

🖈 Do not confuse
with **faun** *fawn in
colour • a deer and its
fawn • Courtiers fawn
on the king*

fawning
fax
 faxes

fear
 feared
 fearing
fearful
fearfully
fearless
fearlessly
fearlessness
fearsome
feasibility
feasible
feasibly
feast
feat

🖈 Do not confuse
with **feet** *a difficult feat*

feather
feathered
featherweight
feathery
feature
 featured
 featuring
featureless
febrile
feckless
fed
federal
federalism
federalist
federate
 federated
 federating
federated
federation
fee
feeble
feeble-minded
feebleness
feebly
feed

Can't find your word? Try looking under **PH**

fed
feeding
feedback
feeder
feel
 felt
 feeling
feeler
feelgood
feeling
feet

> ●* Do not confuse
> with **feat** *These shoes
> hurt my feet • five feet in
> length*

feign
feint

> ●* Do not confuse
> with **faint** *make a feint
> to deceive your
> opponent*

feisty
felicitation
felicitous
felicity
 felicities
feline
fell
fellow
fellowship
felon
felony
 felonies
felt
female
feminine
femininity
feminism
feminist
femme fatale
 femmes fatales

femur
fen
fence
 fenced
 fencing
fencer
fencing
fend
fender
feng shui
fennel
fenugreek
feral
ferment

> ●* Do not confuse
> with **foment** *to ferment
> beer • in a ferment of
> excitement*

fermentation
fern
ferocious
ferociously
ferociousness
ferocity
ferret
 ferreted
 ferreting
ferric
Ferris wheel
ferrous
ferry
 ferries
 ferried
 ferrying
fertile
fertilisation
 another spelling of
 fertilization
fertilise
 another spelling of
 fertilize

fertiliser
 another spelling of
 fertilizer
fertility
**fertilization,
 fertilisation**
fertilize, fertilise
 fertilized, fertilised
 fertilizing, fertilising
fertilizer, fertiliser
fervent
fervently
fervour
fester
 festered
 festering
festival
festive
festively
festivity
 festivities
festoon
 festooned
 festooning
feta
fetal
 another spelling of
 foetal
fetch
fetching
fête, fete

> ●* Do not confuse
> with **fate** *a stall at the
> summer fête*

fetid, foetid
fetish
 fetishes
fetlock
fetters
fettle
fettuccine

Can't find your word? Try looking under **PH**

fetus
another spelling of
 foetus
feud
feudal
feudalism
fever
fevered
feverish
few
fez
 fezzes
fiancé

> ♦* Do not confuse
> with **fiancée** *He is her
> fiancé*

fiancée

> ♦* Do not confuse
> with **fiancé** *She is his
> fiancée*

fiasco
 fiascos
fib
 fibbed
 fibbing
fibber
fibre
fibreglass
fibre-optic
fibre optics
fibrous
fickle
fickleness
fiction
fictional
fictitious
fiddle
 fiddled
 fiddling
fiddler
fiddlesticks

fiddly
fidelity
fidget
 fidgeted
 fidgeting
fidgety
field
fielder
field-marshal
fieldmouse
 fieldmice
fieldwork
fiend
fiendish
fierce

> ❶ Fighting is
> especially fierce.

fiercely
fierceness
fiery
fiesta
fifteen
fifteenth
fifth
fifties
fiftieth
fifty
 fifties
fifty-fifty
fig
fight
 fought
 fighting
fighter
figment
figurative
figuratively
figure
 figured
 figuring
figured

figurehead
figurine
filament
filch
file
 filed
 filing
filigree
filing
fill
 filled
 filling
filler
fillet
 filleted
 filleting
filling
filly
 fillies
film
filo
Filofax®
filter
 filtered
 filtering
filth
filthy
 filthier
 filthiest
filtrate
filtration
fin
final

> ♦* Do not confuse
> with **finale** *the final
> chapter • the cup final*

finale

> ♦* Do not confuse
> with **final** *the finale at
> the end of the concert •
> the grand finale*

Can't find your word? Try looking under **PH**

finalisation
another spelling of
finalization
finalise
another spelling of
finalize
finalist
finality
**finalization,
finalisation**
finalize, finalise
finalized, finalised
finalizing, finalising
finally
finance
financed
financing
financial
financially
financier
finch
finches
find
found
finding
finder
findings
fine
fined
fining
finery
finesse
fine-tune
fine-tuned
fine-tuning
finger
fingered
fingering
fingerboard
fingerbowl
fingermark
fingernail

fingerprint
fingertip
finicky
finish
finishes
finished
finite
fiord, fjord
fir

●* Do not confuse
with **fur** *a fir tree • a fir
cone*

fire
fired
firing
firearm
fireball
fire-bomb
firebrand
firecracker
fire-eater
fire-fighter
fire-fighting
firefly
fireflies
fireguard
firelighter
fireman
firemen
fireplace
fireside
firewood
fireworks
firm
firmament
firmly
firmness
first
first-aid
first-class
first-hand

firstly
first-rate
firth
fiscal
fish
fish, fishes
fishcake
fisherman
fishermen
fishery
fisheries
fishing-rod
fishmonger
fishy
fission

●* Do not confuse
with **fissure** *nuclear
fission*

fissure

●* Do not confuse
with **fission** *a fissure in
the rock*

fist
fistful
fisticuffs
fit
fitter
fittest
fitted
fitting
fitful
fitfully
fitness
fitting
five
fiver
fix
fixation
fixative
fixedly
fixer

Can't find your word? Try looking under **PH**

Narratives

One way to remember lists of words that have the same letter pattern, or the same spelling problem, is to make up a short story containing as many of the words as possible.

For example, the following passage contains ten words ending in -o that have the plural -oes:

> Ships carrying cargoes of potatoes and tomatoes were wrecked by tornadoes and enemy torpedoes. The sailors swam to an island where buffaloes roamed the slopes of volcanoes and where they were treated as heroes. They ate mangoes all day in caves full of echoes.

Can you make up a narrative using words containing ei, such as *reign*, *seize*, *neighbour*, *eight* or *foreign*?

fixture
fizz
fizzle
  fizzled
  fizzling
fizzy
  fizzier
  fizziest
fjord
another spelling of
  fiord
flab
flabbergasted
flabbiness
flabby
flaccid
flag
  flagged
  flagging
flageolet
flagon
flagpole
flagrancy
flagrant
flagrantly
flagship

flagstaff
flagstone
flail
  flailed
  flailing
flair

> ●* Do not confuse with **flare** *have a flair for business*

flak
flake
  flaked
  flaking
flaky
  flakier
  flakiest
flamboyance
flamboyant
flame
  flamed
  flaming
flamenco
  flamencos
flamingo
  flamingos,
  flamingoes

flammable
flan
flange
flank
flannel
flannelette
flap
  flapped
  flapping
flapjack
flapper
flare
  flared
  flaring

> ●* Do not confuse with **flair** *a flare as a signal • make the fire flare up • flared trousers*

flash
  flashes
flashback
flashbulb
flasher
flashily
flashlight

Can't find your word? Try looking under **PH**

flashpoint
flashy
 flashier
 flashiest
flask
flat
 flatter
 flattest
flatfish
flatly
flatness
flatten
 flattened
 flattening
flatter
 flattered
 flattering
flatterer
flattery
flatulence
flatulent
flaunt
flautist
flavour
 flavoured
 flavouring
flavouring
flavoursome
flaw
flawed
flawless
flax
flaxen
flay
 flayed
 flaying
flea

✸ Do not confuse with **flee** *bitten by a flea*

fleck

flecked
fled
fledged
fledgling
flee
 fled
 fleeing

✸ Do not confuse with **flea** *to flee from the enemy*

fleece
 fleeced
 fleecing
fleecy
fleet
fleeting
fleetingly
flesh
fleshy
flew

✸ Do not confuse with **flu** or **flue** *The bird flew away*

flex
 flexes
flexibility
flexible
flexitime
flick
flicker
 flickered
 flickering
flier
 another spelling of
 flyer
flies
flight
flightless
flimsiness
flimsy
 flimsier

flimsiest
flinch
fling
 flung
 flinging
flint
flip
 flipped
 flipping
flip-flop
flippancy
flippant
flippantly
flipper
flirt
flirtation
flirtatious
flit
 flitted
 flitting
float
 floated
 floating
flock
floe

✸ Do not confuse with **flow** *an ice floe*

flog
 flogged
 flogging
flood
floodgate
floodlight
 floodlit
 floodlighting
floodlighting
floodlit
floor
 floored
 flooring
floorboard

Can't find your word? Try looking under **PH**

flop
flopped
flopping
floppy
floppy disk
flora
floral
floret
florid
florist
floss
flotation
flotilla
flotsam
flounce
flounced
flouncing
flounder
floundered
floundering
flour

> 💣* Do not confuse
> with **flower** *Bread is
> made with flour*

flourish
flourishes
floury

> 💣* Do not confuse
> with **flowery** *floury
> potatoes • My hands
> are floury*

flout
flouted
flouting
flow

> 💣* Do not confuse
> with **floe** *a flow of
> blood • to flow
> smoothly*

flowchart

flower
flowered
flowering

> 💣* Do not confuse
> with **flour** *pick a flower
> from the garden • plants
> that flower in the spring*

flowerpot
flowery

> 💣* Do not confuse
> with **floury** *flowery
> curtain material •
> flowery language*

flown
flu

> 💣* Do not confuse
> with **flew** or **flue** *a flu
> epidemic*

fluctuate
fluctuated
fluctuating
fluctuation
flue

> 💣* Do not confuse
> with **flew** or **flu** *The
> smoke goes up the flue*

fluency
fluent
fluently
fluff
fluffy
fluffier
fluffiest
fluid
fluidity
fluke
flume
flummox
flummoxed
flung

flunk
fluorescence
fluorescent
fluoridate
fluoridated
fluoridating
fluoridation
fluoride
fluoridize, fluoridise
fluoridized,
fluoridised
fluoridizing,
fluoridising
flurry
flurries
flurried
flurrying
flush
flushes
fluster
flustered
flustering
flute
fluted
fluting
flutter
fluttered
fluttering
fluvial
flux
fly
flies
flew
flown
flying
flyer, flier
fly-fishing
flying
flyleaf
flyleaves
flyover
flysheet

Can't find your word? Try looking under **PH**

fly-spray
flywheel
foal
 foaled
 foaling
foam
 foamed
 foaming
foamy
fob
 fobbed
 fobbing
focaccia
focal
fo'c'sle
 another spelling of
 forecastle
focus
 pl focuses
 focused, focussed
 focusing, focussing
fodder
foe
foetal, fetal
foetid
 another spelling of
 fetid
foetus, fetus
 foetuses, fetuses
fog
 fogged
 fogging
fogey
 fogeys
foggy
 foggier
 foggiest
foghorn
foible
foil
 foiled
 foiling

foist
fold
folder
foliage
folio
 folios
folk
folklore
folksong
follicle
follow
follower
following
follow-up
folly
 follies
foment

♦* Do not confuse
with **ferment** *to foment
a rebellion*

fomentation
fond
fondant
fondle
 fondled
 fondling
fondly
fondness
fondue
font

♦* Do not confuse
with **fount** *the
baptismal font* You can
use **font** or **fount** for
the printing term.

food
foodie
foodstuff
fool
 fooled
 fooling

foolery
foolhardy
foolish
foolishly
foolishness
foolproof
foolscap
foot
 pl feet
 footed
 footing
foot-and-mouth
football
footbridge
foothill
foothold
footing
footlight
footloose
footman
 footmen
footnote
footpath
footprint
footsore
footstep
footstool
footwear
footwork
fop
foppish
for
forage
 foraged
 foraging
foray
forbade
forbear
 forbore
 forbearing
forbearance
forbid

Can't find your word? Try looking under **PH**

forbade
forbidden
forbidding
forbore
force
forced
forcing
force-feed
force-fed
force-feeding
forceful
forcefully
forcefulness
forceps
forcible
forcibly
ford
fore

💧* Do not confuse
with **four** *come to the
fore • The fore parts are
at the front*

forearm
foreboding
forecast
forecast
forecasting
forecastle, fo'c'sle
forecourt
forefather
forefinger
forefront
forego
foregoes
forewent
foregone
foregoing

💧* Do not confuse
with **forgo** *To forego is
to go before*

foregoing

foregone

💧* Do not confuse
with **forgone** *a
foregone conclusion*

foreground
forehand
forehead
foreign

❶ Before **I** go **n**orth to
foreign lands…

foreigner
foreleg
forelock
foreman
foremen
foremost
forensic
forensically
forerunner
foresee
foresaw
foreseen
foreseeing
foreseeable
foreshadow
foreshore
foresight
forest
forestall
forestation
forested
forester
forestry
foretaste
foretell
foretold
foretelling
forethought
foretold
forever
forewarn

forewarning
forewent
forewoman
forewomen
foreword

💧* Do not confuse
with **forward** *Who
wrote the foreword to
the book?*

forfeit
forfeited
forfeiting
forfeiture
forgave
forge
forged
forging
forgery
forgeries
forget
forgot
forgotten
forgetting
forgetful
forgetfully
forgetfulness
forget-me-not
forgivable
forgive
forgave
forgiven
forgiving
forgiveness
forgo
forgoes
forwent
forgone
forgoing

💧* Do not confuse
with **forego** *To forgo is
to give up or do without*

Can't find your word? Try looking under **PH**

forgone

🖋* Do not confuse
with **foregone** *He has
forgone his privileges*

forgot
forgotten
fork
forked
forkful
fork-lift truck
forlorn
form
formal
formaldehyde
formalise
another spelling of
formalize
formality
formalities
formalize, formalise
formalized,
formalised
formalizing,
formalising
formally

🖋* Do not confuse
with **formerly** *formally
dressed for the occasion*

format
formatted
formatting
formation
formative
former
formerly

🖋* Do not confuse
with **formally** *The
building was formerly
used as a school*

formic

Formica®
formidable
formidably
formless
formula
formulae, formulas
formulaic
formulate
formulated
formulating
formulation
forsake
forsook
forsaken
forsaking
forswear
forswore
forsworn
forswearing
fort

🖋* Do not confuse
with **forte** *They
besieged the fort*

forte

🖋* Do not confuse
with **fort** or **forty**
*Cooking is not my forte
• The chord is played
forte*

forth

🖋* Do not confuse
with **fourth** *Smoke
issued forth • from that
day forth • selling
computers and so forth*

forthcoming
forthright
forthwith
forties
fortieth

fortification
fortify
fortifies
fortified
fortifying
fortissimo
fortitude
fortnight
fortnightly
fortress
fortresses
fortuitous
fortuitously
fortunate
fortunately
fortune
fortune-teller
forty
forties

❶ **For**ty **for**gets the **u**.

🖋* Do not confuse
with **forte** *He spent
forty pounds*

forum
forums, fora
forward

🖋* Do not confuse
with **foreword** *a
forward movement • to
forward a letter*

forwards
forwent
fossil
**fossilization,
fossilisation**
fossilize, fossilise
fossilized, fossilised
fossilizing,
fossilising
foster

Can't find your word? Try looking under **PH**

fostered
fostering
fought
foul

* Do not confuse
with **fowl** *the foul smell
of rotting cabbage • foul
play • It's a foul if you
trip another player up*

foul-mouthed
found

* Do not confuse
found, the past form of
find, with **founded**,
the past form of **found**
*He found the missing
key • She founded a
new company*

foundation
founder
foundered
foundering
foundling
foundry
foundries
fount

* Do not confuse
with **font** *the fount of
knowledge* You can use
fount or **font** for the
printing term.

fountain
four

* Do not confuse
with **fore** *She has four
brothers*

four-poster
foursome
fourteen
fourteenth

fourth

* Do not confuse
with **forth** *the fourth of
July • in fourth place*

fourthly
fowl

* Do not confuse
with **foul** *domestic fowl
such as chickens and
turkeys*

fox
foxes
foxglove
foxhound
fox-hunting
foxtrot
foxy
foyer
fracas
fractal
fraction
fractional
fractionally
fractious
fracture
fractured
fracturing
fragile
fragility
fragment
fragmentary
fragmentation
fragrance
fragrant
frail
frailty
frailties
frame
framed
framing
framework

franc

* Do not confuse
with **frank** *the French
franc*

franchise
franchised
franchising
francophone,
Francophone
franglais
frank

* Do not confuse
with **franc** *frank and
honest • to frank a letter*

frankfurter
frankincense
frantic
frantically
fraternal
fraternisation
another spelling of
fraternization
fraternise
another spelling of
fraternize
fraternity
fraternities
fraternization,
fraternisation
fraternize,
fraternise
fraternized,
fraternised
fraternizing,
fraternising
fraud
fraudulent
fraught
fray
frayed
fraying

Can't find your word? Try looking under **PH**

frazzle
freak
freakish
freaky
freckle
freckled
free
 freed
 freeing
freebie
freedom
free-for-all
freehand
freehold
freeholder
freelance
freelancer
freeload
freeloader
freely
Freemason
free-range
freesia
freestyle
freeware
freeway
freewheel
 freewheeled
 freewheeling
freeze
 froze
 frozen
 freezing

♦* Do not confuse
with **frieze** *to freeze
vegetables • a price
freeze • Freeze! shouted
the cop*

freezer
freight
freighter

frenetic
frenetically
frenzied
frenzy
frequency
 frequencies
frequent
fresco
 frescoes, frescos
fresh
freshen
 freshened
 freshening
fresher
freshly
freshness
freshwater
fret
 fretted
 fretting
fretful
fretfully
fretsaw
fretwork
friar

♦* Do not confuse
with **fryer** *A friar
belongs to a religious
order • Friar Tuck*

friary
 friaries
friction
fridge
fried
friend

🛈 Share your **fries**
with your **frie**nd.

friendless
friendliness
friendly
 friendlier

friendliest
friendship
frier
 another spelling of
 fryer
fries
frieze

♦* Do not confuse
with **freeze** *decorate
the wall with a frieze*

frigate
fright
frighten
 frightened
 frightening
frightful
frightfully
frigid
frigidity
frill
frilly
 frillier
 frilliest
fringe
 fringed
 fringing
Frisbee®
frisk
friskily
frisky
frisson
fritter
 frittered
 frittering
frivolity
 frivolities
frivolous
frizz
frizzy
fro
frock

Can't find your word? Try looking under **PH**

frock-coat
frog
frogman
 frogmen
frogmarch
frogspawn
frolic
 frolicked
 frolicking
frolicsome
from
fromage frais
frond
front
frontage
frontal
frontbench
frontbencher
frontier
frontispiece
front-runner
frost
frostbite
frostbitten
frosted
frostily
frosting
frosty
 frostier
 frostiest
froth
frothy
frown
froze
frozen
frugal
frugality
frugally
fruit
fruitcake
fruiterer
fruitful

fruitfully
fruition
fruitless
fruitlessly
fruity
frump
frumpish
frustrate
 frustrated
 frustrating
frustration
fry
 fries
 fried
 frying
fryer, frier

> ✦* Do not confuse
> with **friar** *a deep-fat*
> *fryer for cooking chips*

frying-pan
fuchsia
fuddle
 fuddled
 fuddling
fuddy-duddy
fudge
 fudged
 fudging
fuel
 fuelled
 fuelling
fugitive
fugue
fulcrum
 fulcrums, fulcra
fulfil
 fulfilled
 fulfilling

> ❶ Remember – both
> **full** and **fill** drop extra
> l's.

fulfilment
full
fullback
full-blown
full-blooded
full-circle
full house
full-length
fullness, fulness
full-scale
full stop
full-time
fully
fulmar
fulminate
 fulminated
 fulminating
fulness
 another spelling of
 fullness
fulsome
fumble
 fumbled
 fumbling
fume
 fumed
 fuming
fumes
fumigate
 fumigated
 fumigating
fumigation
fun
function
 functioned
 functioning
functional
functionality
functionally
functionary
 functionaries
fund

Can't find your word? Try looking under **PH**

fundamental
fundamentalism
fundamentalist
fundamentally
funder
funding
funeral

✍* Do not confuse
with **funereal** *the
church where the
funeral was held • the
funeral procession*

funereal

✍* Do not confuse
with **funeral** *playing
solemn, funereal music*

funfair
fungal
fungicidal
fungicide
fungus
 fungi, funguses
funicular railway
funky
funnel
 funnelled
 funnelling
funnily
funny
 funnier
 funniest

fur
 furred
 furring

✍* Do not confuse
with **fir** *a fur coat • a
cat's fur • Hard water
makes kettles fur up*

furbish
furious
furiously
furl
furlong
furnace
furnish
furnishings
furniture
furore
furred
furrier
furring
furrow
furry
further
 furthered
 furthering
furtherance
furthermore
furthest
furtive
furtively
furtiveness

fury
furze
fuse
 fused
 fusing
fuselage
fusilier
fusillade
fusion
fuss
 fusses
fussily
fussiness
fusspot
fussy
 fussier
 fussiest
fustiness
fusty
futile
futilely
futility
futon
future
futurist
futuristic
fuzz
fuzzy
 fuzzier
 fuzziest

Can't find your word? Try looking under **PH**

G g

If the word you're looking for sounds as if it begins with a straightforward **G** but you can't find it, try looking under **GH** for words like *ghastly* and *ghost*, and **GU** for words like *guard* and *guide*.

gab
gabbed
gabbing
gabble
gabbled
gabbling
gable
gadabout
gadget
gadgetry
gaff

💧* Do not confuse with **gaffe** *A gaff is a large hook* • *blow the gaff*

gaffe

💧* Do not confuse with **gaff** *A gaffe is a social blunder*

gag
gagged
gagging
gaga
gaggle
gaiety
gaily
gain
gained
gaining
gainful

gait

💧* Do not confuse with **gate** *walk with a shuffling gait*

gala
galactic
galaxy
galaxies
gale
gall
gallant
gallantry
gall bladder
galleon

💧* Do not confuse with **gallon** *a Spanish galleon on the high seas*

gallery
galleries
galley
galleys
galling
gallivant
gallon

💧* Do not confuse with **galleon** *a gallon of petrol*

gallop
galloped
galloping

gallows
gallstone
galore
galoshes, goloshes
galumph
galvanic
galvanize, galvanise
galvanized,
galvanised
galvanizing,
galvanising
gambit
gamble
gambled
gambling

💧* Do not confuse with **gambol** *People gamble in a casino* • *Our gamble paid off*

gambler
gambol
gambolled
gambolling

💧* Do not confuse with **gamble** *Lambs gambol in the fields*

game
gamekeeper
gaming
gamma

SPELLING *focus*

Games

Fish game

How many words can you write down which end in the letters **-fish**, but which are not the names of different types of fish?

Vanishing opposites

Think about the words *gormless* and *ruthless*. They look like negatives, but neither of them now corresponds to a positive adjective *gorm* or *ruth*. In the same way, you may feel *disgruntled*, but have you ever felt *gruntled*? Write down as many other words as you can think of which seem to be the opposite of non-existent adjectives. If you look in a bigger dictionary, you might find that some of these words did have opposites in the past.

Word snake

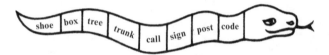

This snake is made up of words which form compounds. For example, *shoe* and *box* make *shoebox*; *box* and *tree* make *box tree* (a type of evergreen tree); *tree* and *trunk* make *tree-trunk*, and so on. What is the longest word snake you can make? (If you get stuck, look in a dictionary for help.)

Clockwise game

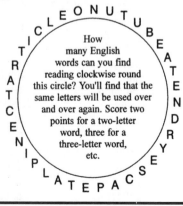

How many English words can you find reading clockwise round this circle? You'll find that the same letters will be used over and over again. Score two points for a two-letter word, three for a three-letter word, etc.

gammon
gammy
gamut
gander
gang
gangland
gangly
gangplank
gangrene
gangrenous
gangster
gangway
gannet
gantry
 gantries
gaol
another spelling of **jail**

> 💣* Do not confuse
> with **goal** *He was sent*
> *to gaol*

gaolbird
another spelling of
jailbird
gaoler
another spelling of
jailer
gap
gape
 gaped
 gaping
gappy
garage
 garaged
 garaging
garam masala
garb
garbage
garble
 garbled
 garbling
garbled

garden
 gardened
 gardening
gardener
gardening
gardenia
gargantuan
gargle
 gargled
 gargling
gargoyle
garish
garishness
garland
garlic
garlicky
garment
garner
 garnered
 garnering
garnet
garnish
 garnishes
garret
garrison
 garrisoned
 garrisoning
garrotte
 garrotted
 garrotting
garrulous
garter
gas
 pl gases
 gassed
 gassing
gaseous
gash
 gashes
gasket
gaslight
gasoline

gasometer
gasp
gassy
gastric
gastritis
gastroenteritis
gastronomic
gastronomy
gastropod
gasworks
gate

> 💣* Do not confuse
> with **gait** *a garden gate*
> • *shut the gate*

gateau, gâteau
 gateaus, gateaux,
 gâteaux
gatecrash
gatecrasher
gated
gateway
gather
 gathered
 gathering
gathering
gauche
gaucho
 gauchos
gaudily
gaudiness
gaudy
 gaudier
 gaudiest
gauge
 gauged
 gauging

> ❶ To **gauge** is to get **a**
> **u**seful **g**eneral
> estimate.

gaunt
gauntlet

---

gauntness
gauze
gave
gavel
gavotte
gawkily
gawkiness
gawky
gawp
gay
gaze
 gazed
 gazing
gazebo
 gazebos, gazeboes
gazelle
gazette
gazetteer
gazpacho
gazump
gear
 geared
 gearing
gearbox
 gearboxes
gecko
gee
geese
geezer

♦ Do not confuse with **geyser** *Geezer is a slang word for a man*

geisha
gel, jell
 gelled, jelled
 gelling, jelling

♦ The spelling **jell** is only used for the verb *hair gel • The plan began to jell*

gelatine, gelatin
gelatinous
geld
gelding
gelignite
gem
gemstone
gen
 genned
 genning
gender
gene
genealogical
genealogist
genealogy
 genealogies
genera
general
generalisation
 another spelling of
 generalization
generalise
 another spelling of
 generalize
generality
 generalities
generalization,
 generalisation
generalize,
 generalise
 generalized,
 generalised
 generalizing,
 generalising
generally
generate
 generated
 generating
generation
generative
generator
generic

generosity
generous
generously
genesis
genetic
genetically
geneticist
genetics
genial
geniality
genially
genie
 genii

♦ Do not confuse with **genius** *The genie granted her wishes*

genital
genitalia
genitals
genitive
genius
 geniuses

♦ Do not confuse with **genie** or **genus** *He is clever but not a genius*

genocide
genome
genre
gent
genteel

♦ Do not confuse with **gentile** or **gentle** *a genteel tea party*

genteelly
gentian
gentile

♦ Do not confuse with **genteel** or **gentle** *Jews and gentiles*

gentility

Can't find your word? Try looking under **GH** or **GU**

gentle

> ♦* Do not confuse with **genteel** or **gentile** *She has a gentle nature* • *a gentle breeze*

gently
gentleman
 gentlemen
gentlemanly
gentleness
gentrification
gentrify
 gentrifies
 gentrified
 gentrifying
gentry
gents
genuflect
genuflection
genuine

> ❶ Word breakdown: gen-u-ine

genuinely
genuineness
genus
 genera

> ♦* Do not confuse with **genius** *To what genus does that plant belong?*

geode
geographer
geographic
geographical
geographically
geography
geological
geologically
geologist
geology

geometric
geometrical
geometrically
geometry
geophysics
geothermal
geranium
gerbil
geriatric
germ
germicide
germinate
 germinated
 germinating
germination
gerund
gestate
gestation
gesticulate
 gesticulated
 gesticulating
gesticulation
gesture
 gestured
 gesturing
get
 got
 getting
getaway
gettable
get-together
get-up-and-go
geyser

> ♦* Do not confuse with **geezer** *a geyser in Yellowstone Park*

ghastliness
ghastly

> ❶ Go home and stay there, little yob!

ghee

gherkin
ghetto
 ghettos
ghetto-blaster
ghillie
 another spelling of
 gillie
ghost

> ❶ Gasp with horror when you see a ghost!

ghostliness
ghostly
ghoul
ghoulish
giant
giantess
 giantesses
gibber
 gibbered
 gibbering
gibberish
gibbet
gibbon
gibe
 another spelling of
 jibe
giblets
giddiness
giddy
gift
gifted
gift-wrap
 gift-wrapped
 gift-wrapping
gig
gigabyte
gigantic
giggle
 giggled
 giggling
giggly

Can't find your word? Try looking under **GU**

gild

> ●* Do not confuse
> with **guild** *to gild a*
> *brooch*

gill
gillie, ghillie
gilt

> ●* Do not confuse
> with **guilt** *pictures in*
> *gilt frames*

gilt-edged
gimlet
gimmick
gimmicky
gin
ginger
gingerbread
gingerly
gingham
gingivitis
ginormous
ginseng
gipsy
another spelling of
gypsy
giraffe
gird
girder
girdle
girl
girlfriend
girlhood
girlie
girlish
giro
giros
girth
gist
give
gave
given

giving
giveaway,
give-away
gizzard
glacé
glacial
glaciation
glacier

> ●* Do not confuse
> with **glazier** *The*
> *glacier is melting*

glad
gladden
gladdened
gladdening
glade
gladiator
gladiatorial
gladly
gladness
glamorize,
glamorise
glamorized,
glamorised
glamorizing,
glamorising
glamorous
glamour
glance
glanced
glancing
gland
glandular
glare
glared
glaring
glaringly
glass
glasses
glasshouse
glassily

glassy
glaucoma
glaze
glazed
glazing
glazier

> ●* Do not confuse
> with **glacier** *The*
> *glazier mended the*
> *window*

gleam
gleamed
gleaming
glean
gleaned
gleaning
glebe
glee
gleeful
gleefully
glen
glib
glibly
glibness
glide
glided
gliding
glider
glimmer
glimmered
glimmering
glimpse
glimpsed
glimpsing
glint
glisten
glistened
glistening
glitch
glitches
glitter

Can't find your word? Try looking under **GH** or **GU**

glittered
glittering
glittery
glitz
glitzy
gloaming
gloat
gloated
gloating
global
globally
globe
globetrotter
globular
globule
glockenspiel
gloom
gloomily
gloomy
gloomier
gloomiest
glorification
glorify
glorifies
glorified
glorifying
glorious
glory
glories
gloss
glosses
glossary
glossaries
glossily
glossiness
glossy
glossier
glossiest
glove
glow
glower
glowered

glowering
glowing
glow-worm
glucose
glue
glued
gluing
gluey
glum
glumly
glut
glutted
glutting
glutamate
gluten
glutinous

> ✒* Do not confuse
> with **gluttonous** *a*
> *sticky, glutinous*
> *substance*

glutton
gluttonous

> ✒* Do not confuse
> with **glutinous**
> *gluttonous eaters*

gluttony
glycerine
gnarled
gnash
gnashers
gnat
gnaw
gnocchi
gnome
gnomish
gnu
gnu, gnus
go
pl goes
went
gone

going
goad
go-ahead
goal

> ✒* Do not confuse
> with **gaol** *He scored a*
> *goal*

goalie
goalkeeper
goalpost
goat
goatee
gob
gobble
gobbled
gobbling
gobbledegook,
gobbledygook
go-between
goblet
goblin
gobsmacked
gobstopper
god
godchild
godchildren
goddaughter
goddess
goddesses
godfather
God-fearing
god-forsaken
godless
godlike
godliness
godly
godmother
godparent
godsend
godson
goer

Can't find your word? Try looking under **GH** or **GU**

go-getter
goggle
goggled
goggling
goggles
going
goitre
go-kart
gold
golden
goldfinch
 goldfinches
goldfish
gold-plated
golf
golfer
golfing
golly
goloshes
 another spelling of
 galoshes
gondola
gondolier
gone
goner
gong
gonorrhoea
goo
good
 better
 best
goodbye, good-bye
good-day
good-for-nothing
goodies
goodly
good-natured
goodness
goodnight
goods
goodwill
goody-goody

gooey
goof
goofy
googly
 googlies
goon
goose
 geese
gooseberry
 gooseberries
goose-pimples
gopher
gore
 gored
 goring
gorge
 gorged
 gorging
gorgeous

🛈 Word within word:
gorge-ous

gorgeousness
gorgon
Gorgonzola
gorilla

💧* Do not confuse
with **guerrilla** *A gorilla
is an ape*

gormless
gorse
gory
 gorier
 goriest
gosh
gosling
gospel
gossamer
gossip
 gossiped
 gossiping
gossipy

got
gouge
 gouged
 gouging
goujon
goulash
gourd
gourmand

💧* Do not confuse
with **gourmet** *A
gourmand eats
greedily*

gourmet

💧* Do not confuse
with **gourmand** *A
gourmet likes good
food and wine*

gout
govern
governess
 governesses
government

🛈 Governments
gover**n**.

governmental
governor
gown
grab
 grabbed
 grabbing
grace
 graced
 gracing
graceful
gracefully
gracefulness
graceless
gracious
graciously
graciousness

Can't find your word? Try looking under **GH** or **GU**

gradation

✸ Do not confuse with **graduation**
gradation in order of difficulty

grade
graded
grading
gradient
gradual
gradually
gradualness
graduate
graduated
graduating
graduation

✸ Do not confuse with **gradation**
graduation from university •
graduations marked on the side of a measuring jug

graffiti
graft
grafter
grail
grain
grainy
gram, gramme
grammar

❶ Grand**ma** is good at gram**mar**.

grammarian
grammatical
grammatically
gramme
another spelling of
gram
gramophone

granary
granaries
grand
grandad, granddad
grandchild
grandchildren
granddad
another spelling of
grandad
grand-daughter
grandeur
grandfather
grandiloquence
grandiloquent
grandiose
grandma
grandmother
grandpa
grandparent
grandson
grandstand
grange
granite
granny
grannies
grant
granular
granulated
granule
grape
grapefruit
grapevine
graph
graphic
graphically
graphics
graphite
graphologist
graphology
grapple
grappled
grappling

grasp
grasping
grass
grasses
grasshopper
grassy
grate
grated
grating

✸ Do not confuse with **great** *a fire in the grate • to grate cheese*

grateful
gratefully
grater
gratification
gratify
gratifies
gratified
gratifying
grating
gratis
gratitude
gratuitous
gratuitously
gratuity
gratuities
grave
gravel
gravelly
gravely
graven
gravestone
graveyard
gravitas
gravitate
gravitated
gravitating
gravitation
gravity
gravy

Can't find your word? Try looking under **GH** or **GU**

gravies
graze
grazed
grazing
grease
greased
greasing
greasepaint
greaseproof
greasiness
greasy
greasier
greasiest
great

> ♦* Do not confuse
> with **grate** *a great*
> *writer • a great deal of*
> *trouble*

great-aunt
greatcoat
great-grandfather
great-grandmother
greatly
greatness
great-uncle
grebe
greed
greedily
greediness
greedy
greedier
greediest
green
greenery
greenfinch
greenfinches
greenfly
greenfly
greengage
greengrocer
greenhouse

greenish
greenness
greenstick
greet
greeted
greeting
greeting
gregarious
gremlin
grenade
grenadier
grenadine
grew
grey
greys
greyhound
greyness
grid
griddle
gridiron
grief

> ♦* Do not confuse
> with **grieve** *full of grief*
> *• come to grief*

grievance
grieve
grieved
grieving

> ♦* Do not confuse
> with **grief** *The*
> *bereaved need time to*
> *grieve • It grieves me to*
> *see such waste*

grievous
griffin, griffon
grill

> ♦* Do not confuse
> with **grille** *a grill on a*
> *cooker • a mixed grill •*
> *to grill a steak*

grille

> ♦* Do not confuse
> with **grill** *a metal grille*
> *over a window*

grim
grimace
grimaced
grimacing
grime
grimly
grimness
grimy
grin
grinned
grinning
grind
ground
grinding
grinder
grindstone
grip
gripped
gripping
gripe
griped
griping
griping
gripping
grisly

> ♦* Do not confuse
> with **gristly** or **grizzly**
> *a grisly, horrible sight*

grist
gristle
gristly

> ♦* Do not confuse
> with **grisly** or **grizzly**
> *gristly meat*

grit
gritted

Can't find your word? Try looking under **GH** or **GU**

gritting
gritty
grizzled
grizzly
grizzlies

> ●* Do not confuse
> with **grisly** or **gristly** *a*
> *grizzly bear*

groan
groaned
groaning
groat
grocer
grocery
groceries
grog
groggily
grogginess
groggy
groin
grommet
groom
groomed
grooming
groove
grooved
grooving
groovy
grope
groped
groping

> ●* Do not confuse
> with **group** *to grope*
> *your way • to grope for*
> *a handkerchief*

gross
grossly
grossness
grotesque
grotesquely
grotesqueness

grottiness
grotto
grottoes, grottos
grotty
grottier
grottiest
grouch
grouches
grouchy
ground

> ●* Do not confuse
> **ground**, the past form
> of **grind**, with
> **grounded**, the past
> form of **ground** *I*
> *ground the coffee beans*
> *• They grounded the*
> *planes*

grounding
groundless
groundnut
groundsheet
groundswell
groundwork
group
grouped
grouping

> ●* Do not confuse
> with **grope** *a group of*
> *children • to group*
> *together*

groupie
grouse
pl grouses, grouse
groused
grousing

> ●* The plural **grouse**
> is only used for the
> bird *He shot four*
> *grouse*

grout

grouted
grouting
grove
grovel
grovelled
grovelling
groveller
grow
grew
grown
growing
growl
grown
grown-up
growth
grub
grubbed
grubbing
grubbily
grubbiness
grubby
grubbier
grubbiest
grudge
grudged
grudging
gruel
gruelling
gruesome
gruff
grumble
grumbled
grumbling
grumbler
grump
grumpily
grumpiness
grumpy
grumpier
grumpiest
grunge
grungy

Can't find your word? Try looking under **GH** or **GU**

grunt
Gruyère
guacamole
guano
guarantee
 guaranteed
 guaranteeing

🛈 **G**et **u**p and **rant** about the **gu**arantee.

guarantor
guard

🛈 The **gu**ard has a **gu**n.

guarded
guardedly
guardedness
guardian
guardsman
 guardsmen
guava
guerrilla, guerilla

♦* Do not confuse with **gorilla** *guerrilla warfare* Remember that **gu**errillas often have **gu**ns.

guess
 guesses
guesstimate
guesswork
guest
guesthouse
guff
guffaw
guidance
guide
 guided
 guiding
guidebook
guideline

guild

♦* Do not confuse with **gild** *a guild of craftsmen* • *the Townswomen's Guild*

guile
guileful
guileless
guillemot
guillotine
 guillotined
 guillotining
guilt

♦* Do not confuse with **gilt** *The evidence proved her guilt*

guiltily
guilty

🛈 **Y**ou [**u**] and **I** are gui**l**ty.

guinea
guinea-fowl
guinea-pig
guise
guitar
guitarist
gulf
 gulfs
gull
gullet
gullible
gullibly
gully
 gullies
gulp
gum
 gummed
 gumming
gumboot
gumdrop

gummy
gumption
gun
 gunned
 gunning
gunboat
gunfire
gunge
gung-ho
gungy
gunk
gunman
 gunmen
gunmetal
gunnel
 another spelling of
 gunwale
gunner
gunpoint
gunpowder
gunshot
gunwale, gunnel
guppy
 guppies
gurgle
 gurgled
 gurgling
guru
 gurus
gush
gusset
gust
gustily
gusto
gusty
gut
 gutted
 gutting
guts
gutsy
gutted
gutter

Can't find your word? Try looking under **GH**

guttering
guttural
gutturally
guv
guy
guys
guzzle
guzzled
guzzling
guzzler

gym
gymkhana
gymnasium
  gymnasiums,
  gymnasia
gymnast
gymnastic
gymnastics
gynaecological
gynaecologist

gynaecology
gypsy, gipsy
  gypsies, gipsies
gypsum
gyrate
  gyrated
  gyrating
gyration
gyratory
gyroscope

Can't find your word? Try looking under **GH**

If you can't find the word you're looking for under **H**, it could be that it starts with a different letter. Try looking under **WH** for words like *who*, *whole* and *whom*.

ha
haberdasher
haberdashery
habit
habitable
habitat
habitation
habitual
habitually
habituate
 habituated
 habituating
habituation
hacienda
hack
hacker
hacking
hackles
hackney
hackneyed
hacksaw
had
haddock
Hades
hadj, haj, hajj
hadn't
haematologist
haematology
haemoglobin
haemophilia
haemophiliac

haemorrhage
 haemorrhaged
 haemorrhaging

❶ **Haemorrhage** – an emergency often requiring rapid hospital attention.

haemorrhoid
hag
haggard
haggardly
haggardness
haggis
 haggises
haggle
 haggled
 haggling
haggler
ha-ha
haiku
 haiku, haikus
hail
 hailed
 hailing

🖋️ Do not confuse with **hale** *hail and snow* • *to hail a taxi* • *Hail Mary*

hailstone
hailstorm

hair

🖋️ Do not confuse with **hare** *a girl with red hair* • *You're just splitting hairs*

hairbrush
 hairbrushes
haircut
hairdo
 hairdos
hairdresser
hairdryer, hairdrier
hairgrip
hairless
hairline
hairpin
hair-raising
hair slide
hair-splitting
hairspray
hairstyle
hairy
 hairier
 hairiest
haj
 another spelling of
 hadj
hajj
 another spelling of
 hadj
hake

halal
hale

> ◆* Do not confuse with **hail** *hale and hearty*

half
halves

> ◆* Do not confuse with **halve** *half an apple • cut in half • Two halves make a whole*

halfback
half-baked
half-board
half-brother
half-hearted
half-life
halfpenny
halfpennies
half-sister
half-term
half-timbered
half-time
halfway
halfwit
halibut
halitosis
hall
hallelujah
hallmark
hallo

another spelling of
hello

> ◆* Do not confuse with **hallow** or **halo** *Hallo! How are you?*

hallow

> ◆* Do not confuse with **hallo** or **halo** *to hallow a shrine*

hallowed
hallucinate
hallucinated
hallucinating
hallucination
hallucinatory
hallucinogen
hallucinogenic
hallway
halo
haloes, halos

> ◆* Do not confuse with **hallo** or **hallow** *a saint's halo*

halogen
halt
halter
halting
halve
halved
halving

> ◆* Do not confuse with **half** *to halve an apple*

halves
ham
hamburger
ham-fisted
hamlet
hammer
hammered
hammering
hammock
hamper
hampered
hampering
hamster
hamstring
hamstrung
hamstringing
hand

handbag
handball
handbill
handbook
handbrake
handcuffs
handful
handfuls
hand grenade
handgun
handicap
handicapped
handicapping
handicapped
handicraft
handily
handiness
handiwork
handkerchief
handkerchiefs,
handkerchieves
handle
handled
handling
handlebars
handler
handmade
hand-me-down
handout
handover
hand-picked
handshake
hands-off
handsome
handsomely
handsomeness
hands-on
handwriting
handwritten
handy
handyman
handymen

Can't find your word? Try looking under **WH**

hang
hung, hanged
hanging

🔾* The past form **hanged** is only used for the meaning 'put to death' *They hanged the murderer • he hung the painting in the gallery*

hangar

🔾* Do not confuse with **hanger** *an aeroplane in its hangar*

hangdog
hanger

🔾* Do not confuse with **hangar** *a coat on its hanger*

hanger-on
hangers-on
hang-glider
hang-gliding
hanging
hangman
hangmen
hangnail
hangover
hank
hanker
hankered
hankering
hankie, hanky
hankies
hanky-panky
haphazard
haphazardly
hapless
happen
happened
happening

happily
happiness
happy
happier
happiest
happy-go-lucky
hara-kiri
harangue
harangued
haranguing
harass
harassment
harbinger
harbour
harboured
harbouring
hard
hard-and-fast
hardback
hardcore
hard disk
harden
hardened
hardening
hard-hearted
hard-hitting
hardier
hardiest
hardily
hardiness
hardline
hardliner
hardly
hardness
hard-nosed
hard-pressed
hard-pushed
hardship
hardware
hardy
hardier
hardiest

hare

🔾* Do not confuse with **hair** *A hare is like a large rabbit*

harebell
hare-brained
hare-lip
harem
hark
harlequin
harm
harmful
harmfully
harmless
harmonic
harmonica
harmonious
harmonisation
another spelling of **harmonization**
harmonise
another spelling of **harmonize**
harmonium
harmonization, harmonisation
harmonize, harmonise
harmonized, harmonised
harmonizing, harmonising
harmony
harmonies
harness
harnesses
harp
harpist
harpoon
harpooned
harpooning

Can't find your word? Try looking under **WH**

harpsichord
harpy
 harpies
harrier
harrow
harrowing
harry
 harries
 harried
 harrying
harsh
harshly
harshness
hart

💣* Do not confuse
with **heart** *A hart is a
deer*

harum-scarum
harvest
harvester
has
has-been
hash
 hashes
hashish
hasn't
hassle
 hassled
 hassling
hassock
haste
hasten
 hastened
 hastening
hastily
hastiness
hasty
hat
hatch
 hatches
hatchback

hatchery
 hatcheries
hatchet
hatching
hatchway
hate
 hated
 hating
hateful
hatefully
hatpin
hatstand
hatred
hatter
haughtily
haughtiness
haughty
haul
 hauled
 hauling
haulage
haulier
haunch
 haunches
haunt
haunted
haunting
haute couture
haute cuisine
have
 had
 having
haven
haven't
haversack
havoc
haw
hawk
hawker
hawk-eyed
hawkish
hawthorn

hay

💣* Do not confuse
with **hey** *hay for the
cattle • make hay while
the sun shines*

hay fever
haystack
haywire
hazard
hazardous
haze
hazel
hazelnut
hazily
haziness
hazy
he
head
headache
headband
headboard
headdress
 headdresses
header
headfirst
headgear
headhunter
headhunting
heading
headlamp
headland
headless
headlight
headline
headlong
headmaster
headmistress
 headmistresses
head-on
headphones
headquarters

Can't find your word? Try looking under **WH**

headrest

headroom

headscarf

  headscarves

headset

headstone

headstrong

headway

headwind

headword

heady

heal

  healed

  healing

> 💧* Do not confuse
> with **heel** *to heal a*
> *wound*

healer

healing

health

healthily

healthy

  healthier

  healthiest

heap

  heaped

  heaping

hear

  heard

  hearing

> 💧* Do not confuse
> with **here** *She can't*
> *hear you* Remember
> that you h**ear** with
> your **ears**.

heard

> 💧* Do not confuse
> with **herd** *I heard a*
> *strange noise • I've*
> *never heard of him*

hearing

hearsay

hearse

heart

> 💧* Do not confuse
> with **hart** *heart disease*
> *• a loving heart*

heartache

heartbreaking

heartbroken

heartburn

hearten

  heartened

  heartening

heartfelt

hearth

heartily

heartland

heartless

heart-rending

heartstrings

heart-throb

heart-to-heart

hearty

heat

  heated

  heating

heater

heath

heathen

heather

heating

heatstroke

heat wave

heave

  heaved

  heaving

heaven

heavenly

heavens

heavily

heaviness

heavy

  heavier

  heaviest

heavy-duty

heavy-handed

heavyweight

heckle

  heckled

  heckling

heckler

hectare

hectic

hectically

hector

  hectored

  hectoring

he'd

hedge

  hedged

  hedging

hedgehog

hedgerow

hedonism

hedonist

hedonistic

heebie-jeebies

heed

heedless

heel

  heeled

  heeling

> 💧* Do not confuse
> with **heal** *the heel of a*
> *shoe • to heel a shoe*

hefty

hegemony

heifer

height

> ❶ Height – everyone
> is guessing how tall.

Can't find your word? Try looking under **WH**

heighten
heightened
heightening
heinous
heir

> ✏ Do not confuse
> with **air** *heir to the*
> *throne* • *heir to a*
> *fortune*

heiress
heiresses
heirloom
held
helicopter
helipad
heliport
helium
helix
helixes, helices
he'll
hell
hell-bent
hellish
hellishly
hello, hallo, hullo
helm
helmet
helmsman
helmsmen
help
helper
helpful
helpfully
helpfulness
helping
helpless
helplessly
helplessness
helter-skelter
hem
hemmed

hemming
hemisphere
hemispherical
hemline
hemlock
hemp
hen
hence
henceforth
henchman
henchmen
henna
henpecked
hepatitis
heptagon
heptagonal
her
herald
heraldic
heraldry
herb
herbaceous
herbal
herbalism
herbalist
herbicide
herbivore
herbivorous
Herculean
herd

> ✏ Do not confuse
> with **heard** *a herd of*
> *cattle*

herdsman
herdsmen
here

> ✏ Do not confuse
> with **hear** *Here you*
> *are* • *I left it here*
> Remember **here** and
> **there**.

hereabouts
hereafter
hereby
hereditary
heredity
herein
hereinafter
heresy
heresies
heretic
heretical
heretically
hereto
heretofore
hereupon
herewith
heritage
hermaphrodite
hermetically
hermit
hermitage
hernia
hernias
hero
heroes
heroic
heroically
heroin

> ✏ Do not confuse
> with **heroine** *heroin*
> *addicts*

heroine

> ✏ Do not confuse
> with **heroin** *She is the*
> *heroine of the story*

heroism
heron
herpes
herring
herringbone
hers

Can't find your word? Try looking under **WH**

herself
hertz
he's
hesitancy
hesitant
hesitate
 hesitated
 hesitating
hesitation
hessian
heterodox
heterogeneous
heterosexual
heterosexuality
het up
hew
 hewed
 hewed, hewn
 hewing

✸ Do not confuse with **hue** *to hew down a tree*

hex
 hexes
hexagon
hexagonal
hey

✸ Do not confuse with **hay** *Hey! Look at this!*

heyday
hi
hiatus
 hiatuses
hibernate
 hibernated
 hibernating
hibernation
hiccup, hiccough
 hiccuped,
 hiccoughed

hiccuping,
 hiccoughing
hickory
 hickories
hid
hidden
hide
 hid
 hidden
hide-and-seek
hidebound
hideous
hideously
hideout
hiding
hierarchical
hierarchy
hieroglyphics
hi-fi
 hi-fis
higgledy-piggledy
high
highball
highbrow
high-chair
higher

✸ Do not confuse with **hire** *at a higher level • studying for her Highers*

high fidelity
high-flier, high-flyer
high-flown
high-handed
highjack
 another spelling of
 hijack
highjacker
 another spelling of
 hijacker
high jinks

highland
highlight
 highlighted
 highlighting
highlighter
highly
highly-strung
Highness
 Highnesses
high-pitched
high-rise
high-risk
high-spirited
high-tech, hi-tech
highway
highwayman
 highwaymen
hijack, highjack
hijacker, highjacker
hike
 hiked
 hiking
hiker
hilarious
hilarity
hill
hillock
hillside
hilly
hilt
him

✸ Do not confuse with **hymn** *She married him*

himself
hind
hinder
 hindered
 hindering
hindmost
hindrance

Can't find your word? Try looking under **WH**

hindsight
Hindu
 Hindus
Hinduism
hinge
 hinged
 hinging, hingeing
hint
hinterland
hip
hip-hop
hippie, hippy
 hippies
hippo
 hippos
hippodrome
hippopotamus
 hippopotamuses,
 hippopotami
hippy
another spelling of
 hippie
hipsters
hire
 hired
 hiring

> ●* Do not confuse
> with **higher** *to hire a*
> *nanny • cars for hire*

hire-purchase
hirsute
his
hiss
 hisses
histamine
histogram
historian
historic
historical
historically
history

histories
hit
 hit
 hitting
hit-and-miss
hit-and-run
hitch
 hitches
hitchhike
 hitchhiked
 hitchhiking
hitchhiker
hi-tech
 another spelling of
 high-tech
hither
hitherto
hitman
 hitmen
hitter
hitting
HIV
hive
hoard

> ●* Do not confuse
> with **horde** *to hoard*
> *food • a hoard of*
> *treasure*

hoarder
hoarding
hoar-frost
hoarse

> ●* Do not confuse
> with **horse** *She is*
> *hoarse from shouting*

hoarsely
hoary
hoax
 hoaxes
hob
hobbit

hobble
 hobbled
 hobbling
hobby
 hobbies
hobby-horse
hobgoblin
hobnail
hobnailed
hobnob
 hobnobbed
 hobnobbing
hock
hockey
hocus-pocus
hod
hodgepodge
hoe
 hoed
 hoeing
hog
 hogged
 hogging
hogwash
hogweed
hoi polloi
hoisin
hoist
hoity-toity
hold
 held
 holding
holdall
holder
holding
hold-up
hole

> ●* Do not confuse
> with **whole** *a hole in the*
> *ground • a hole in her*
> *sock*

Can't find your word? Try looking under **WH**

holey

> ♦* Do not confuse
> with **holy** or **wholly**
> *holey socks*

holiday
holidaymaker
holier
holiest
holiness
holistic
holler
hollow
holly
hollyhock
holocaust
hologram
holster
holt
holy
holier
holiest

> ♦* Do not confuse
> with **holey** or **wholly** *a*
> *holy shrine*

homage
home
homed
homing

> ♦* Do not confuse
> with **hone** *to home in*
> *on a target • stay at*
> *home*

home-coming
homeland
homeless
homelessness
homeliness
homely
home-made
homeopath,

homeopath
homeopathic,
homoeopathic
homeopathy,
homoeopathy
homeostasis,
homoeostasis
homesick
homesickness
homespun
homestead
homeward
homewards
homework
homicidal
homicide
homily
homilies
homing
homoeopath
another spelling of
homeopath
homoeopathic
another spelling of
homeopathic
homoeopathy
another spelling of
homeopathy
homoeostasis
another spelling of
homeostasis
homogeneity
homogeneous
homogenization,
homogenisation
homogenize,
homogenise
homogenized,
homogenised
homogenizing,
homogenising
homogenous

homograph
homonym
homophobia
homophone
Homo sapiens
homosexual
homosexuality
hone
honed
honing

> ♦* Do not confuse
> with **home** *to hone a*
> *knife • to hone your*
> *football skills*

honest
honestly
honesty
honey
honeycomb
honeyed
honeymoon
honeysuckle
honk
honky-tonk
honorary

> ♦* Do not confuse
> with **honourable** *He is*
> *honorary secretary of*
> *the club*

honorific
honour
honoured
honouring
honourable

> ♦* Do not confuse
> with **honorary** *He is an*
> *honest and honourable*
> *man*

honourably
hooch

Can't find your word? Try looking under **WH**

SPELLING *focus* Homonyms and Homophones

Homonyms

Homonyms are words that are spelt the same but have different meanings, for example *light* meaning 'not heavy' and *light* meaning 'not dark'. Some homonyms also have different pronunciations. For example, the word *lead* can rhyme with *bed* and be a type of metal or rhyme with *seed* and be a verb meaning 'go in front'. Can you guess the following homonym pairs from the clues given?

- **One pronunciation rhymes with *cheer*; the other means 'rip'**
- **One pronunciation rhymes with *go*; the other means 'argument'**
- **One pronunciation rhymes with *crowned*; the other means 'injure'**

Can you think of any sentences which use homonyms?

He couldn't *bear* to hurt the *bear*.

The violinist put down her *bow* and gave a *bow*.

Homophones

Homophones are words that sound the same but have different spellings, and usually different meanings. Throughout this book you will find boxes alerting you to the danger of confusing them. Here are some examples:

cent, scent and **sent**	**road, rode** and **rowed**
hear and **here**	**write, right** and **rite**

Homophones can cause major spelling problems, because they do not look like a misspelling to you – or to your computer spellchecker! You can sometimes find ways to help you remember which spelling to use, for example by associating *hear* with *ear* and *here* with *there*.

In the following sentence there are eleven wrong homophones – can you spot them all and put them right?

> My brother likes too reed allowed at knight – eye
> tolled hymn two stop butt it maid know difference.

Can you make up a similar sentence of your own?

hood
hoodlum
hoodwink
hoof
 hooves, hoofs
hoofed
hoo-ha
hook
hookah, hooka
hooked
hooker
hookey
hooligan
hooliganism
hoop

> ♦* Do not confuse
> with **whoop** *a hoop*
> *round a barrel*

hooray
hoot
 hooted
 hooting
hooter
Hoover®
hoover
 hoovered
 hoovering
hooves
hop
 hopped
 hopping
hope
 hoped
 hoping
hopeful
hopefully
hopefulness
hopeless
hopelessly
hopelessness
hopped

hopper
hopping
hopscotch
horde

> ♦* Do not confuse
> with **hoard** *a horde of*
> *noisy children* • *hordes*
> *of tourists*

horizon
horizontal
horizontally
hormonal
hormone
horn
hornbill
horned
hornet
hornpipe
horny
horoscope
horrendous
horrible
horribly
horrid
horrific
horrifically
horrify
 horrifies
 horrified
 horrifying
horror
horror-stricken
horror-struck
hors d'oeuvre
 hors d'oeuvres, hors
 d'oeuvre
horse

> ♦* Do not confuse
> with **hoarse** *ride a*
> *horse*

horseback

horsefly
 horseflies
horseplay
horsepower
horse-racing
horseradish
horseshoe
horsey, horsy
horticultural
horticulture
horticulturist
hosanna
hose
 hosed
 hosing
hosepipe
hosiery
hospice
hospitable
hospitably
hospital
hospitalisation
 another spelling of
 hospitalization
hospitalise
 another spelling of
 hospitalize
hospitality
hospitalization,
 hospitalisation
hospitalize,
 hospitalise
 hospitalized,
 hospitalised
 hospitalizing,
 hospitalising
host
hostage
hostel
hostelry
 hostelries
hostess

Can't find your word? Try looking under **WH**

hostesses
hostile
hostilely
hostility
hostilities
hot
hotter
hottest
hotbed
hotchpotch
hotchpotches
hot dog
hotel
hotelier
hotfoot
hot-headed
hothouse
hotline
hotplate
hotpot
hotter
hottest
hot-wire
hot-wired
hot-wiring
hound
hour
hour-glass
hour-glasses
hourly
house
housed
housing
houseboat
housebound
housecoat
household
householder
housekeeper
housekeeping
house-proud
house-train

house-trained
house-training
house-warming
housewife
housewives
housework
housing
hovel
hover
hovered
hovering
hovercraft
hove
how
howdy
however
howl
howler
hub
hubbub
hubby
huddle
huddled
huddling
hue

> ☙* Do not confuse
> with **hew** *different hues
> of paint* • *a hue and cry*

huff
huffy
hug
hugged
hugging
huge
hugely
hugeness
huh
hula-hoop
hulk
hulking
hull

hullabaloo
hullo
another spelling of
hello
hum
hummed
humming
human

> ☙* Do not confuse
> with **humane** *a human
> being*

humane

> ☙* Do not confuse
> with **human** *the
> humane killing of a sick
> animal*

humanely
humanisation
another spelling of
humanization
humanise
another spelling of
humanize
humanism
humanist
humanitarian
humanity
humanization,
humanisation
humanize, humanise
humanized,
humanised
humanizing,
humanising
humankind
humble
humbly
humbug
humdrum
humid
humidifier

Can't find your word? Try looking under **WH**

humidify
humidifies
humidified
humidifying
humidity
humiliate
humiliated
humiliating
humiliation
humility
hummed
humming
hummingbird
hummus

✎* Do not confuse
with **humus** *hummus is
made from chickpeas*

humongous,
humungous
humorist
humorous

ⓘ Word breakdown:
hu-mor-ous

humour
humoured
humouring
humourless
hump
humpback
humpbacked
humph
humungous
another spelling of
humongous
humus

✎* Do not confuse
with **hummus** *humus
is decomposed organic
matter*

hunch

hunches
hunchback
hunchbacked
hundred
hundredth
hundredweight
hung
hunger
hungered
hungering
hungrily
hungry
hungrier
hungriest
hunk
hunky
hunky-dory
hunt
hunter
huntress
huntresses
huntsman
huntsmen
huntswoman
huntswomen
hurdle
hurdled
hurdling
hurdler
hurdygurdy
hurl
hurling
hurly-burly
hurrah
hurray
hurricane
hurried
hurriedly
hurry
hurries
hurried
hurrying

hurt
hurtful
hurtfully
hurtfulness
hurtle
hurtled
hurtling
husband
husbandry
hush
hushed
hush-hush
husk
huskily
husky
huskies
hussar
hussy
hussies
hustings
hustle
hustled
hustling
hustler
hut
hutch
hutches
hyacinth
hyaena
another spelling of
hyena
hybrid
hydra
hydrangea
hydrant
hydrate
hydrated
hydrating
hydraulic
hydro
hydros
hydrocarbon

Can't find your word? Try looking under **WH**

hydrochloric
hydroelectric
hydroelectricity
hydrofoil
hydrogen
hydrogenate
 hydrogenated
 hydrogenating
hydrophobia
hydrotherapy
hydroxide
hyena, hyaena
hygiene

ℹ️ You get **ill** unless you follow the rules of hyg**i**ene.

hygienic
hygienically
hymen
hymn

💣* Do not confuse with **him** *The choir sang a hymn*

hype
 hyped
 hyping
hyper
hyperactive

hyperactivity
hyperbole
hyperglycaemia
hypermarket
hypernym
hypersensitive
hypertension
hyperventilate
 hyperventilated
 hyperventilating
hyperventilation
hyphen
hyphenate
 hyphenated
 hyphenating
hyphenation
hypnosis
hypnotherapy
hypnotic
hypnotically
hypnotise
 another spelling of
 hypnotize
hypnotism
hypnotist
hypnotize,
 hypnotise
 hypnotized,

hypnotised
hypnotizing,
hypnotising
hypoallergenic
hypochondria
hypochondriac
hypocrisy
hypocrite
hypocritical
hypocritically
hypodermic
hypoglycaemia
hyponym
hypotenuse
hypothermia
hypothesis
 hypotheses
hypothesize,
 hypothesise
hypothetical
hypothetically
hysterectomy
hysteria
hysterical
hysterically
hysterics

Can't find your word? Try looking under **WH**

iambic
ibex
 ibex, ibexes
ibis
 ibises
ibuprofen
ice
 iced
 icing
iceberg
icebreaker
icecap
ice cream, ice-cream
ice-skate
ice-skater
ice-skating
icicle
icily
icing
icon, ikon
icy
 icier
 iciest
id
I'd
idea
ideal
idealisation
 another spelling of
 idealization
idealise
 another spelling of
 idealize
idealism

idealist
idealistic
idealization,
 idealisation
idealize, idealise
 idealized, idealised
 idealizing, idealising
ideally
identical
identically
identifiable
identification
identify
 identifies
 identified
 identifying
Identikit®
identity
 identities
ideological
ideologically
ideology
 ideologies
idiocy
idiom
idiomatic
idiomatically
idiosyncrasy
 idiosyncrasies
idiosyncratic
idiosyncratically
idiot
idiotic
idiotically

idle
 idled
 idling

 ✒* Do not confuse
with **idol** or **idyll** *a slow
and idle worker • idle
chatter • to idle away
time • let the engine idle*

idleness
idler
idly
idol

 ✒* Do not confuse
with **idle** or **idyll** *The
singer is her idol •
worshipping idols*

idolatry
idolization,
 idolisation
idolize, idolise
 idolized, idolised
 idolizing, idolising
idyll

 ✒* Do not confuse
with **idle** or **idol** *a rural
idyll of tranquillity*

idyllic
idyllically
if
iffy
igloo
igneous
ignite

ignited
igniting
ignition
ignoble
ignobly
ignominious
ignoramus
ignoramuses
ignorance
ignorant
ignore
ignored
ignoring
iguana
ikon
another spelling of
icon
ilk
I'll
ill
worse
worst
ill-advised
ill-at-ease
ill-bred
illegal
illegality
illegally
illegibility
illegible

♦* Do not confuse
with **eligible** or
ineligible *untidy and*
illegible handwriting

illegibly
illegitimacy
illegitimate
illegitimately
ill-fated
ill-gotten
ill-humoured

illicit

♦* Do not confuse
with **elicit** *an illicit love*
affair

illicitly
illicitness
ill-informed
illiteracy
illiterate

❶ Word breakdown:
il-lit-er-ate

♦* Do not confuse
with **alliterate** *the boy*
was illiterate

ill-mannered
ill-natured
illness
illnesses
illogical
illogicality
illogically
ill-starred
ill-tempered
ill-timed
ill-treat
ill-treated
ill-treating
ill-treatment
illuminate
illuminated
illuminating
illumination
illusion

♦* Do not confuse
with **allusion** or
delusion *an optical*
illusion • have no
illusions about the
realities of life

illusionist

illusory
illustrate
illustrated
illustrating
illustration
illustrative
illustrator
illustrious
ill-will
I'm
image
imagery
imaginable
imaginary
imagination
imaginative
imaginatively
imagine
imagined
imagining
imam
imbalance
imbecile
imbecility
imbibe
imbibed
imbibing
imbue
imbued
imbuing
imitable
imitate
imitated
imitating
imitation
imitative
imitator
immaculate
immaculately
immaterial
immature
immaturity

immeasurable
immediacy
immediate
immediately

🛈 Word within word:
im-**media**-tely

immemorial
immense
immensely
immensity
immerse
immersed
immersing
immersion
immigrant

✏* Do not confuse
with **emigrant** *an
immigrant to Britain*
Remember that
immigrants come in
from another country.

immigration

✏* Do not confuse
with **emigration**
*immigration into
Britain* Remember
that immigration is
coming in.

imminence
imminent
immobile
immobilise
another spelling of
immobilize
immobility
immobilize,
immobilise
immobilized,
immobilised
immobilizing,

immobilising
immoderate
immodest
immodesty
immoral

✏* Do not confuse
with **amoral** or
immortal *Killing
innocent civilians is
immoral*

immorality

✏* Do not confuse
with **immortality**
*wickedness and
immorality*

immorally
immortal

✏* Do not confuse
with **immoral** *He is
immortal and will
never die*

immortalise
another spelling of
immortalize
immortality

✏* Do not confuse
with **immorality** *the
immortality of God*

immortalize,
immortalise
immortalized,
immortalised
immortalizing,
immortalising
immovable
immovably
immune
immunisation
another spelling of
immunization

immunise
another spelling of
immunize
immunity
immunization,
immunisation
immunize, immunise
immunized,
immunised
immunizing,
immunising
immunodeficiency
immunologist
immunology
immutable
imp
impact
impair
impaired
impairing
impairment
impala
impalas, impala
impale
impaled
impaling
impart
impartial
impartiality
impartially
impassable
impasse
impassioned
impassive
impassively
impassiveness
impassivity
impasto
impatience
impatient
impatiently
impeach

impeachable
impeachment
impeccable
impeccably
impede
impeded
impeding
impediment
impel
impelled
impelling
impending
impenetrable
imperative
imperatively
imperceptible
imperceptibly
imperfect
imperfection
imperfectly
imperial
imperialism
imperialist
imperialistic
imperil
imperilled
imperilling
imperious
imperiousness
imperishable
impermanence
impermanent
impermeable
impersonal
impersonally
impersonate
impersonated
impersonating
impersonation
impersonator
impertinence
impertinent

impertinently
imperturbable
impervious
imperviousness
impetuosity
impetuous

☞ Do not confuse
with **impetus** *rash and*
impetuous

impetus
impetuses

☞ Do not confuse
with **impetuous** *the*
impetus of the blow

impiety
impinge
impinged
impinging
impish
implacable
implant
implantation
implausible
implement
implementation
implicate
implicated
implicating
implication
implicit
implicitly
implode
imploded
imploding
implore
implored
imploring
implosion
imply
implies
implied

implying
impolite
impolitely
import
importance
important
importantly
importation
importer
impose
imposed
imposing
imposing
imposition
impossibility
impossible
impossibly
impostor, imposter
impotence
impotent
impound
impoverish
impoverished
impracticability
impracticable
impracticably
impractical
impracticality
impractically
imprecise
imprecision
impregnable
impregnate
impregnated
impregnating
impregnation
impresario
impresarios
impress
impression
impressionable
impressionism

impressionist
impressive
impressively
imprint
imprison
 imprisoned
 imprisoning
imprisonment
improbability
improbable
improbably
impromptu
improper
impropriety
 improprieties
improve
 improved
 improving
improvement
improvidence
improvident
improvisation
improvise
 improvised
 improvising
impudence
impudent
impudently
impulse
impulsive
impulsively
impulsiveness
impunity
impure
impurity
 impurities
in

> ♦※ Do not confuse
> with **inn** *in the house •*
> *dressed in black •*
> *Come in!*

inability
in absentia
inaccessible
inaccessibly
inaccuracy
 inaccuracies
inaccurate
inaccurately
inaction
inactive
inactivity
inadequacy
 inadequacies
inadequate
inadequately
inadmissible
inadvertent
inalienable
inane
inanely
inanimate
inanity
 inanities
inapplicable
inappropriate
inappropriately
inappropriateness
inapt

> ♦※ Do not confuse
> with **inept** *an inapt*
> *comparison*

inaptitude
inaptness
inarticulate
inasmuch as
inattention
inattentive
inattentively
inaudible
inaudibly
inaugural

inaugurate
 inaugurated
 inaugurating
inauguration
inauspicious
inborn
inbred
inbreed
inbreeding
incalculable
incandescence
incandescent
incantation
incapable
incapacitate
 incapacitated
 incapacitating
incapacitation
incapacity
incarcerate
 incarcerated
 incarcerating
incarceration
incarnate
incarnation
incendiary
incense
 incensed
 incensing
incentive
inception
incessant
incest
incestuous
inch
 inches
incidence
incident
incidental
incidentally
incinerate
 incinerated

incinerating
incineration
incinerator
incipient
incise
incised
incising
incision
incisive
incisively
incisiveness
incisor
incite
incited
inciting
incitement
incivility
incivilities
inclemency
inclement
inclination
incline
inclined
inclining
inclined
include
included
including
inclusion
inclusive
inclusively
incognito
incognitos
incoherence
incoherent
income
incomer
incoming
incommunicado
incomparable
incomparably
incompatibility

incompatible
incompetence
incompetent
incomplete
incomprehensibility
incomprehensible
incomprehensibly
incomprehension
inconceivable
inconceivably
inconclusive
inconclusively
incongruous
incongruously
inconsequent
inconsequential
inconsequentially
inconsiderable
inconsiderate
inconsiderately
inconsistency
inconsistencies
inconsistent
inconsolable
inconspicuous
inconspicuousness
inconstancy
inconstant
incontestable
incontinence
incontinent
incontrovertible
incontrovertibly
inconvenience
inconvenient
incorporate
incorporated
incorporating
incorporation
incorrect
incorrigible
incorrigibly

incorruptible
increase
increased
increasing
increasingly
incredibility
incredible

> ✒ Do not confuse
> with **incredulous** *an*
> *incredible story • That's*
> *incredible!*

incredibly
incredulity
incredulous

> ✒ Do not confuse
> with **incredible** *an*
> *incredulous person • an*
> *incredulous look*

increment
incremental
incriminate
incriminated
incriminating
incrimination
incubate
incubated
incubating
incubation
incubator
incumbency
incumbencies
incumbent
incur
incurred
incurring
incurable
incurably
incursion
indebted
indebtedness
indecency

indecent
indecently
indecipherable
indecision
indecisive
indecisively
indecisiveness
indeed
indefatigable
indefatigably
indefensible
indefensibly
indefinable
indefinably
indefinite
indefinitely
indelible
indelibly
indelicacy
indelicate
indelicately
indemnify
  indemnifies
  indemnified
  indemnifying
indemnity
indent
indentation
indenture
independence
independent

ℹ Word within word: in-**depend**-ent

independently
in-depth
indescribable
indescribably
indestructible
indestructibly
indeterminate
indeterminately

index
  indexes, indices

✎✷ The plural form **indices** is not used for the lists at the end of a book *separate indexes of names mentioned in the text*

indexer
index-linked
indicate
  indicated
  indicating
indication
indicative
indicator
indices
indict
indictment
indie
indifference
indifferent
indigence
indigenous

✎✷ Do not confuse with **indigent** *This plant is not indigenous to Britain*

indigent

✎✷ Do not confuse with **indigenous** *indigent and homeless*

indigestible
indigestion
indignant
indignantly
indignation
indignity
  indignities
indigo

indirect
indirectly
indiscernible
indiscipline
indiscreet
indiscretion
indiscriminate
indiscriminately
indispensable

ℹ Only the most **able** people are indispens**able**.

indispensably
indisposed
indisposition
indisputable
indisputably
indissoluble
indistinct
indistinguishable
indistinguishably
individual
individualise
another spelling of
individualize
individualism
individualist
individuality
individualize,
  individualise
  individualized,
  individualised
  individualizing,
  individualising
individually
indivisible
indoctrinate
  indoctrinated
  indoctrinating
indoctrination
indolence

indolent
indoor
indoors
induce
 induced
 inducing
inducement
induct
induction
inductive
indulge
 indulged
 indulging
indulgence
indulgent
industrial

✺ Do not confuse
with **industrious** *an*
industrial process •
industrial action

industrialisation
another spelling of
industrialization
industrialise
another spelling of
industrialize
industrialism
industrialist
industrialization,
 industrialisation
industrialize,
 industrialise
 industrialized,
 industrialised
 industrializing,
 industrialising
industrially
industrious

✺ Do not confuse
with **industrial** *an*
industrious child

industriousness
industry
 industries
inebriated
inebriation
inedible
ineffable
ineffably
ineffective
ineffectively
ineffectiveness
ineffectual
ineffectually
inefficacious
inefficacy
inefficiency
inefficient
inelegance
inelegant
ineligibility
ineligible

✺ Do not confuse
with **illegible** *ineligible*
for the post because of
lack of qualifications

inept

✺ Do not confuse
with **inapt** *an inept*
attempt • an inept
young man

ineptitude
ineptness
inequality
 inequalities
inequity
inert
inertia
inertness
inescapable
inescapably
inestimable

inestimably
inevitability
inevitable
inevitably
inexact
inexcusable
inexcusably
inexhaustible
inexorable
inexorably
inexpensive
inexpensively
inexperience
inexperienced
inexpert
inexplicable
inexplicably
inexplicit
inexpressible
inexpressibly
inextinguishable
inextricable
inextricably
infallibility
infallible
infallibly
infamous
infamy
infancy
infant
infantile
infantry
infatuated
infatuation
infect
infection
infectious
infer
 inferred
 inferring
inference
inferior

inferiority
infernal
infernally
inferno
 infernos
inferred
inferring
infertile
infertility
infest
infidel
infidelity
in-fighting
infiltrate
 infiltrated
 infiltrating
infiltration
infiltrator
infinite
infinitely
infinitesimal
infinitesimally
infinitive
infinity
infirm
infirmary
 infirmaries
infirmity
 infirmities
inflame
 inflamed
 inflaming
inflammable
inflammation
inflammatory
inflatable
inflate
 inflated
 inflating
inflation
inflationary
inflect

inflection, inflexion
inflexibility
inflexible
inflexion
 another spelling of
 inflection
inflict
infliction
in-flight
influence
 influenced
 influencing
influential
influentially
influenza
influx
info
inform
informal
informality
informally
informant
information
informative
informatively
informer
infraction
infrared
infrastructure
infrequency
infrequent
infringe
 infringed
 infringing
infringement
infuriate
 infuriated
 infuriating
infuse
 infused
 infusing
infusion

ingenious

🖋* Do not confuse
with **ingenuous** *an
ingenious invention*

ingenuity
ingenuous

🖋* Do not confuse
with **ingenious** *young
and ingenuous*

ingenuousness
ingest
ingestion
ingot
ingrained
ingratiate
 ingratiated
 ingratiating
ingratitude
ingredient
ingrowing
ingrown
inhabit
 inhabited
 inhabiting
inhabitable
inhabitant
inhalant
inhalation
inhale
 inhaled
 inhaling
inhaler
inherent
inherit
 inherited
 inheriting
inheritance
inheritor
inhibit
 inhibited
 inhibiting

SPELLING  focus

Inflections

Inflections are changes in the form of a word, such as the past form of a verb or the comparative form of an adjective. Regular inflections follow set patterns, which are discussed in the Spelling Rules on p.390. Irregular inflections, for words such as *be*, *have* and *good*, have to be learnt individually as they do not follow any rules. These are shown in full in the main wordlist.

Doubling consonants

You may wonder why *occurred* has two **r**'s and *offered* has only one, or why *regretting* has two **t**'s but *marketing* has only one.

For words which end in consonant + vowel + consonant, we double the final consonant before adding **-ed**, **-ing**, **-er** or **-est** for one of three reasons:

• the vowel is stressed

• the word has only one syllable

• the final consonant is **l**

Here are some examples:

refer: refers, referred, referring	**fat: fatter, fattest**
bar: bars, barred, barring	**travel: travels, travelled, travelling**

This explains why similar words differ in their inflections. While verbs like *overlap* are stressed on the final syllable and so double the final consonant (*overlapped*), other verbs like *develop* and *benefit* are not stressed on the final syllable, so the final consonant is not doubled (*developed*, *benefited*).

If you forget to double the consonant, you may produce a totally different word, such as *pined* instead of *pinned*, or *hoping* instead of *hopping*. Listen to the sound of the word – if it has a short vowel, a double consonant is needed to keep the sound short when **-ed**, **-ing**, **-er** or **-est** is added.

Remember that there are exceptions to this rule, when the consonant is not doubled: for example, words ending in **w**, **x** and **y** do not double the final consonant. And the final consonant in some words ending in **p**, like *kidnap* and *worship*, is doubled regardless of where the stress falls.

Over to you

Would you put a single or double consonant in the inflections of these words:

tap	**target**	**pedal**

inhibition
inhibitor
inhospitable
inhospitably
inhuman

♦* Do not confuse
with **inhumane** *The
torturing of prisoners is
inhuman • a strange,
inhuman laugh*

inhumane

♦* Do not confuse
with **inhuman**
*protesting about the
inhumane treatment of
animals*

inhumanely
inhumanity
inimical
inimitable
inimitably
iniquitous
iniquity
 iniquities
initial
 initialled
 initialling
initially
initiate
 initiated
 initiating
initiation
initiative
initiator
inject
injection
injudicious
injunction
injure
 injured
 injuring

injured
injurious
injury
 injuries
injustice
ink
inkblot
inkling
inkpad
inkwell
inky
inlaid
inland
in-law
inlay
 inlaid
 inlaying
inlet
inmate
inmost
inn

♦* Do not confuse
with **in** *stay overnight
at an inn*

innards
innate
inner
innermost
innings
innkeeper
innocence
innocent

ⓘ **In no cen**tury have
more **innocent** people
died.

innocuous

ⓘ **Innocu**ous
ingredients are found
in no curry.

innovate

innovated
innovating
innovation
innovator
innuendo
 innuendoes,
 innuendos
innumerable
innumeracy
innumerate
inoculate
 inoculated
 inoculating

ⓘ Can you **inocul**ate a
rh**ino** in **cul**ottes?

inoculation
inoffensive
inoffensively
inoperable
inoperative
inopportune
inopportunely
inordinate
inordinately
inorganic
in-patient
input
inputting
inquest
inquire, enquire
 inquired, enquired
 inquiring, enquiring
inquirer, enquirer
inquiry, enquiry
 inquiries, enquiries
inquisition
inquisitive
inquisitively
inquisitor
inroads
inrush

insalubrious
insane
insanely
insanitary
insanity
insatiability
insatiable
insatiably
inscribe
 inscribed
 inscribing
inscription
inscrutable
inscrutably
insect
insecticide
insectivore
insectivorous
insecure
insecurely
insecurity
inseminate
 inseminated
 inseminating
insemination
insensible
insensitive
insensitively
insensitivity
inseparable
inseparably
insert
insertion
in-service
inset
inshore
inside
insider
insidious
insight
insignia
insignificance

insignificant
insincere
insincerely
insincerity
insinuate
 insinuated
 insinuating
insinuation
insipid
insist
insistence
insistent
in situ
insole
insolence
insolent
insolently
insoluble
insolvency
insolvent
insomnia
insomniac
insomuch
inspect
inspection
inspector
inspectorate
inspiration
inspirational
inspire
 inspired
 inspiring
instability
install, instal
 installed
 installing
installation
instalment

❶ An instalment is a
little payment.

instance

instant
instantaneous
instantly
instead
instep
instigate
 instigated
 instigating
instigation
instigator
instil, instill
 instilled
 instilling
instinct
instinctive
instinctively
institute
 instituted
 instituting
institution
institutional
institutionalise
 another spelling of
 institutionalize
institutionalism
institutionalize,
 institutionalise
 institutionalized,
 institutionalised
 institutionalizing,
 institutionalising
instruct
instruction
instructive
instructively
instructor
instrument
instrumental
instrumentalist
instrumentation
insubordinate
insubordination

insubstantial
insufferable
insufferably
insufficiency
insufficient
insular
insularity
insulate
 insulated
 insulating
insulation
insulin
insult
insulting
insupportable
insurable
insurance
insure
 insured
 insuring

♦* Do not confuse
with **ensure** *to insure
your belongings
against loss or theft*

insurer
insurgence
insurgency
insurgent
insurmountable
insurmountably
insurrection
intact
intake
intangible
intangibly
integer
integral
integrate
 integrated
 integrating
integration

integrity
intellect
intellectual
intellectualize,
 intellectualise
 intellectualized,
 intellectualised
 intellectualizing,
 intellectualising
intellectually
intelligence
intelligent

♦* Do not confuse
with **intelligible** *bright
and intelligent children*

intelligently
intelligentsia
intelligibility
intelligible

♦* Do not confuse
with **intelligent** *a
scarcely intelligible
message*

intelligibly
intemperance
intemperate
intemperately
intend
intense
intensely
intensification
intensifier
intensify
 intensifies
 intensified
 intensifying
intensity
 intensities
intensive
intensively
intent

intention
intentional
intentionally
intentness
inter
 interred
 interring
interact
interaction
interactive
interbreed
 interbred
 interbreeding
intercede
 interceded
 interceding
intercept
interception
interceptor
intercession
interchange
 interchanged
 interchanging
interchangeable
intercom
interconnect
intercontinental
intercourse
interdependence
interdependent
interdict
interdiction
interdisciplinary
interest
interested
interesting
interface
interfere
 interfered
 interfering
interference
intergalactic

interim
interior
interject
interjection
interlace
  interlaced
  interlacing
interlink
interlock
interlocutor
interloper
interlude
intermarriage
intermarry
  intermarries
  intermarried
  intermarrying
intermediary
  intermediaries
intermediate
interment

♦* Do not confuse
with **internment** *the
interment of the corpse*

interminable
interminably
intermingle
  intermingled
  intermingling
intermission
intermittent
intermittently
intern
internal
internalize,
  internalise
  internalized,
  internalised
  internalizing,
  internalising
internally

international
internationalism
internationalist
internationally
internee
internet, Internet
internment

♦* Do not confuse
with **interment** *the
internment of the
prisoners*

internship
interpersonal
interplay
Interpol
interpolate
  interpolated
  interpolating
interpolation
interpret
  interpreted
  interpreting
interpretation
interpreter
interracial
interred
interregnum
  interregnums,
  interregna
interrelate
interrelated
interrogate
  interrogated
  interrogating
interrogation
interrogative
interrogator
interrupt

❶ It's really rude to
interrupt.

interruption

intersect
intersection
intersperse
  interspersed
  interspersing
intertwine
  intertwined
  intertwining
interval
intervene
  intervened
  intervening
intervention
interventionism
interventionist
interview
interviewee
interviewer
interweave
  interwove
  interwoven
  interweaving
intestate
intestinal
intestines
intifada
intimacy
intimate
  intimated
  intimating
intimately
intimation
intimidate
  intimidated
  intimidating
intimidation
into
intolerable
intolerably
intolerance
intolerant
intonation

intone
 intoned
 intoning
intoxicant
intoxicate
 intoxicated
 intoxicating
intoxication
intractable
intramural
intransigence
intransigent
intransitive
intravenous
in-tray
intrepid
intrepidity
intricacy
 intricacies
intricate
intricately
intrigue
 intrigued
 intriguing
intrinsic
intrinsically
introduce
 introduced
 introducing
introduction
introductory
introspection
introspective
introspectively
introversion
introvert
intrude
 intruded
 intruding
intruder
intrusion
intrusive

intrusively
intrust
 another spelling of
 entrust
intuition
intuitive
intuitively
inundate
 inundated
 inundating
inundation
inure
 inured
 inuring
invade
 invaded
 invading
invader
invalid
invalidate
 invalidated
 invalidating
invalidation
invalidity
invaluable
invaluably
invariable
invariably
invasion
invasive
invective
inveigle
 inveigled
 inveigling
invent
invention
inventive
inventiveness
inventor
inventory
 inventories
inverse

inversely
inversion
invert
invertebrate

♦* Do not confuse
with **inveterate** *A
worm is an invertebrate
animal*

inverted commas
invest
investigate
 investigated
 investigating
investigation
investigative
investigator
investiture
investment
investor
inveterate

♦* Do not confuse
with **invertebrate** *an
inveterate liar*

invidious
invigilate
 invigilated
 invigilating
invigilator
invigorate
 invigorated
 invigorating
invincibility
invincible
inviolable
inviolate
invisibility
invisible
invisibly
invitation
invite
 invited

inviting
inviting
in vitro
invocation
invoice
invoiced
invoicing
invoke
invoked
invoking
involuntary
involuntarily
involve
involved
involving
involvement
inward
inwardly
inwards
iodine
ion

🌢* Do not confuse
with **iron** *An ion is an*
electrically charged
particle

ionic
ionization,
 ionisation
ionize, ionise
 ionized, ionised
 ionizing, ionising
ionizer, ioniser
ionosphere
iota
IOU
irascibility
irascible
irascibly
irate
irately
ire

iridescence
iridescent
iris
 irises
irk
irksome
iron
 ironed
 ironing

🌢* Do not confuse
with **ion** *iron and steel •*
to iron a shirt

ironic
ironical
ironically
ironing
ironmonger
ironwork
irony
 ironies
irradiate
 irradiated
 irradiating
irradiation
irrational
irrationality
irrationally
irreconcilability
irreconcilable
irrecoverable
irrecoverably
irredeemable
irrredeemably
irrefutable
irrefutably
irregular
irregularity
 irregularities
irregularly
irrelevance
irrelevancy

irrelevant
irrelevantly
irremediable
irreparable
irreparably
irreplaceable
irrepressible
irrepressibly
irreproachable
irreproachably
irresistible

❶ Word within word:
ir-**resist**-ible

irresistibly
irresolute
irresolutely
irrespective
irrespectively
irresponsible
irresponsibly
irretrievable
irreverence
irreverent
irreversible
irrevocable
irrevocably
irrigate
 irrigated
 irrigating
irrigation
irritable
irritably
irritant
irritate
 irritated
 irritating
irritation
is
Islam
Islamic
island

islander
isle

💧✷ Do not confuse
with **aisle** *sail to the Isle
of Man*

islet
isn't
isobar
isolate
  isolated
  isolating
isolation
isomer
isometric
isosceles
isotope
I-Spy
issue
  issued
  issuing

it
italic
italicize, italicise
  italicized, italicised
  italicizing,
  italicising
italics
itch
  itches
itchiness
itchy
it'd
item
itemize, itemise
  itemized, itemised
  itemizing, itemising
itinerant
itinerary
  itineraries
it'll

it's

💧✷ **It's** is a short form
of **it is** or **it has**. Do not
confuse with **its** *It's
raining • It's got tiny
paws*

its

💧✷ **Its** means
'belonging to it'. Do
not confuse with **it's** *its
leg • its bed*

itself
itsy-bitsy
I've
ivory
  ivories
ivy
  ivies

J

If you can't find the word you're looking for under **J**, it could be that it starts with a different letter. Try looking under **G** for words like *gem*, *gin* and *gymnast*.

jab
 jabbed
 jabbing
jabber
 jabbered
 jabbering
jack
jackal
jackass
 jackasses
jackboot
jackdaw
jacket
jack-in-the-box
jack-knife
 pl jack-knives
 jack-knifed
 jack-knifing
jack-of-all-trades
jackpot
Jacuzzi®
jade
jaded
jag
jagged
jaguar
jail, gaol
 jailed, gaoled
 jailing, gaoling
jailbird, gaolbird
jailer, gaoler

Jain
jalopy
 jalopies
jam
 jammed
 jamming

✒* Do not confuse with **jamb** *strawberry jam • in a jam • the machine jammed • musicians jamming together*

jamb

✒* Do not confuse with **jam** *the door jamb*

jamboree
jammy
jam-packed
jangle
 jangled
 jangling
janitor
jape
japonica
jar
 jarred
 jarring
jargon
jasmine
jaundice

jaundiced
jaunt
jauntily
jaunty
javelin
jaw
jawbone
jay
jaywalk
jaywalker
jaywalking
jazz
jazzily
jazzy
jealous

❶ I'm not **jealous** of your **lousy jeans**!

jealousy
jeans
jeep
jeer
 jeered
 jeering
Jekyll and Hyde
jell
 another spelling of **gel**
jellied
jelly
 jellies
jellyfish

jemmy
jemmies
jeopardize,
jeopardise
jeopardized,
jeopardised
jeopardizing,
jeopardising
jeopardy
jerk
jerkily
jerkiness
jerkin
jerky
jersey
jerseys
jest
jester
jesting
jet
jetted
jetting
jet-black
jetfoil
jet-lag
jet-lagged
jetsam
jet set
jet-setter
jettison
jettisoned
jettisoning
jetty
jetties
Jew

♦* Do not confuse
with **dew** or **due** *Jews*
worship at the
synagogue

jewel
jeweller

jewellery

❶ A jew**eller** is a s**eller**
of jew**eller**y.

Jewish
jib
jibbed
jibbing

♦* Do not confuse
with **jibe** *to jib at*
paying a lot • hoist the
jib

jibe, gibe
jibed, gibed
jibing, gibing

♦* Do not confuse
with **jib** *to sneer and*
jibe

jiffy
jig
jigged
jigging
jiggery-pokery
jiggle
jiggled
jiggling
jigsaw
jihad
jilt
jingle
jingled
jingling
jingoism
jingoistic
jinx
jinxes
jitterbug
jitters
jittery
jive
job

jobber
jobbing
job centre,
Jobcentre
jobless
joblessness
job-sharing
jockey
pl jockeys
jockeyed
jockeying
jockstrap
jocular
jocularity
jodhpurs

❶ Remember the
hidden **h** for **h**orse.

jog
jogged
jogging
jogger
joggle
joggled
joggling
joie de vivre
join
joined
joining
joiner
joinery
joint
jointly
joist
jojoba
joke
joked
joking
joker
jokey, joky
jokiness
jokingly

Can't find your word? Try looking under **G**

Visualization and Shapes

You can use the shape or sound of the letters in a word to help you picture the word in your mind. For example:

- Remember the two **i**'s of *definite* by seeing them as two eyes on either side of the **n** (the nose)

- You might see the two **e**'s of *elephant* as two ears on either side of the **l**, its long trunk

Can you think of any more animals that can be visualized like this?

You can also think about the shape of a word by imagining drawing a line around its outline. Does it have lots of tall letters? Is it long or short? Does it have many letters which descend below the line? This makes what is called a 'spelling silhouette' and can help you to decide if the word looks right when you write it down yourself.

---

joky
another spelling of
jokey
jollification
jollily
jollity
jolly
  jollier
  jolliest
jolt
josh
joss-stick
jostle
  jostled
  jostling
jot
  jotted
  jotting
jotter
joule
journal
journalese
journalism
journalist

journey
  pl journeys
  journeyed
  journeying
joust
jovial
jovially
jowl
joy
joyful
joyfully
joyfulness
joyless
joyous
joyride
joyrider
joyriding
joystick
jubilant
jubilation
jubilee
Judaism
judder
  juddered

  juddering
judge
  judged
  judging
judgement
judgment
judicial

💣* Do not confuse
with **judicious** *a*
judicial inquiry

judiciary
judicious

💣* Do not confuse
with **judicial** *a*
*judicious choice of
books*

judo
jug
juggernaut
juggle
  juggled
  juggling
juggler

Can't find your word? Try looking under **G**

jugular (vein)
juice
juicer
juiciness
juicy
 juicier
 juiciest
ju-jitsu
jukebox
 jukeboxes
julep
jumble
 jumbled
 jumbling
jumble sale
jumbo
 jumbos
jump
jumper
jump-start
jumpsuit
jumpy

junction

💧* Do not confuse
with **juncture** *a road
junction*

juncture

💧* Do not confuse
with **junction** *I have
nothing to add at this
juncture*

jungle
junior
juniper
junk
junket
junketing
junkie, junky
 junkies
jurisdiction
jurist
juror
jury

 juries
just
justice
justiciary
justifiable
justifiably
justification
justify
 justifies
 justified
 justifying
justly
jut
 jutted
 jutting
jute
juvenile
juxtapose
 juxtaposed
 juxtaposing
juxtaposition

Can't find your word? Try looking under **G**

K k

If you can't find the word you're looking for under **K**, it could be that it starts with a different letter. Try looking under **C** for words like *can*, **CH** for words like *character*, and **Q** for words like *quite*. Also don't forget **KH** for words like *khaki*.

kaftan
another spelling of
 caftan
kaiser
kale
kaleidoscope
kaleidoscopic
kaleidoscopically
kamikaze
kangaroo
kaolin
kapok
karaoke
karate
karma
kart

> ☙* Do not confuse
> with **cart** *a go-kart*

kayak
kazoo
kebab
kedgeree
keel
 keeled
 keeling
keelhaul
 keelhauled
 keelhauling
keen
 keened

keening
keenly
keenness
keep
 kept
 keeping
keeper
keeping
keepsake
keg
kelp
kelvin
ken
kendo
kennel
kept
kerb

> ☙* Do not confuse
> with **curb** *She stepped
> off the kerb into the
> road*

kerbstone
kernel

> ☙* Do not confuse
> with **colonel** *the kernel
> of a nut*

kerosine, kerosene
kestrel
ketch

ketches
ketchup
kettle
kettledrum
key
 pl keys
 keyed
 keying

> ☙* Do not confuse
> with **quay** *the key to the
> door*

keyboard
keyboarder
keyed-up
keyhole
keynote
keypad
key-ring
keystroke
keyword
khaki
kibbutz
 kibbutzim
kibosh
kick
kicker
kick-off
kick-start
kid
 kidded

kidding

kidnap
 kidnapped
 kidnapping
kidnapper
kidnapping
kidney
 kidneys
kill
killer
killing
killjoy
kiln
kilo
 kilos
kilobyte
kilocalorie
kilogram,
 kilogramme
kilohertz
kilometre
kilowatt
kilt
kilter
kimono
 kimonos
kin
kind
kindergarten
kind-hearted
kindle
 kindled
 kindling
kindliness
kindling
kindly
kindness
kindred
kinesis
kinetic
kinetically
kinetics

king
kingdom
kingfisher
kingly
kingpin
kink
kinky
kinsfolk
kinship
kinsman
 kinsmen
kinswoman
 kinswomen
kiosk
kip
 kipped
 kipping
kipper
kiss
 kisses
kissable
kisser
kissogram
kit
 kitted
 kitting
kitbag
kitchen
kitchenette
kite
kith and kin
kitsch
kitten
kittenish
kittiwake
kitty
 kitties
kiwi
 kiwis
klaxon
kleptomania
kleptomaniac

knack
knacker
knackered
knapsack
knapweed
knave

♦* Do not confuse
with **nave** *A knave is a
rogue • the knave of
hearts*

knavery
knavish
knead

♦* Do not confuse
with **kneed** or **need**
Knead the dough well

knee
 kneed
 kneeing
kneecap
 kneecapped
 kneecapping
kneed

♦* Do not confuse
with **knead** or **need**
*She kneed him in the
stomach*

knee-deep
knee-jerk
kneel
 knelt
 kneeling
knees-up
knell
knelt
knew

♦* Do not confuse
with **new** *I knew he was
lying*

knickerbockers

Can't find your word? Try looking under **C**, **CH**, **Q** or **KH**

knickers
knick-knack,
nick-nack
knife
  pl knives
  knifed
  knifing
knight

> 💣* Do not confuse
> with **night** *a knight in
> shining armour*

knighted
knighthood
knightly
knit
  knitted
  knitting

> 💣* Do not confuse
> with **nit** *to knit a
> cardigan*

knitting
knitwear
knives
knob
knock
knockdown

knocker
knock-kneed
knock-on
knockout
knoll
knot
  knotted
  knotting

> 💣* Do not confuse
> with **not** *tie a knot • to
> knot the string*

knotty

> 💣* Do not confuse
> with **naughty** *a knotty
> problem*

know
  knew
  known
  knowing

> 💣* Do not confuse
> with **no** *I know her well*

know-all
know-how
knowing
knowingly

knowledge

> ❶ Word within word:
> **know-ledge**

knowledgeable
knowledgeably
known
knuckle
  knuckled
  knuckling
koala bear
kohl

> 💣* Do not confuse
> with **coal** *Kohl is a
> powder used as eyeliner*

kookaburra
Koran, Qur'an
kosher
kowtow
krill
krypton
kudos
kung-fu

Can't find your word? Try looking under **C, CH, Q** or **KH**

Ll

la
lab
label
 labelled
 labelling
laboratory
 laboratories
laborious
labour
 laboured
 labouring
laboured
labourer
labrador
laburnum
labyrinth
lace
 laced
 lacing
lacerate
 lacerated
 lacerating
laceration
lace-up
lack
lackey
 lackeys
lacklustre
laconic
laconically
lacquer
 lacquered
 lacquering
lacrosse

lactate
 lactated
 lactating
lactation
lactic
lactose
lad
ladder
 laddered
 laddering
laden
ladies
lading
ladle
 ladled
 ladling
lady
 ladies
ladybird
ladylike
ladyship
lag
 lagged
 lagging
lager
lagging
lagoon
laid
laid-back
lain

♦* Do not confuse
with **lane** *He has lain
down*

lair

♦* Do not confuse
with **layer** *a wolf's lair*

laird
laissez-faire
laity
lake
lama

♦* Do not confuse
with **llama** *A lama is a
Buddhist priest*

lamb
lambada
lambast, lambaste
 lambasted
 lambasting
lambswool
lame
 lamed
 laming
lamé
lamely
lameness
lament
lamentable
lamentation
laminate
 laminated
 laminating
lamination
lamp
lampoon
 lampooned

lampooning
lamppost
lamprey
lampreys
lampshade
lance
lanced
lancing
lance-corporal
lancet
land
landed
landing
landlady
landladies
landlocked
landlord
landlubber
landmark
landmass
landmasses
landowner
landscape
landslide
landslip
lane

❧* Do not confuse
with **lain** *a country
lane • the inside lane of
the motorway*

language
languid
languish
languor
languorous
languorously
lank
lanky
lanolin
lantern
lap

lapped
lapping
lapdog
lapel
lapse
lapsed
lapsing
laptop
lapwing
larceny
larch
larches
lard
larder
large
largely
largeness
largesse
largo
lark
larkspur
larva
larvae
laryngitis
larynx
larynxes, larynges
lasagne
lascivious
laser
lash
lashes
lass
lasses
lassitude
lasso
lassos, lassoes
last
lastly
latch
latches
latchkey
latchkeys

late
lately
latency
lateness
latent
lateral
laterally

❧* Do not confuse
with **latterly** *A crab
moves laterally*

latex
lath

❧* Do not confuse
with **lathe** *A lath is a
thin strip of wood*

lathe

❧* Do not confuse
with **lath** *A lathe is a
machine for woodwork
and metalwork*

lather
lathered
lathering
lathery
latitude
latitudinal
latrine
latter
latterly

❧* Do not confuse
with **laterally** *Latterly
he has grown senile*

lattice
laud
laudable
laudably
laugh
laughable
laughably
laughing-stock

laughter

ℹ Loud and uncontrolled giggling has turned into laughter.

launch
launches
launder
laundered
laundering
**launderette,
   laundrette**
laundry
laundries
laureate
laurel
lava
lavatorial
lavatory
lavatories
lavender
lavish
law
law-abiding
lawful
lawfully
lawless
lawlessness
lawn
lawnmower
lawsuit
lawyer
lax
laxative
laxity
lay
laid
laying
layabout
lay-by, layby
lay-bys, laybys

layer
layered
layering

✒* Do not confuse with **lair** *two layers of cloth*

layette
layman
laymen
layout
layperson
laywoman
laywomen
laze
lazed
lazing
lazily
laziness
lazy
lazier
laziest
lazy-bones
lea

✒* Do not confuse with **lee** *the grassy lea*

leach

✒* Do not confuse with **leech** *to leach harmful substances into the water*

lead
led
leading

✒* Do not confuse **lead** with **led**, the past form of the verb *to lead the way • lead pipes • a pencil lead*

leaden
leader

leadership
leading
leaf
pl leaves
leafed
leafing
leafless
leaflet
leafy
league
leak

✒* Do not confuse with **leek** *a gas leak • Does this boat leak?*

leakage
leaky
lean
leant, leaned
leaning
leaning
leanness
leant

✒* Do not confuse with **lent** *She leant her head on my shoulder*

lean-to
lean-tos
leap
leapt, leaped
leaping
leapfrog
leapt
learn
learnt, learned
learning
learned
learner
learning
learnt
lease
leased

leasing
leasehold
leaseholder
leash
leashes
least
leather
leathered
leathering
leathery
leave
left
leaving
leaven
leavened
leavening
leaver
leaves
leavings
lecher
lecherous
lechery
lecithin
lectern
lecture
lectured
lecturing
lecturer
led

💠 Do not confuse
with **lead** *He led the
team to victory • She
has led them astray*

lederhosen
ledge
ledger
lee

💠 Do not confuse
with **lea** *in the lee of the
wall • the lee side of the
boat*

leech
leeches

💠 Do not confuse
with **leach** *clinging like
a leech • Leeches were
used in medicine*

leek

💠 Do not confuse
with **leak** *leek soup*

leer
leered
leering
lees
leeward
leeway
left
left-hand
left-handed
left-handedness
left-hander
leftism
leftist
leftover
leftovers
left-wing
left-winger
leg
legacy
legacies
legal
legalisation
another spelling of
legalization
legalise
another spelling of
legalize
legality
legalities
legalization,
legalisation
legalize, legalise

legalized, legalised
legalizing, legalising
legally
legend
legendary
leggings
leggy
legibility
legible
legibly
legion
legionnaire
legislate
legislated
legislating
legislation
legislative
legislator
legislature
legitimacy
legitimate
legitimately
legitimize,
legitimise
legitimized,
legitimised
legitimizing,
legitimising
legless
legroom
leisure

❶ It's our **lei**sure time,
so let's enjoy it!

leisured
leisurely
leitmotiv
lemming
lemon
lemonade
lemony
lemur

SPELLING *focus*

Letter Patterns

The English language has many different letter patterns. A letter pattern is a sequence of the same letters in the same order which can be found in many words. For example **-ight** is a common letter pattern found in words like *bright*, *height*, *light*, *straight* and *weight*. Few letter patterns sound the same in every word. For example, **-ear** is pronounced differently in *near*, *bear* and *heart*.

The letter string **-ough** probably has the most different sounds: 'oh' in *dough*, 'ow' in *bough*, 'oo' in *through*, 'off' in *cough*, 'uff' in *enough*, 'aw' in *brought*, 'uh' in *thorough* and several more. Can you think of other words containing **-ough** that rhyme with each of these?

Not only can the same letters be pronounced in many different ways, but the same sound can be written with many different letter patterns:

'oan': **loan, bone, grown, sewn**
'eer': **veer, mere, hear, pier**
'ite': **kite, byte, fight, height**
'erd': **herd, bird, curd, word, heard, furred**
'tion': **station, fashion, electrician, session, Russian**

How many different ways can you find to spell the long 'a' sound, as in *tray* and *gate*?

Using letter patterns

Use your knowledge of letter patterns to help you spell unfamiliar or difficult words. For example, if you know the letter pattern **-our** from words like *sour*, *flour* and *pour*, you can apply it to work out the spelling of longer words like *flavour*, *armour*, *colour* and *honour*.

You may find it useful to learn sets of letter patterns that are often used to spell the same sound, such as **ee** and **ea** (*beech*, *teach*), **ou** and **ow** (*doubt*, *down*), **sc** and **ps** (*science*, *psychic*) and **kn** and **gn** (*knight*, *gnat*).

If there is a word that you always find difficult to spell, think of another word with the same letter pattern and make up a sentence containing both. It does not matter if the letter patterns are pronounced differently – this can still help you to remember them:

Her d*augh*ter c*augh*t the ball.
My fr*ien*d is an al*ien*.

Letter Patterns continued

Many words are spelt and pronounced in a logical way. More information can be found in the Spelling Rules on p.390. Here are some extra guidelines:

- The letter **h** often occurs with another consonant in combinations such as **ch** (*chick*), **tch** (*watch*), **sh** (*fashion*), **sch** (*school*), **th** (*myth*), **wh** (*white*), **gh** (*sigh* and *ghost*) and **ght** (*daughter*). Learn the letter patterns **tch**, **sch** and **ght** and do not put the **h** in the wrong place. Beware of the **phth** combination, found in words like *ophthalmic* and *diphtheria*, and do not miss out an **h**.

- **CC** is sometimes pronounced like **x** in the middle of a word – remember that you need two **c**'s, one for the 'k' sound and one for the 's' sound: *accent*, *accept*, *eccentric*, *succeed*, *succinct*, *vaccine*.

- When a short 'o' sound follows **w** or **qu** it is usually spelt with an **a**: *wash*, *wasp*, *swan*, *swat*, *quash*, *squat*, *squabble*. (Exceptions include *wok* and *wobble*.) Similarly, the 'or' sound is usually spelt **ar** after **w** or **qu**: *warm*, *warn*, *swarm*, *dwarf*, *towards*, *quarter*.

Over to you

The answers to the following clues are groups of words containing the same letter patterns, which may or may not have the same sound in each word. The first one has been done – can you solve the rest?

---

not heavy / battle / scare / ugly

    -ight: light / fight / frighten / unsightly

---

seat / animal's den / place where milk is processed / list of questions

---

sixty minutes / bitter / sightseer / grieve

Make a note of common patterns, like **-our-**, **-ight-**, **-ous** and **-ial** in your Spelling Journal. Make lists under each heading of words which have this pattern as you come across them.

lend
lent
lending
length
lengthen
lengthened
lengthening
lengthily
lengthiness
lengthways
lengthwise
lengthy
lenience
leniency
lenient
lens
lenses
lent

🖋* Do not confuse
with **leant** *He lent me
£20*

lentil
leopard

ℹ️ **Leo pard**oned the
leopard for eating his
sister.

leotard
leper
leprechaun
leprosy
lesbian
lesbianism
lesion
less
lessen
lessened
lessening

🖋* Do not confuse
with **lesson** *to lessen
the pain*

lesser
lesson

🖋* Do not confuse
with **lessen** *a French
lesson*

lest
let
let
letting
lethal
lethargic
lethargically
lethargy
letter
lettered
letterhead
lettering
letting
lettuce
leukaemia
level
levelled
levelling
level-headed
lever
levered
levering
leverage
leviathan
levitate
levitated
levitating
levitation
levity
levy
levies
levied
levying
lewd
lewdness
lexical

lexicographer
lexicography
lexicon
liability
liabilities
liable

🖋* Do not confuse
with **libel** *You are
liable to slip on ice •
liable for her debts*

liaise
liaised
liaising

ℹ️ You need two eyes
[two **i**'s] to **liaise**
properly.

liaison
liar

🖋* Do not confuse
with **lyre** *He's a liar
and a cheat*

libel
libelled
libelling

🖋* Do not confuse
with **liable** *guilty of
libel • Did the
newspaper libel him?*

libellous
liberal
liberally
liberalisation
another spelling of
liberalization
liberalise
another spelling of
liberalize
liberalism
liberality
liberalization,

liberalisation
liberalize, liberalise
liberalized,
liberalised
liberalizing,
liberalising
liberate
liberated
liberating
liberation
liberator
liberty
liberties
libido
libidos
librarian
librarianship
library
libraries
libretto
libretti, librettos
lice
licence

◆* Do not confuse
with **license** *a TV
licence • poetic licence*

license
licensed
licensing

◆* Do not confuse
with **licence** *to license a
TV • a licensed
restaurant*

licensee
licentiate
licentious
licentiousness
lichen
lichgate
another spelling of
lychgate

lick
lid
lido
lidos
lie
lay, lied
lain, lied
lying

◆* The past forms **lay**
and **lain** are used for
all meanings except
'tell an untruth' *It lay
undisturbed for months
• He has lain down •
She lied about her age*

liege
lie-in
lieu

◆* Do not confuse
with **loo** *in lieu of
payment*

lieutenant

❶ The **lieut**enant will
lie utterly still.

life
lives
lifebelt
life-blood
lifeboat
life-cycle
lifeguard
life-jacket
lifeless
lifelike
lifeline
lifelong
lifer
life-saver
lifespan
lifestyle

lifetime
lift
lift-off
ligament
ligature
light
lit, lighted
lighting
lighten
lightened
lightening

◆* Do not confuse
lightening with
lightning *lightening
the load*

lighter
light-headed
light-hearted
lighthouse
lighting
lightly
lightness
lightning

◆* Do not confuse
with **lightening**
thunder and lightning

lightweight
light-year
like
liked
liking
likeable, likable
likelihood
likely
like-minded
liken
likened
likening
likeness
likewise
lilac

Lilliputian, lilliputian
lilt
lily
 lilies
lily-of-the-valley
limb
limber
 limbered
 limbering
limbless
limbo
lime
limelight
limerick
limestone
limit
 limited
 limiting
limitation
limitless
limo
 limos
limousine
limp
limpet
limpid
limpness
linchpin
line
 lined
 lining
lineage
lineal
lineally
linear
linen
liner
linesman
 linesmen
lineswoman
 lineswomen
line-up

linger
 lingered
 lingering
lingerer
lingerie
lingua franca
 lingua francas
linguist
linguistic
linguistically
linguistics
liniment
lining
link
links
link-up
linnet
lino
linocut
linoleum
linseed
lint
lintel
lion
lioness
 lionesses
lionize, lionise
 lionized, lionised
 lionizing, lionising
lip
lipid
lipogram
liposuction
lip-read
 lip-read
 lip-reading
lip-reader
lip-service
lipstick
liquefaction
liquefy
 liquefies

liquefied
liquefying
liqueur

♠* Do not confuse
with **liquor** *Cointreau
is an orange liqueur*

liquid
liquidate
 liquidated
 liquidating
liquidation
liquidator
liquidize, liquidise
 liquidized,
 liquidised
 liquidizing,
 liquidising
liquidizer, liquidiser
liquor

♠* Do not confuse
with **liqueur** *banned
from selling alcoholic
liquor*

liquorice

❶ Is water **liqu**id **or
ice**?

lisp
lissom, lissome
list
listen
 listened
 listening
listener
listening

❶ Word within word:
listen-ing

listeria
listless
lit
litany

litanies
literacy
literal

> ♦* Do not confuse
> with **literary** or
> **literate** *a literal*
> *translation*

literally
literary

> ♦* Do not confuse
> with **literal** or **literate**
> *What are her literary*
> *tastes?*

literate

> ♦* Do not confuse
> with **literal** or **literary**
> *He is scarcely literate*

literati
literature
lithe
litheness
lithium
lithograph
lithographer
lithography
litigant
litigate
litigated
litigating
litigation
litigious
litmus
litre
litter
littered
littering
little
littoral
liturgical
liturgy

liturgies
live
lived
living
liveable, livable
livelihood
liveliness
livelong
lively
livelier
liveliest
liven
livened
livening
liver
liveried
livery
liveries
lives
livestock
livid
living
living-room
lizard
llama

> ♦* Do not confuse
> with **lama** *A llama is a*
> *South American*
> *animal*

lo

> ♦* Do not confuse
> with **low** *lo and behold*
> • *Lo! It's vanished!*

loach
load

> ♦* Do not confuse
> with **lode** *a heavy load*
> *to carry* • *to load the*
> *lorry with coal*

loaded

loaf
pl loaves
loafed
loafing
loafer
loam
loamy
loan
loaned
loaning

> ♦* Do not confuse
> with **lone** *a book on*
> *loan* • *a bank loan* • *to*
> *loan paintings to a*
> *gallery*

loath, loth

> ♦* Do not confuse
> with **loathe** *He was*
> *loath to go*

loathe
loathed
loathing

> ♦* Do not confuse
> with **loath** *I loathe*
> *cruelty*

loathing
loathsome
loaves
lob
lobbed
lobbing
lobby
lobbies
lobbied
lobbying
lobbyist
lobe
lobelia
lobotomy
lobotomies

lobster
lobster-pot
local

> ♦* Do not confuse
> with **locale** *local people*
> *• a pub lunch at his local*

locale

> ♦* Do not confuse
> with **local** *the locale of*
> *the film*

localise
another spelling of
localize
locality
localities
localize, localise
localized, localised
localizing, localising
locally
locate
located
locating
location
loch
lochs
loci
lock
lockable
locker
locket
lockjaw
lockout
locksmith
lockup
locomotion
locomotive
locum
locus
loci
locust
locution

lode

> ♦* Do not confuse
> with **load** *A lode is a*
> *vein in rock containing*
> *metal*

lodestar
lodestone
lodge
lodged
lodging
lodger
lodgings
lo-fi
loft
loftily
loftiness
lofty
log
logged
logging
loganberry
loganberries
logarithm
logbook
loggerheads
logic
logical
logically
logistic
logistical
logistics
logo
logos
loin
loincloth
loiter
loitered
loitering
loiterer
loll
lollipop

lollop
lolloped
lolloping
lolly
lollies
lone

> ♦* Do not confuse
> with **loan** *a lone*
> *cottage • a lone star*
> Remember that **lone**
> describes **one** thing by
> itself.

loneliness
lonely
lonesome
long
longboat
longbow
longevity
longhand
longing
longitude
longship
long-sighted
long-standing
long-suffering
long-term
long-winded
loo

> ♦* Do not confuse
> with **lieu** *I'm dying to*
> *go to the loo*

loofah
look
lookalike, look-alike
look-in
lookout
loom
loomed
looming
loony

loop
looped
looping
loophole
loose
loosed
loosing

✒* Do not confuse
with **lose** *This screw is
loose • at a loose end •
He threatened to loose
the guard dogs*

loosely
loosen
loosened
loosening
looseness
loot
looted
looting

✒* Do not confuse
with **lute** *the burglar's
loot • The rioters looted
the shops*

looter
lop
lopped
lopping
lope
loped
loping
lop-eared
lop-sided
loquacious
loquacity
lord
lordly
lordship
lore
lorry
lorries

lose
lost
losing

✒* Do not confuse
with **loose** *to lose a
glove • to lose weight •
to lose time*

loser
loss
losses
lost
lot
loth
another spelling of
loath
lotion
lottery
lotteries
lotto
lotus
lotuses
loud
loudhailer
loudly
loudness
loudspeaker
lounge
lounged
lounging
lour
another spelling of
lower
louse
lice
lousy
lout
lovable
love
loved
loving
lovebird

loveless
loveliness
lovelorn
lovely
lovelier
loveliest
lover
lovesick
loving
lovingly
low

✒* Do not confuse
with **lo** *a low wall •
Cows low*

lower, lour
lowered, loured
lowering, louring

✒* The spelling **lour**
is only used for the
verb meaning 'become
dark' or 'frown' *louring
skies • She loured at us*

lower-case
lowland
lowlander
lowliness
lowly
lowlier
lowliest
lowness
loyal
loyalist
loyally
loyalty
lozenge
lubricant
lubricate
lubricated
lubricating
lubrication
lucid

lucidity
lucidly
luck
luckily
luckless
lucky
 luckier
 luckiest
lucrative
lucre
Luddite
ludicrous
ludo
lug
 lugged
 lugging
luge
luggage
lukewarm
lull
lullaby
 lullabies
lumbar

> ♦* Do not confuse
> with **lumber** *lumbar*
> *pain • a lumbar*
> *puncture*

lumber
lumbered
lumbering

> ♦* Do not confuse
> with **lumbar** *rubbish*
> *and lumber •*
> *Elephants lumber*
> *through the forests • to*
> *lumber us with it*

lumberjack
luminary
luminescence
luminescent
luminosity
luminous
lump
lumpectomy
lumpy
lunacy
lunar
lunatic
lunch
 lunches
luncheon
lunchtime
lung
lunge
 lunged
 lunging
lupin
lurch
 lurches
lurcher
lure
 lured
 luring
lurid
lurk
lurking
luscious
lush
lust
lustful
lustfully
lustily

lustre
lustrous
lusty
lute

> ♦* Do not confuse
> with **loot** *play music on*
> *a lute*

luxuriance
luxuriant
luxuriate
 luxuriated
 luxuriating
luxurious
luxury
 luxuries
lychgate, lichgate
lychee
Lycra®
lying
lymph
lymphatic
lynch
lynx
 lynxes
lyre

> ♦* Do not confuse
> with **liar** *A lyre is like a*
> *harp*

lyric
lyrical
lyrically
lyricism
lyricist

ma'am
mac, mack
macabre
macaroni

> ♦* Do not confuse
> with **macaroon**
> *macaroni cheese*

macaroon

> ♦* Do not confuse
> with **macaroni**
> *coconut macaroons*

macaw
mace
machete
Machiavellian
machine
  machined
  machining
machine-gun
machinery
machinist
machismo
Mach number
macho
mack
  another spelling of
  mac
mackerel
mackintosh
  mackintoshes
macro
  macros
macrobiotic

macrocosm
macroeconomics
mad
  madder
  maddest
madam
madcap
madden
  maddened
  maddening
made

> ♦* Do not confuse
> with **maid** *I made a
> mistake • a statue
> made of bronze*

Madeira
madhouse
madly
madman
  madmen
madness
madrigal
madwoman
  madwomen
maelstrom
maestro
  maestros
magazine
magenta
maggot
maggoty
magic
magical

magically
magician
magisterial
magistrate
magma
magnanimity
magnanimous
magnanimously
magnate

> ♦* Do not confuse
> with **magnet** *He is a
> shipping magnate*

magnesia
magnesium
magnet

> ♦* Do not confuse
> with **magnate** *A
> magnet attracts iron*

magnetic
magnetically
magnetisation
  another spelling of
  magnetization
magnetise
  another spelling of
  magnetize
magnetism
magnetization,
  magnetisation
magnetize,
  magnetise
  magnetized,
  magnetised

magnetizing,
magnetising
magneto
magnetos
magnification
magnificence
magnificent
magnify
magnifies
magnified
magnifying
magnitude
magnolia
magnum
magpie
magus
magi
Maharajah
mah-jong
mahogany
maid

📍* Do not confuse
with **made** *The maid
served the tea*

maiden
mail
mailed
mailing

📍* Do not confuse
with **male** *first-class
mail • to mail a letter • a
coat of mail*

mailbag
mailbox
mailboxes
mailing list
mail order
mail shot
maim
maimed
maiming

main

📍* Do not confuse
with **mane** *the main
points of his speech • a
main road • a gas main*

mainframe
mainland
mainline
mainly
mainsail
mainstay
mainstream
maintain
maintained
maintaining
maintenance

🛈 The **main tent** is
where the d**ance** is
held.

maisonette
maize

📍* Do not confuse
with **maze** *fields of
maize*

majestic
majestically
majesty
majesties
major
majorette
majority
majorities
make
made
making
make-believe
maker
makeshift
make-up
making

malachite
maladjusted
malady
maladies
malaise
malaria
malarkey
male

📍* Do not confuse
with **mail** *male and
female*

malediction
maledictory
maleness
malevolence
malevolent
malevolently
malformation
malformed
malfunction
malfunctioned
malfunctioning
malice
malicious
maliciously
malign
malignant
malinger
malingered
malingering
malingerer
mall
mallard
malleable
mallet
mallow
malnutrition
malpractice
malt
maltreat
maltreated

maltreating
maltreatment
mama, mamma
mamba
mambo
mamma
another spelling of
mama
mammal
mammalian
mammary
mammogram
mammoth
man
pl men
manned
manning
manacle
manacled
manacling
manage
managed
managing
manageable

❶ Word within word:
man-age-able

management
manager
manageress
manageresses
managerial
mandarin
mandate
mandatory
mandible
mandolin,
mandoline
mane

♦* Do not confuse
with **main** *a horse's
mane*

manful
manfully
manga
manganese
mange
manger
mangetout
mangle
mangled
mangling
mango
mangoes
mangrove
mangy
manhandle
manhandled
manhandling
manhole
manhood
manhunt
mania
maniac

♦* Do not confuse
with **manic** *The
murderer was a maniac*

maniacal
manic

♦* Do not confuse
with **maniac** *manic
depression*

manicure
manicured
manicuring
manicurist
manifest
manifestation
manifesto
manifestos,
manifestoes
manifold
manipulate

manipulated
manipulating
manipulation
mankind
manky
manliness
manly
manna
manned
mannequin
manner

♦* Do not confuse
with **manor** *a manner
of speaking • Don't
forget your manners!*

mannerism
mannerly
manning
mannish
manoeuvrability
manoeuvrable
manoeuvre
manoeuvred
manoeuvring

❶ **Manoeuvre** the
canoe up violent
rapids.

manor

♦* Do not confuse
with **manner** *the lord of
the manor • a manor
house*

manorial
manpower
manse
mansion
manslaughter
mantelpiece
mantis
mantis, mantises

mantle
mantra
manual
manually
manufacture
　manufactured
　manufacturing
manufacturer
manure
　manured
　manuring
manuscript
Manx cat
many
map
　mapped
　mapping
maple
mar
　marred
　marring
maracas
maraschino
　maraschinos
marathon
maraud
marauder
marauding
marble
march
　marches
marchioness
　marchionesses
mare

♦* Do not confuse
with **mayor** *a mare and
her foal*

margarine
margin
marginal
marginalize,

marginalise
marginalized,
marginalised
marginalizing,
marginalising
marginally
marigold
marijuana,
　marihuana
marimba
marina
marinade
　marinaded
　marinading
marinate
　marinated
　marinating
marine
mariner
marionette
marital
maritally
maritime
marjoram
mark
marked
markedly
marker
market
　marketed
　marketing
marketable
marketing
marksman
　marksmen
marksmanship
markswoman
　markswomen
marl
marmalade
marmoset
marmot

maroon
　marooned
　marooning
marquee
marquess, marquis
　marquesses,
　marquises
marquetry
marred
marriage

🛈 Can you get
married at any **age**?

marriageable
marring
marrow
marrowbone
marry
　marries
　married
　marrying
marsh
　marshes
marshal
　marshalled
　marshalling

♦* Do not confuse
with **martial** *a marshal
in the armed forces • to
marshal the troops*

marshmallow
marshy
marsupial
marten

♦* Do not confuse
with **martin** *the fur of a
marten*

martial

♦* Do not confuse
with **marshal** *martial
law • martial arts*

martin

💧* Do not confuse with **marten** *a martin's nest*

martyr
martyred
martyring

ℹ Word within word: m-**arty**-r

martyrdom
marvel
marvelled
marvelling
marvellous
Marxism
Marxist
marzipan
mascara
mascarpone
mascot
masculine
masculinity
mash
mask

💧* Do not confuse with **masque** *The burglar wore a mask • to mask her ignorance*

masked
masochism
masochist
masochistic
mason
masonic
masonry
masque

💧* Do not confuse with **mask** *A masque is an old form of entertainment*

masquerade
masqueraded
masquerading
masquerader
mass
masses
massacre
massacred
massacring
massage
massaged
massaging
masseur
masseuse
massive
mass-produce
mass-produced
mass-producing
mass production
mast
mastectomy
master
mastered
mastering
masterful
masterfully
masterliness
masterly
mastermind
masterpiece
mastery
masthead
mastic
masticate
masticated
masticating
mastication
mastiff
mat
matted
matting
matador

match
matches
matchbox
matchboxes
matchless
matchmaker
matchstick
mate
mated
mating
material
materialisation
another spelling of **materialization**
materialise
another spelling of **materialize**
materialism
materialistic
materialization, materialisation
materialize, materialise
materialized, materialised
materializing, materialising
materially
maternal
maternally
maternity
mathematical
mathematically
mathematician
mathematics
maths
matinée, matinee
matins
matriarch
matriarchs
matriarchal
matrices

matriculate
matriculated
matriculating
matriculation
matrimonial
matrimony
matrix
matrices, matrixes
matron
matronly
matt, matte, mat
matted
matter
mattered
mattering
matter-of-fact
matting
mattress
mattresses
mature
matured
maturing
maturity
maudlin
maul
mauled
mauling
mausoleum
mauve
maverick
maw
mawkish
maxim
maximal
maximize, maximise
maximized,
maximised
maximizing,
maximising
maximum
maxima
may

might
maybe
mayday
mayfly
mayflies
mayhem
mayonnaise

🛈 Word breakdown:
may-on-naise

mayor

◆* Do not confuse
with **mare** *elect a
mayor • the Lord
Mayor of London*

mayoress
mayoresses
maypole
maze

◆* Do not confuse
with **maize** *lost in a
maze*

me
mead
meadow
meagre
meagrely
meal
mealy-mouthed
mean
meant
meaning

◆* Do not confuse
with **mien** *a mean old
miser • What does the
word mean?*

meander
meandered
meandering
meaning
meaningful

meaningfully
meaningless
meanness
means
meant
meantime
meanwhile
measles
measly
measurable
measure
measured
measuring
measurement
meat

◆* Do not confuse
with **meet** or **mete**
*Vegetarians don't eat
meat*

meatball
meaty
meatier
meatiest
mechanic
mechanical
mechanically
mechanics
mechanisation
another spelling of
mechanization
mechanise
another spelling of
mechanize
mechanism
**mechanization,
mechanisation**
**mechanize,
mechanise**
mechanized,
mechanised
mechanizing,

mechanising
medal

💧* Do not confuse
with **meddle** *a gold
medal*

medallion
medallist
meddle
meddled
meddling

💧* Do not confuse
with **medal** *to meddle
in other people's affairs*

meddler
meddlesome
meddling
media
mediaeval
another spelling of
medieval
medial
median
mediate
mediated
mediating

💧* Do not confuse
with **meditate** *to
mediate in a dispute*

mediation
mediator
medic
medical
medically
medicate
medicated
medicating
medicated
medication
medicinal
medicinally

medicine

❶ I see [c] I need some
med**i**cine.

medieval, mediaeval
mediocre
mediocrity
meditate
meditated
meditating

💧* Do not confuse
with **mediate** *I
meditate every day*

meditation
meditative
medium
media, mediums

💧* The plural form
mediums is only used
for spiritualists
*Mediums are psychic •
art works created using
various media*

medley
medleys
meek
meekly
meet
met
meeting

💧* Do not confuse
with **meat** or **mete**
*They meet in the church
hall*

mega
megabyte
megalith
megalomania
megalomaniac
megaphone
megaton

melamine
melancholic
melancholy
melanin
melanoma
mêlée
mellow
melodic
melodious
melodrama
melodramatic
melodramatically
melody
melodies
melon
melt
meltdown
melting-pot
member
membership
membrane
membranous
memento
mementos,
mementoes

💧* Do not confuse
with **momentum** *a
memento of your visit*

memo
memos
memoirs
memorabilia
memorable
memorably
memorandum
memoranda
memorial
memorize,
memorise
memorized,
memorised

memorizing,
memorising
memory
memories
men
menace
menaced
menacing
menacing
menagerie
mend
mendacious
mendacity
mendicant
menfolk
menhir
menial
meningitis
menopausal
menopause
menses
menstrual
menstruate
menstruated
menstruating
menstruation
mental
mentally
mentality
mentalities
menthol
mentholated
mention
mentioned
mentioning
mentor
menu
menus
mercantile
mercantilism
mercenary
mercenaries

merchandise
merchant
merciful
mercifully
merciless
mercurial
mercury
mercy
mercies
mere
merely
merge
merged
merging
merger
meridian
meridional
meringue
merino
merinos
merit
merited
meriting
meritocracy
meritocracies
meritorious
mermaid
merman
mermen
merrily
merriment
merry
merrier
merriest
merry-go-round
merrymaking
mesh
meshes
mesmeric
mesmerise
another spelling of
mesmerize

mesmerism
mesmerize,
mesmerise
mesmerized,
mesmerised
mesmerizing,
mesmerising
mess
messes
message
messenger
messily
messy
messier
messiest
met
metabolic
metabolise
another spelling of
metabolize
metabolism
metabolize,
metabolise
metabolized,
metabolised
metabolizing,
metabolising
metal

◆* Do not confuse
with **mettle** *a metal
box*

metallic
metallurgist
metallurgy
metamorphose
metamorphosed
metamorphosing
metamorphosis
metamorphoses
metaphor
metaphorical

metaphorically
metaphysical
metaphysics
metatarsal
mete
 meted
 meting

✐* Do not confuse
with **meat** or **meet** *to
mete out punishment*

meteor
meteoric
meteorite
meteorological
meteorologically
meteorologist
meteorology
meter
 metered
 metering

✐* Do not confuse
with **metre** *a gas meter
• a parking meter*

methadone
methane
methanol
method
methodical
methodically
Methodist
methodology
meths
methylated spirits
meticulous
meticulously
metonymy
metre

✐* Do not confuse
with **meter** *a metre of
cloth • poetic metre*

metric
metrical
metricate
 metricated
 metricating
metrication
metronome
metropolis
 metropolises
metropolitan
mettle

✐* Do not confuse
with **metal** *That horse
has plenty of mettle •
You must be on your
mettle at the interview*

mew
mews

✐* Do not confuse
with **muse** *a mews flat •
Horses were kept in the
mews*

mezzanine
mezzo-soprano
 mezzo-sopranos
miaow
mica
mice
mickey
micro
 micros
microbe
microbiologist
microbiology
microchip
microclimate
microcomputer
microcosm
microfiche
microfilm
microlight

micrometer
micro-organism
microphone
microprocessor
microscope
microscopic
microsecond
microsurgeon
microsurgery
microwave
microwaveable,
 microwavable
mid-air
midday
midden
middle
middle-aged
middleman
 middlemen
middleweight
middling
midfield
midge
midget
midnight
midpoint
midriff
midst
midstream
midsummer
midway
midweek
midwife
 midwives
midwifery
midwinter
mien

✐* Do not confuse
with **mean** *She had a
solemn mien*

miffed

might

●* Do not confuse
with **mite** *the might of
the army • It might rain*

mightily
mightiness
mightn't
mighty
 mightier
 mightiest
migraine
migrant
migrate
 migrated
 migrating
migration
migratory
mike
mild
mildew
mildly
mile
mileage
**mileometer,
 milometer**
milestone
milieu
 milieus, milieux
militancy
militant
military
militate
 militated
 militating
militia
milk
milkmaid
milkman
 milkmen
milk-shake
milky

mill
millennium
 millennia

❶ A millennium is
a lot longer than
ninety-nine years.

miller
millet
millibar
**milligram,
 milligramme**
millilitre
millimetre
million
millionaire
millionairess
 millionairesses
millipede
millisecond
millpond
millstone
milometer
 another spelling of
 mileometer
mime
 mimed
 miming
mimic
 mimicked
 mimicking
mimicry
minaret
mince
 minced
 mincing
mincemeat
mincer
mind
mind-blowing
minder
mindful

mindless
mine
 mined
 mining
minefield
miner

●* Do not confuse
with **minor** or **myna**
*miners working at the
coalface*

mineral
mineralogical
mineralogist
mineralogy
minestrone
minesweeper
mingle
 mingled
 mingling
mingy
Mini®
 Minis
miniature

❶ Word breakdown:
min-i-a-ture

**miniaturize,
 miniaturise**
 miniaturized,
 miniaturised
 miniaturizing,
 miniaturising
minibus
 minibuses
minicab
minim
minimal
minimalism
minimalist
minimize, minimise
 minimized,
 minimised

minimizing,
minimising
minimum
minima
mining
minion
miniskirt
minister
ministered
ministering

🖊* Do not confuse
with **minster** *a
minister of the church* •
the prime minister • *to
minister to her needs*

ministerial
ministerially
ministration
ministry
ministries
mink
minnow
minor

🖊* Do not confuse
with **miner** or **myna** *of
minor importance* • *the
key of E minor* •
*Legally, she is still a
minor*

minority
minorities
minster

🖊* Do not confuse
with **minister** *York
Minster*

minstrel
mint
minty
minuet
minus

minuscule
minute
minutiae
minx
minxes
miracle
miraculous
miraculously
mirage
mire
mirror
mirrored
mirroring
mirth
mirthful
mirthless
misadventure
misanthropic
misanthropist
misanthropy
misappropriate
misappropriated
misappropriating
misappropriation
misbehave
misbehaved
misbehaving
misbehaviour
miscalculate
miscalculated
miscalculating
miscalculation
miscarriage
miscarry
miscarries
miscarried
miscarrying
miscellaneous

ⓘ Word breakdown:
mis-cell-a-ne-ous

miscellany

miscellanies
mischance
mischief

ⓘ Causing havoc is
excellent fun!

mischievous
misconception
misconduct
misconstrue
misconstrued
misconstruing
misdeed
misdemeanour
miser
miserable
miserably
miserly
misery
miseries
misfire
misfired
misfiring
misfit
misfortune
misgiving
misguided
mishandle
mishandled
mishandling
mishap
mishear
misheard
mishearing
mishmash
misinform
misinformation
misinterpret
misinterpreted
misinterpreting
misjudge
misjudged

misjudging

mislay
mislaid
mislaying

mislead
misled
misleading

mismanage
mismanaged
mismanaging

mismatch
mismatches

misnomer

misogynist

misogynous

misplace
misplaced
misplacing

misprint

mispronounce
mispronounced
mispronouncing

misquote
misquoted
misquoting

misread
misread
misreading

misrepresent

miss
misses

missal

✸ Do not confuse with **missile** *read a prayer from the missal*

misshapen

missile

✸ Do not confuse with **missal** *a nuclear missile*

missing

mission

missionary
missionaries

missive

misspell
misspelled, misspelt
misspelling

ⓘ Don't **miss** an s out of **miss**pell.

misspelling

misspent

mist

mistake
mistook
mistaken
mistaking

mistaken

mister

mistletoe

mistook

mistral

mistreat
mistreated
mistreating

mistress
mistresses

mistrust

misty

misunderstand
misunderstood
misunderstanding

misunderstanding

misuse
misused
misusing

mite

✸ Do not confuse with **might** *a poor little mite*

mitigate
mitigated

mitigating

mitigation

mitre
mitred
mitring

mitt

mitten

mix
mixes

mixed

mixer

mixture

mnemonic

moan
moaned
moaning

✸ Do not confuse with **mown** *to moan in pain • the moan of the wind*

moat

mob
mobbed
mobbing

mobile

mobilisation
another spelling of **mobilization**

mobilise
another spelling of **mobilize**

mobility

mobilization, mobilisation

mobilize, mobilise
mobilized, mobilised
mobilizing, mobilising

Möbius strip

moccasin

SPELLING *focus*

Misspellings

Why are some words especially difficult to spell?

Silent letters

There are at least ten consonants that can lurk silently in a word, tricking you into misspelling it:

silent b: thumb, debt, subtle
silent g: reign, sign, gnome
silent l: talk, calm, would
silent m: mnemonic
silent n: solemn, column, autumn
silent t: mortgage

Can you identify the others, and think of some words which include them?

One way to learn and remember these is to make up sentences containing examples of words with the same silent letter – the sillier the better. For example, for a silent **h** you could say 'an *honest ghost* will tell you *when* the *chorus rhymes*'. Another way is to think of similar or related words where the silent letter is sounded, for example *sign* and *signal*, or *doubt* and *dubious*.

Spellings that break the rules

Words that are exceptions to rules are often difficult. One rule says that a **g** with a soft 'j' sound must be followed by **e**, **i** or **y**, as in *general*, *engine*, *energy*, *changeable* and *gyrate*. The word *margarine* breaks this rule.

Words that are not spelt as they sound

Words that have come into English from French or other languages are sometimes the most difficult to spell. The word *manoeuvre*, for example, sounds as if it should be spelt 'manoover', and words like *reconnaissance* just have to be learnt.

Other problems

Words might also be difficult to spell because they have tricky vowel combinations (like *biscuit*), difficult inflections (like *occurring*), difficult plurals (like *buses*), awkward prefixes (like *misspell*), or because you are not sure whether they have double or single consonants in the middle (like *accommodate*). More information on these topics can be found in other panels or in the Spelling Rules on p.390.

mocha
mock
mockery
mocking
mockingbird
mock-up
modal

> ◕* Do not confuse
> with **model** or **module**
> *a modal verb*

mode
model
 modelled
 modelling

> ◕* Do not confuse
> with **modal** or **module**
> *a model aeroplane • a*
> *fashion model*

modem
moderate
 moderated
 moderating
moderately
moderation
moderato
moderator
modern
modernisation
 another spelling of
 modernization
modernise
 another spelling of
 modernize
moderniser
 another spelling of
 modernizer
modernity
modernization,
 modernisation
modernize,
 modernise

modernized,
 modernised
modernizing,
 modernising
modernizer,
 moderniser
modest
modesty
modicum
modification
modify
 modifies
 modified
 modifying
modish
modular
modulate
 modulated
 modulating
modulation
module

> ◕* Do not confuse
> with **modal** or **model** *a*
> *space module •*
> *complete another*
> *module of the course*

mogul
mohair
Mohican
moist
moisten
 moistened
 moistening
moistness
moisture
moisturize,
 moisturise
 moisturized,
 moisturised
 moisturizing,
 moisturising

moisturizer,
 moisturiser
molar
molasses
mole
molecular
molecule
molehill
moleskin
molest
mollification
mollify
 mollifies
 mollified
 mollifying
mollusc
mollycoddle
 mollycoddled
 mollycoddling
molten
moment
momentarily
momentary
momentous
momentum
 momenta

> ◕* Do not confuse
> with **memento** *It*
> *gathers momentum as*
> *it rolls down the hill*

monarch
 monarchs
monarchist
monarchy
 monarchies
monastery
 monasteries
monastic
monasticism
monetarism
monetarist

monetary

money

moneyed, monied

mongoose

mongooses

mongrel

monied

another spelling of

moneyed

monitor

monitored

monitoring

monk

monkey

pl monkeys

monkeyed

monkeying

monkfish

monochrome

monocle

monogamous

monogamy

monogram

monolingual

monolith

monolithic

monologue

monopolize,

monopolise

monopolized,

monopolised

monopolizing,

monopolising

monopoly

monopolies

monorail

monosodium

monosyllabic

monosyllable

monotone

monotonous

monotony

monoxide

monsoon

monster

monstrosity

monstrosities

monstrous

montage

month

monthly

monthlies

monument

monumental

moo

mooed

mooing

mooch

mood

moodiness

moody

moodier

moodiest

moon

mooned

mooning

moonbeam

moonlight

moonlighting

moonlit

moonshine

moonstone

moor

moored

mooring

moorhen

moorings

moorland

moose

moose

> ♦* Do not confuse
> with **mouse** or **mousse**
> *the antlers of a moose*

moot point

mop

mopped

mopping

mope

moped

moping

moped

moraine

moral

> ♦* Do not confuse
> with **morale** *the moral
> of the story* • *moral
> support*

morale

> ♦* Do not confuse
> with **moral** *Morale was
> low in the army*

moralise

another spelling of

moralize

moraliser

another spelling of

moralizer

moralist

morality

> ♦* Do not confuse
> with **mortality**
> *goodness and morality*

moralize, moralise

moralized,

moralised

moralizing,

moralising

moralizer, moraliser

morally

morass

morasses

moratorium

moratoria,

moratoriums
moray
morbid
morbidity
morbidly
mordant
more
moreish, morish
moreover
morgue
moribund
morish
another spelling of
moreish
morn
mornay
morning
moron
moronic
morose
morosely
moroseness
morpheme
morphia
morphine
morphological
morphology
morris dance
morris dancer
morris dancing
morrow
Morse code
morsel
mortal
mortality

🌢* Do not confuse
with **morality** *the
mortality rate in road
accidents*

mortally
mortar

mortarboard
mortgage
mortgaged
mortgaging

ⓘ We took out a
mortgage on the
mortar for the **garage**.

mortice
another spelling of
mortise
mortician
mortification
mortify
mortifies
mortified
mortifying
mortise, mortice
mortuary
mortuaries
mosaic
Moses basket
mosque
mosquito
mosquitoes,
mosquitos
moss
mosses
mossy
most
mostly
motel
moth
mothball
moth-eaten
mother
mothered
mothering
motherboard
motherhood
mother-in-law
mothers-in-law

motherland
motherliness
motherly
mother-of-pearl
motif
motifs

🌢* Do not confuse
with **motive** *a
decorative motif*

motion
motioned
motioning
motionless
motivate
motivated
motivating
motive

🌢* Do not confuse
with **motif** *a motive for
murder*

motley
motocross
motor
motored
motoring
motorbike
motorcade
motorcycle
motorcyclist
motoring
motorise
another spelling of
motorize
motorist
motorize, motorise
motorized,
motorised
motorizing,
motorising
motorway
mottled

motto
mottoes
mould
moulder
mouldered
mouldering
moulding
mouldy
mouldier
mouldiest
moult
mound
mount
mountain
mountaineer
mountaineering
mountainous
mourn
mourner
mournful
mournfully
mourning
mouse
mice

💧* Do not confuse
with **moose** or **mousse**
*The cat chased the
mouse • a computer
mouse*

mousetrap
moussaka
mousse

💧* Do not confuse
with **moose** or **mouse**
*lemon mousse • styling
mousse for your hair*

moustache

ℹ Your **moustache**
looks like a **mou**se with
stomach **ache**!

mousy
mouth
mouthful
mouthfuls
mouth-organ
mouthpiece
mouthwash
movable, moveable
move
moved
moving
movement
mover
movie
moving
mow
mowed
mowed, mown
mowing
mower
mown

💧* Do not confuse
with **moan** *a neatly
mown lawn*

mozzarella
Mr
Mrs
Ms
much
muck
mucous

💧* Do not confuse
with **mucus** *a slimy,
mucous substance*

mucus

💧* Do not confuse
with **mucous** *mucus
from the nose*

mud
muddle

muddled
muddling
muddy
muddier
muddiest
muddies
muddied
muddying
mudguard
mudpack
muesli
muezzin
muff
muffin
muffle
muffled
muffling
muffler
mufti
mug
mugged
mugging
mugger
mugginess
muggins
muggy
mugshot
mulberry
mulberries
mulch
mule
mulish
mull
mulled
mullet
mulligatawny
multicoloured
multicultural
multilingual
multimedia
multimillionaire
multinational

multiple

> ♦* Do not confuse
> with **multiply** *multiple
> injuries • 8 is a multiple
> of 4*

multiplex
 multiplexes
multiplication
multiplicity
multiply
 multiplies
 multiplied
 multiplying

> ♦* Do not confuse
> with **multiple** *multiply
> the figure by 10*

multipurpose
multiracial
multistorey
multitasking
multitude
multitudinous
mum
mumble
 mumbled
 mumbling
mumbo-jumbo
mummification
mummify
 mummifies
 mummified
 mummifying
mummy
 mummies
mumps
munch
munchies
mundane
municipal
municipality
 municipalities

munificence
munificent
munitions
mural
murder
 murdered
 murdering
murderer
murderess
 murderesses
murderous
murkiness
murky
murmur
 murmured
 murmuring
muscatel
muscle

> ♦* Do not confuse
> with **mussel** *exercises
> to develop your muscles*

muscular
muse
 mused
 musing

> ♦* Do not confuse
> with **mews** *to muse on
> the beauty of nature*

museum
mush
mushroom
 mushroomed
 mushrooming
mushy
music
musical
musically
musician
musicologist
musicology
musk

musket
musketeer
musky
Muslim
muslin
mussel

> ♦* Do not confuse
> with **muscle** *mussels
> and other shellfish*

must
mustang
mustard
muster
 mustered
 mustering
mustiness
mustn't
musty
mutability
mutable
mutant
mutate
 mutated
 mutating
mutation
mute
muted
mutilate
 mutilated
 mutilating
mutilation
mutineer
mutinous
mutiny
 mutinies
 mutinied
 mutinying
mutter
 muttered
 muttering
mutton

mutual
mutuality
mutually
Muzak®
muzzle
 muzzled
 muzzling
muzzy
my
myna, mynah

✎* Do not confuse
with **miner** or **minor** *a
myna bird*

myopia
myopic
myriad

myrrh
myrtle
myself
mysterious
mysteriously
mystery
 mysteries
mystic

✎* Do not confuse
with **mystique** *mystics
meditating on spiritual
things*

mystical
mystically
mysticism
mystification

mystify
 mystifies
 mystified
 mystifying
mystique

✎* Do not confuse
with **mystic** *The
cinema has lost some of
its mystique*

myth
mythical
mythically
mythological
mythologically
mythology
myxomatosis

N n

If you can't find the word you're looking for under **N**, it could be that it starts with a different letter. Try looking under **KN** for words like *knot* and *know*, **GN** for words like *gnat*, **PN** for words like *pneumonia*, and **MN** for words like *mnemonic*.

nab
nabbed
nabbing
nadir
naff
nag
nagged
nagging
naiad
nail
nailed
nailing
naive, naïve

🛈 **Nai**ve people are **a**wfully **i**nexperienced.

naivety, naïvety
naked
nakedness
namby-pamby
name
named
naming
name-drop
name-dropped
name-dropping
name-dropper
nameless
namely
namesake
nana, nanna

nanny
nannies
nanny-goat
nap
napped
napping
napalm
nape
napkin
nappy
nappies
narcissism
narcissistic
narcissus
narcissi, narcissuses
narcotic
nark
narky
narrate
narrated
narrating
narration
narrative
narrator
narrow
narrow-gauge
narrowly
narrow-minded
narrow-mindedness
narrowness

nasal
nasalize, nasalise
nasalized, nasalised
nasalizing,
nasalising
nascent
nastily
nastiness
nasturtium
nasty
nastier
nastiest
natal
nation
national
nationalisation
another spelling of
nationalization
nationalise
another spelling of
nationalize
nationalism
nationalist
nationalistic
nationality
nationalities
nationalization,
nationalisation
nationalize,
nationalise

nationalized,
nationalised
nationalizing,
nationalising
nationally
nationwide
native
nativity
natter
nattered
nattering
natterjack
nattily
natty
natural
naturalisation
another spelling of
naturalization
naturalise
another spelling of
naturalize
naturalist
naturalization,
naturalisation
naturalize,
naturalise
naturalized,
naturalised
naturalizing,
naturalising
naturally
naturalness
nature
naturism
naturist
naturopathy
naught

> ✎* Do not confuse
> with **nought** *Our plans
> came to naught*

naughtily

naughtiness
naughty
naughtier
naughtiest

> ✎* Do not confuse
> with **knotty** *a naughty
> child*

nausea
nauseate
nauseated
nauseating
nauseating
nauseatingly
nauseous
nautical
naval

> ✎* Do not confuse
> with **navel** *a naval
> battle • a naval officer*

nave

> ✎* Do not confuse
> with **knave** *the nave of
> a church*

navel

> ✎* Do not confuse
> with **naval** *Your navel
> is your belly-button • a
> navel orange*

navigability
navigable
navigate
navigated
navigating
navigation
navigational
navigator
navvy
navvies
navy
navies

nay

> ✎* Do not confuse
> with **née** or **neigh** *Nay,
> he will not come*

Nazi
Nazism
neap
near
neared
nearing
nearby
nearly
nearness
nearside
near-sighted
neat
neaten
neatened
neatening
neatly
neatness
nebula
nebulae, nebulas
nebulous
necessarily
necessary

> ❶ One **c**ollar and two
> **s**leeve**s** are ne**c**e**ss**ary
> on a shirt.

necessitate
necessitated
necessitating
necessity
necessities
neck
neckerchief
neckerchiefs,
neckerchieves
necklace
neckline
nectar

Can't find your word? Try looking under **KN**, **GN**, **PN** or **MN**

nectarine

née

♠* Do not confuse with **nay** or **neigh** *Ann Smith, née Jones*

need

♠* Do not confuse with **knead** or **kneed** *Plants need water • Do you need any help?*

needful
needle
needlecord
needlepoint
needless
needlewoman
 needlewomen
needlework
needn't
needy
 needier
 neediest
ne'er
ne'er-do-well
nefarious
negate
 negated
 negating
negation
negative
neglect
neglectful
negligée
negligence
negligent

♠* Do not confuse with **negligible** *a careless, negligent mother*

negligently

negligible

♠* Do not confuse with **negligent** *a negligible amount*

negligibly
negotiable
negotiate
 negotiated
 negotiating
negotiation
negotiator
neigh

♠* Do not confuse with **nay** or **née** *to neigh like a horse*

neighbour

❶ We invited **eigh**t of **our** n**eigh**bours.

neighbourhood
neighbouring
neighbourliness
neighbourly
neither
nemesis
neoclassical
Neolithic
neologism
neon
neonatal
neophyte
nephew
nephritis
nephrology
nepotism
nerd
nerve
nerve-racking,
 nerve-wracking
nervous
nervously

nervousness
nervy
nest
nestle
 nestled
 nestling
nestling
net, nett
 netted
 netting

♠* The spelling **nett** is only used for the meanings 'remaining after deductions' or 'not including packaging' *nett profit • nett weight*

netball
nether
nett
 another spelling of **net**
netting
nettle
 nettled
 nettling
network
neuralgia
neurone
neurosis
neurotic
neuter
 neutered
 neutering
neutral
neutralisation
 another spelling of **neutralization**
neutralise
 another spelling of **neutralize**
neutrality

Can't find your word? Try looking under **KN**, **GN**, **PN** or **MN**

neutralization,
neutralisation
neutralize,
neutralise
neutralized,
neutralised
neutralizing,
neutralising
neutrally
neutron
never
nevertheless
new

♦* Do not confuse
with **knew** *a new dress*

newborn
newcomer
newfangled
newly
newness
news
newsagent
newscaster
newsflash
newsflashes
newsletter
newspaper
newsreader
newsy
newt
newton
next
niacin
nib
nibble
nibbled
nibbling
niblick
nice
nicely
nicety

niceties
niche
nick
nickel
nick-nack
another spelling of
knick-knack
nickname
nicotine
niece

❶ My **n**iece is **n**ice.

niff
niffy
nifty
niggardly
niggle
niggled
niggling
nigh
night

♦* Do not confuse
with **knight** *I woke up
during the night*

nightcap
nightclub
nightdress
nightdresses
nightfall
nightie
nightingale
nightjar
nightlife
nightly
nightmare
nightmarish
nightshade
nightshirt
night-time
night-watchman
night-watchmen

nihilistic
nil
nimble
nimbly
nimbus
nimbi, nimbuses
nincompoop
nine
ninepins
nineteen
nineteenth
ninetieth
ninety
nineties
ninja
ninny
ninnies
ninth
nip
nipped
nipping
nipper
nipple
nippy
nirvana, Nirvana
nit

♦* Do not confuse
with **knit** *a stupid nit •
nits in her hair*

nit-picking
nitrate
nitric
nitrogen
nitroglycerine
nitty-gritty
nitwit
no
noes

♦* Do not confuse
with **know** *We have no
money • No, I won't!*

Can't find your word? Try looking under **KN, GN, PN** or **MN**

Words Within Words

Many tricky words have other words inside them, or at their beginning or end. For example, the word *favourite* contains *our* and *rite*, and the word *mother* contains *moth*, *other*, *the*, *he* and *her*. Finding and remembering these 'words within words' can help you to learn a difficult spelling.

• The words *something* and *constable* contain at least seven words each – can you find them all?

• How many words can you find in *unprecedented* and *dishonourable*?

Looking for 'words within words' can be particularly useful for remembering the spelling of unstressed or silent vowels, for example thinking of *get* in *vegetable* or *sin* in *business*.

---

no-ball
nobble
 nobbled
 nobbling
nobility
noble
nobleman
 noblemen
noblewoman
 noblewomen
nobly
nobody
 nobodies
nocturnal
nocturnally
nod
 nodded
 nodding
node
nodule
noise
noiseless
noisily
noisy
 noisier
 noisiest
nomad
nomadic

no-man's-land
nom de plume
 noms de plume
nomenclature
nominal
nominally
nominate
 nominated
 nominating
nomination
nominative
nominee
nonagenarian
nonagon
nonchalance
nonchalant
nonchalantly
non-commissioned
non-committal
nonconformism
nonconformist
nondescript
none
nonentity
 nonentities
nonetheless
non-event
non-existent

non-fiction
non-flammable
no-no
no-nonsense
nonplussed
nonsense
nonsensical
nonsensically
non sequitur
non-starter
non-stick
non-stop
noodle
nook
noon
no-one, no one
noose
nor
norm
normal
normalcy
normalisation
 another spelling of
 normalization
normalise
 another spelling of
 normalize
normality

Can't find your word? Try looking under **KN**, **GN**, **PN** or **MN**

normalization,
  normalisation
normalize,
  normalise
 normalized,
  normalised
 normalizing,
  normalising
normally
Norman
north
northbound
north-east
north-easterly
north-eastern
northerly
northern
northerner
northernmost
northward
northwards
north-west
north-westerly
north-western
nose
 nosed
 nosing
nosebag
nosedive
 nosedived
 nosediving
nosey, nosy
nosh
nosily
nosiness
nostalgia
nostalgic
nostalgically
nostril
nosy
 another spelling of
 nosey

not

♦* Do not confuse
with **knot** *He is not
here*

notability
 notabilities
notable
notably
notary
 notaries
notation
notch
 notches
note
 noted
 noting
notebook
noted
notelet
notepad
notepaper
noteworthy
nothing
nothingness
notice
 noticed
 noticing
noticeable

❶ Word within word:
not-ice-able

noticeably
notice-board
notifiable
notification
notify
 notifies
 notified
 notifying
notion
notional
notoriety

notorious
notwithstanding
nougat

♦* Do not confuse
with **nugget** *Nougat is
a sticky sweet*

nought

♦* Do not confuse
with **naught** *The
telephone number
contains two noughts*
Remember that the **o**
of nought is like a zero.

noun
nourish
nourishing
nourishment
nous
nouveau riche
 nouveaux riches
nouvelle cuisine
nova
 novas
novel
novelist
novella
novelty
 novelties
novice
now
nowadays
nowhere
no-win
noxious
nozzle
nuance
nub
nubile
nuclear
nucleus
 nuclei

Can't find your word? Try looking under **KN, GN, PN** or **MN**

nude
nudge
 nudged
 nudging
nudism
nudist
nudity
nugget

> ♦* Do not confuse
> with **nougat** *a gold*
> *nugget*

nuisance

> ⓘ This new umbrella
> is a nuisance.

null
nullification
nullify
 nullifies
 nullified
 nullifying
numb
number
 numbered

numbering
numbness
numbskull
 another spelling of
 numskull
numeracy
numeral
numerate
numerator
numerical
numerically
numerology
numerous
numskull, numbskull
nun
nunnery
 nunneries
nuptial
nurse
 nursed
 nursing
nursery
 nurseries

nurture
 nurtured
 nurturing
nut
nutcase
nutcrackers
nuthatch
 nuthatches
nutmeg
nutrient
nutriment
nutrition
nutritional
nutritious
nutritive
nutshell
nutter
nutty
nuzzle
 nuzzled
 nuzzling
nylon
nymph

Can't find your word? Try looking under **KN**, **GN**, **PN** or **MN**

o
another spelling of **oh**
oaf
 oafs
oafish
oafishly
oafishness
oak
oak-apple
oar

> ♦* Do not confuse
> with **ore** *an oar for a*
> *boat*

oarsman
 oarsmen
oarsmanship
oarswoman
 oarswomen
oasis
 oases
oast house
oatcake
oath
oatmeal
oats
obedience
obedient
obediently
obelisk
obese
obesity
obey
 obeyed

 obeying
obituary
 obituaries
object
objection
objectionable
objectionably
objective
objectively
objectivity
objector
obligate
 obligated
 obligating
obligation
obligatory
obligatorily
oblige
 obliged
 obliging
oblique
obliquely
obliqueness
obliterate
 obliterated
 obliterating
obliteration
oblivion
oblivious
obliviously
oblong
obnoxious
oboe
oboist

obscene

> ❶ He will cut any
> **scene** he considers
> ob**scene**.

obscenely
obscenity
 obscenities
obscure
obscurely
obscurity
obsequious
obsequiousness
observable
observance
observant
observation
observational
observatory
 observatories
observe
 observed
 observing
observer
obsess
obsession
obsessional
obsessive
obsessively
obsessiveness
obsolescence
obsolescent
obsolete
obstacle

obstetric
obstetrical
obstetrician
obstetrics
obstinacy
obstinate
obstinately
obstreperous
obstruct
obstruction
obstructive
obtain
 obtained
 obtaining
obtainable
obtrude
obtrusion
obtrusive
obtrusively
obtuse
obtusely
obverse
obvious
obviously
ocarina
occasion

> ❶ It's an occasion to seize [two **c**'s] an **s**.

occasional
occasionally
occidental
occult
occultism
occultist
occupancy
occupant
occupation
occupier
occupy
 occupies
 occupied

occupying
occur
 occurred
 occurring
occurrence

> ❶ Crimson cats and red rabbits are rare occurrences.

ocean
oceanic
oceanographer
oceanography
ocelot
ochre
o'clock
octagon
octagonal
octagonally
octahedron
octane
octant
octave
octet
octogenarian
octopus
 octopuses
odd
oddball
oddity
 oddities
oddly
oddment
oddness
odds
ode
odious
odium
odorous
odour
odourless
odyssey

odysseys
oesophagus
 oesophagi
oestrogen
oestrus
of

> ✹ Do not confuse with **off** *a cup of tea • made of silver • to die of hunger*

off

> ✹ Do not confuse with **of** *to switch off a light • to run off • badly off • The meat is off*

offal
offbeat
off-chance
off-colour
offcut
offence
offend
offender
offensive
offensively
offer
 offered
 offering
offering
offhand
office
officer
official

> ✹ Do not confuse with **officious** *official action • official duties*

officialdom
officialese
officially
officiate

officiated
officiating
officious

♦* Do not confuse
with **official** *rude and
officious*

offing
off-licence
off-line
offload
off-peak
off-putting
offset
 offset
 offsetting
offshoot
offshore
offside
offspring
oft
often
ogle
 ogled
 ogling
ogre
oh, o
ohm
oil
 oiled
 oiling
oilfield
oiliness
oil paint
oil painting
oil rig
oilskin
oily
 oilier
 oiliest
oink
ointment

OK, okay
 OK'd, OKed, okayed
 OK'ing, OKing,
 okaying
okey-dokey
okra
old
olden
old-fashioned
oldie
olfactory
olive
ombudsman
 ombudsmen
omega
omelette, omelet
omen
ominous
omission

♦* Do not confuse
with **emission** *the
omission of her name
from the list*

omit
 omitted
 omitting
omnibus
 omnibuses
omnipotence
omnipotent
omnipresence
omnipresent
omniscience
omniscient
omnivore
omnivorous
on
once
oncologist
oncology
oncoming

one
one-liner
onerous
oneself
one-sided
one-upmanship
one-way
ongoing
onion
on-line
onlooker
only
onomatopoeia
onomatopoeic
onrush
onset
onshore
onslaught
onto
onus
 onuses
onward
onwards
onyx
oodles
oomph
oops
ooze
 oozed
 oozing
opacity
opal
opalescent
opaque
opaqueness
open
 opened
 opening
open-cast
opener
opening
openly

open-minded
open-mindedness
openness
open-plan
opera
operable
operate
 operated
 operating
operatic
operation
operational
operative
operator
operetta
ophthalmic
ophthalmologist
opiate
opinion
opinionated
opium
opossum
opponent
opportune
opportunism
opportunist
opportunistic
opportunity
 opportunities

---

❶ **P**ick the **p**erfect
op**portun**ity to make
your f**ortun**e.

---

oppose
 opposed
 opposing
opposer
opposite
opposition
oppress
oppression
oppressive

oppressor
opt
optic
optical
optically
optician
optics
optimal
optimise
 another spelling of
 optimize
optimism
optimist
optimistic
optimistically
optimize, optimise
 optimized,
 optimised
 optimizing,
 optimising
optimum
option
optional
optionally
optometrist
opulence
opulent
opus
 opuses, opera
or
oracle
oracular
oral

✏* Do not confuse
with **aural** *The dentist
spoke about oral
hygiene* Remember
that oral has to do with
the mouth and
speaking – the **o** looks
like an open mouth.

---

orally
orange
orang-utan,
 orang-outang
oration
orator
oratorio
 oratorios
oratory
 oratories
orb
orbit
 orbited
 orbiting
orbital
orchard
orchestra
orchestral
orchestrate
 orchestrated
 orchestrating
orchestration
orchid
ordain
 ordained
 ordaining
ordeal
order
 ordered
 ordering
orderly
 orderlies
ordinal
ordinance
ordinarily
ordinary
ordination
Ordnance Survey
ore

✏* Do not confuse
with **oar** *iron ore*

oregano
organ
organic
organically
organisation
another spelling of
organization
organise
another spelling of
organize
organiser
another spelling of
organizer
organism
organist
organization,
organisation
organize, organise
organized,
organised
organizing,
organising
organizer, organiser
orgasm
orgy
orgies
orient
oriental
orientate
orientated
orientating
orientation
oriented
orienteering
orifice
origami
origin
original
originality
originally
originate
originated

originating
originator
ornament
ornamental
ornamentally
ornamentation
ornate
ornithological
ornithologist
ornithology
orphan
orphanage
orphaned
orthodontic
orthodontist
orthodox
orthodoxy
orthographic
orthographical
orthography
orthopaedic
orthopaedics
oscillate
oscillated
oscillating
oscillation
osmosis
osprey
ospreys
ostensible
ostensibly
ostentation
ostentatious
osteopath
osteopathic
osteopathy
osteoporosis
ostinato
ostracise
another spelling of
ostracize
ostracism

ostracize, ostracise
ostracized,
ostracised
ostracizing,
ostracising
ostrich
ostriches
other
otherwise
otter
ottoman
ottomans
ouch
ought
ounce
our

❢* Do not confuse
with **are** *our house •
our ideas*

ours
ourselves
oust
out
outback
outboard
outbreak
outbuilding
outburst
outcast
outcome
outcrop
outcry
outdated
outdo
outdid
outdone
outdoing
outdoor
outdoors
outer
outermost

outfit
outfitter
outgoing
outgoings
outgrow
outgrew
outgrown
outgrowing
outhouse
outing
outlandish
outlaw
outlay
outlet
outline
outlined
outlining
outlive
outlived
outliving
outlook
outlying
outmoded
outnumber
outnumbered
outnumbering
out-patient
outpost
outpouring
output
outrage
outraged
outraging
outrageous
outright
outset
outshine
outshone
outshining
outside
outsider
outsize

outskirts
outspoken
outstanding
outstay
outstayed
outstaying
outstretched
outstrip
outstripped
outstripping
out-take
out-tray
outvote
outvoted
outvoting
outward
outwardly
outwards
outweigh
outwit
outwitted
outwitting
ova
oval
ovarian
ovary
ovaries
ovation
oven
ovenproof
over
overact
overall
overarm
overawe
overawed
overawing
overbalance
overbalanced
overbalancing
overbearing
overboard

overcame
overcast
overcharge
overcharged
overcharging
overcoat
overcome
overcame
overcome
overcoming
overcrowded
overcrowding
overdo
overdid
overdone
overdoing
overdose
overdosed
overdosing
overdraft
overdrawn
overdrive
overdue
overestimate
overestimated
overestimating
overexpose
overexposed
overexposing
overexposure
overflow
overgrown
overhang
overhung
overhanging
overhaul
overhauled
overhauling
overhead
overheads
overhear
overheard

Word Webs

A word web is a diagram showing how one word may be linked to several other groups of words. For example, the word *insignificant* can be linked to words with the prefix in- (for example *informal*), words with the suffix -ant (for example *arrogant*), words containing the root sign (for example *designer*), and words related to *significant* (for example *significance*).

To make a word web, place the key word in a box in the centre, with arrows leading out to boxes containing the other word groups.

Sometimes the word web has a short root word at the centre:

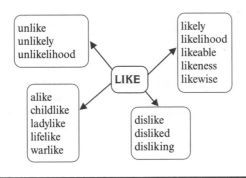

overhearing	**overnight**	overruled
overheat	**overpass**	overruling
overheated	overpasses	**overrun**
overheating	**overpower**	overran
overjoyed	overpowered	overrun
overkill	overpowering	overrunning
overland	**overpowering**	**overseas**
overlap	**overran**	**oversee**
overlapped	**overrate**	oversaw
overlapping	overrated	overseen
overlay	overrating	overseeing
overlaid	**overreach**	**overseer**
overlaying	**overreact**	**overshadow**
overleaf	**override**	**oversight**
overload	overrode	**oversimplify**
overlook	overridden	oversimplifies
overly	overriding	oversimplified
overmuch	**overrule**	oversimplifying

oversleep
 overslept
 oversleeping
overstatement
overstep
 overstepped
 overstepping
overt
overtake
 overtook
 overtaken
 overtaking
overthrow
 overthrew
 overthrown
 overthrowing
overtime
overtook
overtone
overture

overturn
overview
overweight
overwhelm
overwhelming
overwork
overworked
overwrite
overwrought
ovulate
 ovulated
 ovulating
ovulation
ovum
 ova
owe
 owed
 owing
owl
owlish

own
owner
ownership
ox
 oxen
oxidant
oxide
oxidize, oxidise
 oxidized, oxidised
 oxidizing, oxidising
oxtail
oxygen
oxygenate
 oxygenated
 oxygenating
oxymoron
oyster
oystercatcher
ozone

pace
paced
pacing
pacemaker
pacesetter
pacifier
pacifism
pacifist
pacify
pacifies
pacified
pacifying
pack
package
packaged
packaging
packaging
packed

> ☙* Do not confuse
> with **pact** *We packed
> the cases • a packed
> hall*

packer
packet
packing
pact

> ☙* Do not confuse
> with **packed** *We made
> a pact • a pact between
> nations*

pad
padded
padding

padding
paddle
paddled
paddling
paddler
paddle-steamer
paddock
paddy-field
padlock
paediatrician
paediatrics
paedophile
paedophilia
paella
pagan
paganism
page
paged
paging
pageant
pageantry
pageboy
pager
paginate
paginated
paginating
pagination
pagoda
paid
pail

> ☙* Do not confuse
> with **pale** *a pail of
> water*

pain
pained
paining

> ☙* Do not confuse
> with **pane** *a pain in his
> chest • take pains to get
> it right*

pained
painful
painfully
painkiller
painless
painlessly
painstaking
painstakingly
paint
paintbrush
paintbrushes
painter
painting
pair
paired
pairing

> ☙* Do not confuse
> with **pare** or **pear** *a
> pair of shoes*

pakora
pal
palace
Palaeolithic
palaeontologist
palaeontology
palatable

palate

> ♦* Do not confuse
> with **palette** or **pallet**
> *The palate is the roof of
> the mouth*

palatial
palaver
pale
 paled
 paling

> ♦* Do not confuse
> with **pail** *thin and pale*
> • *a pale colour* • *to pale
> into insignificance* •
> *beyond the pale*

paleness
palette

> ♦* Do not confuse
> with **palate** or **pallet**
> *an artist's palette*

palindrome
palindromic
paling
palisade
pall
palladium
pallbearer
pallet

> ♦* Do not confuse
> with **palate** or **palette**
> *a straw pallet*

palliative
pallid
pallor
palm
palmist
palmistry
palomino
 palominos
palpable

palpably
palpate
 palpated
 palpating
palpation
palpitate
 palpitated
 palpitating
palpitation
palsy
paltry
pampas
pamper
 pampered
 pampering
pamphlet
pan
 panned
 panning
panacea
panache
pancake
pancreas
panda
pandemic
pandemonium
pander
 pandered
 pandering
pane

> ♦* Do not confuse
> with **pain** *a pane of
> glass*

panel
 panelled
 panelling
panelling
panellist
pang
panic
 panicked

 panicking
panicky
panic-stricken
pannier
panorama
panoramic
panpipes
pansy
 pansies
pant
pantheism
pantheist
pantheon
panther
panties
pantomime
pantry
 pantries
pants
papa
papacy
papal
paparazzo
 paparazzi
papaya
paper
 papered
 papering
paperback
paperweight
paperwork
papier-mâché
papoose
paprika
papyrus
par

> ♦* Do not confuse
> with **parr** *not up to par* •
> *feeling below par* • *on a
> par with his brother*

parable

parabola
parabolic
paracetamol
parachute
 parachuted
 parachuting
parachutist
parade
 paraded
 parading
paradigm
paradise
paradox
 paradoxes
paradoxical
paradoxically
paraffin
paraglider
paragliding
paragon
paragraph
parakeet
parallel

❶ Word within word:
par-**all**-el

parallelogram
paralyse
 paralysed
 paralysing
paralysis
paralytic
paramedic
paramedical
parameter
paramilitary
paramount
paranoia
paranoid
paranormal
parapet
paraphernalia

paraphrase
 paraphrased
 paraphrasing
paraplegia
paraplegic
parascending
parasite
parasitic
parasol
paratrooper
paratroops
parboil
 parboiled
 parboiling
parcel
 parcelled
 parcelling
parch
parched
parchment
pardon
 pardoned
 pardoning
pardonable
pare
 pared
 paring

🖋 Do not confuse
with **pair** or **pear** *to*
pare an apple • *to pare*
your toenails

parent
parentage
parental
parenthesis
 parentheses
parenthood
par excellence
pariah
parish
 parishes

parishioner
parity
park
parka
parkin
parlance
parley
 pl parleys
 parleyed
 parleying
parliament

❶ Liam is a Member
of Parli**am**ent.

parliamentary
parlour
parlourmaid
Parmesan
parochial
parody
 parodies
 parodied
 parodying
parole
 paroled
 paroling
paroxysm
parquet
parr

🖋 Do not confuse
with **par** *A parr is a*
young salmon

parrot
parry
 parries
 parried
 parrying
parse
 parsed
 parsing
parsimonious
parsimony

parsley
parsnip
parson
parsonage
part
partake
 partook
 partaken
 partaking
partial
partiality
partially
participant
participate
 participated
 participating
participation
participatory
participial
participle
particle
particular
particularly
parting
partisan
partition
partly
partner
 partnered
 partnering
partnership
partook
partridge
part-time
part-timer
party
 parties
pascal
pass
 passed
 passing
passable

passage
passageway
passata
passé
passed

> ✎* Do not confuse
> with **past** *The boat had*
> *passed out of sight •*
> *The feeling soon passed*

passenger
passer-by
 passers-by
passim
passing
passion
passionate
passionately
passive
passively
passiveness
passivity
passport
password
past

> ✎* Do not confuse
> with **passed** *We walked*
> *past the church • The*
> *weeks flew past •*
> *thinking about the past*

pasta
paste
pastel

> ✎* Do not confuse
> with **pastille** *pastel*
> *colours*

pasteurization,
pasteurisation
pasteurize,
pasteurise
 pasteurized,

pasteurised
pasteurizing,
pasteurising
pastiche
pastille

> ✎* Do not confuse
> with **pastel** *a throat*
> *pastille*

pastime
pastiness
pastor
pastoral
pastrami
pastry
 pastries
pasturage
pasture
pasty
 pasties
pat
 patted
 patting
patch
 patches
patchouli
patchwork
patchy
pate

> ✎* Do not confuse
> with **pâté** *a bald pate*

pâté

> ✎* Do not confuse
> with **pate** or **patty** *pâté*
> *on toast*

patent
patently
paternal
paternalism
paternalistic
paternally

paternity
path
pathetic
pathetically
pathogen
pathological
pathologist
pathology
pathos
pathway
patience
patient
patiently
patina
patio
 patios
patisserie
patois
patriarch
 patriarchs
patriarchal
patriarchy
patrician
patrimony
patriot
patriotic
patriotically
patriotism
patrol
 patrolled
 patrolling
patron
patronage
patronize, patronise
 patronized,
 patronised
 patronizing,
 patronising
patted
patter
 pattered
 pattering

pattern
patterned
patting
patty
 patties

💣* Do not confuse
with **pâté** *a fried meat
patty*

paucity
paunch
 paunches
pauper
pause
 paused
 pausing
pave
 paved
 paving
pavement
pavilion
paving
pavlova
paw
pawn
pawnbroker
pawnshop
pawpaw
pay
 paid
 paying
payable
payee
payment
payphone
payroll
pea
peace

💣* Do not confuse
with **piece** *peace and
quiet • make peace with
your enemies*

peaceable
peaceably
peaceful
peacefully
peacemaker
peacetime
peach
 peaches
peacock
peahen
peak

💣* Do not confuse
with **peek** or **pique** *a
mountain peak • the
peak of his cap • Prices
peaked in July*

peakiness
peaky
peal
 pealed
 pealing

💣* Do not confuse
with **peel** *a peal of bells
• peals of laughter •
Bells peal*

peanut
pear

💣* Do not confuse
with **pair** or **pare** *an
apple and a pear*

pearl

💣* Do not confuse
with **purl** *a pearl
necklace*

pearly
peasant

💣* Do not confuse
with **pheasant** *a
peasant working on the
land*

peashooter
peat
peaty
pebble
pebbledash
pebbly
pecan
peccadillo
 peccadillos,
 peccadilloes
peck
pecker
peckish
pectin
pectoral
peculiar
peculiarity
 peculiarities
peculiarly
pecuniary
pedagogic
pedagogical
pedal
 pedalled
 pedalling

💧* Do not confuse with **peddle** *a bicycle pedal • to pedal uphill*

pedalo
 pedalos, pedaloes
pedant
pedantic
pedantically
pedantry
peddle
 peddled
 peddling

💧* Do not confuse with **pedal** *to peddle your wares • to peddle drugs*

peddler

💧* Do not confuse with **pedlar** *a drug peddler*

pedestal
pedestrian
pedestrianize,
 pedestrianise
 pedestrianized,
 pedestrianised
 pedestrianizing,
 pedestrianising
pedicure
pedigree
pedlar

💧* Do not confuse with **peddler** *pedlars selling their wares*

pedometer
pee
 peed
 peeing
peek

💧* Do not confuse with **peak** or **pique** *to peek through the window • Take a peek at this!*

peel
 peeled
 peeling

💧* Do not confuse with **peal** *orange peel • to peel a potato • to peel the label off*

peeler
peelings
peep
 peeped
 peeping

peephole
peer
 peered
 peering

💧* Do not confuse with **pier** *to peer through the window • a peer of the realm • a peer group • peer pressure*

peerage
peerless
peeve
 peeved
 peeving
peeved
peevish
peevishness
peewit, pewit
peg
 pegged
 pegging
pejorative
pelican
pellet
pell-mell
pelmet
pelt
pelvis
pen
 penned
 penning
penal
penalize, penalise
 penalized, penalised
 penalizing,
 penalising
penalty
 penalties
penance
pence

penchant
pencil
  pencilled
  pencilling
pendant

> ✦* Do not confuse
> with **pendent** *a silver*
> *pendant*

pendent

> ✦* Do not confuse
> with **pendant** *a*
> *pendent light*

pending
pendulous
pendulum
penetrable
penetrate
  penetrated
  penetrating
penetration
pen-friend
penguin
penicillin
peninsula

> ✦* Do not confuse
> with **peninsular** *A*
> *peninsula is almost*
> *surrounded by water*

peninsular

> ✦* Do not confuse
> with **peninsula**
> *Peninsular is an*
> *adjective •* the
> *Peninsular War*

penis
  penises
penitence
penitent
penknife
  penknives

pen-name
pennant
pennies
penniless
penny
  pence, pennies

> ✦* Use the plural
> form **pence** for an
> amount of money and
> **pennies** for a number
> of coins *It only costs ten*
> *pence • Does this*
> *machine take pennies?*

penny-farthing
penny-pinching
pennyworth
pen-pal
pen-pusher
pension
  pensioned
  pensioning
pensionable
pensioner
pensive
pensively
pentagon
pentathlete
pentathlon
pentatonic
penthouse
pent-up
penultimate
penury
peony
  peonies
people
  peopled
  peopling

> ❶ **People** enjoy other
> people's laughter
> everyday.

pep
  pepped
  pepping
pepper
  peppered
  peppering
peppercorn
peppermill
peppermint
peppery
peptic
per
perambulation
perambulator
per annum
per capita
perceivable
perceive
  perceived
  perceiving
per cent
percentage
percentile
perceptible
perceptibly
perception
perceptive
perch
  perches
percolate
  percolated
  percolating
percolator
percussion
percussive
perdition
peregrine
peremptorily
peremptory
perennial
perennially
perestroika

Spellcheckers

Computer spellcheckers are a useful way of picking up spelling mistakes. However, you should also be aware of their limitations:

• They will not tell you if you have used the wrong homophone, for example *there* instead of *their*, because *there* is not a misspelling, just the wrong word in the wrong place. For the same reason, they will not tell you if you have accidentally typed the wrong word, for example *that* instead of *than*.

• The list of words that the computer checks against does not contain every word in the English language. Some correctly spelt words may be marked as wrong, simply because they are not on its list.

• Make sure that the language is set to British English rather than American English, or it will tell you that words like *theatre* are incorrect.

Remember not to rely on spellcheckers, as there will be times when you won't be able to use one, for example in exams.

perfect
perfectible
perfection
perfectionism
perfectionist
perfidious
perfidy
perforate
 perforated
 perforating
perforated
perforation
perforce
perform
performance
performer
perfume
 perfumed
 perfuming
perfumery
perfunctorily
perfunctory
perhaps
peril

perilous
perilously
perimeter
period
periodic
periodically
periodical
peripatetic
peripheral
periphery
 peripheries
periscope
perish
perishable
peristalsis
peritonitis
periwinkle
perjure
 perjured
 perjuring
perjurer
perjury
perk
perky

perm
permafrost
permanence
permanency
permanent

❶ The **man ent**ered the country as a per**manent** resident.

permanently
permanganate
permeable
permeate
 permeated
 permeating
permissible
permission
permissive
permissiveness
permit
 permitted
 permitting
permutation
pernicious

pernickety
Pernod®
peroxide
perpendicular
perpetrate
 perpetrated
 perpetrating

💣* Do not confuse
with **perpetuate** *to
perpetrate a crime*

perpetration
perpetrator
perpetual
perpetually
perpetuate
 perpetuated
 perpetuating

💣* Do not confuse
with **perpetrate** *to
perpetuate a tradition*

perpetuation
perpetuity
perplex
perplexedly
perplexedness
perplexing
perplexingly
perplexity
 perplexities
perquisite

💣* Do not confuse
with **prerequisite** *A
company car is one of
the perquisites of the
job*

persecute
 persecuted
 persecuting
persecution
persecutor

perseverance

ℹ Word breakdown:
per-sev-er-ance

persevere
 persevered
 persevering
persist
persistence
persistent
persistently
person
personable
personage
personal

💣* Do not confuse
with **personnel** *She is
his personal assistant •
a personal letter*

personalise
 another spelling of
 personalize
personality
 personalities
personalize,
personalise
 personalized,
 personalised
 personalizing,
 personalising
personally
personification
personify
 personifies
 personified
 personifying
personnel

💣* Do not confuse
with **personal** *the
personnel department •
military personnel*

perspective

💣* Do not confuse
with **prospective** *The
drawing is out of
perspective • get things
into perspective • from a
different perspective*

Perspex®
perspiration
perspire
 perspired
 perspiring
persuade
 persuaded
 persuading
persuasion
persuasive
persuasively
pert
pertain
 pertained
 pertaining
pertinence
pertinent
pertness
perturb
perturbation
perusal
peruse
 perused
 perusing
pervade
 pervaded
 pervading
pervasive
perverse
perversely
perversion
perversity
pervert
pesky

pessimism
pessimist
pessimistic
pessimistically
pest
pester
 pestered
 pestering
pesticide
pestilence
pestilent
pestilential
pestle
pesto
pet
 petted
 petting
petal
petard
peter
 petered
 petering
petite
petition
 petitioned
 petitioning
petitioner
petrel

🖋* Do not confuse
with **petrol** *A petrel is a
seabird*

petrify
 petrifies
 petrified
 petrifying
petrochemical
petrol

🖋* Do not confuse
with **petrel** *The car ran
out of petrol*

petroleum

petticoat
pettily
pettiness
pettish
petty
 pettier
 pettiest
petulance
petulant
petunia
pew
pewit
 another spelling of
 peewit
pewter
peyote
phalanx
 phalanxes,
 phalanges
phantom
Pharaoh

🛈 Pyramids **h**ouse
ancient relics and
other **h**istorical items.

pharmaceutical
pharmacist
pharmacological
pharmacologist
pharmacology
pharmacy
 pharmacies
phase
 phased
 phasing
pheasant

🖋* Do not confuse
with **peasant** *The
pheasant flew away •
pheasant feathers*

phenomenal
phenomenally

phenomenon
 phenomena

🛈 Word breakdown:
phen-o-men-on

pheromone
phew
phial
philander
 philandered
 philandering
philanderer
philanthropic
philanthropically
philanthropist
philanthropy
philatelist
philately
philharmonic
philistine
philological
philologist
philology
philosopher
philosophical
philosophically
philosophize,
 philosophise
 philosophized,
 philosophised
 philosophizing,
 philosophising
philosophy
 philosophies
phlegm

🛈 People have **phlegm**
in their throats, not
their **legs**.

phlegmatic
phobia
phobic
phoenix

phoenixes
phone
phonecard
phoneme
phonemic
phonetic
phonetically
phonetics
phoney, phony
phonic
phonological
phonologically
phonology
phony
another spelling of
 phoney
phosphate
phosphorescence
phosphorescent
phosphorus
photo
 photos
photocopiable
photocopier
photocopy
 photocopies
 photocopied
 photocopying
Photofit®
photogenic
photogenically
photograph
photographer
photographic
photographically
photography
photon
photosensitive
photosynthesis
photosynthesize,
 photosynthesise
 photosynthesized,

photosynthesised
 photosynthesizing,
 photosynthesising
phrasal
phrase
 phrased
 phrasing
phraseology
phylum
 phyla
physical

> ❶ Practice helps your
> sporty **physical** fitness.

physically
physician
physicist
physics
physiognomy
physiological
physiologically
physiologist
physiology
physiotherapist
physiotherapy
physique
pi
pianissimo
pianist
piano
 pianos
pianoforte
piazza

> ◆* Do not confuse
> with **pizza** *a café in the*
> *piazza*

pibroch
 pibrochs
picaresque
piccolo
 piccolos
pick

pickaxe
picker
picket
 picketed
 picketing
pickle
 pickled
 pickling
pick-me-up
pick 'n' mix
pickpocket
picky
picnic
 picnicked
 picnicking
picnicker
pictogram
pictorial
pictorially
picture
 pictured
 picturing
picturesque
picturesquely
piddling
pidgin

> ◆* Do not confuse
> with **pigeon** *a pidgin*
> *language*

pie
piebald
piece
 pieced
 piecing

> ◆* Do not confuse
> with **peace** *a piece of*
> *paper*

pièce de résistance
piecemeal
piecework
pied

pied-à-terre
 pieds-à-terre
pie-eyed
pier

> ♦* Do not confuse
> with **peer** *the pier at the*
> *seaside*

pierce
 pierced
 piercing
piety
piffle
pig
pigeon

> ♦* Do not confuse
> with **pidgin** *The pigeon*
> *flew away*

pigeon-hole
 pigeon-holed
 pigeon-holing
piggery
 piggeries
piggish
piggy
piggyback
pig-headed
piglet
pigment
pigmentation
pigmy
 another spelling of
 pygmy
pigskin
pigsty
 pigsties
pigswill
pigtail
pike
pikestaff
pilau
pilchard

pile
 piled
 piling
piles
pile-up
pilfer
 pilfered
 pilfering
pilferer
pilgrim
pilgrimage
pill
pillage
pillar
pillbox
 pillboxes
pillion
pillory
 pillories
 pilloried
 pillorying
pillow
pillowcase
pillowslip
pilot
 piloted
 piloting
pimp
pimpernel
pimple
pimply
pin
 pinned
 pinning
pinafore
pinball
pince-nez
pincers
pinch
 pinches
pinched
pin-cushion

pine
 pined
 pining
pineapple
ping
ping-pong
pinhead
pinion
 pinioned
 pinioning
pink
pinkie
pinkish
pinnacle
pinned
pinnie
pinning
pinpoint
pin-prick
pint
pioneer
 pioneered
 pioneering
pious
pip
 pipped
 pipping
pipe
 piped
 piping
pipe-cleaner
pipeline
piper
pipette
piping
pipistrelle
pipped
pippin
pipping
pipsqueak
piquancy
piquant

pique
piqued
piquing

♦* Do not confuse
with **peak** or **peek** *to
resign out of pique • to
pique their curiosity*

piracy
piranha
pirate
pirated
pirating
piratical
pirouette
pirouetted
pirouetting
pistachio
pistachios
piste
pistil

♦* Do not confuse
with **pistol** *the pistil of a
flower*

pistol

♦* Do not confuse
with **pistil** *She shot
him with a pistol*

piston
pit
pitted
pitting
pitch
pitches
pitch-black
pitchblende
pitcher
pitchfork
piteous
pitfall
pith

pithy
pitiable
pitiful
pitifully
pitiless
pit stop
pitta
pittance
pitted
pitting
pituitary
pity
pities
pitied
pitying
pivot
pivoted
pivoting
pivotal
pixel
pixie, pixy
pixies
pizza

♦* Do not confuse
with **piazza** *a cheese
and tomato pizza*

pizzazz
pizzeria
pizzicato
placard
placate
placated
placating
placatory
place
placed
placing

♦* Do not confuse
with **plaice** *a place to
live • to place the book
on the table*

placebo
placebos
placement
placenta
placid
placidity
plagiarise
another spelling of
plagiarize
plagiarism
plagiarist
plagiarize, plagiarise
plagiarized,
plagiarised
plagiarizing,
plagiarising
plague
plagued
plaguing
plaice

♦* Do not confuse
with **place** *plaice and
chips*

plaid
plain

♦* Do not confuse
with **plane** *a vast,
treeless plain • a plain
dress*

plainly
plainness
plainsong
plaintiff

♦* Do not confuse
with **plaintive** *The
plaintiff lost the case*

plaintive

♦* Do not confuse
with **plaintiff** *a
plaintive cry*

plait
plaited
plaiting

●* Do not confuse
with **plate** *to plait hair •*
plaited rope

plan
planned
planning

plane

●* Do not confuse
with **plain** *The plane*
landed • A plane is a
tool used in carpentry •
A plane is a tree with
broad leaves • A plane
surface is level • to
plane wood

planet
planetarium
planetaria,
planetariums
planetary
plank
plankton
planned
planner
planning
plant
plantain
plantation
planter
plaque
plasma
plaster
plastered
plastering
plasterboard
plasterer
plastic
Plasticine®

plasticity
plate
plated
plating

●* Do not confuse
with **plait** *a plate of*
food • plated with silver

plateau
plateaux, plateaus
plateful
platefuls
platelet
platform
plating
platinum
platitude
platonic
platonically
platoon
platter
platypus
platypuses
plaudit
plausibility
plausible
plausibly
play
played
playing
playback
playboy
player
playful
playfully
playground
playgroup
playing-card
playmate
playpen
playschool
plaything

playwright

❶ A play**wright** has to
spell words **right**.

plaza
plea
plead
pleasant
pleasantly
pleasantness
pleasantry
pleasantries
please
pleased
pleasing
pleasurable
pleasurably
pleasure
pleat
pleated
pleating
pleb
plebeian
plebiscite
plectrum
plectrums, plectra
pledge
pledged
pledging
plenary
plenitude
plenteous
plentiful
plentifully
plenty
plethora
pleurisy
plexus
plexus, plexuses
pliability
pliable
pliant

pliers
plight
plimsoll
plinth
plod
 plodded
 plodding
plodder
plonk
plop
 plopped
 plopping
plot
 plotted
 plotting
plough
ploughshare
plover
ploy
pluck
plucky
 pluckier
 pluckiest
pluckily
plug
 plugged
 plugging
plughole
plum

♦* Do not confuse
with **plumb** *a ripe,
juicy plum*

plumage
plumb

♦* Do not confuse
with **plum** *to plumb the
depths*

plumber
plumbing
plumbline
plume

plummet
 plummeted
 plummeting
plummy
plump
plunder
 plundered
 plundering
plunderer
plunge
 plunged
 plunging
plunger
pluperfect
plural
pluralise
 another spelling of
 pluralize
pluralism
pluralist
plurality
pluralize, pluralise
 pluralized,
 pluralised
 pluralizing,
 pluralising
plus
plush
plutonium
ply
 plies
 plied
 plying
plywood
pneumatic
pneumatically
pneumonia

❶ People never expect
us to get **pneu**monia.

poach
poacher

pocket
 pocketed
 pocketing
pockmark
pockmarked
pod
podgy
podiatrist
podiatry
podium
 podiums, podia
poem
poet
poetic
poetical
poetically
poetry
po-faced
pogo stick
pogrom
poignancy
poignant
point
point-blank
pointed
pointedly
pointedness
pointer
pointless
poise
 poised
 poising
poised
poison
 poisoned
 poisoning
poisoner
poisonous
poke
 poked
 poking
poker

poker-faced
poky
polar
polarisation
another spelling of
  polarization
polarise
another spelling of
  polarize
polarity
polarization,
  polarisation
polarize, polarise
  polarized, polarised
  polarizing,
  polarising
pole
polecat
polemic
polemical
polemicist
polemics
polenta
police
  policed
  policing
policeman
  policemen
policewoman
  policewomen
policy
  policies
polio
poliomyelitis
polish
  polishes
polisher
polite
politely
politeness
politic
political

politically
politician
politicize, politicise
  politicized,
  politicised
  politicizing,
  politicising
politics
polka
poll
pollard
pollen
pollinate
  pollinated
  pollinating
pollination
pollster
pollutant
pollute
  polluted
  polluting
pollution
polo
poltergeist
polyester
polygamist
polygamous
polygamy
polyglot
polygon
polygraph
polymath
polymer
polyp
polyphonic
polyphony
polystyrene
polysyllabic
polysyllable
polytechnic
polythene
polyunsaturated

polyurethane
pomander
pomegranate
pomelo
pommel
pomp
pompom, pompon
pomposity
pompous
poncho
  ponchos
pond
ponder
  pondered
  pondering
ponderous
pong
pongy
pontiff
pontifical
pontificate
  pontificated
  pontificating
pontoon
pony
  ponies
pony-trekking
poo
poodle
pooh-pooh
pool
  pooled
  pooling
poop
poor
poorly
pop
  popped
  popping
popadom,
  popadum,
  poppadom,

poppadum
popcorn
pope
poplar

> ◑* Do not confuse
> with **popular** *The*
> *poplar is a tall tree*

poppadom
another spelling of
  popadom
poppadum
another spelling of
  popadom
popper
poppet
poppy
  poppies
populace
popular

> ◑* Do not confuse
> with **poplar** *a popular*
> *entertainer*

popularise
another spelling of
  popularize
popularity
popularize,
  popularise
  popularized,
  popularised
  popularizing,
  popularising
popularly
populate
  populated
  populating
population
populist
populous
porcelain
porch

porches
porcine
porcupine
pore
  pored
  poring

> ◑* Do not confuse
> with **pour** *the pores of*
> *the skin* • *He pored over*
> *his books*

pork
porky
porn
pornographic
pornography
porosity
porous
porpoise
porridge
port
portable
portal
portcullis
  portcullises
portend
portent
porter
portfolio
  portfolios
port-hole
portico
  porticos, porticoes
portion
  portioned
  portioning
portly
portrait
portraiture
portray
  portrayed
  portraying

portrayal
pose
  posed
  posing
poser
posh
position
  positioned
  positioning
positive
positively
positivism
positivist
positron
posse
possess
possessed
possession

> ❶ I'm in possession of
> four s's.

possessive
possessively
possessiveness
possessor
possibility
  possibilities
possible
possibly
possum
post
postage
postal
postbag
postbox
  postboxes
postcard
postcode
postdate
  postdated
  postdating
poster

poste restante
posterior
posterity
postern
postgraduate
post-haste
posthumous
postman
 postmen
postmark
postmaster
postmeridian
postmistress
 postmistresses
postmortem
postnatal
postpone
 postponed
 postponing
postponement
postscript
postulate
 postulated
 postulating
posture
postwar
postwoman
 postwomen
posy
 posies
pot
 potted
 potting
potash
potassium
potato
 potatoes
pot-bellied
pot-belly
potency
potent
potentate

potential
potentiality
 potentialities
potentially
pothole
potholer
potholing
potion
potpourri
potted
potter
 pottered
 pottering
pottery
 potteries
potting
potty
 potties
pouch
 pouches
pouffe
poultice
poultry
pounce
 pounced
 pouncing
pound
pour
 poured
 pouring

 ◆* Do not confuse
with **pore** *to pour milk
from a jug* • *The rain
poured down*

pout
 pouted
 pouting
poverty
poverty-stricken
powder
 powdered

 powdering
powdery
power
powerboat
powered
powerful
powerfully
powerhouse
powerless
pow-wow
pox
practicable
practical
practicality
practically
practice

 ◆* Do not confuse
with **practise** *We have
choir practice on
Thursdays* • *Practice
makes perfect* • *a
doctor's practice*
Remember that **ice** is a
noun.

practise
 practised
 practising

 ◆* Do not confuse
with **practice** *You must
practise your dance
steps* • *to practise
medicine*

practitioner
pragmatic
pragmatism
pragmatist
prairie
praise
 praised
 praising
praiseworthy

praline
pram
prance
  pranced
  prancing
prang
prank
prankster
prate
  prated
  prating
prattle
  prattled
  prattling
prawn
pray
  prayed
  praying

> ♦* Do not confuse
> with **prey** *We will pray
> for his safe return*

prayer
preach
preacher
preamble
prearrange
  prearranged
  prearranging
precarious
precaution
precautionary
precede
  preceded
  preceding

> ❶ To prec**ede** is to be
> plac**ed** ahead.

> ♦* Do not confuse
> with **proceed** *May
> precedes June*

precedence

precedent
preceding
precept
precinct
precious
precipice
precipitate
  precipitated
  precipitating
precipitation
precipitous
précis
  précis
precise
precisely
preciseness
precision
preclude
  precluded
  precluding
preclusion
precocious
precocity
preconceive
  preconceived
  preconceiving
preconception
precondition
precook
precursor
predate
  predated
  predating
predator
predatory
predecessor
predestine
  predestined
  predestining
predestined
predetermine
  predetermined

predetermining
predetermined
predicament
predicate
predict
predictable
predictably
prediction
predilection
predispose
  predisposed
  predisposing
predisposition
predominance
predominant
predominantly
predominate
  predominated
  predominating
pre-eminence
pre-eminent
pre-empt
pre-emptive
preen
  preened
  preening
prefab
prefabricated
preface
  prefaced
  prefacing
prefect
prefer
  preferred
  preferring
preferable
preferably
preference
preferential
preferment
prefix
  prefixes

SPELLING *focus*

Prefixes

A *prefix* is a set of letters at the beginning of a word that gives it a particular meaning. For example, the **pre-** at the beginning of *prefix*, *precede*, *predict* and *preface* means 'before'. You can also add prefixes to words to change their meaning:

lucky + un → unlucky   **spell + mis → misspell**

Can you match the prefixes in the top row with the words in the bottom row to make six new words?

non-	super-	tele-	inter-	auto-	de-
phone	biography	national	sense	value	structure

Adding prefixes

Many prefixes are simply attached to the beginning of a word with no other change of spelling. For example, **dis-** + *appear* = *disappear*; **dis-** + *satisfied* = *dissatisfied*. This means that double letters are often created, as in *unnatural* or *immobile*.

The prefix **in-** changes to **il-** before words beginning with **l**, to **im-** before words beginning with **b**, **m** or **p**, and to **ir-** before words beginning with **r**. This creates words like:

- **inability**   **innumerable**   **inorganic**
- **illegal**   **illegitimate**   **illogical**
- **imbalance**   **immoral**   **impatient**
- **irrational**   **irregular**   **irresistible**

Once again, the spelling of the root word stays the same.

Prefixes with hyphens

Most prefixes are attached without hyphens. Hyphens are sometimes used when a prefix ending in a vowel is attached to a word beginning with a vowel, especially the same vowel, for example *anti-aircraft*, *re-elect*, *co-operate*, *pre-eminent* and *micro-organism*. They are also used when a prefix is attached to a word beginning with a capital letter, for example *anti-Semitism*. Words with the prefix **self-** always have hyphens, for example *self-confident* and *self-defence*. Sometimes a hyphen is also added to avoid creating a misleading letter combination, such as **ew** in *pre-war*.

Prefixes continued

Antonym prefixes

There are a number of prefixes that can be added to words to reverse their meaning. They include **un-**, **dis-**, **non-**, and the **in-/il-/im-/ir-** group. For example, *able* + **un-** = *unable*, and *please* + **dis-** = *displease*. Which prefix is used to create the antonym of each of the following words?

patient _____	certain _____	legible _____
existent _____	contented _____	regular _____

Other meanings of prefixes

Here are some common prefixes with their meanings. Many come from ancient Greek or Latin words with this meaning. Understanding the meaning of prefixes can help you to spell new words.

aqua 'water': **aquarium**
de 'undo': **dehydrate**
ex 'out of': **extract**

mis 'wrong': **mislead**
re 'again': **revisit**
tele 'distant': **telescope**

The prefixes **ante-** and **anti-** can cause spelling problems. **Ante-** means 'before', as in *antedate*, *antenatal* and *anteroom*. **Anti-** means 'against' or 'opposite', as in *anticlockwise*, *antifreeze* and *antisocial*.

Over to you

Here are some more groups of words with prefixes. Can you work out what each prefix means?

bicycle, binary, binoculars, biplane	_____
interaction, intercept, interlude, international	_____
microcosm, microfilm, microscope, microsurgery	_____

Making new words

New words are often created by adding prefixes to existing words. In recent years, the **eco-** prefix has given us *ecofriendly* and *ecotourism*, and the new prefix **e-**, meaning 'electronic', has given us *e-mail*, *e-commerce* and more.

It might be helpful to make a list of prefixes and their meanings in your Spelling Journal, and 'collect' lists of words that begin with each of them.

pregnancy
 pregnancies
pregnant
preheat
prehensile
prehistoric
prehistorically
prehistory
prejudge
 prejudged
 prejudging
prejudice
 prejudiced
 prejudicing

❶ People **reject** **u**nfair **dice.**

prejudiced
prejudicial
prelate
preliminary
 preliminaries
prelude
premarital
premature
prematurely
premedication
premeditate
 premeditated
 premeditating
premeditated
premeditation
premenstrual
premier

🌢* Do not confuse
with **première** *Who is
the Italian premier?*

première

🌢* Do not confuse
with **premier** *the
première of the play*

premise, premiss
 premises, premisses

🌢* The plural form
premisses is only used
for the meaning
'statements from
which a conclusion is
drawn' *The theory is
based on false
premisses*

premises

🌢* Do not confuse
with **premisses** *They
moved to new premises*

premiss
another spelling of
 premise
premium
premolar
premonition
prenatal
preoccupation
preoccupied
preoccupy
 preoccupies
 preoccupied
 preoccupying
preordain
 preordained
 preordaining
preorder
prep
prepacked
prepaid
preparation
preparatory
prepare
 prepared
 preparing
prepared
prepay

prepaid
prepaying
prepayment
preposition
prepositional
prepossessing
preposterous
prerequisite

🌢* Do not confuse
with **perquisite**
*Patience is a
prerequisite for
teaching*

prerogative
presage
 presaged
 presaging
Presbyterian
presbytery
 presbyteries
preschool
prescient
prescribe
 prescribed
 prescribing

🌢* Do not confuse
with **proscribe**
*Doctors prescribe
drugs for their patients*

prescription
prescriptive
presence
present
presentable
presentably
presentation
presenter
presently
preservation
preservative
preserve

preserved
preserving
preset
preset
presetting
preside
presided
presiding
presidency
presidencies
president
presidential
press
presses
pressing
press-up
pressure
pressurize,
pressurise
pressurized,
pressurised
pressurizing,
pressurising
prestige
prestigious
presto
presumably
presume
presumed
presuming
presumption
presumptive
presumptuous
presuppose
presupposed
presupposing
presupposition
pretence
pretend
pretender
pretension
pretentious

pretext
prettily
prettiness
pretty
prettier
prettiest
pretzel
prevail
prevailed
prevailing
prevailing
prevalence
prevalent
prevaricate
prevaricated
prevaricating
prevarication
prevaricator
prevent
preventable
preventative
prevention
preventive
preview
previous
previously
pre-war
prey
preyed
preying

💥* Do not confuse
with **pray** *animals
hunting their prey •
Owls prey on mice*

price
priced
pricing

💥* Do not confuse
with **prise** *What is the
price of that house? •
jackets priced at £50*

priceless
pricey, pricy
prick
prickle
prickled
prickling
prickly
pricy
another spelling of
pricey
pride
prided
priding
pried
pries
priest
priestess
priestesses
priesthood
priestly
prig
priggish
prim
primacy
prima donna
primaeval
another spelling of
primeval
primal
primarily
primary
primate
prime
primed
priming
primer
primeval, primaeval
primitive
primitively
primness
primogeniture
primordial

primp
primrose
primula
prince
princedom
princely
princess
princesses
principal

♦* Do not confuse
with **principle** *the*
principal of the college

principality
principalities
principally
principle

♦* Do not confuse
with **principal** *the*
principle of the steam
engine • a man of
principle

principled
print
printable
printed
printer
printing
printing-press
printout, print-out
prior
prioress
prioresses
prioritize, prioritise
prioritized,
prioritised
prioritizing,
prioritising
priority
priorities
priory
priories

prise
prised
prising

♦* Do not confuse
with **price** or **prize** *to*
prise open a lid • to prise
information from
someone who doesn't
want to tell

prism
prison
prisoner
prisoner of war
prissy
pristine
privacy
private

♦* Do not confuse
with **privet** *private*
information • a private
secretary

privately
privateer
privation
privatization,
  privatisation
privatize, privatise
privatized,
privatised
privatizing,
privatising
privet

♦* Do not confuse
with **private** *a privet*
hedge

privilege

❶ Word within word:
privi-**leg**-e

privileged
privy

prize
prized
prizing

♦* Do not confuse
with **prise** *I never win a*
prize • to prize a
possession dearly

pro
pros
proactive
probability
probabilities
probable
probably
probate
probation
probationary
probationer
probe
probed
probing
probity
problem
problematic
problematical
proboscis
proboscises,
proboscides
procedural
procedure
proceed

❶ Proceed carefully,
examining every
detail.

♦* Do not confuse
with **precede**
Passengers should
proceed to gate 14 • The
baby proceeded to
scream

proceedings
proceeds
process
processes

ℹ The process needs
care for success.

procession
processor
proclaim
proclaimed
proclaiming
proclamation
procrastinate
procrastinated
procrastinating
procrastination
procreate
procreated
procreating
procreation
procure
procured
procuring
procurement
procurer
prod
prodded
prodding
prodigal
prodigality
prodigious
prodigy
prodigies
produce
produced
producing
producer
product
production
productive
productively

productivity
profane
profanely
profanity
profanities
profess
professed
profession
professional
professionalism
professionally
professor

ℹ Word breakdown:
pro-fes-sor

professorial
professorship
proffer
proffered
proffering
proficiency
proficient
profile
profit
profited
profiting

✒* Do not confuse
with **prophet** *profit and
loss • to profit from the
experience*

profitability
profitable
profitably
profiteer
profiteered
profiteering
profiterole
profligacy
profligate
pro forma
profound
profoundly

profundity
profuse
profusely
profusion
progenitor
progeny
progesterone
prognosis
prognoses
program
programmed
programming

✒* Do not confuse
with **programme** *a
computer program • to
program a computer*

programmable
programme

✒* Do not confuse
with **program** *a theatre
programme • a
television programme*

programmer
progress
progression
progressive
progressively
prohibit
prohibited
prohibiting
prohibition
prohibitionist
prohibitive
prohibitively
prohibitory
project
projectile
projection
projectionist
projector
prolapse

prolapsed
prolapsing
proletarian
proletariat
pro-life
proliferate
proliferated
proliferating
proliferation
prolific
prolifically
prologue
prolong
prom
promenade
promenaded
promenading
promenader
prominence
prominent
prominently
promiscuity
promiscuous
promise
promised
promising
promising
promissory
promontory
promontories
promote
promoted
promoting
promoter
promotion
promotional
prompt
prompter
prompting
promptly
promptness
promulgate

promulgated
promulgating
promulgation
prone
prong
pronged
pronoun
pronounce
pronounced
pronouncing
pronounceable
pronounced
pronouncement
pronouncer
pronto
pronunciation

❶ Word breakdown:
pro-nun-ci-a-tion

proof
proofs

♦* Do not confuse
with **prove** *We have
proof of his guilt* • *proof
against attack*

proofread
proofread
proofreading
proofreader
prop
propped
propping
propaganda
propagandist
propagate
propagated
propagating
propagation
propagator
propane
propel
propelled

propelling
propellant

♦* Do not confuse
with **propellent** *a
rocket propellant* • *a
propellant used in
aerosols*

propellent

♦* Do not confuse
with **propellant**
*Propellent means
'driving' or 'propelling'* •
propellent force

propeller
propensity
propensities
proper
properly
propertied
property
properties

♦* Do not confuse
with **propriety** *lost
property* • *property
development* • *the
properties of gases*

prophecy
prophecies

♦* Do not confuse
with **prophesy** *make a
prophecy about the
future*

prophesy
prophesies
prophesied
prophesying

♦* Do not confuse
with **prophecy** *to
prophesy about the
future*

prophet

🔥* Do not confuse with **profit** *an Old Testament prophet • a prophet of doom*

prophetic
prophetically
prophylactic
propitious
proponent
proportion
proportional
proportionally
proportionate
proportionately
proposal
propose
 proposed
 proposing
proposer
proposition
propound
propped
propping
proprietary
proprietor
proprietorial
proprietress
 proprietresses
propriety
 proprieties

🔥* Do not confuse with **property** *She behaved with dignity and propriety*

propulsion
propulsive
pro rata
prosaic
prosaically
prosciutto

proscribe
 proscribed
 proscribing

🔥* Do not confuse with **prescribe** *The authorities proscribe books they consider unsuitable*

proscription
proscriptive
prose
prosecute
 prosecuted
 prosecuting
prosecution
prosecutor
prosodic
prosody
prospect
prospective

🔥* Do not confuse with **perspective** *a prospective buyer*

prospector
prospectus
 prospectuses
prosper
 prospered
 prospering
prosperity
prosperous
prosperously
prostate

🔥* Do not confuse with **prostrate** *the prostate gland*

prosthesis
 prostheses
prostitute
prostitution

prostrate
 prostrated
 prostrating

🔥* Do not confuse with **prostate** *He lay prostrate on the floor • They prostrated themselves before the emperor*

prostration
protagonist
protect
protection
protectionism
protectionist
protective
protectively
protector
protectorate
protégé

🔥* Do not confuse with **protégée** *He is the governor's protégé*

protégée

🔥* Do not confuse with **protégé** *She is the governor's protégée*

protein
protest
Protestant
protestation
protester
protocol
proton
prototype
Protozoa
protozoan
 protozoans,
 protozoa
protract

protracted
protractor
protrude
protruded
protruding
protrusion
protuberance
protuberant
proud
prove
proved
proving

♦* Do not confuse with **proof** *I can prove that she's lying*

provenance
proverb
proverbial
proverbially
provide
provided
providing
providence
provident
providential
providentially
provider
province
provincial
provincially
provision
provisional
provisionally
proviso
provisos
provisory
provocation
provocative
provocatively
provoke
provoked

provoking
provost
prow
prowess
prowl
prowler
proximity
proxy
proxies
prude
prudence
prudent
prudently
prudery
prudish
prudishness
prune
pruned
pruning
prurience
prurient
pry
pries
pried
prying
psalm
psalmist
psalter
pseud
pseudo
pseudonym
psoriasis
psych
psyche
psychedelic
psychiatric
psychiatrist
psychiatry
psychic
psychical
psycho
psychoanalyse

psychoanalysed
psychoanalysing
psychoanalysis
psychoanalyst
psychological
psychologically
psychologist
psychology
psychopath
psychosis
psychoses
psychosomatic
psychotherapist
psychotherapy
psychotic
ptarmigan
pterodactyl
pub
puberty
pubescence
pubescent
pubic
pubis
pubises
public
publican
publication
publicise
another spelling of
publicize
publicity
publicize, publicise
publicized,
publicised
publicizing,
publicising
publicly

❶ He was publicly cleared of all blame.

publish
publisher

publishing
puce
puck
pucker
 puckered
 puckering
pudding
puddle
puerile
puerility
puff
puffin
puffy
pug
pugnacious
pugnacity
pug-nosed
puke
 puked
 puking
pukka
pull
pullet
pulley
 pulleys
pullover
pulmonary
pulp
pulpit
pulsar
pulsate
 pulsated
 pulsating
pulse
 pulsed
 pulsing
pulverize, pulverise
 pulverized,
 pulverised
 pulverizing,
 pulverising
puma

pumice stone
pummel
 pummelled
 pummelling
pump
pumpernickel
pumpkin
pun
 punned
 punning
punch
 punches
punchy
punctilious
punctual
punctuality
punctually
punctuate
 punctuated
 punctuating
punctuation
puncture
 punctured
 puncturing
pundit
pungent
punish
punishable
punishing
punishment
punitive
punk
punned
punnet
punning
punt
punter
puny
 punier
 puniest
pup
pupa

pupae
pupate
 pupated
 pupating
pupil
puppet
puppeteer
puppetry
puppy
 puppies
purchase
 purchased
 purchasing
purchaser
purdah
pure
purée
 puréed
 puréeing
purely
purgative
purgatory
purge
 purged
 purging
purification
purifier
purify
 purifies
 purified
 purifying
purism
purist
puritan
puritanical
puritanically
purity
purl

◆* Do not confuse
with **pearl** *knit one,*
purl one

purloin
 purloined
 purloining
purple
purport
purpose
 purposed
 purposing
purposeful
purposefully
purposeless
purposely
purr
purse
 pursed
 pursing
purser
pursue
 pursued
 pursuing
pursuer
pursuit
purvey
 purveyed
 purveying
purveyor
pus
push
 pushes

push-chair
pusher
push-over
pushy
 pushier
 pushiest
pussy
 pussies
pussyfoot
 pussyfooted
 pussyfooting
pussyfooting
pustule
put
 put
 putting

💣* Do not confuse
with **putt** *to put a cup
on the table*

putative
putrefaction
putrefy
 putrefies
 putrefied
 putrefying
putrid
putsch
 putsches

putt
 putted
 putting

💣* Do not confuse
with **put** *to putt a golf
ball*

putter
putting
putty
puzzle
 puzzled
 puzzling
puzzlement
pygmy, pigmy
 pygmies, pigmies
pyjamas

ⓘ **P**ut your **py**jamas
on.

pylon
pyramid
pyre
Pyrex®
pyrite
pyromania
pyromaniac
pyrotechnics
Pyrrhic
python

qi
quack
quackery
quad
quadrangle
quadrangular
quadrant
quadraphonic,
  quadrophonic
quadriceps
quadrilateral
quadrille
quadriplegia
quadriplegic
quadrophonic
another spelling of
  quadraphonic
quadruped
quadruple
 quadrupled
 quadrupling
quadruplet
quaff
quagmire
quail
 quailed
 quailing
quaint
quake
 quaked
 quaking
Quaker
qualification
qualified

qualifier
qualify
 qualifies
 qualified
 qualifying
qualitative
quality
 qualities
qualm
quandary
 quandaries
quango
 quangos
quantify
 quantifies
 quantified
 quantifying
quantitative
quantity
 quantities
quantum
quarantine
 quarantined
 quarantining
quark
quarrel
 quarrelled
 quarrelling
quarrelsome
quarry
 quarries
 quarried
 quarrying
quart

quarter
quarterly
quartermaster
quartet
quartile
quarto
quartz
quasar
quash

♦* Do not confuse
with **squash** *to quash
the judge's decision*

quasi
quaver
 quavered
 quavering
quay

♦* Do not confuse
with **key** *boats moored
at the quay*

queasily
queasiness
queasy
queen
queenly
queer
quell
quench
querulous
query
 queries
 queried
 querying

quest
question
 questioned
 questioning
questionable
questionably
questioner
questionnaire

ⓘ There are **no** **new** questions in this questio**nn**aire.

queue
 queued
 queuing, queueing

ⓘ There are two **u**gly **e**lves in the q**ue**ue.

✒* Do not confuse with **cue** *a queue for the cinema • jump the queue • to queue for tickets*

quibble
 quibbled
 quibbling
quiche
quick
quicken
 quickened
 quickening
quicklime
quickly
quickness
quicksand

quicksilver
quickstep
quid
quiescence
quiescent
quiet

✒* Do not confuse with **quite** *a shy, quiet child • peace and quiet*

quieten
 quietened
 quietening
quietly
quietness
quietude
quiff
quill
quilt
quilted
quin
quince
quinine
quintessence
quintessential
quintet
quintuplet
quip
 quipped
 quipping
quirk
quirky
quisling
quit

 quitted, quit
 quitting
quite

✒* Do not confuse with **quiet** *It's quite easy • I quite forgot*

quits
quiver
 quivered
 quivering
quixotic
quixotically
quiz
 pl quizzes
 quizzed
 quizzing
quizmaster
quizzical
quizzically
quoits
quorate
quorum
quota
quotable
quotation
quote
 quoted
 quoting
quotient
Qur'an
 another spelling of
 Koran

R r

If you can't find the word you're looking for under **R**, it could be that it starts with a different letter. Try looking under **WR** for words like *wrist* and *wrong*. Also, don't forget **RH** for words like *rhyme* and *rhinoceros*.

rabbi
  rabbis
rabbit
  rabbited
  rabbiting
rabble
rabid
rabidity
rabidly
rabidness
rabies
raccoon, racoon
race
  raced
  racing
racecard
racecourse
racegoer
racehorse
racer
racetrack
racial
racialism
racialist
racially
racily
raciness
racing
racing car
racist

rack

💣* Do not confuse with **wrack** *put your luggage on the rack • Prisoners were tortured on the rack* You can use **rack** or **wrack** for phrases like *rack and ruin, racked with guilt* and *rack your brains*, but **rack** is the usual spelling.

racket, racquet

💣* The spelling **racquet** is only used for the bat *a tennis racquet • Stop making such a racket!*

racketeer
racketeering
raconteur
racoon
  another spelling of
  raccoon
racquet
  another spelling of
  racket
racy
  racier
  raciest

radar

💣* Do not confuse with **raider** *on the radar screen*

radial
radian
radiance
radiant
radiate
  radiated
  radiating
radiation
radiator
radical
radically
radii
radio
  pl radios
  radioed
  radioing
radioactive
radioactivity
radiographer
radiography
radiologist
radiology
radiotherapist
radiotherapy
radish
  radishes

radium

radius
 radii

raffia

raffish

raffle
 raffled
 raffling

raft

rafter

rag
 ragged
 ragging

ragamuffin

rage
 raged
 raging

ragga

ragged

raging

ragout

ragtime

raid

raider

❥* Do not confuse
with **radar** *The police
caught the raider*

rail
 railed
 railing

railcard

railing

railroad

railway

rain
 rained
 raining

❥* Do not confuse
with **reign** or **rein** *wind
and rain • to rain
heavily*

rainbow

raincoat

rainfall

rainforest

rainy
 rainier
 rainiest

raise
 raised
 raising

❥* Do not confuse
with **raze** *to raise a
family • to raise your
arm*

raisin

raita

rajah

rake
 raked
 raking

rakish

rakishly

rakishness

rally
 rallies
 rallied
 rallying

ram
 rammed
 ramming

ramble
 rambled
 rambling

rambler

rambling

ramekin, ramequin

ramification

ramp

rampage
 rampaged
 rampaging

rampant

❥* Do not confuse
with **rampart** *Violence
is rampant • rampant
inflation*

rampart

❥* Do not confuse
with **rampant** *the
rampart round the
castle*

ram-raid

ramrod

ramshackle

ran

❥* Do not confuse
with **run** *I ran all the
way home*

ranch
 ranches

rancher

rancid

rancorous

rancour

rand

randy

random

rang

❥* Do not confuse
with **rung** *I rang the
bell*

range
 ranged
 ranging

ranger

rank

rankle
 rankled
 rankling

ransack

ransom

Can't find your word? Try looking under **WR** or **RH**

ransomed
ransoming
rant
rap
rapped
rapping

> ✸ Do not confuse
> with **wrap** *Rap on the
> door • rap music • take
> the rap for somebody
> else's mistake*

rape
raped
raping
rapid
rapidity
rapidly
rapids
rapist
rapped

> ✸ Do not confuse
> with **rapt** or **wrapped**
> *He rapped on the door*

rapper
rapping
rapport
rapt

> ✸ Do not confuse
> with **rapped** or
> **wrapped** *gazing with
> rapt attention*

rapture
rapturous
rare
rarefied
rarely
raring
rarity
rarities
rascal

rascally
rash
rashes
rasher
rashly
rashness
rasp
raspberry
raspberries
rasping
Rasta
Rastafarian
rat
ratted
ratting
ratatouille
rate
rated
rating
rateable
rather
ratification
ratify
ratifies
ratified
ratifying
rating
ratio
ratios
ration
rationed
rationing
rational

> ✸ Do not confuse
> with **rationale** *It was a
> rational question*

rationale

> ✸ Do not confuse
> with **rational** *A
> rationale is an
> underlying principle*

rationalisation
another spelling of
rationalization
rationalise
another spelling of
rationalize
rationalism
rationalist
rationality
rationalization,
rationalisation
rationalize,
rationalise
rationalized,
rationalised
rationalizing,
rationalising
rationally
rattan
ratted
ratting
rattle
rattled
rattling
rattlesnake
ratty
raucous
raunchy
ravage
ravaged
ravaging
rave
raved
raving
raven
ravenous
raver
ravine
raving
ravioli
ravishing
raw

Can't find your word? Try looking under **WR** or **RH**

rawness
ray
ray-gun
rayon
raze
 razed
 razing

💧* Do not confuse
with **raise** *to raze a city
to the ground*

razor
razzle
razzmatazz
reach
 reaches
reachable
react
reaction
reactionary
 reactionaries
reactivation
reactivate
 reactivated
 reactivating
reactive
reactor
read
 read
 reading

💧* Do not confuse
with **reed** or **red** *to read
a magazine* • *He read
out a list of names* •
*Have you read this
book?*

readable
reader
readership
readily
readiness
ready

real

💧* Do not confuse
with **reel** *a real
diamond* • *a real friend*

realign
realignment
realisation
 another spelling of
 realization
realise
 another spelling of
 realize
realism
realist
realistic
realistically
reality
 realities
realization,
 realisation
realize, realise
 realized, realised
 realizing, realising
really
realm
ream
reap
 reaped
 reaping
reaper
reapply
 reapplies
 reapplied
 reapplying
rear
 reared
 rearing
rearguard
rearm
rearmament
reason

reasoned
reasoning
reasonable
reasonably
reassurance
reassure
 reassured
 reassuring
rebate
rebel
 rebelled
 rebelling
rebellion
rebellious
rebirth
reboot
 rebooted
 rebooting
reborn
rebound
rebuff
rebuild
 rebuilt
 rebuilding
rebuke
 rebuked
 rebuking
rebut
 rebutted
 rebutting
rebuttal
recall
recant
recantation
recap
 recapped
 recapping
recapitulate
 recapitulated
 recapitulating
recapitulation
recapture

Can't find your word? Try looking under **WR** or **RH**

recaptured
recapturing
recede
receded
receding
receding
receipt

---

❶ I want a receipt for the cash I paid them.

---

receive
received
receiving

---

❶ Receive follows the rule: **i** before **e**, except after **c**.

---

receiver
receivership
recent
recently
receptacle
reception
receptionist
receptive
recess
  recesses
recession
recessive
recipe
recipient
reciprocal
reciprocally
reciprocate
  reciprocated
  reciprocating
reciprocation
reciprocity
recital
recitalist
recitation
recite
  recited

reciting
reckless
recklessly
recklessness
reckon
reckoned
reckoning
reckoning
reclaim
reclaimed
reclaiming
reclaimable
reclamation
recline
reclined
reclining
recliner
recluse
recognisable
another spelling of
recognizable
recognisably
another spelling of
recognizably
recognise
another spelling of
recognize
recognition
recognizable,
recognisable
recognizably,
recognisably
recognize, recognise
recognized,
recognised
recognizing,
recognising
recoil
recoiled
recoiling
recollect
recollection

recommend

---

❶ I recommend cooked marshmallows.

---

recommendation
recompense
recompensed
recompensing
reconcile
reconciled
reconciling
reconciliation
recondition
reconnaissance
reconnoitre
reconnoitred
reconnoitring
reconsider
reconsidered
reconsidering
reconstitute
reconstituted
reconstituting
reconstitution
reconstruct
reconstruction
record
recorder
recording
recorded
recount, re-count

◆✳ The spelling **re-count** is only used in the sense of counting again *to re-count the votes* • *The loser demanded a re-count* • *She recounted what had happened*

---

recoup
recouped

Can't find your word? Try looking under **WR** or **RH**

recouping
recourse
recover, re-cover
recovered,
re-covered
recovering,
re-covering

> ◆* The spelling
> **re-cover** is only used
> in the sense of
> covering again *to
> re-cover the book in
> brown paper • He never
> recovered*

recoverable
recovery
recoveries
recreate
recreated
recreating
**recreation,
re-creation**

> ◆* The spelling
> **re-creation** is only
> used in the sense of
> creating again *the
> re-creation of a
> medieval town • swings
> at the recreation
> ground*

recreational
recrimination
recriminatory
recruit
recruited
recruiting
recruitment
rectal
rectangle
rectangular
rectifiable

rectify
rectifies
rectified
rectifying
rectitude
recto
rector
rectory
rectories
rectum
rectums, recta
recumbent
recuperate
recuperated
recuperating
recuperation
recuperative
recur
recurred
recurring
recurrence
recurrent
recyclable
recycle
recycled
recycling
red

> ◆* Do not confuse
> with **read** *a red dress*

redbreast
redcurrant
redden
reddened
reddening
redeem
redeemed
redeeming
redeemer
redeeming
redemption
redemptive

redeploy
redeployed
redeploying
redeployment
redevelop
redeveloped
redeveloping
redevelopment
red-handed
redhead
redness
redo
redid
redone
redoing
redolence
redolent
redouble
redoubled
redoubling
redoubtable
redress
reduce
reduced
reducing
reducible
reduction
redundancy
redundancies
redundant
redwood
reed

> ◆* Do not confuse
> with **read** *a reed
> growing by the pond •
> the reed of a musical
> instrument*

reedy
reef
reefs
reefer

Can't find your word? Try looking under **WR** or **RH**

reek

💧* Do not confuse with **wreak** *the reek of stale tobacco smoke • Your socks reek*

reel
reeled
reeling

💧* Do not confuse with **real** *a reel of thread • dance a Scottish reel • to reel drunkenly • to reel off a list of names*

re-elect
re-entry
refectory
refectories
refer
referred
referring
referee
refereed
refereeing
reference
referendum
referenda,
referendums
referential
referral
referred
referring
refill
refillable
refine
refined
refining
refinement
refinery
refineries
refit

refitted
refitting
reflect
reflection
reflective
reflectively
reflector
reflex
reflexes
reflexive
reflexologist
reflexology
reform
reformable
reformation
reformatory
reformatories
reformer
reformism
refract
refraction
refractory
refrain
refrained
refraining
refresh
refresher
refreshing
refreshingly
refreshment
refrigerate
refrigerated
refrigerating
refrigeration
refrigerator

ℹ️ There's a **fr**ightened **ti**ger in the re**frige**rator.

refuel
refuelled
refuelling

refuge

💧* Do not confuse with **refugee** *take refuge from danger • a refuge for battered wives*

refugee

💧* Do not confuse with **refuge** *refugees fleeing the war zone • a refugee camp*

refund
refundable
refurbish
refurbishment
refusal
refuse
refused
refusing
refutable
refutation
refute
refuted
refuting
regain
regained
regaining
regal

💧* Do not confuse with **regale** *She walks with regal bearing • regal splendour*

regale
regaled
regaling

💧* Do not confuse with **regal** *to regale them with humorous stories*

regalia

Can't find your word? Try looking under **WR** or **RH**

regally
regard
regarding
regardless
regards
regatta
regency
 regencies
regenerate
 regenerated
 regenerating
regeneration
regenerative
regent
reggae
regime, régime
regiment
regimental
region
regional
regionally
register
 registered
 registering
registrar
registration
registry
 registries
regress
regression
regressive
regret
 regretted
 regretting
regretful
regretfully
regrettable
regrettably
regular
regularisation
another spelling of
 regularization

regularise
another spelling of
 regularize
regularity
regularization,
 regularisation
regularize,
 regularise
 regularized,
 regularised
 regularizing,
 regularising
regularly
regulate
 regulated
 regulating
regulation
regulator
regurgitate
regurgitation
rehabilitate
 rehabilitated
 rehabilitating
rehabilitation
rehash
rehearsal
rehearse
 rehearsed
 rehearsing
reheat
 reheated
 reheating
reign

❶ Rulers everywhere **ign**ore their subjects.

🖋 Do not confuse with **rain** or **rein** *during Queen Victoria's reign • a reign of terror • He reigned for twenty years*

reiki
reimburse
 reimbursed
 reimbursing
rein
 reined
 reining

🖋 Do not confuse with **rain** or **reign** *the reins of a horse • give free rein to your imagination • to rein in expenditure*

reincarnate
 reincarnated
 reincarnating
reincarnation
reindeer
 reindeer
reinforce
 reinforced
 reinforcing
reinforcement
reinstate
 reinstated
 reinstating
reinstatement
reiterate
 reiterated
 reiterating
reiteration
reiterative
reject
rejection
rejoice
 rejoiced
 rejoicing
rejoinder
rejuvenate
 rejuvenated
 rejuvenating

Can't find your word? Try looking under **WR** or **RH**

rejuvenation
relapse
 relapsed
 relapsing
relate
 related
 relating
related
relation
relationship
relative
relatively
relativism
relativity
relax
relaxant
relaxation
relaxed
relaxing
relay
 relayed
 relaying
release
 released
 releasing
relegate
 relegated
 relegating
relegation
relent
relentless
relentlessly
relentlessness
relevance
relevant
reliability
reliable
reliably
reliance
reliant
relic
relied

relief

 ❶ Relief follows the
rule: **i** before **e**, except
after **c**.

 💧 Do not confuse
with **relieve** *a sigh of
relief • a relief worker*

relies
relieve
 relieved
 relieving

 💧 Do not confuse
with **relief** *to relieve the
pain • relieved to hear
they were safe*

religion
religious
relinquish
relish
 relishes
relive
 relived
 reliving
reload
relocate
 relocated
 relocating
relocation
reluctance
reluctant
reluctantly
rely
 relies
 relied
 relying
remain
 remained
 remaining
remainder
remains

remake
 remade
 remaking
remand
remark
remarkable
remarkably
remarry
 remarries
 remarried
 remarrying
remedial
remedy
 remedies
 remedied
 remedying
remember
 remembered
 remembering

 ❶ Word breakdown:
re-mem-ber

remembrance
remind
reminder
reminisce
 reminisced
 reminiscing
reminiscence
reminiscent
remiss
remission
remit
 remitted
 remitting
remittance
remix
remnant
remonstrance
remonstrate
 remonstrated
 remonstrating

Can't find your word? Try looking under **WR** or **RH**

remonstration
remorse
remorseful
remorsefully
remorseless
remote
remote-controlled
remotely
remoteness
remould
removable
removal
remove
  removed
  removing
remover
remunerate
  remunerated
  remunerating
remuneration
remunerative
renaissance
renal
rename
  renamed
  renaming
rend
render
  rendered
  rendering
rendezvous
  rendezvous
rendition
renegade
renege
  reneged
  reneging
renew
renewable
renewal
rennet
renounce

renounced
renouncing
renouncement
renovate
  renovated
  renovating
renovation
renown
renowned
rent
rental
renunciation
reorganization,
  reorganisation
reorganize,
  reorganise
reorganized,
  reorganised
reorganizing,
  reorganising
rep
repaid
repair
  repaired
  repairing
repairable

> ♦* Do not confuse
> with **reparable** *The car
> is not repairable*

repaper
reparable

> ♦* Do not confuse
> with **repairable** *The
> loss is not reparable*

reparation
repartee
repast
repatriate
  repatriated
  repatriating
repatriation

repay
repaid
repaying
repayment
repeal
repealed
repealing
repeat
repeated
repeating
repeatable
repeatedly
repel
repelled
repelling
repellent, repellant
repent
repentance
repentant
repercussion
repertoire
repertory
repetition

> ❶ A parrot is a **pet** that
> loves re**pet**ition.

repetitious
repetitive
repetitively
replace
replaced
replacing
replaceable
replacement
replay
replayed
replaying
replenish
replenishment
replete
replica
replicate

Can't find your word? Try looking under **WR** or **RH**

replicated
replicating
reply
 replies
 replied
 replying
report
reportedly
reporter
repose
 reposed
 reposing
repository
 repositories
repossess
 repossessed
 repossessing
repossession
reprehensible
reprehensibly
represent
representation
representative
repress
repression
repressive
reprieve
 reprieved
 reprieving
reprimand
reprint
reprisal
reproach
 reproaches
reproachful
reproachfully
reprobate
reproduce
 reproduced
 reproducing
reproduction
reproductive

reproof

💧* Do not confuse
with **reprove** *a look of
reproof*

reprove
 reproved
 reproving

💧* Do not confuse
with **reproof** *to reprove
the naughty child*

reptile
reptilian
republic
republican
republicanism
repudiate
 repudiated
 repudiating
repudiation
repugnance
repugnant
repulse
 repulsed
 repulsing
repulsion
repulsive
repulsively
reputable
reputation
repute
reputed
reputedly
request
requiem
require
 required
 requiring
requirement
requisite
requisition
 requisitioned

requisitioning
requite
 requited
 requiting
reroute
 rerouted
 rerouteing, rerouting
rerun
 reran
 rerun
 rerunning
resat
rescind
rescue
 rescued
 rescuing
rescuer
research
 researches
researcher
resemblance
resemble
 resembled
 resembling
resent
resentful
resentfully
resentment
reservation
reserve
 reserved
 reserving
reserved
reservist
reservoir

ℹ The **reservoir**
provides a **reserve** of
i**c**y **r**ainwater.

reshuffle
 reshuffled
 reshuffling

Can't find your word? Try looking under **WR** or **RH**

reside
 resided
 residing
residence
resident
residential
residual
residue
resign
resignation
resigned
resilience
resilient
resin
resinous
resist
resistance
resistant
resistible
resistor
resit
 resat
 resitting
resolute
resolutely
resolution
resolve
 resolved
 resolving
resonance
resonant
resonate
 resonated
 resonating
resort
resound
resounding
resource
 resources
resourceful
respect
respectability

respectable
respectably
respectful

> ♦* Do not confuse
> with **respective** *a
> respectful salute*

respectfully
respective

> ♦* Do not confuse
> with **respectful** *They
> returned to their
> respective homes*

respectively
respiration
respirator
respiratory
respire
 respired
 respiring
respite
resplendent
respond
respondent
response
responsibility
 responsibilities
responsible
responsibly
responsive
rest

> ♦* Do not confuse
> with **wrest** *take a rest •
> rest in peace*

restaurant

> ❶ My **aunt rants** about
> this rest**aurant**.

restaurateur
restful
restfully
restitution

restive
restively
restless
restlessness
restorable
restoration
restorative
restore
 restored
 restoring
restorer
restrain
 restrained
 restraining
restraint
restrict
restriction
restrictive
result
resultant
resume
 resumed
 resuming
résumé
resumption
resurgence
resurgent
resurrect
resurrection
resuscitate
 resuscitated
 resuscitating
resuscitation
retail
 retailed
 retailing
retailer
retain
 retained
 retaining
retainer
retake

Can't find your word? Try looking under **WR** or **RH**

retook
retaken
retaking
retaliate
retaliated
retaliating
retaliation
retard
retardant
retardation
retarded
retch

> ♦* Do not confuse
> with **wretch** *The sight
> of blood makes him
> retch*

retention
retentive
rethink
rethought
rethinking
reticence
reticent
retina
retinas, retinae
retinue
retiral
retire
retired
retiring
retired
retirement
retiring
retook
retort
retrace
retraced
retracing
retract
retractable
retraction

retrain
retrained
retraining
retreat
retreated
retreating
retrench
retrenchment
retribution
retrievable
retrieval
retrieve
retrieved
retrieving
retriever
retro
retrograde
retrospect
retrospective
retrospectively
return
returnable
reunion
reunite
reunited
reuniting
rev
revved
revving
revamp
reveal
revealed
revealing
reveille
revel
revelled
revelling
revelation
revelatory
reveller
revelry
revenge

revenged
revenging
revengeful
revenue
reverberate
reverberated
reverberating
reverberation
revere
revered
revering
reverence
Reverend
reverent
reverential
reverentially
reverie
reversal
reverse
reversed
reversing
reversible
reversion
revert
review

> ♦* Do not confuse
> with **revue** *His new
> book got a good review •
> We'll review the
> situation tomorrow*

reviewer
revile
reviled
reviling
revilement
revise
revised
revising
revision
revisionism
revisionist

Can't find your word? Try looking under **WR** or **RH**

revisit
revitalize, revitalise
 revitalized,
 revitalised
 revitalizing,
 revitalising
revival
revivalist
revive
 revived
 reviving
revoke
 revoked
 revoking
revolt
revolting
revolution
revolutionary
 revolutionaries
revolutionize,
 revolutionise
 revolutionized,
 revolutionised
 revolutionizing,
 revolutionising
revolve
 revolved
 revolving
revolver
revue

> ✦ Do not confuse
> with **review**
> *performing in a revue*

revulsion
revved
revving
reward
rewarding
rewind
 rewound
 rewinding

rewire
 rewired
 rewiring
reword
rewrite
 rewrote
 rewritten
 rewriting
rhapsodic
rhapsodize,
 rhapsodise
 rhapsodized,
 rhapsodised
 rhapsodizing,
 rhapsodising
rhapsody
 rhapsodies
rhesus
rhetoric
rhetorical
rhetorically
rheumatic
rheumatism
rheumatoid
rhinestone
rhinoceros
 rhinoceroses
rhododendron
rhombus
 rhombuses, rhombi
rhubarb
rhyme
 rhymed
 rhyming

> ℹ **R**emember how you
> begin to **rh**yme.

rhythm

> ℹ **Rh**ythm helps you
> to hear **m**usic.

rhythmic

rhythmical
rhythmically
rib
ribald
ribaldry
ribbed
ribbon
riboflavin
rice
rich
riches
richly
richness
Richter scale
rickets
rickety
rickshaw
ricochet
 ricocheted
 ricocheting
rid
 rid
 ridding
riddance
ridden
riddle
 riddled
 riddling
ride
 rode
 ridden
 riding
rider
ridge
ridged
ridicule
 ridiculed
 ridiculing
ridiculous
ridiculously
ridiculousness
riding

Can't find your word? Try looking under **WR**

rife
riff-raff
rifle
 rifled
 rifling
rift
rig
 rigged
 rigging
rigging
right

> ✎* Do not confuse
> with **rite** or **write** *the
> road on the right • the
> right answer • the right
> to vote • to right a wrong*

righteous

> 🛈 Each of us is
> right**e**ous.

righteousness
rightful
rightfully
right-hand
right-handed
right-handedness
right-wing
right-winger
rigid
rigidity
rigidly
rigmarole
rigor mortis
rigorous
rigorously
rigour
rile
 riled
 riling
rim
rimmed
rind

ring
 rang, ringed
 rung, ringed
 ringing

> ✎* Do not confuse
> with **wring** *to ring the
> bells • Ring the correct
> answer • an
> engagement ring • a
> ringing sound* The past
> form **ringed** is only
> used for the meaning
> 'put or make a ring
> round' *I ringed the
> correct answer • The
> phone rang • I have
> rung the bell*

ringer
ringleader
ringlet
ring-pull
rink
rinse
 rinsed
 rinsing
riot
 rioted
 rioting
rioter
riotous
rip
 ripped
 ripping
ripe
ripen
 ripened
 ripening
ripeness
rip-off
riposte
ripped
ripping

ripple
 rippled
 rippling
rip-roaring
rise
 rose
 risen
 rising
risible
rising
risk
risky
 riskier
 riskiest
risotto
rissole
rite

> ✎* Do not confuse
> with **right** or **write**
> *perform a religious rite
> • rites of passage*

ritual
ritualist
ritualistic
ritually
rival
 rivalled
 rivalling
rivalry
 rivalries
river
rivet
 riveted
 riveting
rivulet
roach
 roaches
road

> ✎* Do not confuse
> with **rode** or **rowed**
> *drive along the road*

Can't find your word? Try looking under **WR** or **RH**

SPELLING *focus*

Root Words

A *root word* is one to which prefixes and suffixes can be added to form different words. These new words are derived from the root word and are called *derivatives* or *derivations*. The root word *help*, for example, can be built up into the derivatives *helpful*, *unhelpful*, *helpless*, *helper* and more.

Grouping words into families with the same root can help you to remember difficult spellings. For example, the root word *sign* is found in *signal*, *significant* and *signature*. The 'g' sound in these three words should help you to remember the silent **g** in *sign*.

The root word *press* is found in *pressure*, *impress*, *depression* and others. Can you think of at least three words derived from each of the following root words?

part	_____	_____	_____
joy	_____	_____	_____
pass	_____	_____	_____
hand	_____	_____	_____

Foreign roots

Many roots come from ancient Greek or Latin words, and so are not whole words in English. For example, the root *spect*, found in *spectacle*, *spectator*, *inspection* and *retrospect*, comes from a Latin verb meaning 'look at'. You may recognize some roots as French words: for example *fin*, meaning 'end', found in *finish*, *final*, *definite* and *infinity*.

Can you work out the roots of the following groups of words and what they mean?

dictate, diction, predict, contradict	_____
vocabulary, vocal, vocation, advocate	_____
novelty, innovation, novice, renovate	_____
pedal, pedestrian, impede, expedition	_____

Spelling changes

A root can sometimes change its spelling in different words. For example, the root *ann*, which comes from the Latin word for 'year', is found in *annual* and *anniversary* but changes to *enn* in *millennium* and *perennial*.

Root Words continued

Log

Log is an interesting root. It comes from the Greek word *logos*, meaning 'word', 'speech' or 'reason', and is found in the English words *logic*, *logo*, *dialogue*, *analogous* and others. It is also found in the suffix **-logy** and its derivatives, as in *ecology*, *astrologer*, *psychologist* and *zoological*.

Building words

Knowledge of foreign root words, prefixes and suffixes can help you to build words up and take them apart. For example, **auto-** means 'self', **bio-** means 'life', **graph-** means 'write', and **-er** means 'somebody who does something'. So an *autobiographer* is a person who writes about his or her own life. If you know that **hydro-** means 'water' and **-phobia** means 'fear', you should have no difficulty in creating the word for 'fear of water'. If you know that **pseudo-** means 'false' and **-nym** means 'name', you should not need to use a dictionary to find out what a *pseudonym* is.

How many new words can you make from these 'building blocks'?

> tele   ped   ion   dict   photo
>
> contra   graph   ition   ex   vis

Here are some pairs of words that you can 'mix and match' to make a different pair with the same roots. Can you think of any more pairs like these?

> biography, geology → biology, geography
>
> telephone, microscope → telescope, microphone

Help with spelling

Knowledge of foreign root words can help with spelling. The words *pneumatic* and *pneumonia* share the root *pneum*, which means 'air' or 'breath': *pneumatic* tyres are filled with air, and *pneumonia* is a disease of the lungs, through which we breathe. The root *scien*, which means 'knowing', is a difficult letter pattern that is found in words such as *science*, *scientific*, *conscience* and *conscientious*.

roadie
roadside
roadster
roadworthy
roam
 roamed
 roaming
roar
 roared
 roaring
roast
rob
 robbed
 robbing
robber
robbery
 robberies
robe
 robed
 robing
robin
robot
robotic
robotics
robust
rock
rock-and-roll, rock
 'n' roll
rocker
rockery
 rockeries
rocket
 rocketed
 rocketing
rocking-chair
rocking-horse
rock 'n' roll
 another spelling of
 rock-and-roll
rocky
rococo
rod

rode

🖋* Do not confuse
with **road** or **rowed** *He
rode his bicycle home*

rodent
rodeo
 rodeos
roe

🖋* Do not confuse
with **row** *a roe deer •
cod roe*

rogue
roguish
role, rôle

🖋* Do not confuse
with **roll** *the starring
role in the film • a role
model • a role-playing
exercise*

roll

🖋* Do not confuse
with **role** *a roll of carpet
• to roll a ball • The
instructor called the roll*

roller
rollercoaster
roller-skate
 roller-skated
 roller-skating
rollicking
rolling-pin
rollmop
roll-on
roly-poly
romance
 romanced
 romancing
romantic
romantically
romanticize,

romanticise
 romanticized,
 romanticised
 romanticizing,
 romanticising
romp
rompers
rondo
 rondos
rood
roof
 pl roofs
 roofed
 roofing
roofing
rooftop
rook
rookery
 rookeries
room
room-mate
roomy
roost
rooster
root
 rooted
 rooting

🖋* Do not confuse
with **route** *the root of a
plant • the root of the
problem • to root
through her handbag*

rope
 roped
 roping
ropy
rosary
 rosaries
rose
rosé
rosehip

Can't find your word? Try looking under **WR** or **RH**

rosemary
rosette
rosewood
roster
rostrum
rostrums, rostra
rosy
rosier
rosiest
rot
rotted
rotting
rota
rotary
rotate
rotated
rotating
rotation
rote

> ✒* Do not confuse
> with **wrote** *He learnt
> the answers by rote*

rotisserie
rotor
rotted
rotten
rotter
rotting
Rottweiler
rotund
rotundity
rouble, ruble
rouge
rough

> ✒* Do not confuse
> with **ruff** *a rough
> surface • a rough sea • a
> rough draft*

roughage
roughen
roughened

roughening
roughshod
roulette
round
roundabout
roundel
rounders
Roundhead
roundly
roundworm
rouse
roused
rousing
rout
routed
routing

> ✒* Do not confuse
> with **route** *to rout the
> enemy • Napoleon's
> army was put to rout*

route
routed
routeing, routing

> ✒* Do not confuse
> with **root** or **rout** *the
> quickest route to
> Edinburgh • to route
> the bus along the main
> road*

routine
routinely
roux
rove
roved
roving
rover
row

> ✒* Do not confuse
> with **roe** *a row of chairs
> • to row a boat*

rowan
rowdy
rowdier
rowdiest
rowdiness
rowdyism
rowed

> ✒* Do not confuse
> with **road** or **rode** *She
> rowed the boat across
> the lake*

rower
rowing
rowing-boat
rowlock
royal
royalist
royally
royalty
royalties
rub
rubbed
rubbing
rubber
rubbery
rubbish
rubble
rubella
ruble
another spelling of
rouble
rubric
ruby
rubies
ruche
ruched
rucksack
ruction
rudder
ruddy
rude

Can't find your word? Try looking under **WR** or **RH**

rudely
rudeness
rudimentary
rudiments
rue
 rued
 ruing
rueful
ruefully
ruff

> ♦* Do not confuse
> with **rough** *a ruff
> round the neck*

ruffian
ruffle
 ruffled
 ruffling
rug
rugby
rugged
ruin
 ruined
 ruining
ruination
ruined
ruinous
ruinously
rule
 ruled
 ruling
ruler
ruling
rum
rumba
rumble
 rumbled
 rumbling
rumbustious
ruminant

ruminate
 ruminated
 ruminating
rumination
rummage
 rummaged
 rummaging
rummy
rumour
 rumoured
 rumouring
rump
rumple
 rumpled
 rumpling
rumpus
run
 ran
 run
 running

> ♦* Do not confuse
> **run** with **ran** *Walk,
> don't run!* • *He has run
> away* • *I ran all the way
> home*

runaway
run-down
rune
rung

> ♦* Do not confuse
> with **rang** or **wrung** *I
> have rung the bell* • *the
> first rung of the ladder*

runic
run-in
runner
runner-up
 runners-up

running
runny
run-of-the-mill
runt
run-up
runway
rupee
rupture
 ruptured
 rupturing
rural
ruse
rush
 rushes
rusk
russet
rust
rustic
rusticity
rustiness
rustle
 rustled
 rustling
rustler
rustproof
rusty
 rustier
 rustiest
rut
 rutted
 rutting
ruthless
ruthlessness
rye

> ♦* Do not confuse
> with **wry** *bread made
> from rye*

Can't find your word? Try looking under **WR** or **RH**

If you can't find the word you're looking for under **S**, perhaps it starts with a different letter. Try looking under **C** for words like *century* and *city*, and **PS** for words like *psychology*. Also, don't forget **SC** for words like *scent*, **SCH** for words like *schism*, and **SW** for words like *sword*. If the word you're looking for sounds as if it begins *sh* but you can't find it there, remember that **CH** is sometimes pronounced *sh* (as in *chivalry* and *chic*), as is **SCH** (*schnapps*).

Sabbath
sabbatical
sable
sabotage
  sabotaged
  sabotaging
saboteur
sabre
sac

> 💣* Do not confuse with **sack** *a fluid-filled sac in the body*

saccharine,
saccharin

> 💣* The spelling **saccharin** is only used for the noun *sweetened with saccharin • a saccharine smile*

sachet
sack

> 💣* Do not confuse with **sac** *a sack of potatoes • give an employee the sack*

sackcloth

sacking
sacrament
sacred
sacrifice
  sacrificed
  sacrificing
sacrificial
sacrilege
sacrilegious
sad
  sadder
  saddest
sadden
  saddened
  saddening
saddle
  saddled
  saddling
saddler
sadism
sadist
sadistic
sadistically
sadly
sadness
safari
  safaris
safe

safes
safely
safeguard
safekeeping
safety
saffron
sag
  sagged
  sagging
saga
sage
sagely
saggy
sago
said
sail
  sailed
  sailing

> 💣* Do not confuse with **sale** *a sail round the bay • to sail a boat*

sailboard
sailboarding
sailor
saint
sainthood
saintliness

saintly
sake
salaam
salable
another spelling of
saleable
salacious
salad
salamander
salami
salaried
salary
salaries
sale

> ✱ Do not confuse
> with **sail** *a furniture*
> *sale • a house for sale*

saleable, salable
salesman
salesmen
salesperson
saleswoman
saleswomen
salient
saline
saliva
salivary
salivate
salivated
salivating
sallow
sally
sallies
sallied
sallying
salmon
salmonella
salon

> ✱ Do not confuse
> with **saloon** *a*
> *hairdressing salon*

saloon

> ✱ Do not confuse
> with **salon** *a saloon car*
> *• a saloon bar*

salopettes
salsa
salt
salted
saltiness
salty
salutary
salutation
salute
saluted
saluting
salvage
salvaged
salvaging
salvation
salve
salved
salving
salver
salvo
salvos, salvoes
samba
same
sameness
samey
samosa
samovar
sampan
sample
sampled
sampling
sampler
samurai
samurai
sanatorium
sanatoriums,
sanatoria

sanctify
sanctifies
sanctified
sanctifying
sanctimonious
sanction
sanctioned
sanctioning
sanctity
sanctuary
sanctuaries
sanctum
sand
sandal
sandalwood
sandbag
sandblast
sander
sandpaper
sandpit
sandstone
sandwich
sandwiches
sandy
sane
sanely
saneness
sang

> ✱ Do not confuse
> with **sung** *We sang the*
> *chorus*

sangfroid
sangria
sanguine
sanguinely
sanitary
sanitation
sanitization,
sanitisation
sanitize, sanitise
sanitized, sanitised

Can't find your word? Try looking under **C**, **CH**, **PS**, **SC**, **SCH** or **SW**

sanitizing, sanitising
sanity
sank

> 💣* Do not confuse
> with **sunk** *The ship*
> *sank*

sanserif
sap
 sapped
 sapping
sapling
sapphire
sarcasm
sarcastic
sarcastically
sarcophagus
 sarcophagi,
 sarcophaguses
sardine
sardonic
sardonically
sari
 saris
sarong
sartorial
sash
 sashes
sat
Satan
satanic
satanism
satchel
sated
satellite

---
❶ **Tell** me what a
sa**tell**ite is.
---

satiable
satiate
 satiated
 satiating
satin

satire
satirical
satirically
satirist
satirize, satirise
 satirized, satirised
 satirizing, satirising
satisfaction
satisfactorily
satisfactory
satisfy
 satisfies
 satisfied
 satisfying
satsuma
saturate
 saturated
 saturating
saturation
sauce

> 💣* Do not confuse
> with **source** *do you*
> *want sauce on your*
> *chips?*

saucepan
saucer
saucily
sauciness
saucy
 saucier
 sauciest
sauerkraut
sauna
saunter
 sauntered
 sauntering
sausage

---
❶ **Sausages** are
usually **s**picy.
---

sauté
savage

savaged
savaging
savagely
savagery
savannah, savanna
save
 saved
 saving
savings
saviour

> 💣* Do not confuse
> with **savour** *our*
> *saviour*

savoir-faire
savour
 savoured
 savouring

> 💣* Do not confuse
> with **saviour** *to savour*
> *the delicious soup*

savoury
 savouries
savoy
savvy
saw
 sawed
 sawn
 sawing
sawdust
sawn
saxophone
saxophonist
say
 said
 saying
scab
scabbard
scabby
scabies
scaffold
scaffolding

Can't find your word? Try looking under **C**, **CH**, **PS**, **SCH** or **SW**

scald
scale
 scaled
 scaling
scalene
scallop
scalloped
scallywag
scalp
scalpel
scaly
scam
scamp
scamper
 scampered
 scampering
scampi
scan
 scanned
 scanning
scandal
scandalize,
 scandalise
 scandalized,
 scandalised
 scandalizing,
 scandalising
scandalous
scanner
scansion
scant
scantily
scanty
scapegoat
scar
 scarred
 scarring
scarab
scarce
scarcely
scarcity
 scarcities

scare
 scared
 scaring
scarecrow
scared
scaremonger
scaremongering
scarey
 another spelling of
 scary
scarf
 scarves, scarfs
scarlet
scarper
 scarpered
 scarpering
scarred
scarring
scarves
scary, scarey
 scarier
 scariest
scathing
scathingly
scatter
 scattered
 scattering
scatterbrained
scattered
scattering
scatty
scavenger
scenario
 scenarios
scene

●* Do not confuse
with **seen** *the first scene
of the play* • *the scene of
the crime*

scenery
scenic

scent

●* Do not confuse
with **cent** or **sent** *the
scent of spring flowers* •
to scent danger

sceptic

●* Do not confuse
with **septic** *A sceptic is
someone who doubts
what they are told*

sceptical
sceptically
scepticism
sceptre
schedule
 scheduled
 scheduling
schematic
scheme
 schemed
 scheming
schemer
scheming
schism
schizophrenia
schizophrenic
schmaltz
schmaltzy
schnapps
scholar
scholarly
scholarship
school
 schooled
 schooling
schoolfellow
schooling
schoolmaster
schoolmistress
 schoolmistresses
schoolteacher

Can't find your word? Try looking under **C, CH, PS** or **SW**

Dictionaries

There are ways to speed up how quickly you can find the word you want in a dictionary.

- Think of the dictionary as having four parts (called 'quartiles'), approximately *a-d*, *e-l*, *m-r* and *s-z*. If you are looking for the word *catapult*, open the dictionary in the first quartile; if you are looking for *mysterious*, open it just past the middle. Use the second and third letters of the word to home in on the page you need as quickly as possible.

- Remember that dictionaries sometimes put words with suffixes at the end of the entry for the word they are derived from, rather than giving every single word an entry of its own. So if you are looking for *efficiency*, for example, you may not find the entry for it above *efficient* (where you might expect it to be), but at the end of the entry for *efficient*, along with *efficiently*.

schooner	**scorch**	**Scrabble**®
sciatic	**scorcher**	**scrabble**
sciatica	**scorching**	scrabbled
science	**score**	scrabbling
scientific	scored	**scrag**
scientifically	scoring	**scragginess**
scientist	**scoreboard**	**scraggy**
sci-fi	**scorer**	**scram**
scintillate	**scorn**	**scramble**
scintillated	**scornful**	scrambled
scintillating	**scornfully**	scrambling
scion	**scorpion**	**scrap**
scissors	**scotch**	scrapped
	scot-free	scrapping
❶ She cut it snipping	**scoundrel**	**scrapbook**
swiftly – ouch!	**scour**	**scrape**
	scoured	scraped
sclerosis	scouring	scraping
scoff	**scourer**	**scraper**
scold	**scourge**	**scrapie**
scolding	scourged	**scrapped**
scone	scourging	**scrappy**
scoop	**scout**	**scratch**
scooped	scouted	scratches
scooping	scouting	**scratchy**
scooter	**scowl**	**scrawl**
scope		

Can't find your word? Try looking under **C**, **CH**, **PS** or **SW**

scrawny
scream
 screamed
 screaming
scree
screech
 screeches
screed
screen
 screened
 screening
screenplay
screen-saver
screw
screwdriver
scribble
 scribbled
 scribbling
scribbler
scribe
scrimp
script
scripture
scriptwriter
scroll
scrotum
 scrota, scrotums
scrounge
 scrounged
 scrounging
scrounger
scrub
 scrubbed
 scrubbing
scrubby
scrubland
scruff
scruffily
scruffy
 scruffier
 scruffiest
scrum

scrummage
scrummy
scrumptious
scrumpy
scrunch
scrunchie
scruple
 scrupled
 scrupling
scrupulous
scrupulously
scrutineer
scrutinize, scrutinise
 scrutinized,
 scrutinised
 scrutinizing,
 scrutinising
scrutiny
scuba
scud
 scudded
 scudding
scuff
scuffle
scull

♦* Do not confuse
with **skull** *A scull is a
short oar*

scullery
 sculleries
sculpt
sculptor

♦* Do not confuse
with **sculpture** *He is a
painter and a sculptor*

sculpture

♦* Do not confuse
with **sculptor** *a
beautiful piece of
sculpture*

scum
scummy
scupper
 scuppered
 scuppering
scurrilous
scurry
 scurries
 scurried
 scurrying
scurvy
scuttle
 scuttled
 scuttling
scythe
sea

♦* Do not confuse
with **see** *swim in the sea
• all at sea • a sea of
faces*

sea anemone
sea-bed
seaboard
seafarer
seafaring
seafood
seafront
seagoing
seagull
seahorse
seal
 sealed
 sealing
sealant
sealed
sealing

♦* Do not confuse
with **ceiling** *sealing
wax • I'm sealing the
envelope*

sealskin

Can't find your word? Try looking under **C, CH, PS, SCH** or **SW**

seam

⬥* Do not confuse
with **seem** *to sew a
seam • a coal seam*

seaman
 seamen
seamanship
seamless
seamstress
 seamstresses
seamy
séance
sear
 seared
 searing

⬥* Do not confuse
with **seer** *to sear meat
in hot fat*

search
 searches
searching
searchlight
searing
seashell
seashore
seasick
seasickness
seaside
season
 seasoned
 seasoning
seasonable
seasonal
seasonally
seasoned
seasoning
seat
 seated
 seating
seating
seaweed

seaworthy
sebaceous
secateurs
secede
 seceded
 seceding
secession
secluded
seclusion
second
secondary
seconder
second-hand
secondly
secondment
second-rate
secrecy
secret

⬥* Do not confuse
with **secrete** *Can you
keep a secret? • a secret
plan*

secretarial
secretariat
secretary
 secretaries

❶ Can your **secret**ary
keep a **secret**?

secrete
 secreted
 secreting

⬥* Do not confuse
with **secret** *glands that
secrete hormones • He
secreted a dagger
under his cloak*

secretion
secretive
secretively
secretiveness

sect
sectarian
sectarianism
section
 sectioned
 sectioning
sectional
sector
secular
secularism
secularize,
 secularise
 secularized,
 secularised
 secularizing,
 secularising
secure
 secured
 securing
securely
security
 securities
sedan
sedate
 sedated
 sedating
sedately
sedation
sedative
sedentary
sedge
sediment
sedimentary
sedition
seditious
seduce
 seduced
 seducing
seducer
seduction
seductive
seductively

Can't find your word? Try looking under **C, CH, PS, SC, SCH** or **SW**

see
saw
seen
seeing

❖ Do not confuse
with **sea** *Did you see
him? • to see clearly • a
bishop's see*

seed
seedless
seedling
seedy
seedier
seediest
seek
sought
seeking
seem
seemed
seeming

❖ Do not confuse
with **seam** *They seem
friendly*

seemingly
seemly
seen

❖ Do not confuse
with **scene** *Have you
seen this film before? •
Otters may be seen
round the coastline*

seep
seeped
seeping
seepage
seer

❖ Do not confuse
with **sear** *The seer
foretold her death*

seersucker

seesaw
seethe
seethed
seething
seething
segment
segregate
segregated
segregating
segregation
seismic
seismograph
seismography
seismological
seismologist
seismology
seize
seized
seizing

❶ To **seize** is to snatch
eagerly in.

seizure
seldom
select
selection
selective
selector
self
selves
self-addressed
self-appointed
self-assurance
self-assured
self-catering
self-centred
self-confessed
self-confidence
self-confident
self-conscious
self-contained
self-control

self-defence
self-effacing
self-employed
self-esteem
self-evident
self-explanatory
self-help
self-importance
self-important
self-indulgence
self-indulgent
self-interest
selfish
selfishness
selfless
selflessness
self-made
self-pity
self-portrait
self-raising
self-respect
self-righteous
selfsame
self-satisfied
self-service
self-sufficient
sell
sold
selling

❖ Do not confuse
with **cell** *to sell flowers*

seller

❖ Do not confuse
with **cellar** *The seller
raised the price • a
seller of stolen goods*

Sellotape®
sell-out
selvage, selvedge
selves
semaphore

Can't find your word? Try looking under **C**, **CH**, **PS**, **SC**, **SCH** or **SW**

semblance
semen
semester
semibreve
semicircle
semicolon
semi-detached
semi-final
seminal
seminar
semiquaver
semitone
semolina
senate
senator
send
 sent
 sending
sender
senile
senility
senior
seniority
senna
sensation
sensational
sensationalist
sensationally
sense
 sensed
 sensing
senseless
sensibility
 sensibilities
sensible
sensibly
sensitise
 another spelling of
 sensitize
sensitive
sensitively
sensitivity

sensitize, sensitise
 sensitized, sensitised
 sensitizing,
 sensitising
sensor

🖋* Do not confuse
with **censor** *a heat
sensor*

sensory
sensual
sensuality
sensually
sensuous
sent

🖋* Do not confuse
with **cent** or **scent** *I
sent her a postcard*

sentence
 sentenced
 sentencing
sententious
sentient
sentiment
sentimental
sentimentality
sentimentally
sentinel
sentry
 sentries
sepal
separable
separate
 separated
 separating

❶ To se**para**te things is
to keep them a**par**t.

separately
separation
separatism
separatist

sepia
septet
septic

🖋* Do not confuse
with **sceptic** *The
wound went septic • a
septic tank*

septicaemia
septuagenarian
sepulchral
sepulchre
sequel
sequence
sequential
sequestered
sequestrate
 sequestrated
 sequestrating
sequestration
sequin
seraph
 seraphs, seraphim
seraphic
serenade
 serenaded
 serenading
serendipity
serene
serenely
serenity
serf
 serfs
serfdom
serge

🖋* Do not confuse
with **surge** *wearing a
serge suit*

sergeant

❶ Word within word:
serge-ant

Can't find your word? Try looking under **C, CH, PS, SC, SCH** or **SW**

serial

*✸ Do not confuse with **cereal** *a television serial* • *a serial killer* Remember that a **seri**al is a **seri**es of episodes.*

serialization, serialisation
serialize, serialise
serialized, serialised
serializing, serialising
series
series

*✸ Do not confuse with **serious** *a series of plays**

serious

*✸ Do not confuse with **series** *in a serious mood**

seriously
seriousness
sermon
serpent
serpentine
serrated
serried
serum
servant
serve
served
serving
server
service
serviceable
serviceman
servicemen
serviette

servile
servilely
servility
serving
servitude
sesame
session
set
set
setting
setback
settee
setter
settle
settled
settling
settlement
settler
seven
seventeen
seventeenth
seventh
seventieth
seventy
seventies
sever
severed
severing
several
severance
severe
severely
severity
sew
sewed
sewn
sewing

*✸ Do not confuse with **so** or **sow** *to sew a seam**

sewage

sewer

*✸ Do not confuse with **sower** *I'm not a sewer or a knitter* • *Waste water passes through the sewer**

sewerage
sewing
sewn

*✸ Do not confuse with **sown** *I've sewn the hem**

sex
sexes
sexagenarian
sexily
sexiness
sexism
sexist
sextant

*✸ Do not confuse with **sexton** *A sailor uses a sextant**

sextet
sexton

*✸ Do not confuse with **sextant** *The sexton tolled the bell**

sextuplet
sexual
sexuality
sexually
sexy
sexier
sexiest
shabbily
shabby
shack
shackle
shackled

Can't find your word? Try looking under **C, CH, PS, SC, SCH** or **SW**

shackling
shackles
shade
shaded
shading
shading
shadow
shady
shadier
shadiest
shaft
shag
shaggy
shake
shook
shaken
shaking
shaker
shakily
shaky
shale
shall
should
shallot
shallow
sham
shammed
shamming
shaman
shamans
shamanism
shambles
shambolic
shame
shamed
shaming
shamefaced
shameful
shamefully
shameless
shammy
another spelling of

chamois
shampoo
shampooed
shampooing
shamrock
shandy
shandies
shank
shan't
shanty
shanties
shape
shaped
shaping
shapeless
shapely
shard
share
shared
sharing
shareholder
shareware
shark
sharp
sharpen
sharpened
sharpening
sharpener
sharply
shatter
shattered
shattering
shave
shaved
shaving
shaven
shaver
shavings
shawl
she
sheaf
sheaves

shear
sheared
shorn
shearing

> 🖋 Do not confuse
> with **sheer** *to shear*
> *sheep • He sheared the*
> *sheep*

shearer
shears
sheath

> 🖋 Do not confuse
> with **sheathe** *put a*
> *sword in its sheath •*
> *covered with a*
> *protective sheath*

sheathe
sheathed
sheathing

> 🖋 Do not confuse
> with **sheath** *to sheathe*
> *a sword • The cat*
> *sheathes its claws*

sheaves
shebang
she'd
shed
sheen
sheep
sheepdog
sheepish
sheepshank
sheepskin
sheer
sheered
sheering

> 🖋 Do not confuse
> with **shear** *a sheer drop*
> *• sheer delight • The car*
> *sheered off the road*

Can't find your word? Try looking under **C**, **CH**, **PS**, **SC**, **SCH** or **SW**

sheet
sheikh
shekel
shelf
 shelves

💧* Do not confuse
with **shelve** *the books
on the shelf*

she'll
shell
shellfish
shelter
 sheltered
 sheltering
shelve
 shelved
 shelving

💧* Do not confuse
with **shelf** *to shelve the
project • The cliff
shelves slightly*

shelves
shelving
shenanigans
shepherd
shepherdess
 shepherdesses
sherbet
sheriff
sherry
 sherries
shiatsu
shied
shield
shier
shies
shiest
shift
shiftily
shiftless
shifty

shilling
shimmer
 shimmered
 shimmering
shin
shindig
shine
 shone
 shining
shingle
shingles
shining
Shinto
Shintoism
Shintoist
shinty
shiny
 shinier
 shiniest
ship
 shipped
 shipping
shipment
shipping
shipshape
shipwreck
shipwrecked
shipyard
shire
shirk
shirker
shirt
shirty
shiver
 shivered
 shivering
shivery
shoal
shock
shocking
shod
shoddily

shoddiness
shoddy
shoe
 shod
 shoeing

💧* Do not confuse
with **shoo** *a pair of new
shoes • to shoe a horse*

shoebox
shoelace
shoestring
shone
shoo
 shooed
 shooing

💧* Do not confuse
with **shoe** *to shoo the
birds away*

shook
shoot
 shot
 shooting

💧* Do not confuse
with **chute** *a shoot of a
plant • to shoot a deer*

shop
 shopped
 shopping
shopkeeper
shoplift
shoplifter
shoplifting
shopper
shopping
shore
 shored
 shoring
shorn
short
shortage

Can't find your word? Try looking under **C**, **CH**, **PS**, **SC**, **SCH** or **SW**

shortbread
short-circuit
  short-circuited
  short-circuiting
shortcoming
shorten
  shortened
  shortening
shortfall
shorthand
short-lived
shortly
shorts
short-sighted
short-tempered
short-term
shot
shotgun
should
shoulder
  shouldered
  shouldering
shouldn't
should've
shout
  shouted
  shouting
shove
  shoved
  shoving
shovel
  shovelled
  shovelling
show
  showed
  shown
  showing
showbiz
showcase
showdown
shower
  showered

  showering
showery
showily
showjumping
shown
showroom
showy
shrank

💧* Do not confuse with **shrunk** *My jumper shrank in the wash*

shrapnel
shred
  shredded
  shredding
shredder
shrew
shrewd
shrewish
shriek

❶ I tried to shriek.

shrill
shrilly
shrimp
shrine
shrink
  shrank
  shrunk
  shrinking
shrinkage
shrink-wrap
  shrink-wrapped
  shrink-wrapping
shrivel
  shrivelled
  shrivelling
shroud
shrub
shrubbery
  shrubberies

shrug
  shrugged
  shrugging
shrunk

💧* Do not confuse with **shrank** *These jeans have shrunk*

shrunken
shudder
  shuddered
  shuddering
shuffle
  shuffled
  shuffling
shufti
shun
  shunned
  shunning
shunt
shut
  shut
  shutting
shutter
shuttle
shuttlecock
shy
  shyer
  shyest
  shies
  shied
  shying
shyly
shyness
sibilant
sibling
sick
sicken
  sickened
  sickening
sickening
sickle

Can't find your word? Try looking under **C, CH, PS, SC, SCH** or **SW**

sickly
sickness
side
 sided
 siding
sideboard
sideburn
sidecar
sidekick
sideline
sidelong
sideshow
sidestep
 sidestepped
 sidestepping
sidetrack
sideways
siding
sidle
 sidled
 sidling
siege

ⓘ Stuck **i**nside,
everyone **g**ot **e**xcited.

sienna
sierra
siesta
sieve
 sieved
 sieving
sift
sigh
sight

♦* Do not confuse
with **cite** or **site** *He lost
his sight in the accident
• a sight for sore eyes • to
sight land from a ship*

sighted
sighting
sightless

sightseeing
sightseer
sign
signal
 signalled
 signalling
signalman
 signalmen
signatory
 signatories
signature
signet

♦* Do not confuse
with **cygnet** *a signet
ring*

significance
significant
signify
 signifies
 signified
 signifying
signpost
Sikh
Sikhism
silage
silence
 silenced
 silencing
silencer
silent
silhouette
 silhouetted
 silhouetting

ⓘ The **silent hou**se
was in **silhou**ette.

silicon

♦* Do not confuse
with **silicone** *a silicon
chip • Silicon is a
common element*

silicone

♦* Do not confuse
with **silicon** *silicone
polish*

silk
silken
silkworm
silky
sill
silly
 sillier
 silliest
silo
 silos
silt
silver
 silvered
 silvering
silverfish
silversmith
silvery
simian
similar
similarity
 similarities
similarly
simile
simmer
 simmered
 simmering
simper
 simpered
 simpering
simple
simpleton
simplicity
simplification
simplify
 simplifies
 simplified
 simplifying

Can't find your word? Try looking under **C, CH, PS, SC, SCH** or **SW**

simplistic
simply
simulate
 simulated
 simulating
simulated
simulation
simulator
simulcast
simultaneous
simultaneously
sin
 sinned
 sinning
since
sincere
sincerely

❶ Word within word:
since-rely

sincerity
sinew
sinewy
sinful
sinfully
sing
 sang
 sung
 singing

◐* Do not confuse
singing with singeing
singing a song

singe
 singed
 singeing

◐* Do not confuse
singeing with singing
*singeing the shirt with
the iron*

singer
single

singled
singling
single-handed
single-minded
singleness
singlet
singly
singsong, sing-song
singular
singularity
singularly
sinister
sink
 sank
 sunk
 sinking
sinner
sinuous

◐* Do not confuse
with sinus *sinuous
curves*

sinus
 sinuses

◐* Do not confuse
with sinuous *He has
sinus trouble*

sinusitis
sip
 sipped
 sipping
siphon, syphon
 siphoned, syphoned
 siphoning,
 syphoning
sir
sire
siren
sirloin
sisal
sissy
 another spelling of

cissy
sister
sisterhood
sister-in-law
 sisters-in-law
sisterly
sit
 sat
 sitting
sitar
sitcom
site
 sited
 siting

◐* Do not confuse
with cite or sight *a
building site • decide
where to site the new
factory*

sit-in
sitting
sitting-room
situate
 situated
 situating
situated
situation
six
 sixes
sixpence
sixteen
sixteenth
sixth
sixtieth
sixty
 sixties
size
 sized
 sizing
sizeable, sizable
sizzle

Can't find your word? Try looking under C, CH, PS, SC, SCH or SW

sizzled
sizzling
ska
skate
skated
skating
skateboard
skateboarding
skater
skein
skeletal
skeleton
sketch
sketches
sketchily
sketchy
skew
skewer
skewered
skewering
skew-whiff
ski
pl skis
skied
skiing
skid
skidded
skidding
skier
skies

❧* Do not confuse
with **skis** *cloudier skies
• praise him to the skies*

skiff
skilful

❶ Remember – both
skill and **full** drop
extra l's.

skilfully
skill
skilled

skillet
skim
skimmed
skimming
skimp
skimpily
skimpy
skin
skinned
skinning
skinflint
skinful
skinhead
skinny
skinnier
skinniest
skint
skip
skipped
skipping
skipper
skipping
skirl
skirmish
skirmishes
skirt
skirting
skirting-board
skis

❧* Do not confuse
with **skies** *He put his
skis on • She skis very
well*

skit
skittish
skittle
skive
skived
skiving
skiver
skivvy

skivvies
skulduggery
skulk
skull

❧* Do not confuse
with **scull** *He had a
fractured skull*

skunk
sky
skies
sky-diving
skylark
skylight
skyline
skyscraper
slab
slack
slacken
slackened
slackening
slacks
slag
slagged
slagging
slain
slake
slaked
slaking
slalom
slam
slammed
slamming
slander
slandered
slandering
slanderous
slang
slant
slanting
slap
slapped

Can't find your word? Try looking under **C, CH, PS, SC, SCH** or **SW**

slapping
slapdash
slapstick
slash
slashes
slat
slate
slated
slating
slatted
slattern
slaughter
slaughtered
slaughtering
slaughterhouse
slave
slaved
slaving
slaver
slavered
slavering
slavery
slavish
slay
slew
slain
slaying

💧* Do not confuse
with **sleigh** *to slay the
enemy*

sleaze
sleazy
sled
sledded
sledding
sledge
sledged
sledging
sledgehammer
sleek
sleep

slept
sleeping
sleeper
sleepily
sleeping
sleepless
sleepwalk
sleepwalker
sleepwalking
sleepy
sleet
sleeve
sleeveless
sleigh

💧* Do not confuse
with **slay** *travel across
the snow in a sleigh*

sleight of hand
slender
slept
sleuth
slew
slice
sliced
slicing
slicer
slick
slide
slid
sliding
slight
slightly
slightness
slim
slimmed
slimming
slime
slimy
sling
slung
slinging

slingback
slink
slunk
slinking
slinkily
slinky
slip
slipped
slipping
slipknot
slip-on
slipper
slippery
slipshod
slipstream
slip-up
slipway
slit
slit
slitting
slither
slithered
slithering
sliver
slob
slobber
slobbered
slobbering
slobbish
sloe

💧* Do not confuse
with **slow** *A sloe is a
small black fruit*

slog
slogged
slogging
slogan
sloop
slop
slopped
slopping

Can't find your word? Try looking under **C, CH, PS, SC, SCH** or **SW**

slope
 sloped
 sloping
sloppily
sloppy
slosh
slot
 slotted
 slotting
sloth
slothful
slothfully
slouch
slough
slovenly
slow

> 💧* Do not confuse
> with **sloe** *a slow train* •
> *to slow down*

slowcoach
 slowcoaches
slow-worm
sludge
slug
sluggish
sluice
 sluiced
 sluicing
slum
slumber
 slumbered
 slumbering
slump
slung
slunk
slur
 slurred
 slurring
slurp
slurry
slush

slushy
sly
slyly
slyness
smack
smacker
small
smallholder
smallness
smallpox
smarmy
smart
smarten
 smartened
 smartening
smash
 smashes
smashing
smattering
smear
 smeared
 smearing
smell
 smelt, smelled
 smelling
smelly
 smellier
 smelliest
smelt
smelter
smelting
smile
 smiled
 smiling
smirch
smirk
smite
 smote
 smitten
 smiting
smithereens
smithy

 smithies
smitten
smock
smocking
smog
smoke
 smoked
 smoking
smokeless
smoker
smokescreen
smoky
smooch
smooth
smoothie
smote
smother
 smothered
 smothering
smoulder
 smouldered
 smouldering
smudge
 smudged
 smudging
smug
smuggle
 smuggled
 smuggling
smuggler
smut
smutty
snack
snag
 snagged
 snagging
snail
snake
 snaked
 snaking
snakebite
snap

Can't find your word? Try looking under **C**, **CH**, **PS**, **SC**, **SCH** or **SW**

snapped
snapping
snapdragon
snapper
snappily
snappy
snapshot
snare
snared
snaring
snarl
snatch
snatches
snazzy
sneak
sneakers
sneaky
sneer
sneered
sneering
sneeze
sneezed
sneezing
snicker
snickered
snickering
snide
sniff
sniffle
sniffled
sniffling
snigger
sniggered
sniggering
snip
snipped
snipping
snipe
sniped
sniping
sniper
snippet

snitch
snitches
snivel
snivelled
snivelling
snob
snobbery
snobbish
snobby
snog
snogged
snogging
snood
snooker
snoop
snooped
snooping
snooty
snootier
snootiest
snooze
snoozed
snoozing
snore
snored
snoring
snorkel
snorkelling
snort
snot
snotty
snout
snow
snowball
snowboard
snowboarding
snowbound
snowdrift
snowdrop
snowfall
snowflake
snowman

snowmen
snowplough
snowy
snub
snubbed
snubbing
snuff
snuffbox
snuffboxes
snuffle
snuffled
snuffling
snug
snuggle
snuggled
snuggling
so

> ✎* Do not confuse
> with **sew** or **sow** *so*
> *beautiful • so much • I*
> *think so*

soak
soaking
so-and-so
soap
soaped
soaping
soapbox
soapiness
soapstone
soapsuds
soapy
soar
soared
soaring

> ✎* Do not confuse
> with **sore** *to soar high*
> *in the air • Prices will*
> *soar*

sob
sobbed

Can't find your word? Try looking under **C**, **CH**, **PS**, **SC**, **SCH** or **SW**

sobbing
sober
sobered
sobering
soberness
sobriety
so-called
soccer
sociability
sociable
sociableness
sociably
social
socialise
another spelling of
socialize
socialism
socialist
socialite
socialize, socialise
socialized,
socialised
socializing,
socialising
socially
society
societies
sociological
sociologist
sociology
sock
socket
soda
sodden
sodium
sofa
soft
soften
softened
softening
softener
soft-hearted

software
soggy
soil
soiled
soiling
sojourn
solace
solaced
solacing
solar
sold
solder
soldered
soldering

> ◆* Do not confuse with **soldier** *to solder metal*

soldier
soldiered
soldiering

> ◆* Do not confuse with **solder** *The soldier left the army • She soldiered on alone*

sole
soled
soling

> ◆* Do not confuse with **soul** *the sole of the foot • lemon sole • He is the sole survivor • to sole a shoe*

solely
solemn
solemnise
another spelling of
solemnize
solemnity
solemnize,
solemnise

solemnized,
solemnised
solemnizing,
solemnising
solemnly
solenoid
sol-fa
solicit
solicited
soliciting
solicitor
solicitous
solicitude
solid
solidarity
solidify
solidifies
solidified
solidifying
solidity
soliloquy
soliloquies
solitaire
solitary
solitude
solo
solos
soloist
solstice
solubility
soluble
solution
solve
solved
solving
solvency
solvent
sombre
sombrely
sombreness
sombrero
sombreros

Can't find your word? Try looking under **C**, **CH**, **PS**, **SC**, **SCH** or **SW**

some

> **⚫*** Do not confuse with **sum** *some people*

somebody
somehow
someone
somersault
something
sometime
sometimes
somewhat
somewhere
son

> **⚫*** Do not confuse with **sun** *a son and a daughter* Remember her **only** son.

sonar
sonata
song
songbird
songster
songstress
 songstresses
sonic
son-in-law
 sons-in-law
sonnet
sonny
soon
sooner
soot

> **⚫*** Do not confuse with **suit** *soot in the chimney*

soothe
 soothed
 soothing
soothsayer
sooty

sop
sophisticated
sophistication
sophistry
sophomore
soporific
sopping
soppy
 soppier
 soppiest
soprano
 sopranos
sorbet
sorcerer
sorceress
 sorceresses
sorcery
sordid
sore

> **⚫*** Do not confuse with **soar** *a sore leg • a sight for sore eyes • a cold sore*

sorely
soreness
sorghum
sorority
 sororities
sorrel
sorrow
sorrowful
sorrowfully
sorry
sort
sortie
SOS
so-so
sotto voce
soufflé
sought
souk

soul

> **⚫*** Do not confuse with **sole** *heart and soul • the soul of discretion • a dear old soul • soul music*

soulful
soulfully
soulless
sound
soundbite
soundproof
soundtrack
soup
sour
 soured
 souring
source
 sourced
 sourcing

> **⚫*** Do not confuse with **sauce** *the source of the leak*

sourpuss
 sourpusses
souse
 soused
 sousing
south
southbound
south-east
south-easterly
south-eastern
southerly
southern
southerner
southernmost
southward
southwards
south-west
south-westerly

Can't find your word? Try looking under **C, CH, PS, SC, SCH** or **SW**

south-western
souvenir
sou'wester
sovereign
sovereignty
sow
sowed
sown, sowed
sowing

> ✪* Do not confuse
> with **sew** or **so** *to sow*
> *seeds • a sow in the*
> *pigsty*

sower

> ✪* Do not confuse
> with **sewer** *a sower of*
> *seeds*

sown

> ✪* Do not confuse
> with **sewn** *I've sown*
> *some parsley seeds*

soy
soya
spa
space
spaced
spacing
spacecraft
spaceman
spacemen
spacewoman
spacewomen
spacious
spaciousness
spade
spaghetti

> ❶ You can't **h**ide the
> elephant's **t**wo **t**runks
> in spag**hetti**.

Spam®

spam
spammed
spamming
span
spanned
spanning
spangle
spangled
spangling
spaniel
spank
spanking
spanner
spar
sparred
sparring
spare
spared
sparing
sparing
sparingly
spark
sparkle
sparkled
sparkling
sparkler
sparkling
sparred
sparring
sparrow
sparse
sparsely
spartan
spasm
spasmodic
spasmodically
spastic
spat
spate
spatial
spats
spatter

spattered
spattering
spatula
spawn
spay
spayed
spaying
speak
spoke
spoken
speaking
speakeasy
speaker
spear
speared
spearing
spearhead
spearmint
special
specialisation
another spelling of
specialization
specialise
another spelling of
specialize
specialism
specialist
speciality
specialities

> ✪* Do not confuse
> with **specialty** *Cream*
> *cakes are their*
> *speciality*

specialization,
specialisation
specialize, specialise
specialized,
specialised
specializing,
specialising
specially

Can't find your word? Try looking under **C**, **CH**, **PS**, **SC**, **SCH** or **SW**

specialty
specialties

♦* Do not confuse
with **speciality** *a*
medical specialty

species
species

♦* Do not confuse
with **specious** *animals*
of different species

specific
specifically
specification
specify
specifies
specified
specifying
specimen
specious

♦* Do not confuse
with **species** *a specious*
argument

speck
speckle
speckled
spectacle
spectacles
spectacular
spectacularly
spectator
spectral
spectre
spectrum
spectrums, spectra
speculate
speculated
speculating
speculation
speculative
speculatively

speculator
speculum
sped
speech
speeches
speechless
speed
sped, speeded
speeding

♦* The past form
sped is used for the
meaning 'go quickly'
and **speeded** for the
meaning 'exceed the
speed limit' *They sped*
along the path • She
often speeded on the
motorway

speedboat
speedily
speeding
speedometer
speedway
speedy
spell
spelt, spelled
spelling
spellbinding
spellbound
spellchecker,
  spellcheck
spelling
spelt
spend
spent
spending
spendthrift
spent
sperm
spermatozoon
spermatozoa

spermicide
spew
sphere
spherical
sphinx
sphinxes

🛈 Some pyramids
have a **sph**inx.

spice
spiciness
spick-and-span
spicy
spicier
spiciest
spider
spidery
spied
spiel
spies
spike
spiked
spiking
spiky
spill
spilt, spilled
spilling
spillage
spilt
spin
spun
spinning
spina bifida
spinach
spinal
spindle
spindly
spin-dryer,
  spin-drier
spine
spine-chilling
spineless

Can't find your word? Try looking under **C, CH, PS, SC, SCH** or **SW**

spinet
spinner
spinneret
spinney
spinneys
spin-off
spinster
spiny
spiral
spiralled
spiralling
spire
spirit
spirited
spiriting
spirited
spiritual
spiritualism
spiritualist
spirituality
spiritually
spit
spat
spitting
spite
spiteful
spitefully
spittle
spittoon
splash
splashes
splat
splatter
splattered
splattering
splay
splayed
splaying
splay-footed
spleen
splendid
splendidly

splendour
splice
spliced
splicing
splint
splinter
splintered
splintering
split
split
splitting
splodge
splurge
splurged
splurging
splutter
spluttered
spluttering
spoil
spoilt, spoiled
spoiling
spoiler
spoilsport
spoilt
spoke
spoken
spokesman
spokesmen
spokesperson
spokeswoman
spokeswomen
sponge
sponged
sponging
sponger
spongy
sponsor
sponsored
sponsoring
sponsorship
spontaneity
spontaneous

spoof
spoofs
spooky
spookier
spookiest
spool
spoon
spooned
spooning
spoonbill
spoonerism
spoon-feed
spoon-fed
spoon-feeding
spoonful
spoonfuls
spoor

●* Do not confuse
with **spore** *follow the
deer's spoor*

sporadic
sporadically
spore

●* Do not confuse
with **spoor** *the spores of
a plant*

sporran
sport
sporting
sportsman
sportsmen
sportsmanlike
sportsmanship
sportswoman
sportswomen
sporty
spot
spotted
spotting
spotless
spotlight

Can't find your word? Try looking under **C**, **CH**, **PS**, **SC**, **SCH** or **SW**

spot-on
spotted
spotting
spotty
spouse
spout
spouted
spouting
sprain
sprained
spraining
sprang

> ❋ Do not confuse
> with **sprung** *He sprang*
> *to his feet*

sprat
sprawl
spray
sprayed
spraying
spread
spread
spreading
spread-eagled
spreadsheet
spree
sprig
sprightliness
sprightly
spring
sprang
sprung
springing
springboard
springbok
spring-clean
spring-cleaned
spring-cleaning
springer
springtime
springy

sprinkle
sprinkled
sprinkling
sprinkler
sprint
sprinter
sprite
spritzer
sprocket
sprout
sprouted
sprouting
spruce
spruced
sprucing
sprucely
sprung

> ❋ Do not confuse
> with **sprang** *It has*
> *sprung a leak*

spry
spryly
spud
spume
spun
spur
spurred
spurring
spurious
spurn
spurt
sputnik
sputter
sputtered
sputtering
spy
spies
spied
spying
spyhole
squabble

squabbled
squabbling
squad
squaddie, squaddy
squaddies
squadron
squalid
squall
squally
squalor
squander
squandered
squandering
square
squared
squaring
squarely
squash
squashes

> ❋ Do not confuse
> with **quash** *to squash*
> *the fruit • a game of*
> *squash*

squat
squatted
squatting
squatter
squaw
squawk
squeak
squeaky
squeal
squealed
squealing
squeamish
squeegee
squeeze
squeezed
squeezing
squelch
squelchy

Can't find your word? Try looking under **C, CH, PS, SC, SCH** or **SW**

squib
squid
squiffy
squiggle
squiggly
squint
squire
squirm
squirrel
squirt
stab
 stabbed
 stabbing
stabilise
 another spelling of
 stabilize
stabiliser
 another spelling of
 stabilizer
stability
stabilize, stabilise
 stabilized, stabilised
 stabilizing,
 stabilising
stabilizer, stabiliser
stable
 stabled
 stabling
staccato
stack
stadium
 stadiums, stadia
staff
stag
stage
 staged
 staging
stagecoach
 stagecoaches
stagger
 staggered
 staggering

staging
stagnant
stagnate
 stagnated
 stagnating
stagnation
staid

💧* Do not confuse
with **stayed** *She is staid
and respectable*

stain
 stained
 staining
stainless
stair

💧* Do not confuse
with **stare** *climb the
stairs*

staircase
stairway
stairwell
stake
 staked
 staking

💧* Do not confuse
with **steak** *a wooden
stake • a stake in the
firm • Her life is at stake
• to stake a claim*

stalactite
stalagmite
stale
stalemate
stalk
stalker
stall
stallion
stalwart
stamen
stamina

stammer
 stammered
 stammering
stamp
stampede
 stampeded
 stampeding
stance
stanch
stand
 stood
 standing
standard
standardization,
 standardisation
standardize,
 standardise
 standardized,
 standardised
 standardizing,
 standardising
standby
stand-in
standing
stand-offish
standpipe
standpoint
standstill
stank

💧* Do not confuse
with **stunk** *The bag
stank of fish*

stanza
staple
 stapled
 stapling
stapler
star
 starred
 starring
starboard

Can't find your word? Try looking under **C, CH, PS, SC, SCH** or **SW**

starch
starches
starchy
stardom
stare
stared
staring

✎* Do not confuse **stare** with **stair** *a disapproving stare • to stare in amazement*

starfish
stark
starkers
starlet
starling
starlit
starred
starring
starry
start
starter
startle
startled
startling
startling
starvation
starve
starved
starving
stash
stashes
state
stated
stating
stately
statement
state-of-the-art
statesman
statesmen
statesmanlike

statesmanship
stateswoman
stateswomen
static
station
stationed
stationing
stationary

✎* Do not confuse with **stationery** *The train was stationary* Remember that a **car** can be statio**na**ry.

stationer
stationery

✎* Do not confuse with **stationary** *pens, paper and other stationery* Remember that stationery includes **e**nvelopes.

statistical
statistically
statistician
statistics
statue

✎* Do not confuse with **statute** *a bronze statue*

statuesque
statuette
stature
status
statuses
status quo
statute

✎* Do not confuse with **statue** *a parliamentary statute*

statutory

staunch
stave
staved, stove
staving
stay
stayed
staying

✎* Do not confuse **stayed** with **staid** *We stayed at a hotel • She has stayed unmarried*

stead
steadfast
steadily
steadiness
steady
steadies
steadied
steadying
steak

✎* Do not confuse with **stake** *steak and chips*

steakhouse
steal
stole
stolen
stealing

✎* Do not confuse with **steel** *Did he steal the jewels? • to steal away unnoticed*

stealth
stealthily
stealthy
steam
steamed
steaming
steam-boat
steamer

Can't find your word? Try looking under **C, CH, PS, SC, SCH** or **SW**

steamroller
steamy
steed
steel
steeled
steeling

> ●* Do not confuse
> with **steal** *iron and*
> *steel • to steel yourself*
> *for the battle ahead*

steelworks
steely
steep
steeped
steeping
steeple
steeplechase
steer
steered
steering
steering-wheel
stellar
stem
stemmed
stemming
stench
stenches
stencil
stencilled
stencilling
step
stepped
stepping

> ●* Do not confuse
> with **steppe** *climb the*
> *steps to the front door •*
> *a step in the right*
> *direction*

stepbrother
stepchild
stepchildren

stepdaughter
stepfather
stepladder
stepmother
steppe

> ●* Do not confuse
> with **step** *the vast,*
> *treeless steppes of*
> *Russia*

stepping-stone
stepson
stereo
stereos
stereophonic
stereotype
stereotyped
stereotypical
sterile
sterilisation
another spelling of
sterilization
sterilise
another spelling of
sterilize
sterility
sterilization,
sterilisation
sterilize, sterilise
sterilized, sterilised
sterilizing,
sterilising
sterling
stern
sternly
sternness
sternum
sternums, sterna
steroid
stethoscope
stetson
stew

steward
stewardess
stewardesses
stick
stuck
sticking
stickiness
stick-in-the-mud
stickleback
stickler
sticky
stickier
stickiest
stiff
stiffen
stiffened
stiffening
stiffness
stifle
stifled
stifling
stifling
stigma
stigmas, stigmata
stigmatize,
stigmatise
stigmatized,
stigmatised
stigmatizing,
stigmatising
stile

> ●* Do not confuse
> with **style** *Climb over*
> *the stile into the next*
> *field*

stiletto
stilettos
still
stillborn
stillness
stilt

Can't find your word? Try looking under **C**, **CH**, **PS**, **SC**, **SCH** or **SW**

stilted
Stilton
stilts
stimulant
stimulate
 stimulated
 stimulating
stimulation
stimulus
 stimuli
sting
 stung
 stinging
stingray
stingy
stink
 stank
 stunk
 stinking
stint
stipend
stipendiary
stipple
 stippled
 stippling
stipulate
 stipulated
 stipulating
stipulation
stir
 stirred
 stirring
stir-fry
 stir-fries
 stir-fried
 stir-frying
stirring
stirrup
stitch
 stitches
stoat
stock

stockade
stockbroker
stocked

> ♦* Do not confuse
> with **stoked** *We
> stocked up on food for
> the party • a
> well-stocked bookshop*

stockily
stockiness
stocking
stockinged
stockist
stockpile
 stockpiled
 stockpiling
stockroom
stock-still
stocktaking
stocky
stodge
stodginess
stodgy
stoic
stoical
stoically
stoicism
stoke
 stoked
 stoking

> ♦* Do not confuse
> **stoked** with **stocked**
> *He stoked the fire*

stoker
stole
stolen
stolid
stolidity
stomach
 stomachs
stomach-ache

stomp
stone
 stoned
 stoning
stonechat
stoned
stonemason
stonewall
stonewashed
stonily
stony
stood
stooge
stool
stoop
 stooped
 stooping
stop
 stopped
 stopping
stopcock
stopgap
stopover
stoppage
stopper
stopwatch
 stopwatches
storage
store
 stored
 storing
storey
 storeys

> ♦* Do not confuse
> with **story** *a building of
> four storeys*

stork
storm
stormily
stormtrooper
stormy

Can't find your word? Try looking under **C, CH, PS, SC, SCH** or **SW**

story
stories

📍* Do not confuse
with **storey** *a fairy
story*

storyline
stout
stoutness
stove
stow
stowaway
straddle
straddled
straddling
straggle
straggled
straggling
straggler
straggly
straight

📍* Do not confuse
with **strait** *a straight
line • go straight home*

straighten
straightened
straightening

📍* Do not confuse
straightened with
straitened *The dentist
straightened my teeth*

straightforward
straightness
strain
strained
straining
strainer
strait

📍* Do not confuse
with **straight** *sail
across the strait*

straitened

📍* Do not confuse
with **straightened** *in
straitened
circumstances*

straitjacket
strait-laced
strand
stranded
strange
strangely
strangeness
stranger
strangle
strangled
strangling
stranglehold
strangler
strangulation
strap
strapped
strapping
strata
stratagem
strategic
strategically
strategist
strategy
strategies
strathspey
stratification
stratified
stratosphere
stratum
strata
stratus
straw
strawberry
strawberries
stray
strayed

straying
streak
streaked
streaker
streakiness
streaky
stream
streamed
streaming
streamer
streamline
streamlined
streamlining
street
streetwise
strength

ℹ Stretches never
gain them height.

strengthen
strengthened
strengthening
strenuous
stress
stresses
stressed
stressful
stress-mark
stretch
stretches
stretcher
stretchy
strew
strewed
strewn, strewed
strewing
stricken
strict
strictly
stricture
stride
strode

Can't find your word? Try looking under **C, CH, PS, SC, SCH** or **SW**

stridden
striding
stridency
strident
strife

●* Do not confuse
with **strive** *trouble and*
strife

strike
struck
striking
striker
striking
string
strung
stringing
stringed
stringency
stringent
stringy
strip
stripped
stripping
stripe
striped
striping
striped
stripling
stripped
stripper
stripping
striptease
stripy
strive
strove
striven
striving

●* Do not confuse
with **strife** *to strive to*
do better

strobe

strode
stroke
stroked
stroking
stroll
strong
stronghold
strongly
strontium
strop
stropped
stropping
stroppy
strove
struck
structural
structuralism
structuralist
structurally
structure
structured
strudel
struggle
struggled
struggling
strum
strummed
strumming
strung
strut
strutted
strutting
strychnine
stub
stubbed
stubbing
stubble
stubbly
stubborn
stubbornly
stubbornness
stubby

stucco
stuck
stuck-up
stud
studded
studding
student
studied
studies
studio
studios
studious
studiously
studiousness
study
studies
studied
studying
stuff
stuffing
stuffy
stultify
stultifies
stultified
stultifying
stumble
stumbled
stumbling
stumbling-block
stump
stumpy
stun
stunned
stunning
stung
stunk

●* Do not confuse
with **stank** *The fridge*
has stunk for days

stunner
stunning

Can't find your word? Try looking under **C, CH, PS, SC, SCH** or **SW**

stunt
stunted
stuntman
 stuntmen
stuntwoman
 stuntwomen
stupefaction
stupefy
 stupefies
 stupefied
 stupefying
stupendous
stupid
stupidity
stupor
sturdily
sturdiness
sturdy
 sturdier
 sturdiest
sturgeon
stutter
 stuttered
 stuttering
sty, stye
 sties, styes

◆* The spelling **stye**
is only used for a
swelling on the eyelid
*ointment for his stye • a
pig in its sty*

style
 styled
 styling

◆* Do not confuse
with **stile** *style of dress
• literary style • to style
hair*

stylised
another spelling of
stylized

stylish
stylist
stylistic
stylistics
stylized, stylised
stylus
 styluses
stymie
 stymied
 stymieing, stymying
suave
suavely
suavity
subaqua
subcommittee
subconscious
subcontinent
subcontract
subcontractor
subculture
subdirectory
subdivide
 subdivided
 subdividing
subdivision
subdue
 subdued
 subduing
subject
subjection
subjective
subjectively
subjectiveness
subjectivity
subjugate
 subjugated
 subjugating
subjugation
subjunctive
sublet
 sublet
 subletting

sublieutenant
sublime
sublimely
subliminal
submarine
submerge
 submerged
 submerging
submergence
submersible
submersion
submission
submissive
submissively
submit
 submitted
 submitting
subnormal
subordinate
 subordinated
 subordinating
subordination
subplot
subpoena
 subpoenaed
 subpoenaing
subscribe
 subscribed
 subscribing
subscriber
subscription
subsequent
subservience
subservient
subset
subside
 subsided
 subsiding
subsidence
subsidiary
 subsidiaries
subsidize, subsidise

Can't find your word? Try looking under **C**, **CH**, **PS**, **SC**, **SCH** or **SW**

subsidized,
subsidised
subsidizing,
subsidising
subsidy
subsidies
subsist
subsistence
subsoil
substance
substandard
substantial
substantially
substantiate
substantiated
substantiating
substantiation
substantive
substitute
substituted
substituting
substitution
subsume
subsumed
subsuming
subterfuge
subterranean
subtext
subtitle
subtitled
subtle

ℹ There's a silent **u**nexpected **b** to learn in **subtle**.

subtlety
subtleties
subtly
subtotal
subtract
subtraction
subtropical

suburb
suburban
suburbia
subvention
subversion
subversive
subversively
subvert
subway
succeed

ℹ Two **c**'s and two **e**'s will help you su**cce**ed.

success
successes

ℹ Can **c**ats use si**x**th sense for su**cce**ss?

successful
successfully
succession
successive
successively
successor
succinct
succinctly
succour
succoured
succouring
succulence
succulent
succumb
such
such-and-such
suchlike
suck
sucker
suckle
suckled
suckling
sucrose
suction

sudden
suddenly
suddenness
suds
sue
sued
suing
suede

♦* Do not confuse with **swede** *a suede jacket*

suet
suffer
suffered
suffering
sufferance
sufferer
suffering
suffice
sufficed
sufficing
sufficiency
sufficient
sufficiently
suffix
suffixes
suffocate
suffocated
suffocating
suffocation
suffrage
suffragette
suffuse
suffused
suffusing
sugar
sugared
sugaring
sugar beet
sugared
sugary

Can't find your word? Try looking under **C**, **CH**, **PS**, **SC**, **SCH** or **SW**

SPELLING *focus*

Suffixes

A *suffix* is a set of letters at the end of a word that gives it a particular meaning or that changes its part of speech. For example, the suffix **-ly** changes an adjective to an adverb (for example, *clear* to *clearly*) and the suffix **-ness** changes an adjective to a noun (for example, *good* to *goodness*). Here are some other examples of suffixes, with their uses:

-able, -ible, -ic, -ous, -ful, -less
create *adjectives*: **allowable, helpful, useless**

-ion, -tion, -ment, -ity, -hood, -ship
create *nouns*: **education, stupidity, childhood**

-en, -ate, -ify, -ise, -ize
create *verbs*: **lengthen, domesticate, intensify**

A word may have more than one suffix: **help** + **-less** + **-ly** = *helplessly*, and *hope* + **-ful** + **-ness** = *hopefulness*.

Remember that the suffix **-ly** cannot be directly attached to adjectives ending in **-ic** so you must add **-ally** instead. For example, *tragic* becomes *tragically*, and *fantastic* becomes *fantastically*. The exception to this is *public* which becomes *publicly*.

Spelling changes

In most cases suffixes do not change the spelling at the end of the word they are attached to, especially if the suffix begins with a consonant. However, sometimes the word does change, for example by dropping an **e**, or doubling a consonant. These changes are like those made for verb and adjective inflections (see the Spelling Rules on p.390 for more information).

Sometimes the root word changes in a less predictable way. Can you spot the difference in these examples?

horror → horrify	curious → curiosity
abdomen → abdominal	pronounce → pronunciation

-ant or -ent?

Where there are two forms of a word, one ending with the suffix **-ant** and the other with **-ent**, the **-ant** word is usually the noun (*dependant*) and the **-ent** word is usually the adjective (*dependent*). However, you cannot rely on this as a rule, and for most words you must simply learn the correct spelling.

Suffixes continued

Shun sounds

Many words end with a 'shun' sound, which can be spelled in several ways.

-tion and -sion

The most common 'shun' suffix is **-tion**. **-sion** is often used where the base word ends in **d** or **de**, or **s** or **se**. These suffixes are often used when you form nouns from verbs:

explode → explosion   subtract → subtraction
confuse → confusion   introduce → introduction

-ation, -etion, -ition, -otion and -ution

'Shun' often follows a vowel sound as **-ation**, **-etion**, **-ition**, **-otion** or **-ution**. Where a base word has a clearly pronounced vowel, the same vowel sound is often heard in the new word. Say these words out loud to hear the similarities:

educate → education   dilute → dilution
promote → promotion   complete → completion

-cian

If you are changing a word which ends in **-ic**, **-ics** or **-ical**, you often add the suffix **-cian** to make the 'shun' sound. This often relates to people's occupations:

electric → electrician   mathematics → mathematician

Over to you

Turn the words in bold type into words with a 'shun' suffix. Remember to use the right one!

There was a **collide**_____ with another car. Dad had a **confront**_____ with the other driver, who shouted that Dad should see an **optic**_____. Dad said he drove with **considerate**_____ but he had a furious **express**_____ on his face. He said it would need a **magic**_____ to fix it, not a mechanic.

There are other, less common ways of spelling 'shun'. Can you think of any words which end with these 'shun' sounds:

-sian   -tian   -cion   -xion   -cean

suggest
suggestible
suggestion
suggestive
suggestively
suicidal
suicide
suit
  suited
  suiting

> ♦* Do not confuse
> with **soot** or **suite** *a*
> *suit of clothes • a suit of*
> *playing-cards • Does*
> *Wednesday suit you*
> *better?*

suitability
suitable
suitably
suitcase
suite

> ♦* Do not confuse
> with **suit** or **sweet** *a*
> *suite of rooms • a*
> *bedroom suite • a ballet*
> *suite*

suitor
sulk
sulkily
sulkiness
sulky
sullen
sullenness
sully
  sullies
  sullied
  sullying
sulphate
sulphur
sulphuric
sulphurous

sultan
sultana
sultrily
sultriness
sultry
sum
  summed
  summing

> ♦* Do not confuse
> with **some** *a difficult*
> *sum • to sum up*

summarily
summarize,
  summarise
  summarized,
  summarised
  summarizing,
  summarising
summary
  summaries

> ♦* Do not confuse
> with **summery** *a*
> *summary of the plot*

summer
summerhouse
summertime
summery

> ♦* Do not confuse
> with **summary** *a*
> *summery day • a*
> *summery dress*

summing-up
summit
summon
  summoned
  summoning
summons
  summonses
sumo
sumptuous

sun
  sunned
  sunning

> ♦* Do not confuse
> with **son** *The sun shone*
> *brightly • to sun*
> *yourself on the beach*

sunbathe
  sunbathed
  sunbathing
sunbeam
sunbed
sunburn
sunburned,
  sunburnt
sundae
sundial
sundries
sundry
sunflower
sung

> ♦* Do not confuse
> with **sang** *Have you*
> *ever sung this song*
> *before?*

sunglasses
sunk

> ♦* Do not confuse
> with **sank** *The ship has*
> *sunk*

sunken
sunlight
sunlit
sunnily
sunny
  sunnier
  sunniest
sunrise
sunroof
  sunroofs

Can't find your word? Try looking under **C**, **CH**, **PS**, **SC**, **SCH** or **SW**

sunset
sunshade
sunshine
sunspot
sunstroke
suntan
suntanned
suntrap
sup
 supped
 supping
super
superannuated
superannuation
superb
superbly
supercilious
superficial
superficiality
superficially
superfluity
superfluous
superhuman
superimpose
 superimposed
 superimposing
superintend
superintendence
superintendent
superior
superiority
superlative
superlatively
superman
 supermen
supermarket
supernatural
supernaturally
supernova
 supernovas
superpower
superscript

supersede
 superseded
 superseding

> **❶** Semi-**de**tached houses will super**sede** all others.

supersonic
superstar
superstition
superstitious
superstitiously
superstructure
supervise
 supervised
 supervising
supervision
supervisor
supervisory
superwoman
 superwomen
supper
supplant
supple
supplement
supplementary
suppleness
suppliant
supplicant
supplicate
 supplicated
 supplicating
supplication
supplier
supply
 supplies
 supplied
 supplying
support
supporter
supportive
suppose

supposed
supposing
supposed
supposedly
supposition
suppository
suppress
suppression
supremacy
supreme
supremely
surcharge
sure
sure-fire
sure-footed
surely
surety
 sureties
surf
surface
 surfaced
 surfacing
surfboard
surfeit
surfer
surfing
surge
 surged
 surging

> **☀** Do not confuse with **serge** *a surge of enthusiasm • The crowd surged forward*

surgeon
surgery
 surgeries
surgical
surgically
surliness
surly
 surlier

Can't find your word? Try looking under **C**, **CH**, **PS**, **SC**, **SCH** or **SW**

surliest
surlily
surmise
surmised
surmising
surmount
surmountable
surname
surpass
surplice

💧* Do not confuse with **surplus** *a priest's surplice*

surplus
surpluses

💧* Do not confuse with **surplice** *a surplus of butter • surplus staff*

surprise
surprised
surprising

ⓘ You are [**u r**] in for a sur**prise** – I'm giving you a **rise**!

surprised
surprising
surreal
surrealism
surrealist
surrender
surrendered
surrendering
surreptitious
surrogacy
surrogate
surround
surroundings
surtax
surtitle
surveillance

survey
pl surveys
surveyed
surveying
surveyor
survival
survive
survived
surviving
survivor
susceptibility
susceptible
sushi
suspect
suspend
suspender
suspense
suspension
suspicion
suspicious
suspiciously
suss
sustain
sustained
sustaining
sustenance
suture
sutured
suturing
svelte
swab
swabbed
swabbing
swaddle
swaddled
swaddling
swag
swagger
swaggered
swaggering
swallow
swallowtail

swam

💧* Do not confuse with **swum** *She swam to his rescue*

swamp
swampy
swan
swank
swanky
swap, swop
swapped, swopped
swapping, swopping
swarm
swarthy
swashbuckling
swastika
swat
swatted
swatting

💧* Do not confuse with **swot** *to swat a fly*

swatch
swatches
swathe, swath
swathed
swathing

💧* The spelling **swath** is only used for the meaning 'a broad strip' *cut a swath*

swathed
sway
swayed
swaying
swear
swore
sworn
swearing
swear-word
sweat

Can't find your word? Try looking under **C, CH, PS, SC** or **SCH**

sweated
sweating
sweater
sweatshirt
sweaty
sweatier
sweatiest
swede

💣* Do not confuse
with **suede** *turnips and*
swedes

sweep
swept
sweeping
sweeper
sweeping
sweepstake
sweet

💣* Do not confuse
with **suite** *a sweet smile*
• a sweet orange •
sucking a sweet

sweetcorn
sweeten
sweetened
sweetening
sweetener
sweetheart
sweetie
sweetly
sweetmeat
sweetness
sweet-toothed
swell
swelled
swollen
swelling
swelling
swelter
sweltered
sweltering

swept
swerve
swerved
swerving
swift
swiftly
swiftness
swig
swigged
swigging
swill
swim
swam
swum
swimming
swimmer
swimming
swimming-bath
swimming costume
swimmingly
swimming-pool
swimsuit
swindle
swindled
swindling
swindler
swine
swing
swung
swinging
swingeing

💣* Do not confuse
with **swinging**
swingeing cuts in
expenditure

swinger
swinging

💣* Do not confuse
with **swingeing** *the*
swinging sixties •
swinging her arms

swipe
swiped
swiping
swirl
swish
switch
switches
switchback
switchboard
swivel
swivelled
swivelling
swizz
swollen
swoon
swooned
swooning
swoop
swooped
swooping
swop
another spelling of
swap
sword
swordfish
swordsman
swordsmen
swordsmanship
swore
sworn
swot
swotted
swotting

💣* Do not confuse
with **swat** *to swot for an*
exam

swum

💣* Do not confuse
with **swam** *He has*
swum eight lengths

swung

Can't find your word? Try looking under **C**, **CH**, **PS**, **SC** or **SCH**

SPELLING  focus

Syllables and Phonemes

Syllables

A *syllable* is a word or part of a word containing a single vowel sound, often with a consonant at one or both ends.

The word *happiness* has three syllables (*hap-pi-ness*); the word *painful* has two syllables (*pain-ful*); the word *find* has one syllable. The syllables of a word are like the beats of music. Breaking a word down into separate syllables can help you to learn its spelling.

• How many syllables does the word *education* have?

• Can you think of a word with six syllables?

• Name at least four birds with two syllables each, and at least three fruits and vegetables with three syllables each.

• Look around you and make a list of everything you can see that has four syllables.

Phonemes

A *phoneme* is the smallest unit of sound in a word. Phonemes are often spelt with single letters, but can also be spelt with combinations of letters making a single sound, such as **sh**, **ch**, **ea** or **oo**. (A combination of two letters that make a single sound is called a *digraph*.) The word *cat* has three phonemes (*c-a-t*), and so does the word *mouse* (*m-ou-se*). The word *stop* has four phonemes (*s-t-o-p*), and so does the word *rhythm* (*rh-y-th-m*). How many phonemes does the word *elephant* have?

Can you put the following words into pairs with the same number of phonemes (for example *t-w-i-g* and *s-n-a-tch*)?

> twig committee hip through snatch
>
> out ability two remember engines

Phonemes can cause spelling problems because the same phoneme may be spelt in different ways: **f** and **ph**, **ch** and **tch**, **ee** and **ea**, and **ow** and **ou**. The panels on Letter Patterns and Vowels both give further information about different spellings of the same sound.

sycamore
sycophant
sycophantic
syllabic
syllable
syllabub
syllabus
syllabuses, syllabi
sylph
symbiosis
symbiotic
symbol

♦ Do not confuse
with **cymbal** *a*
mathematical symbol •
a symbol of the king's
authority

symbolic
symbolically
symbolise
another spelling of
symbolize
symbolism
symbolize,
symbolise
symbolized,
symbolised
symbolizing,
symbolising
symmetrical
symmetrically
symmetry
sympathetic
sympathetically
sympathize,

sympathise
sympathized,
sympathised
sympathizing,
sympathising
sympathy
sympathies
symphonic
symphony
symphonies
symposium
symposia,
symposiums
symptom
symptomatic
synagogue
synchronic
synchronization,
synchronisation
synchronize,
synchronise
synchronized,
synchronised
synchronizing,
synchronising
syncopate
syncopated
syncopating
syncopation
syndicate
syndrome
synergy
synod
synonym
synonymous

synopsis
synopses
syntactic
syntactical
syntax
synthesis
synthesize,
synthesise
synthesized,
synthesised
synthesizing,
synthesising
synthesizer,
synthesiser
synthetic
synthetically
syphilis
syphon
another spelling of
siphon
syringe
syringed
syringing
syrup
syrupy
system
systematic
systematically
systematize,
systematise
systematized,
systematised
systematizing,
systematising
systemic

Can't find your word? Try looking under **C, CH, PS, SC, SCH** or **SW**

Tt

If you can't find the word you're looking for under **T**, it could be that it starts with a different letter. Try looking under **PT** for words like *pterodactyl*. Also, don't forget **TH** for words like *thyme*.

ta
tab
tabby
 tabbies
tabernacle
table
 tabled
 tabling
tableau
 tableaux
tablecloth
tablespoon
tablespoonful
 tablespoonfuls
tablet
tableware
tabloid
taboo
tabular
tabulate
 tabulated
 tabulating
tabulation
tachograph
tacit
taciturn
tack
tackle
 tackled
 tackling
tacky

taco
tact
tactful
tactfully
tactic
tactical
tactically
tactician
tactics
tactile
tactless
tactlessly
tadpole
tae kwon do
taffeta
tag
 tagged
 tagging
tagliatelle
t'ai chi, tai chi
tail
 tailed
 tailing

> ●* Do not confuse
> with **tale** *a dog's tail* •
> *Did the police tail him?*

tailback
tailless
tailor
 tailored
 tailoring

tailor-made
taint
take
 took
 taken
 taking
takeaway
take-off
takeover
takings
talc
talcum powder
tale

> ●* Do not confuse
> with **tail** *a fairy tale*

talent
talented
talisman
 talismans
talk
talkative
tall
tallboy
tallness
tallow
tally
 tallies
 tallied
 tallying
tally-ho

talon
tamarind
tambourine
tame
 tamed
 taming
tamely
tamer
tamper
 tampered
 tampering
tampon
tan
 tanned
 tanning
tandem
tandoori
tang
tangent
tangential
tangerine
tangible
tangibly
tangle
 tangled
 tangling
tango
 pl tangos
 tangoed
 tangoing
tangy
tank
tankard
tanker
tanned
tannery
 tanneries
tannin
tanning
tantalize, tantalise
 tantalized,
 tantalised

tantalizing,
 tantalising
**tantalizing,
 tantalising**
tantamount
tantrum
tap
 tapped
 tapping
tapas
tap-dance
 tap-danced
 tap-dancing
tap-dancer
tape
 taped
 taping
taper
 tapered
 tapering

♦* Do not confuse
with **tapir** *a lighted
taper • to taper to a
point*

tape recorder
tape recording
tapestry
 tapestries
tapeworm
tapioca
tapir

♦* Do not confuse
with **taper** *A tapir
resembles a large pig*

tapped
tapping
tar
 tarred
 tarring
taramasalata
tarantula

tardily
tardy
target
 targeted
 targeting
tariff
tarmac
 tarmacked
 tarmacking
tarn
tarnish
tarot
tarpaulin
tarragon
tarred
tarring
tarry
 tarries
 tarried
 tarrying
tart
tartan
tartar
task
taskmaster
tassel
 tasselled
taste
 tasted
 tasting
tasteful
tastefully
tasteless
taster
tasty
 tastier
 tastiest
tattered
tatters
tattle
 tattled
 tattling

Can't find your word? Try looking under **PT** or **TH**

tattoo
tattooed
tattooing
tattooist
tatty
tattier
tattiest
taught

💧 Do not confuse
with **taut** *She taught French*

taunt
taunting
taut

💧 Do not confuse
with **taught** *The rope is taut*

tauten
tautened
tautening
tautological
tautologous
tautology
tavern
taverna
tawdry
tawny
tax
taxes
taxable
taxation
taxi
pl taxis
taxied
taxiing, taxying
taxicab
taxidermist
taxidermy
taxonomic
taxonomy
taxpayer

tea

💧 Do not confuse
with **tee** *a cup of tea*

teacake
teach
taught
teaching
teachable
teacher
teaching
tea cosy
teacup
teak
teal
team
teamed
teaming

💧 Do not confuse
with **teem** *a football team • to team up with one of your classmates*

teamwork
teapot
tear
tore
torn
tearing

💧 Do not confuse
with **tier** *He wiped a tear from his eye • tear gas*

tearaway
teardrop
tearful
tear-jerker
tea room
tease
teased
teasing
teasel

teaser
teaspoon
teaspoonful
teaspoonfuls
teat
technical
technicality
technicalities
technically
technician
technique

ℹ What's your technique for choosing nice questions?

techno
technocrat
technological
technologically
technologist
technology
technologies
tectonics
teddy
teddies
tedious
tedium
tee
teed
teeing

💧 Do not confuse
with **tea** *a golf tee • to tee off at the first hole*

teem
teemed
teeming

💧 Do not confuse
with **team** *to teem with rain • to teem with fish*

teen
teenage

Can't find your word? Try looking under **PT** or **TH**

teenager
teens
teeny
teenybopper
teeny-weeny
teepee
another spelling of
tepee
tee-shirt, T-shirt
teeter
teetered
teetering
teeth

> ✎* Do not confuse
> with **teethe** *Brush your
> teeth after meals*

teethe
teethed
teething

> ✎* Do not confuse
> with **teeth** *The baby
> has begun to teethe*

teetotal
teetotaller
telebanking
telecommunication
telecommunications
telecommuting
teleconferencing
telegram
telegraph
telegraphic
telemarketing
telepathic
telepathically
telepathy
telephone
telephoned
telephoning
telephonist
telephoto

telesales
telescope
telescoped
telescoping
telescopic
telescopically
teletext
televise
televised
televising
television
televisual
teleworker
teleworking
telex
telexes
tell
told
telling
teller
telling
telly
tellies
temerity
temp
temper
tempered
tempering
temperament
temperamental
temperamentally
temperance
temperate
temperature

> ⓘ Don't lose your
> **temper** at high
> **temper**atures.

tempest
tempestuous
template
temple

tempo
tempos
temporal
temporary
temporize,
  temporise
temporized,
temporised
temporizing,
temporising
tempt
temptation
tempter
tempting
temptress
temptresses
tempura
ten
tenable
tenacious
tenacity
tenancy
tenancies
tenant
tend
tendency
tendencies
tender
tendered
tendering
tenderize, tenderise
tenderized,
tenderised
tenderizing,
tenderising
tenderizer,
  tenderiser
tendinitis,
  tendonitis
tendon
tendril
tenement

Can't find your word? Try looking under **PT** or **TH**

tenet
tenner

> ●* Do not confuse
> with **tenor** or **tenure**
> *Can you give me
> change for a tenner?*

tennis
tenor

> ●* Do not confuse
> with **tenner** or **tenure** *a
> tenor and a soprano* •
> *The general tenor of the
> report was optimistic*

tenpin bowling
tense
 tensed
 tensing
tensely
tensile
tension
tent
tentacle
tentative
tentatively
tenterhooks
tenth
tenuous
tenure

> ●* Do not confuse
> with **tenner** or **tenor**
> *land tenure*

tepee, teepee
tepid
tequila
tercentenary
term
terminal
terminate
 terminated
 terminating

termination
terminology
terminus
 terminuses, termini
termite
tern
ternary
terrace
terraced
terracing
terracotta
terra firma
terrain
terrapin
terrestrial
terrible
terribly
terrier
terrific
terrifically
terrify
 terrifies
 terrified
 terrifying
terrine
territorial
territory
 territories
terror
terrorise
 another spelling of
 terrorize
terrorism
terrorist
terrorize, terrorise
 terrorized,
 terrorised
 terrorizing,
 terrorising
terse
tersely
terseness

tertiary
tessellate
 tessellated
 tessellating
tessellation
test
testament
testator
test-drive
 test-drove
 test-driven
 test-driving
tester
testes
testicle
testicular
testify
 testifies
 testified
 testifying
testily
testimonial

> ●* Do not confuse
> with **testimony** *a
> testimonial from her
> previous employer*

testimony
 testimonies

> ●* Do not confuse
> with **testimonial** *the
> testimony of the witness*

testiness
testing
testosterone
testy
tetanus
tetchy
tête-à-tête
tether
 tethered
 tethering

Can't find your word? Try looking under **PT** or **TH**

text
textbook
textile
textual
texture
than
thank
thankful
thankfully
thankless
thanks
thanksgiving
that
thatch
thaw
the
theatre
theatrical
theatricality
theatrically
thee
theft
their

🖋* Do not confuse
with **there** or **they're**
They lost their way

theirs
theism
theist
them
theme
themselves
then
thence
thenceforth
theocracy
theocratic
theologian
theological
theology
theorem

theoretic
theoretical
theoretically
theorist
theorize, theorise
 theorized, theorised
 theorizing,
 theorising
theory
 theories
therapeutic
therapist
therapy
 therapies
there

🖋* Do not confuse
with **their** or **they're**
There is nobody there
Remember **here** and
there.

thereabouts
thereafter
thereby
therefore
therein
thereof
thereto
thereunder
thereupon
therm
thermal
thermometer
thermonuclear
Thermos®
thermostat
thesaurus
 thesauruses,
 thesauri
these
thesis
 theses

thespian
they
they'd
they'll
they're

🖋* **They're** is a short
form of **they are**. Do
not confuse with **their**
or **there** *They're
coming today*

they've
thiamine
thick
thicken
 thickened
 thickening
thicket
thickhead
thick-headed
thickness
 thicknesses
thickset
thick-skinned
thief
 thieves
thieving
thievish
thigh
thimble
thin
 thinner
 thinnest
 thinned
 thinning
thine
thing
thingummy
thingummybob
thingummyjig
think
 thought

Can't find your word? Try looking under **PT**

thinking
thinly
thinness
third
third-rate
thirst
thirstily
thirsty
thirstier
thirstiest
thirteen
thirteenth
thirtieth
thirty
thirties
this
thistle
thither
thong
thorax
thoraxes, thoraces
thorn
thorny
thorough

💧* Do not confuse
with **through** *a
thorough search*

thoroughbred
thoroughfare
thoroughgoing
thoroughly
those
thou
though
thought
thoughtful
thoughtfully
thoughtfulness
thoughtless
thousand
thousandth

thrall
thrash

💧* Do not confuse
with **thresh** *Did he
thrash you?* • *to thrash
out a problem*

thread
threadbare
threat
threaten
threatened
threatening
three
threepence
threepenny
thresh

💧* Do not confuse
with **thrash** *to thresh
corn*

thresher
threshold
threw

💧* Do not confuse
with **through** *He threw
the ball*

thrice
thrift
thriftily
thrifty
thriftier
thriftiest
thrill
thriller
thrilling
thrive
thrived, throve
thrived, thriven
thriving
throat
throaty

throb
throbbed
throbbing
throes

💧* Do not confuse
with **throws** *in the
throes of moving house*

thrombosis
throne

💧* Do not confuse
with **thrown** *the king
on his throne*

throng
throttle
throttled
throttling
through

💧* Do not confuse
with **thorough** or
threw *through the door*

throughout
throw
pl throws
threw
thrown
throwing

💧* Do not confuse
throws with **throes**
three throws of the dice

throwaway
throwback
thrown

💧* Do not confuse
with **throne** *I've
thrown it away*

thrush
thrushes
thrust
thrust

Can't find your word? Try looking under **PT**

thrusting
thud
thudded
thudding
thug
thuggery
thuggish
thumb
thumbscrew
thumbtack
thump
thunder
thundered
thundering
thunderbolt
thunderclap
thunderous
thunderstorm
thunderstruck
thundery
thus
thwack
thwart
thy
thyme

♦* Do not confuse with **time** *season the sauce with thyme*

thyroid
tiara
tic

♦* Do not confuse with **tick** *a nervous tic*

tick

♦* Do not confuse with **tic** *I'll be ready in a tick • bitten by a tick • to tick the correct answer • Clocks tick*

ticker

ticker-tape
ticket
ticking
ticking-off
tickle
tickled
tickling
ticklish
tickly
tidal
tiddler
tiddlywinks
tide
tided
tiding
tidemark
tidily
tidiness
tidings
tidy
tidier
tidiest
tidies
tidied
tidying
tie
tied
tying
tie-breaker
tie-dyed
tiepin
tier

♦* Do not confuse with **tear** *a tier of seats in the theatre • a wedding cake with three tiers*

tiff
tiger
tight
tighten

tightened
tightening
tight-fisted
tight-lipped
tightly
tightness
tightrope
tights
tigress
tigresses
tikka
tile
tiled
tiling
tiler
till
tiller
tilt
timber

♦* Do not confuse with **timbre** *The timber is rotting*

timbre

♦* Do not confuse with **timber** *the timbre of his voice*

time
timed
timing

♦* Do not confuse with **thyme** *What time is it? • to time a race*

timekeeper
timeless
timely
timepiece
timer
time-share
time-sharing
timetable

Can't find your word? Try looking under **PT**

timetabled
timetabling
timid
timidity
timidly
timorous
timpani, tympani
timpanist,
 tympanist
tin
 tinned
 tinning
tincture
tinder
tine
tinfoil
tinge
 tinged
 tinging, tingeing
tingle
 tingled
 tingling
tingly
tinker
 tinkered
 tinkering
tinkle
 tinkled
 tinkling
tinned
tinning
tinnitus
tinny
tin-opener
tinsel
tint
tiny
 tinier
 tiniest
tip
 tipped
 tipping

tip-off
Tipp-Ex®
tipple
 tippled
 tippling
tippler
tipsy
tiptoe
 tiptoed
 tiptoeing
tiptop
tirade
tire
 tired
 tiring

💧* Do not confuse
with **tyre** *The runner
began to tire • Did the
journey tire you?*

tired
tiredness
tireless
tiresome
tiring
tiro, tyro
 tiros, tyros
'tis
tissue
tit
titanic
titanium
titbit
tithe
titillate
 titillated
 titillating
titillation
title
 titled
titter
 tittered

tittering
tittle-tattle
titular
tizzy
to

💧* Do not confuse
with **too** or **two** *I have
to go to the bank*

toad
toad-in-the-hole
toadstool
toady
 toadies
 toadied
 toadying
toast
toasted
toaster
tobacco
tobacconist
toboggan
 tobogganed
 tobogganing
toccata
today
toddle
 toddled
 toddling
toddler
toddy
 toddies
to-do
 to-dos
toe
 toed
 toeing

💧* Do not confuse
with **tow** *She stubbed
her toe on a rock*

toenail
toff

Can't find your word? Try looking under **PT** or **TH**

toffee
tofu
toga
together
togetherness
toggle
 toggled
 toggling
toil
 toiled
 toiling
toilet
toiletries
token
tokenism
told
tolerable
tolerably
tolerance
tolerant
tolerate
 tolerated
 tolerating
toleration
toll
tollgate
tomahawk
tomato
 tomatoes
tomb

> ♦* Do not confuse
> with **tome** *A tome is a
> large book*

tombola
tomboy
tombstone
tomcat
tome

> ♦* Do not confuse
> with **tomb** *A tomb is
> the tomb of the late king*

tomfoolery
tomorrow

> ⓘ **Toma**toes **r**ipen in
> **rows.**

tomtom
ton

> ♦* Do not confuse
> with **tonne** or **tun** *a ton
> of coal* • *A ton is 2240
> pounds*

tonal
tone
 toned
 toning
tone-deaf
tongs
tongue
tongue-tied
tongue-twister
tonic
tonight
tonnage
tonne

> ♦* Do not confuse
> with **ton** or **tun** *a tonne
> is 1000 kilograms* A
> **tonne** is also called a
> **metric ton**.

tonsil
tonsillectomy
tonsillitis
tonsure
too

> ♦* Do not confuse
> with **to** or **two** *My
> sister wants some too* •
> *too much work*
> Remember that **too**
> means 'also', so add
> another **o**.

took
tool
toolbox
 toolboxes
toolkit
toot
 tooted
 tooting
tooth
 teeth
toothache
toothbrush
 toothbrushes
toothless
toothpaste
toothpick
toothy
tootle
 tootled
 tootling
top
 topped
 topping
topaz
top-heavy
topiary
topic
topical
topically
topless
topmost
top-notch
topographical
topography
topped
topping
topple
 toppled
 toppling
top-secret
topside
topsoil

Can't find your word? Try looking under **PT** or **TH**

topspin
topsy-turvy
torch
  torches
torchlight
torchlit
tore
toreador
torment
tormentor
torn
tornado
  tornadoes
torpedo
  pl torpedoes
  torpedoed
  torpedoing
torpid
torpor
torrent
torrential
torrid
torsion
torso
  torsos
tortilla
tortoise
tortoiseshell
tortuous

> ♦* Do not confuse
> with **torturous** *a*
> *tortuous road through*
> *the mountains • a novel*
> *with a tortuous plot*

torture
  tortured
  torturing
torturous

> ♦* Do not confuse
> with **tortuous** *a*
> *torturous ordeal*

Tory
  Tories
toss
  tosses
toss-up
tot
  totted
  totting
total
  totalled
  totalling
totalitarian
totality
totally
totem
totter
  tottered
  tottering
toucan
touch
  touches
touch-and-go
touchdown
touché
touched
touchily
touchiness
touching
touchline
touchpaper
touch-type
  touch-typed
  touch-typing
touchy
tough
toughen
  toughened
  toughening
toughness
toupee
tour
  toured

touring
tourism
tourist
touristy
tournament
tourniquet
tousled
tout
  touted
  touting
tow

> ♦* Do not confuse
> with **toe** *to tow a car*

toward
towards
towbar
towel
  towelled
  towelling
towelling
tower
  towered
  towering
towering
town
township
towpath
towrope
toxic
toxicity
toxicologist
toxicology
toxin
toy
  toyed
  toying
trace
  traced
  tracing
traceable
tracery

Can't find your word? Try looking under **PT** or **TH**

Proofreading your Work

No matter how good you are at spelling, you should always proofread what you have written. This does not mean a quick glance over the text – you must read each word slowly and carefully, preferably with a ruler under the line, paying particular attention to tricky words such as homophones.

You may sometimes find it useful to cover half of a long word with your finger while you read the other half, or to read it syllable by syllable to make sure there are no letters missing, for example *artifical* for *artificial* or *accomodate* for *accommodate*.

trachea	**tragic**	**tramp**
tracing	**tragically**	**trample**
track	**tragicomedy**	trampled
tracksuit	**trail**	trampling
tract	trailed	**trampoline**
tractable	trailing	**tramway**
traction	**trailblazer**	**trance**
tractor	**trailer**	**tranquil**
trade	**train**	**tranquillise**
traded	trained	*another spelling of*
trading	training	**tranquillize**
trademark	**trainee**	**tranquilliser**
tradename	**trainer**	*another spelling of*
trader	**training**	**tranquillizer**
tradesman	**trainspotter**	**tranquillity**
tradesmen	**trainspotting**	**tranquillize,**
trade union	**traipse**	**tranquillise**
trade unionist	traipsed	tranquillized,
tradition	traipsing	tranquillised
traditional	**trait**	tranquillizing,
traditionalism	**traitor**	tranquillising
traditionalist	**traitorous**	**tranquillizer,**
traditionally	**trajectory**	**tranquilliser**
traffic	trajectories	**tranquilly**
trafficked	**tram**	**transact**
trafficking	**tramcar**	**transaction**
trafficker	**tramline**	**transatlantic**
tragedian	**trammel**	**transcend**
tragedy	trammelled	**transcendence**
tragedies	trammelling	**transcendent**

Can't find your word? Try looking under **PT** or **TH**

transcendental
transcribe
transcribed
transcribing
transcript
transcription
transept
transfer
transferred
transferring
transferable
transference
transfiguration
transfigure
transfigured
transfiguring
transfix
transform
transformation
transformer
transfuse
transfused
transfusing
transfusion
transgress
transgression
transgressor
transience
transient
transistor
transit
transition
transitional
transitive
transitorily
transitory
translate
translated
translating
translation
translator
transliterate

transliterated
transliterating
transliteration
translucence
translucent
transmissible
transmission
transmit
transmitted
transmitting
transmitter
transmute
transmuted
transmuting
transparency
transparencies
transparent
transpire
transpired
transpiring
transplant
transplantation
transport
transportation
transporter
transpose
transposed
transposing
transposition
transverse
transvestite
trap
trapped
trapping
trapdoor
trapeze
trapezium
trapeziums, trapezia
trapezoid
trapper
trappings
trash

trashy
trauma
traumatic
traumatize,
traumatise
traumatized,
traumatised
traumatizing,
traumatising
travel
travelled
travelling
traveller
travelogue
traverse
traversed
traversing
travesty
travesties
trawl
trawler
tray
treacherous
treachery
treacheries
treacle
tread
trod
trodden
treadle
treadmill
treason
treasonable
treasure
treasured
treasuring
treasurer
treasury
treasuries
treat
treated
treating

Can't find your word? Try looking under **PT** or **TH**

treaties

> ♦* Do not confuse with **treatise** *treaties signed after the war*

treatise

> ♦* Do not confuse with **treaties** *a philosophical treatise*

treatment
treaty
 treaties
treble
 trebled
 trebling
tree
tree-trunk
trefoil
trek
 trekked
 trekking
trellis
 trellises
tremble
 trembled
 trembling
tremendous
tremolo
 tremolos
tremor
tremulous
trench
 trenches
trenchant
trend
trendsetter
trendy
 trendier
 trendiest
trepidation
trespass
 trespasses

trespasser
tress
 tresses
trestle
triad
trial
triangle
triangular
triangulate
 triangulated
 triangulating
triangulation
triathlete
triathlon
tribal
tribalism
tribe
tribesman
 tribesmen
tribeswoman
 tribeswomen
tribulation
tribunal
tribune
tributary
 tributaries
tribute
trice
triceps
trick
trickery
trickle
 trickled
 trickling
trickster
tricky
 trickier
 trickiest
tricolour
tricycle
trident
tried

triennial
trier
tries
trifle
 trifled
 trifling
trifling
trigger
 triggered
 triggering
trigger-happy
trigonometry
trike
trilby
 trilbies
trilingual
trill
trillion
trilogy
 trilogies
trim
 trimmed
 trimming
trimmer
trimming
Trinity
trinket
trio
 trios
trip
 tripped
 tripping
tripe
triple
 tripled
 tripling
triplet
triplicate
tripod
tripped
tripper
tripping

Can't find your word? Try looking under **PT** or **TH**

tripwire
trisect
trisection
trite
triumph
triumphal
triumphant
triumphantly
trivet
trivia
trivial
triviality
 trivialities
trivialize, trivialise
 trivialized,
 trivialised
 trivializing,
 trivialising
trod
trodden
troll
trolley
 trolleys
trombone
trombonist
troop
 trooped
 trooping

> ♦* Do not confuse
> with **troupe** *a troop of*
> *soldiers* • *to troop out of*
> *the hall*

trooper
trophy
 trophies
tropic
tropical
trot
 trotted
 trotting
trotters

troubadour
trouble
 troubled
 troubling
troublemaker
troubleshooter
troubleshooting
troublesome
trough
trounce
 trounced
 trouncing
troupe

> ♦* Do not confuse
> with **troop** *a troupe of*
> *actors*

trousers
trousseau
 trousseaux,
 trousseaus
trout
trove
trowel
truancy
truant
truce
truck
trucker
trudge
 trudged
 trudging
true
truffle
truism
truly

> ❶ Answer t**ruly** – are
> you [**r u**] **l**ying?

trump
trumpet
 trumpeted
 trumpeting

truncated
truncheon
trundle
 trundled
 trundling
trunk
truss
 trusses
trust
trustee
trustful
trustfully
trusting
trustworthy
trusty
truth
truthful
truthfully
truthfulness
try
 tries
 tried
 trying
tryst
tsar, tzar, czar
tsarina, tzarina,
 czarina
tsetse
T-shirt
 another spelling of
 tee-shirt
tsunami
 tsunami, tsunamis
tub
tuba
tubby
tube
tuber
tuberculin
tuberculosis
tubing
tubular

Can't find your word? Try looking under **PT** or **TH**

tuck
tuffet
tuft
tug
 tugged
 tugging
tug-of-war
tuition
tulip
tulle
tumble
 tumbled
 tumbling
tumbledown
tumble-dryer,
 tumble-drier
tumbler
tumbleweed
tummy
 tummies
tummy-button
tumour
tumult
tumultuous
tumulus
 tumuli
tun

> ◆* Do not confuse
> with **ton** or **tonne** *A tun*
> *is a large cask*

tuna
tundra
tune
 tuned
 tuning
tuneful
tunefully
tuneless
tuner
tungsten
tunic

tuning
tunnel
 tunnelled
 tunnelling
tunny
 tunny, tunnies
tuppence
turban

> ◆* Do not confuse
> with **turbine** *He wore a*
> *turban on his head*

turbid
turbine

> ◆* Do not confuse
> with **turban** *a turbine*
> *engine • a wind turbine*

turbocharged
turbojet
turbot
turbulence
turbulent
tureen
turf
 turfs, turves
turgid
turkey
 turkeys
turmeric
turmoil
turn
turnaround
turncoat
turning
turning-point
turnip
turnoff
turn-on
turnout
turnover
turnpike
turnstile

turntable
turpentine
turpitude
turquoise
turret
turreted
turtle
turtledove
turtleneck
tusk
tussle
 tussled
 tussling
tussock
tut
 tutted
 tutting
tutor
tutorial
tutu
 tutus
tuxedo
 tuxedos, tuxedoes
twaddle
twain
twang
tweak
twee
tweed
tweedy
tweet
 tweeted
 tweeting
tweezers
twelfth
twelve
twentieth
twenty
 twenties
twerp
twice
twiddle

Can't find your word? Try looking under **PT** or **TH**

twiddled
twiddling
twig
twilight
twill
twin
twinned
twinning
twine
twined
twining
twinge
twinkle
twinkled
twinkling
twinkling
twinset
twirl
twist
twisted
twister
twit
twitch
twitches
twitchy
twitter
twittered
twittering
twittery
two

> ✱ Do not confuse with **to** or **too** *two apples*

two-edged
two-faced
twofold
twopence
twopenny

twosome
two-step
two-time
two-timed
two-timing
two-timer
two-way
tycoon

> ✱ Do not confuse with **typhoon** *a business tycoon*

tying
tympani
another spelling of **timpani**
tympanist
another spelling of **timpanist**
type
typed
typing
typecast
typecast
typecasting
typeface
typescript
typeset
typeset
typesetting
typesetter
typewriter
typewritten
typhoid
typhoon

> ✱ Do not confuse with **tycoon** *The ship was sunk in a typhoon*

typhus
typical
typically
typify
typifies
typified
typifying
typing
typist
typo
typographer
typographic
typographical
typography
tyrannical
tyrannically
tyrannize, tyrannise
tyrannized, tyrannised
tyrannizing, tyrannising
tyrannosaur
tyrannous
tyranny
tyrannies
tyrant
tyre

> ✱ Do not confuse with **tire** *a tyre for the car*

tyro
another spelling of **tiro**
tzar
another spelling of **tsar**
tzarina
another spelling of **tsarina**

Can't find your word? Try looking under **PT** or **TH**

U*n*

ubiquitous
ubiquity
udder
ufology
ugh
ugliness
ugly
 uglier
 ugliest
ukulele, ukelele
ulcer
ulcerate
 ulcerated
 ulcerating
ulceration
ulcerous
ulterior
ultimate
ultimately
ultimatum
 ultimatums,
 ultimata
ultramarine
ultrasonic
ultrasound
ultraviolet
umber
umbilical
umbrage
umbrella
umlaut
umpire
 umpired
 umpiring

umpteen
umpteenth
unabashed
unable
unaccountable
unaccountably
unaccustomed
unadulterated
unaffected
unalienable
unanimity
unanimous
unanimously
unapproachable
unarmed
unassuming
unattached
unattended
unaware

> ●* Do not confuse
> with **unawares** *I was
> unaware of his
> presence*

unawares

> ●* Do not confuse
> with **unaware** *The blow
> caught him unawares*

unbalanced
unbearable
unbeknownst
unbelievable
unbelieving
unbend

unbent
unbending
unblock
unborn
unbounded
unbridled
unburden
 unburdened
 unburdening
uncalled for
uncannily
uncanniness
uncanny
uncared for
unceremonious
unceremoniously
uncertain
uncertainty
uncharted
unclasp
uncle
unclean
unclear
unclothed
uncoil
 uncoiled
 uncoiling
uncomfortable
uncommon
uncommonly
uncompromising
unconcern
unconditional
unconscious

unconsciously
unconstitutional
uncork
uncouth
uncover
  uncovered
  uncovering
undaunted
undecided
undeniable
undeniably
under
underachieve
  underachieved
  underachieving
underachiever
under-age
underarm
underbelly
undercarriage
underclothes
undercover
undercurrent
undercut
  undercut
  undercutting
underdeveloped
underdog
underdone
underestimate
  underestimated
  underestimating
underfoot
undergarment
undergo
  underwent
  undergone
  undergoing
undergraduate
underground
undergrowth
underhand

underlay
underlie
  underlay
  underlain
  underlying
underline
  underlined
  underlining
underling
underlying
undermine
  undermined
  undermining
underneath
undernourished
underpants
underpass
  underpasses
underpay
  underpaid
  underpaying
underpin
  underpinned
  underpinning
underprivileged
underrate
  underrated
  underrating
underside
undersigned
undersized
underskirt
understaffed
understand
  understood
  understanding
understandable
understandably
understanding
understate
  understated
  understating

understatement
understood
understudy
  understudies
  understudied
  understudying
undertake
  undertook
  undertaken
  undertaking
undertaker
undertaking
undertone
undertook
undertow
undervalue
  undervalued
  undervaluing
underwater
underwear
underweight
underwent
underworld
underwrite
  underwrote
  underwritten
  underwriting
underwriter
undesirable
undid
undies
undivided
undo
  undid
  undone
  undoing
undone
undoing
undoubted
undoubtedly
undress
undue

Mnemonics

A mnemonic (*ni-mon-ik*) is a rhyme or guide which helps you to remember something. One well-known mnemonic helps you remember the points of the compass clockwise:

Naughty Elephants Squirt Water
(north, east, south, west)

Can you think of any more?

Mnemonics can also help you to remember difficult spellings, which is why the Worst Words Hit List in this book uses them. Think about what makes a good mnemonic. The best are short, simple and catchy, and often make you smile! They create a vivid picture in your head, maybe by using words to do with colours, sounds or animals.

Some of the most helpful mnemonics are ones that you make up yourself. Try to think of a mnemonic for each of these words:

ought   geography   soldier

---

undulate
undulated
undulating
undulation
unduly
undying
unearth
unearthly
unease
uneasily
uneasiness
uneasy
uneconomical
unemployed
unemployment
unenviable
unequal
unequalled
unequivocal
unequivocally
unerring
uneven
uneventful
unexceptionable

unexceptional
unexpected
unfailing
unfair
unfairly
unfaithful
unfasten
  unfastened
  unfastening
unfathomable
unfavourable
unfeeling
unfit
unflagging
unflappable
unflinching
unfold
unforgettable
unforgettably
unfortunate
unfortunately

---
❶ **Tuna** tastes
especially lovely.
---

unfounded
unfunny
unfurl
ungainly
ungracious
ungrateful
ungratefully
unguarded
unhappily
unhappiness
unhappy
  unhappier
  unhappiest
unhealthily
unhealthy
unheard-of
unhelpful
unhinged
unholy
unicorn
unicycle
unidentified
unification
uniform

uniformed
uniformity
unify
 unifies
 unified
 unifying
unilateral
uninhibited
uninitiated
uninspired
uninspiring
uninterested
uninterrupted
union
unionist
unique
uniquely
uniqueness
unisex
unison
unit
unitary
unite
 united
 uniting
united
unity
universal
universally
universe
university
 universities
unkempt
unkind
unknown
unleaded
unleash
unleavened
unless
unlike
unlikely
unlimited

unlit
unload
unlock
unloose
 unloosed
 unloosing
unloved
unluckily
unlucky
 unluckier
 unluckiest
unmade
unmanly
unmarried
unmask
unmentionable
unmistakable,
 unmistakeable
unmistakably,
 unmistakeably
unmitigated
unmoved
unnamed
unnatural
unnecessarily
unnecessary
unnerve
 unnerved
 unnerving
unobtrusive
unobtrusively
unpack
unpaid
unpalatable
unparalleled
unpick
unpleasant
unpleasantness
unplug
 unplugged
 unplugging
unpopular

unpractised
unprecedented
unpremeditated
unprepossessing
unpretentious
unprincipled
unprintable
unprofessional
unqualified
unquestionable
unquestioning
unravel
 unravelled
 unravelling
unreal
unrelenting
unremitting
unrequited
unrest
unrivalled
unruffled
unruliness
unruly
unsafe
unsavoury
unscathed
unscrew
unscrupulous
unseen
unselfish
unsettle
 unsettled
 unsettling
unsettled
unsettling
unsightly
unskilled
unsociable
unsolicited
unsophisticated
unsound
unsounded

unspeakable
unspeakably
unstable
unstinting
unstoppable
unstressed
unstuck
unstudied
unsung
unsure
unsuspecting
unswerving
untamed
untangle
untenable
unthinkable
unthinking
untidy
 untidier
 untidiest
untie
 untied
 untying
until
untimely
unto
untold
untouchable
untoward
untrue
untruth
untruthful
untruthfully
untying
unusual
unusually
unvarnished
unveil
 unveiled
 unveiling
unvoiced
unwaged

unwanted

●* Do not confuse
with **unwonted**
*unwanted children • an
unwanted gift*

unwarranted
unwell
unwieldy

❶ Something that's
unwieldy isn't easily
lifted.

unwilling
unwillingness
unwind
 unwound
 unwinding
unwise
unwitting
unwittingly
unwonted

●* Do not confuse
with **unwanted**
*Unwonted means 'not
usual' • Scrooge's
unwonted generosity*

unworthy
unwound
unwritten
unzip
 unzipped
 unzipping
up
up-and-coming
upbeat
upbraid
upbringing
update
 updated
 updating
upend

upfront, up-front
upgrade
 upgraded
 upgrading
upheaval
upheld
uphill
uphold
 upheld
 upholding
upholder
upholster
 upholstered
 upholstering
upholsterer
upholstery
upkeep
upland
uplifting
up-market
upon
upper
uppercut
uppermost
uppity
upright
uprising
uproar
uproarious
uproot
 uprooted
 uprooting
upset
 upset
 upsetting
upshot
upside-down
upstage
 upstaged
 upstaging
upstairs
upstanding

upstart
upstream
upsurge
uptake
uptight
up-to-date
upward
upwards
uranium
urban

> ♦* Do not confuse
> with **urbane** *an urban*
> *road*

urbane

> ♦* Do not confuse
> with **urban** *an urbane*
> *young man*

urbanisation
another spelling of
urbanization
urbanise
another spelling of
urbanize
urbanity
urbanities
urbanization,
urbanisation
urbanize, urbanise
urbanized,
urbanised
urbanizing,
urbanising
urchin

Urdu
ureter
urethra
urge
urged
urging
urgency
urgent
urgently
urinal
urinary
urinate
urinated
urinating
urination
urine
urn
us
usable
usage
use
used
using
used
useful
usefully
usefulness
useless
uselessness
user
user-friendly
usher
ushered

ushering
usherette
usual
usually
usurp
usurper
usury
utensil
uterus
uteri
utilisation
another spelling of
utilization
utilise
another spelling of
utilize
utilitarian
utility
utilities
utilization,
utilisation
utilize, utilise
utilized, utilised
utilizing, utilising
utmost
utopia
utopian
utter
uttered
uttering
utterance
utterly
U-turn

vacancy
 vacancies
vacant
vacate
 vacated
 vacating
vacation

✎* Do not confuse
with **vocation** *a
university student's
summer vacation*

vaccinate
 vaccinated
 vaccinating
vaccination
vaccine
vacillate
 vacillated
 vacillating
vacillation
vacuous
vacuum

ℹ️ How does one see to
use [one **c** two **u**'s] a
va**cuu**m cleaner at
night?

vacuum-packed
vagabond
vagary
 vagaries
vagina
vaginal
vagrancy

vagrant
vague
vaguely
vagueness
vain

✎* Do not confuse
with **vane** or **vein** *vain
and conceited* • *We
tried in vain*

vainly
valance
vale

✎* Do not confuse
with **veil** *A vale is a
wide valley* • *the Vale of
Evesham*

valediction
valedictory
valency
 valencies
valentine
valet
 valeted
 valeting
valiant
valiantly
valid
validate
 validated
 validating
validation
validity
Valium®

valley
 valleys
valorous
valour
valuable

ℹ️ Unusual **a**ntiques
are often val**ua**ble.

valuation
valuator
value
 valued
 valuing
valueless
valuer
valve
vamp
vampire
van
vandal
vandalise
 another spelling of
 vandalize
vandalism
vandalize, vandalise
 vandalized,
 vandalised
 vandalizing,
 vandalising
vane

✎* Do not confuse
with **vain** or **vein** *a
weather vane*

vanguard

vanilla
vanish
vanity
 vanities
vanquish
vantage
vaporize, vaporise
 vaporized,
 vaporised
 vaporizing,
 vaporising
vaporizer, vaporiser
vapour
variability
variable
variably
variance
variant
variation
varicose
varied
variegated
variety
 varieties
various
variously
varnish
 varnishes
vary
 varies
 varied
 varying
vase
vasectomy
Vaseline®
vast
vat
vaudeville
vault
vaunt
veal
vector

veer
 veered
 veering
vegan
veganism
vegeburger
vegetable
vegetarian
vegetarianism
vegetate
 vegetated
 vegetating
vegetation
vegetative
veggie
vehemence
vehement
vehemently
vehicle

🛈 I get **hic**cups when I'm in a ve**hic**le.

vehicular
veil
 veiled
 veiling

♦* Do not confuse with **vale** *a bride's veil • veiled in mystery*

vein

♦* Do not confuse with **vain** or **vane** *Blood flows through a vein • the veins of a leaf • a vein of cheerfulness*

veined
velocity
 velocities
velour
velvet
velveteen

velvety
venal

♦* Do not confuse with **venial** *corrupt and venal lawyers*

vend
vendetta
vending
vendor
veneer
 veneered
 veneering
venerable
venerate
 venerated
 venerating
veneration
venereal
Venetian blind
vengeance
vengeful
venial

♦* Do not confuse with **venal** *venial sins*

venison
venom
venomous
vent
ventilate
 ventilated
 ventilating
ventilation
ventilator
ventricle
ventriloquism
ventriloquist
venture
 ventured
 venturing
venturesome

venue
veracious
veracity

> ✱ Do not confuse with **voracity** *They doubted the veracity of his statement*

verandah, veranda
verb
verbal
verbalize, verbalise
  verbalized,
  verbalised
  verbalizing,
  verbalising
verbally
verbatim
verbose
verbosity
verdant
verdict
verge
  verged
  verging
verger
verifiable
verification
verify
  verifies
  verified
  verifying
verily
veritable
veritably
verity
vermicelli
vermilion
vermin
verminous
vermouth
vernacular

verruca

> ⓘ Barefoot running round under cover = verruca!

versatile
versatility
verse
versed
versification
versify
  versifies
  versified
  versifying
version
verso
versus
vertebra
  vertebrae
vertebral
vertebrate
vertex
  vertices, vertexes

> ✱ Do not confuse with **vortex** *the vertex of a cone*

vertical
vertically
vertices
vertiginous
vertigo
verve
very
vespers
vessel
vest
vestibule
vestige
vestigial
vestment
vestry
  vestries

vet
  vetted
  vetting
vetch
veteran
veterinarian
veterinary
veto
  pl vetoes
  vetoed
  vetoing
vex
vexation
vexatious
via
viable
viaduct
vibes
vibrant
vibrate
  vibrated
  vibrating
vibration
vibrato
vicar
vicarage
vicarious
vice
vice versa
vicinity
vicious
victim
victimization,
  victimisation
victimize, victimise
  victimized,
  victimised
  victimizing,
  victimising
victor
victorious
victory

victories
video
pl videos
videoed
videoing
videocassette
videotape
vie
vied
vying
view
viewer
viewfinder
viewing
viewpoint
vigil
vigilance
vigilant

♦* Do not confuse
with **vigilante** *remain
vigilant in case of attack*

vigilante

♦* Do not confuse
with **vigilant** *set up a
vigilante group* • *The
vigilantes helped the
police*

vignette
vigorous
vigorously
vigour
viking
vile
vilification
vilify
vilifies
vilified
vilifying
villa
village
villager

villain

❶ A **villain** will cause
pain.

villainous
villainy
villainies
villus
villi
vinaigrette
vindicate
vindicated
vindicating
vindication
vindictive
vindictively
vindictiveness
vine
vinegar
vinegary
vineyard
vintage
vintner
vinyl
viol
viola
violate
violated
violating
violation
violence
violent
violently
violet
violin
violinist
violoncello
violoncellos
viper
viral
virgin
virginal

virginity
virile
virility
virtual
virtually
virtue
virtuosity
virtuoso
virtuosos
virtuous
virtuously
virulence
virulent
virus
viruses
visa
visage
vis-à-vis
viscera
visceral
viscid
viscose
viscosity
viscount
viscountess
viscountesses
viscous
visibility
visible
visibly
vision
visionary
visionaries
visit
visited
visiting
visitation
visitor
visor
vista
visual
visualization,

SPELLING *focus*

Vowels

Vowel sounds often cause spelling problems, because there are so many different ways of spelling the same sound. Here are some examples of different spellings of the short and long sounds 'a', 'e', 'i', 'o', and 'u':

short 'a': cat, plait
short 'e': get, leather, friend
short 'i': fish, mystery, pretty
short 'o': dog, cough, sausage
short 'u': cup, colour, rough

long 'a': game, plain, hay, great, neighbour
long 'e': greed, beat, concede, seize, field
long 'i': time, lie, cycle, height
long 'o': toe, grow, coat, sew
long 'u': flute, true, flew, route

Unstressed vowels

Unstressed vowels are not clearly pronounced in normal speech and so are particularly difficult to spell, because you have no sound to guide you. Examples include the a's at each end of *agenda*, both of which are pronounced with a vague 'uh' sound. To help remember the spelling of unstressed vowels:

- Think of other members of the same word family in which the vowel is stressed. For example, you can remember the unstressed second **a** of *grammar* by thinking of *grammatical*

- Say the word several times to yourself – or out loud – in a way that shows how the unstressed vowel would normally be pronounced, for example *sep-AH-rate, hyp-OH-crite*

Silent vowels

Silent vowels are sometimes used to control the sound of neighbouring consonants. The letters **g** and **c** usually have a hard sound before the vowels **a**, **o** and **u** (for example *gale*, *go* and *cup*) and a soft sound before **e**, **i** and **y** (for example *cell*, *ginger* and *mercy*).

Some words have a silent **u** that keeps the sound hard before **e**, **i** or **y**, as in *guess*, *circuit* and *guy*. Some words have a silent **e** that keeps the sound soft before **a**, **o** or **u**, as in *noticeable*, *surgeon* and *pharmaceutical*.

visualisation
visualize, visualise
visualized,
visualised
visualizing,
visualising
visually
vital
vitalise
another spelling of
vitalize
vitality
vitalize, vitalise
vitalized, vitalised
vitalizing, vitalising
vitally
vitamin
vitreous
vitrification
vitrified
vitrify
vitrifies
vitrified
vitrifying
vitriol
vitriolic
vituperative
vivacious
vivacity
vivid
vividly
vividness
vivisection
vivisectionist
vixen
viz
vizier
vocabulary
vocabularies
vocal
vocalist
vocalize, vocalise

vocalized, vocalised
vocalizing,
vocalising
vocally
vocation

●* Do not confuse
with **vacation** *a
vocation to be a priest*

vocational
vocative
vociferous
vodka
vogue
voice
voiced
voicing
voice-box
voiceless
voice-over
void
volatile
vol-au-vent
volcanic
volcano
volcanoes
vole
volition
volley
pl volleys
volleyed
volleying
volleyball
volt
voltage
voltmeter
volubility
voluble
volubly
volume
voluminous
voluntarily

voluntary
volunteer
volunteered
volunteering
voluptuous
vomit
vomited
vomiting
voodoo
voracious
voracity

●* Do not confuse
with **veracity** *the
voracity of his appetite*

vortex
vortices, vortexes

●* Do not confuse
with **vertex** *the vortex
of a whirlpool*

vote
voted
voting
voter
vouch
voucher
vouchsafe
vouchsafed
vouchsafing
vow
vowel
voyage
voyaged
voyaging
voyager
voyeur
voyeurism
voyeuristic
vulgar
vulgarisation
another spelling of
vulgarization

vulgarise
another spelling of
vulgarize
vulgarity
vulgarization,

vulgarisation
vulgarize, vulgarise
vulgarized,
vulgarised
vulgarizing,

vulgarising
vulnerability
vulnerable
vulture
vying

If the word you're looking for sounds as if it begins with a straightforward **W** but you can't find it, try looking under **WH** for words like *when* and *whether*.

wacky
wackier
wackiest
wad
wadding
waddle
waddled
waddling
wade
waded
wading
wader
wafer
waffle
waffled
waffling
waffler
waft
wag
wagged
wagging
wage
waged
waging
wager
wagged
wagging
waggish
waggle
waggled
waggling

wagon, waggon
wagtail
waif
waifs

> ●* Do not confuse with **waive** or **wave** *a poor little waif • waifs and strays*

waif-like
wail
wailed
wailing
waist

> ●* Do not confuse with **waste** *wear a belt round your waist*

waistband
waistcoat
wait
waited
waiting

> ●* Do not confuse with **weight** *Wait for me! • a long wait for the bus*

waiter
waiting-list
waiting-room
waitress
waitresses

waive
waived
waiving

> ●* Do not confuse with **waif** or **wave** *to waive the right to the throne*

waiver

> ●* Do not confuse with **waver** *I signed a waiver and gave up my rights*

wake
woke, waked
woken
waking
wakeful
waken
wakened
wakening
waking
walk
walkabout
walker
walkie-talkie
Walkman®
Walkmans
walk-out
walk-over
walkway

wall

wallaby
 wallabies
wallet
wallflower
wallop
 walloped
 walloping
wallow
wallpaper
 wallpapered
 wallpapering
wally
walnut
walrus
 walruses
waltz
 waltzes
wan
wand
wander
 wandered
 wandering
wanderer
wanderlust
wane
 waned
 waning
wangle
 wangled
 wangling
wannabe
wanness
want

> ♦* Do not confuse
> with **wont** *for want of
> money • I want a drink*

wanting
wanton
wantonly
wantonness

war
 warred
 warring

> ♦* Do not confuse
> with **wore** *fight in the
> war • a war of words*

warble
 warbled
 warbling
warbler
ward
warden

> ♦* Do not confuse
> with **warder** *a traffic
> warden*

warder

> ♦* Do not confuse
> with **warden** *a prison
> warder*

wardrobe
ware

> ♦* Do not confuse
> with **wear** *earthenware
> • computer software
> and hardware*

warehouse
wares
warfare
warhead
warily
wariness
warlike
warlock
warlord
warm
warm-blooded
warm-hearted
warmly
warmonger
warmth

warn

> ♦* Do not confuse
> with **worn** *to warn of
> danger*

warning
warp
warpaint
warpath
warrant
warranty
 warranties
warred
warren
warring
warrior
warship
wart
wartime
wary
was
wash
 washes
washable
washbasin
washer
washhouse
washing
washing-machine
washing-up
wash-out
washroom
washstand
wasp
waspish
wastage
waste
 wasted
 wasting

> ♦* Do not confuse
> with **waist** *a waste of
> food • to waste time*

Can't find your word? Try looking under **WH**

wasteful
wastefully
wasteland
wastepaper basket
waster
watch
 watches
watchdog
watchful
watchfully
watchfulness
watchman
 watchmen
watchword
water
 watered
 watering
waterborne
watercolour
watercress
waterfall
waterfront
waterhole
watering-can
watering-hole
waterlogged
watermark
watermelon
watermill
waterproof
 waterproofs
watershed
water-ski
 pl water-skis
 water-skied
 water-skiing
watertight
waterway
waterwheel
waterworks
watery
watt

wattage
wattle
wave
 waved
 waving

> 💧* Do not confuse
> with **waive** or **waif** *He
> gave a friendly wave • a
> radio wave • the waves
> of the sea • to wave
> goodbye • Her hair
> waves naturally*

waveband
wavelength
waver
 wavered
 wavering

> 💧* Do not confuse
> with **waiver** *to waver
> and hesitate*

wavy
wax
waxen
waxwork
waxy
way

> 💧* Do not confuse
> with **weigh** or **whey** *the
> way home • the right
> way to do it*

waylay
 waylaid
 waylaying
wayside
wayward
we
weak

> 💧* Do not confuse
> with **week** *a weak child*

weaken

weakened
weakening
weakling
weakly

> 💧* Do not confuse
> with **weekly** *a sick and
> weakly kitten • She
> smiled weakly*

weakness
weal

> 💧* Do not confuse
> with **wheel** *The beating
> left weals across his
> back*

wealth
wealthy
 wealthier
 wealthiest
wean
 weaned
 weaning
weapon
weaponry
wear
 wore
 worn
 wearing

> 💧* Do not confuse
> with **ware** *to wear a hat
> • clothes for casual wear
> • knitwear • footwear*

wearable
wearer
wearily
wearisome
weary
 wearies
 wearied
 wearying
weasel

Can't find your word? Try looking under **WH**

weather
weathered
weathering

✒* Do not confuse with **whether** *fine and sunny weather • to weather the storm*

weatherbeaten
weatherman
weathermen
weatherproof
weave
wove, weaved
woven, weaved
weaving

✒* The past form **weaved** is only used for a winding route *He weaved through the traffic • She wove a basket from twigs*

weaver
web
webbed
webbing
we'd
wed
wedded
wedding
wedding
wedge
wedged
wedging
wee
weed
weeing
wee-wee
wee-weed
wee-weeing
weed
weedkiller

weedy
week

✒* Do not confuse with **weak** *the days of the week*

weekday
weekend
weekly

✒* Do not confuse with **weakly** *a weekly paper • He visits his mother weekly*

weep
wept
weeping
weepy
weevil
weigh

✒* Do not confuse with **way** or **whey** *to weigh the potatoes*

weight

❶ We weigh everything in grams here today.

✒* Do not confuse with **wait** *the weight of the sack*

weightless
weightlessness
weightlifter
weightlifting
weighty
weightier
weightiest
weir
weird

❶ It's w**ei**rd that it's spelt **ei**.

weirdness
weirdo
welcome
welcomed
welcoming
weld
welder
welfare
we'll
well
better
best
well-behaved
wellbeing
wellingtons
well-known
well-meaning
well-meant
well-off
well-to-do
well-wisher
welly
wellies
welt
welter
weltered
weltering
wend
went
wept
we're
were
weren't
werewolf
werewolves
west
westbound
westerly
western
westerner
westward
westwards

Can't find your word? Try looking under **WH**

SPELLING *focus* Weird and Wonderful Words

Long words

What is the longest word you know? Can you spell it correctly? Here are three weird and wonderful long words that you may not have seen before:

antidisestablishmentarianism, which means 'opposition to removing state recognition of an established church'

pneumonoultramicroscopicsilicovolcanoconiosis, which is a lung disease caused by inhaling very fine dust

supercalifragilisticexpialidocious, a word which was featured in the film *Mary Poppins*

Strange spellings

The word *ghoti* was coined to show how illogical English spelling can be. It spells 'fish':

gh = 'f' as in *enough*   **o** = 'i' as in *women*   **ti** = 'sh' as in *nation*

Similarly, *ghoughphtheightteeau* spells 'potato':

gh = 'p' as in *hiccough*   **ough** = 'o' as in *dough*   **phth** = 't' as in the rare word *phthisis*

eigh = 'a' as in *neighbour*   **tte** = 't' as in *gazette*   **eau** = 'o' as in *plateau*

Can you think up any more strange spellings? Can you spell your name in a weird and wonderful way?

Palindromes and anagrams

A palindrome is a word that reads the same forwards and backwards, such as *pip*, *deed*, *civic*, *radar* and *repaper*. Here are some palindromic sentences – can you make up one of your own?

Was it a car or a cat I saw?   **Draw, O coward!**
Stella won no wallets.   **'Tis Ivan on a visit**

There are also many words that can be written backwards to spell a different word. Examples are *desserts* and *stressed*, *deliver* and *reviled*, *straw* and *warts* – can you think of any more?

Anagram pairs, in which one word contains the letters of the other in a different order, can be a useful way of remembering spellings – as long as you rearrange the letters correctly! Here are some examples:

Mate and meat   **Earth and heart**
Generate and teenager   **Orchestra and carthorse**

wet
wetter
wettest
wet, wetted
wetting

♦* Do not confuse
with **whet** *a wet day • to
wet the carpet*

wetness
we've
whack
whale
whaler
whaling
wharf
wharves, wharfs
what
whatever
whatnot
whatsit
whatsoever
wheat
wheatgerm
wheatsheaf
wheedle
wheedled
wheedling
wheedler
wheel
wheeled
wheeling

♦* Do not confuse
with **weal** *the wheels of
the car • to wheel a
trolley • to wheel and
deal*

wheelbarrow
wheelchair
wheeler-dealer
wheeler-dealing
wheelie

wheelwright
wheeze
wheezed
wheezing
wheezy
whelk
whelp
when
whence
whenever
where
whereabouts
whereas
whereby
wherefore
wherein
wheresoever
whereupon
wherever
wherewithal
whet
whetted
whetting

♦* Do not confuse
with **wet** *to whet the
appetite*

whether

♦* Do not confuse
with **weather** *whether
you like it or not*

whey

♦* Do not confuse
with **way** or **weigh**
curds and whey

which

♦* Do not confuse
with **witch** *Which book
is yours?*

whichever
whiff

while
whiled
whiling

♦* Do not confuse
with **wile** *wait a while •
to while away the
afternoon*

whilst
whim
whimper
whimpered
whimpering
whimsical
whimsically
whimsy
whimsies
whine
whined
whining

♦* Do not confuse
with **wine** *the whine of
the machinery • The
dog began to whine*

whinge
whinged
whingeing, whinging
whinny
whinnies
whinnied
whinnying
whip
whipped
whipping
whiplash
whipper-snapper
whippet
whipping
whir
another spelling of
whirr
whirl

whirlpool
whirlwind
whirr, whir
 whirred
 whirring
whisk
whisker
whisky, whiskey
 whiskies, whiskeys
whisper
 whispered
 whispering
whist
whistle
 whistled
 whistling
whistle-stop
whit

✎* Do not confuse
with **wit** *not a whit*

white
whitebait
whiten
 whitened
 whitening
whitener
whiteness
whitewash
whither
whiting
whittle
 whittled
 whittling
whizz, whiz
 whizzed
 whizzing
who
whoa

✎* Do not confuse
with **woe** *He cried
'Whoa!' to the horse*

whodunnit
whoever
whole

✎* Do not confuse
with **hole** *a whole
orange • the whole
household • His work is
good on the whole*

wholefood
wholehearted
wholemeal
wholesale
wholesaler
wholesome
who'll
wholly

❶ **W**as the **holly
wholly** destroyed?

✎* Do not confuse
with **holey** or **holy** *I'm
not wholly convinced*

whom
whoop
 whooped
 whooping

✎* Do not confuse
with **hoop** *She gave a
whoop of joy • to whoop
with joy*

whoopee
whooping-cough
whoops
whopper
whopping
who's

✎* **Who's** is a short
form of **who is** or **who
has**. Do not confuse
with **whose** *Who's
going to the party?*

whose

✎* Do not confuse
with **who's** *Whose
jumper is that?*

whosoever
why
 whys
wick
wicked
wickedly
wickedness
wicker
wicket
wide
wide-eyed
widely
widen
 widened
 widening
widespread
widget
widow
widower
width
wield
wife
 wives
wig
wiggle
 wiggled
 wiggling
wiggly
wigwam
wild
wildcat
wilderness
wildfire
wildfowl
wildlife
wildly
wildness

wile

💣 Do not confuse with **while** *his crafty wiles*

wilful
wilfully
will
willed, would
willing

💣 Do not confuse **willed** with **would** *She willed him to win • He has willed her all his money • I said I would go*

willing
willingness
will-o'-the-wisp
willow
willowy
willpower
willy-nilly
wilt
wily
wimp
win
won
winning
wince
winced
wincing
winch
winches
wind
winded, wound
winding

💣 Do not confuse **winded** with **wound** *The blow winded him • She wound the scarf round her neck*

windbag
windbreak
windcheater
windchill
winder
windfall
winding
windmill
window
windowsill
windpipe
windscreen
windshield
windsock
windsurfer
windsurfing
windswept
windy
windier
windiest
wine
wined
wining

💣 Do not confuse with **whine** *a bottle of red wine • to wine and dine*

wing
winged
wingspan
wink
winkle
winkled
winkling
winner
winning
winnings
winnow
winsome
winter
wintered

wintering
wintry
wipe
wiped
wiping
wiper
wire
wired
wiring
wireless
wiry
wisdom
wise
wisely
wish
wishes
wishbone
wishful
wishy-washy
wisp
wispy
wisteria
wistful
wistfully
wistfulness
wit

💣 Do not confuse with **whit** *cleverness and wit*

witch
witches

💣 Do not confuse with **which** *The witch cast a spell*

witchcraft
with
withdraw
withdrew
withdrawn
withdrawing
withdrawal

Can't find your word? Try looking under **WH**

wither
 withered
 withering
withering
withhold
 withheld
 withholding
within
without
withstand
 withstood
 withstanding
witness
 witnesses
witticism
wittily

> ❉ Do not confuse
> with **wittingly** *He*
> *spoke wittily and*
> *interestingly*

wittingly

> ❉ Do not confuse
> with **wittily** *He did not*
> *wittingly deceive her*

witty
 wittier
 wittiest
wives
wizard
wizardry
wizened
wobble
 wobbled
 wobbling
wobbly
woe

> ❉ Do not confuse
> with **whoa** or **woo**
> *sadness and woe* • *Woe*
> *betide you!*

woebegone
woeful
woefully
woefulness
wok
woke
woken
wolf
 wolves
wolfcub
wolfish
wolfsbane
woman
 women
womanhood
womanize,
 womanise
 womanized,
 womanised
 womanizing,
 womanising
womanizer,
 womaniser
womanly
womb
wombat
women

❶ Why old men enjoy
nagging!

womenfolk
won
wonder
 wondered
 wondering
wonderful
wonderfully
wonderland
wonderment
wondrous
wonky
won't

wont

> ❉ Do not confuse
> with **want** *He left early,*
> *as is his wont* • *It is wont*
> *to break down*

woo
 wooed
 wooing

> ❉ Do not confuse
> with **woe** *to woo a girl*
> *and marry her*

wood

> ❉ Do not confuse
> with **would** or **wooed** *a*
> *beech wood* • *wood for*
> *the fire*

woodcut
woodcutter
wooded
wooden
woodenly
woodenness
woodland
woodlouse
 woodlice
woodpecker
woodwind
woodwork
woodworm
woody
wooed

> ❉ Do not confuse
> with **wood** *He wooed*
> *her ardently*

wooer
woof
 pl woofs
 woofed
 woofing
woofer

Can't find your word? Try looking under **WH**

wooing
wool
woollen
woolly
 woollies
woozy
word
wording
word-perfect
word-processing
word-processor
wordy
 wordier
 wordiest
wore

> ✸ Do not confuse with **war** *She wore her best dress*

work
workable
workaday
workaholic
worker
workforce
workhouse
working
workings
workload
workman
 workmen
workmanship
workout
workplace
workshop
workshy
worktop
world
world-class
worldliness
worldly
worldwide

worm
wormcast
wormwood
worn

> ✸ Do not confuse with **warn** *I've never worn these shoes* • *The carpet is worn*

worried
worrier
worry
 worries
 worried
 worrying
worse
worsen
 worsened
 worsening
worship
 worshipped
 worshipping
worshipful
worshipfully
worshipper
worst
worth
worthily
worthiness
worthless
worthwhile
worthy
 worthies
 worthier
 worthiest
would

> ✸ Do not confuse with **wood** *Would you like a drink?*

would-be
wouldn't
would've

wound
wounded
wove
woven
wow
wrack

> ✸ Do not confuse with **rack** *Wrack is seaweed found on the shore* You can use **wrack** or **rack** for phrases like *rack and ruin, racked with guilt* and *rack your brains*, but **rack** is the usual spelling.

wraith
wrangle
 wrangled
 wrangling
wrap
 wrapped
 wrapping

> ✸ Do not confuse with **rap** *Wrap it up in tissue paper*

wraparound
wrapped

> ✸ Do not confuse with **rapped** or **rapt** *She wrapped the scarf round her neck* • *The box was wrapped in brown paper*

wrapper
wrapping
wrapround
wrath

> ❶ We're really angry.

wrathful

Can't find your word? Try looking under **WH**

wrathfully
wreak
wreaked
wreaking

💣 Do not confuse
with **reek** or **wreck** *to
wreak vengeance • to
wreak havoc*

wreath

💣 Do not confuse
with **wreathe** *a wreath
of flowers*

wreathe
wreathed
wreathing

💣 Do not confuse
with **wreath** *Clouds
wreathe the hilltops •
wreathed in smiles*

wreck

💣 Do not confuse
with **wreak** *the wreck
of the Titanic • a
nervous wreck • to
wreck the car*

wreckage
wren
wrench
wrenches
wrest

💣 Do not confuse
with **rest** *to wrest it
from his grasp*

wrestle
wrestled

wrestling
wrestler
wrestling
wretch
wretches

💣 Do not confuse
with **retch** *The poor
wretch has nowhere to
live*

wretched
wretchedness
wriggle
wriggled
wriggling
wriggly
wring
wrung
wringing

💣 Do not confuse
with **ring** *to wring the
clothes • to wring a
promise from her • Do
that again and I'll
wring your neck! •
wringing wet*

wringer
wrinkle
wrinkled
wrinkling
wrinkly
wrist
wristwatch
wristwatches
writ
write
wrote

written
writing

💣 Do not confuse
with **right** or **rite** *to
write a letter*
Remember that you
write words.

writer
writhe
writhed
writhing
writing
wrong
wrongdoer
wrongdoing
wrong-foot
wrong-footed
wrong-footing
wrongful
wrongfully
wrote

💣 Do not confuse
with **rote** *She wrote her
name on it*

wrought
wrung

💣 Do not confuse
with **rung** *She wrung
the bird's neck to kill it •
He has wrung the
clothes*

wry

💣 Do not confuse
with **rye** *a wry smile • a
wry neck*

Can't find your word? Try looking under **WH**

X-chromosome
xenon
xenophobe
xenophobia

xenophobic
Xerox®
Xeroxes
X-ray

X-rayed
X-raying
xylophone
xylophonist

If you can't find the word you're looking for under **Y**, it could be that it starts with a different letter. Try looking under **EU** for words like *euphemism*, **EW** for words like *ewe*, and **U** for words like *use* and *usual*.

yacht

ℹ **Y**es, **a**ll **c**raft have **t**riangular sails.

yachting
yachtsman
 yachtsmen
yachtswoman
 yachtswomen
yack

♦* Do not confuse with **yak** *To yack is to talk persistently*

yahoo
yak

♦* Do not confuse with **yack** *A yak is a Tibetan animal*

yam
yank
yap
 yapped
 yapping
yappy
yard
yardstick
yarn
yarrow
yashmak
yawn

yawning
Y-chromosome
ye
yeah
year
yearling
yearly
yearn
yeast
yeasty
yell
yellow
yellowish
yellowness
yelp
yen
yeoman
 yeomen
yeomanry
yes
 yeses, yesses
yesterday
yesteryear
yet
Yeti
yew

♦* Do not confuse with **ewe** or **you** *a yew tree*

Y-fronts

yield

ℹ **A**n **i**rate **e**lk will never **y**ield.

yielding
yippee
ylang-ylang
yob
yobbo
 yobbos, yobboes
yodel
 yodelled
 yodelling
yodeller
yoga
yoghurt, yogurt, yoghourt
yogi
yoke
 yoked
 yoking

♦* Do not confuse with **yolk** *the yoke of a plough • the yoke of a dress • to yoke cattle together*

yokel
yolk

♦* Do not confuse with **yoke** *egg yolk*

yonder

yore

🖊* Do not confuse
with **your** or **you're**
days of yore

you

🖊* Do not confuse
with **ewe** or **yew** *you
and I*

you'd
you'll
young
youngster

your

🖊* Do not confuse
with **yore** or **you're**
your house

you're

🖊* **You're** is a short
form of **you are**. Do
not confuse with **your**
or **yore** *You're a good
friend*

yours
yourself
yourselves

youth
youthful
youthfully
you've
Yo-Yo®
Yo-Yos
yucca
yucky
yummy
yum-yum
yuppie, yuppy
yuppies

Can't find your word? Try looking under **EU**, **EW** or **U**

Zz

If you can't find the word you're looking for under **Z**, it could be that it starts with a different letter. Try looking under **X** for words like *xylophone* and *Xerox*.

zany
zap
 zapped
 zapping
zapper
zeal
zealot
zealous
zealously
zebra
zeitgeist
zenith
zephyr
zero
 pl zeros
 zeroed
 zeroing
zest

zestful
zestfully
zigzag
 zigzagged
 zigzagging
zilch
zillion
Zimmer® **frame**
zinc
zing
zip
 zipped
 zipping
zipper
zippy
zither
zodiac
zombie

zonal
zone
 zoned
 zoning
zonked
zoo
zoological

❶ A **zoo** is the **logical** place to find animals.

zoologist
zoology
zoom
 zoomed
 zooming
zucchini
 zucchini, zucchinis
zygote

Appendix: Quick Reference

Days of the Week
Monday
Tuesday
Wednesday
Thursday
Friday
Saturday
Sunday

Planets of the Solar System
Mercury
Venus
Earth
Mars
Jupiter
Saturn
Uranus
Neptune
Pluto

Months of the Year
January
February
March
April
May
June
July
August
September
October
November
December

Signs of the Zodiac
Aries
Taurus
Gemini
Cancer
Leo
Virgo
Libra
Scorpio
Sagittarius
Capricorn
Aquarius
Pisces

Some Cardinal Numbers

one	fifteen	twenty-nine
two	sixteen	thirty
three	seventeen	forty
four	eighteen	fifty
five	nineteen	sixty
six	twenty	seventy
seven	twenty-one	eighty
eight	twenty-two	ninety
nine	twenty-three	hundred
ten	twenty-four	thousand
eleven	twenty-five	million
twelve	twenty-six	billion
thirteen	twenty-seven	trillion
fourteen	twenty-eight	

Some Ordinal Numbers

first	fifteenth	twenty-ninth
second	sixteenth	thirtieth
third	seventeenth	fortieth
fourth	eighteenth	fiftieth
fifth	nineteenth	sixtieth
sixth	twentieth	seventieth
seventh	twenty-first	eightieth
eighth	twenty-second	ninetieth
ninth	twenty-third	hundredth
tenth	twenty-fourth	thousandth
eleventh	twenty-fifth	millionth
twelfth	twenty-sixth	billionth
thirteenth	twenty-seventh	trillionth
fourteenth	twenty-eighth	

Continents and Regions of the World

Africa	Asia	North America
Antarctica	Australasia	Oceania
Arctic	Europe	South America

Some Countries of the World

Afghanistan	Bosnia-	of Independent
Albania	Herzegovina	States (CIS)
Algeria	Botswana	Congo
Andorra	Brazil	Costa Rica
Angola	Brunei	Côte d'Ivoire
Argentina	Bulgaria	Croatia
Armenia	Burkina Faso	Cuba
Australia	Burma	Cyprus
Austria	Burundi	Czech Republic
Azerbaijan	Cambodia	Democratic
The Bahamas	Cameroon	Republic of
Bahrain	Canada	Congo
Bangladesh	Cape Verde	Denmark
Barbados	Central African	Djibouti
Belarus	Republic	Dominica
Belgium	Chad	Dominican
Belize	Chile	Republic
Benin	China	Ecuador
Bhutan	Colombia	Egypt
Bolivia	Commonwealth	$\rightarrow$

Some Countries of the World (cont.)

El Salvador	Lesotho	Qatar
England	Liberia	Romania
Equatorial	Libya	Russia
Guinea	Liechtenstein	Rwanda
Eritrea	Lithuania	Samoa
Estonia	Luxembourg	Saudi Arabia
Ethiopia	Macedonia	Scotland
Fiji	Madagascar	Senegal
Finland	Malawi	Seychelles
France	Malaysia	Sierra Leone
Gabon	Maldives	Singapore
The Gambia	Mali	Slovakia
Georgia	Malta	Slovenia
Germany	Mauritania	Somalia
Ghana	Mauritius	South Africa
Greece	Mexico	South Korea
Grenada	Moldova	Spain
Guatemala	Monaco	Sri Lanka
Guinea	Mongolia	The Sudan
Guinea-Bissau	Morocco	Suriname
Guyana	Mozambique	Swaziland
Haiti	Myanmar	Sweden
Honduras	Namibia	Switzerland
Hungary	Nepal	Syria
Iceland	The Netherlands	Taiwan
India	New Zealand	Tajikistan
Indonesia	Nicaragua	Tanzania
Iran	Niger	Thailand
Iraq	Nigeria	Tonga
Ireland	Northern Ireland	Togo
Israel	North Korea	Trinidad and
Italy	Norway	Tobago
Jamaica	Oman	Tunisia
Japan	Pakistan	Turkey
Jordan	Panama	Turkmenistan
Kazakhstan	Papua New	Uganda
Kenya	Guinea	Ukraine
Kuwait	Paraguay	United Arab
Kyrgyzstan	Peru	Emirates
Laos	Philippines	United Kingdom
Latvia	Poland	(UK)
Lebanon	Portugal	→

Some Countries of the World (cont.)

United States of America (USA)	Vatican	Yemen
	Venezuela	Yugoslavia
Uruguay	Vietnam	Zambia
Uzbekistan	Wales	Zimbabwe

Some Nationalities

Afghan	Cameroonian	Georgian
African	Canadian	German
Albanian	Cape Verdean	Ghanaian
Algerian	Central African	Greek
American	Chadian	Grenadian
Andorran	Chilean	Guatemalan
Angolan	Chinese	Guinean
Argentinian	Colombian	Guyanese
Armenian	Congolese	Haitian
Asian	Costa Rican	Herzegovinian
Australian	Croat	Honduran
Austrian	Cuban	Hungarian
Azerbaijani	Cypriot	Icelander
Bahamian	Czech,	Indian
Bahraini	Czechoslovak	Indonesian
Bangladeshi	Dane, Danish	Iranian
Barbadian	Djiboutian	Iraqi
Basotho (*Lesotho*)	Dominican	Irish
Batswana	Dutch	Israeli
(*Botswana*)	Ecuadorian	Italian
Belarusian	Egyptian	Ivorian
Belgian	Emirati	Jamaican
Belizian	English	Japanese
Beninese	Equatorial	Jordanian
Bhutanese	Guinean	Kazakhstani
Bolivian	Eritrean	Kenyan
Bosnian	Estonian	Kyrgyzstani
Brazilian	Ethiopian	Kuwaiti
Briton, British	European	Laotian
Bruneian	Fijian	Latvian
Bulgarian	Filipino, Filipina	Lebanese
Burkinese	Finn, Finnish	Liberian
Burmese	French	Libyan
Burundian	Gabonese	Liechtensteiner
Cambodian	Gambian	→

Some Nationalities (cont.)

Lithuanian
Luxembourger,
  Luxemburger
Macedonian
Malagasy,
  Madagascan
Malawian
Malaysian
Maldivian
Malian
Maltese
Mauritanian
Mauritian
Mexican
Moldovan
Monégasque,
  Monacan
Mongolian
Moroccan
Mosotho
  (*Lesotho*)
Motswana
  (*Botswana*)
Mozambican
Namibian
Nepalese, Nepali
Netherlander
New Zealander
Nicaraguan
Nigerian
  (*Nigeria*)
Nigerien (*Niger*)

North Korean
Norwegian
Omani
Pakistani
Panamanian
Papua New
  Guinean, Papuan
Paraguayan
Peruvian
Pole, Polish
Portuguese
Qatari
Romanian
Russian
Rwandan
Salvadorean
Samoan
Saudi, Saudi
  Arabian
Scot, Scottish
Senegalese
Seychellois
Sierra Leonian
Singaporean
Slovak
Slovene
Somali
South African
South Korean
Spaniard,
  Spanish
Sri Lankan

Sudanese
Surinamese
Swazi
Swede, Swedish
Swiss
Syrian
Taiwanese
Tajikistani
Tanzanian
Thai
Togolese
Tongan
Trinidadian,
  Tobagan,
  Tobagonian
Tunisian
Turk, Turkish
Turkmen
Ugandan
Ukrainian
Uruguayan
Uzbekistani
Vatican
Venezuelan
Vietnamese
Welsh
Yemeni
Yugoslav,
  Yugoslavian
Zambian
Zimbabwean

Some Seas, Oceans, Lakes and Rivers

Adriatic Sea
Aegean Sea
Amazon
Arabian Sea
Aral Sea
Arctic Ocean
Atlantic Ocean
Baltic Sea

Bay of Bengal
Bering Sea
Black Sea
Caribbean
Caspian Sea
Congo
Coral Sea
Danube

Dead Sea
Ganges
Gulf of Mexico
Hudson Bay
Indian Ocean
Irish Sea
Lake Baikal
                    →

Some Seas, Oceans, Lakes and Rivers (cont.)

Lake Chad	Lake Victoria	Pacific Ocean
Lake Erie	Lake Windermere	Red Sea
Lake Huron	Loch Ness	Rhine
Lake Michigan	Mediterranean Sea	Seine
Lake Ontario	Mississippi	South China Sea
Lake Superior	Nile	Thames
Lake Tanganyika	North Sea	Yangtze

Some Mountains

Alps	Fuji	Lhotse
Annapurna	Helvellyn	Mauna Loa
Ben Nevis	Kangchenjunga	Mont Blanc
Etna	Kilimanjaro	Mount St Helens
Everest	Krakatoa	Vesuvius

Some Deserts

Arabian Desert	Gobi Desert	Nubian Desert
Atacama Desert	Kalahari Desert	Patagonian Desert
Chihuahuan Desert	Mojave Desert	Sahara Desert

Some Festivals and Celebrations

Advent	Hallowe'en,	Pancake Day
All Saints' Day	Halloween	Passover
April Fools' Day	Hanukkah,	Purim
Armistice Day	Chanukkah,	Ramadan
Ash Wednesday	Chanukah	Remembrance
Boxing Day	Harvest Festival	Sunday
Buddha Day	Hogmanay	Rosh Hashanah
Chinese New Year	Id ul-Fitr, Eid	Saint Andrew's
Christmas	ul-Fitr	Day
Christmas Day	Id al-Adha	Saint David's Day
Christmas Eve	Independence Day	Saint George's
Diwali, Divali,	Kumbh Mela	Day
Dewali	Lent	Saint Patrick's Day
Easter	May Day	Shrove Tuesday
Easter Day	Mother's Day	Thanksgiving
Easter Monday	New Year's Day	Valentine's Day
Father's Day	New Year's Eve	Whitsun, Whit
Fourth of July	Noël	Yom Kippur
Good Friday	Palm Sunday	Yule

Glossary of Spelling Terms

abbreviation
a shortened form of a word or group of words, either with some letters missing or with each word represented by its first letter, as in *dept* for *department* and *CD* for *compact disc*

adjective
a word that modifies, or provides more information about, a noun, such as *blue* in *a blue flower*

adverb
a word that can modify, or provide more information about, a verb, an adjective, another adverb or a preposition, such as *quickly* in *he ran quickly to the door*

alternative spelling
a different way of spelling the same word: *judgment* is an alternative spelling of *judgement*

analogy
a similarity between two words, such as a letter pattern, which can help you to spell unfamiliar words by using your knowledge of words that you can spell: for example, using the letter pattern *-eigh* from the word *eight* to spell the more difficult *neighbour*

antonym
a word opposite in meaning to another: *happy* is an antonym of *sad*

antonym prefix
a prefix which can be added to a word to reverse its meaning, such as *anti-* and *un-*

apostrophe
a mark (') indicating possession, as in *the dog's lead*, or a mark indicating that a letter has been missed out, as in *isn't* for *is not*

base word
a word from which other words have developed, eg *like* is the base word of *likeable* and *likely*, or the form of the verb on which inflected forms are based, eg *talk* is the base word of *talked* and *talking*

comparative
the form of an adjective which shows a comparison with something else, such as *bigger*, *happier*

compound word
a word made up of two or more different words, such as *handbag*

conjunction
a word that joins sentences or phrases, such as *and* or *but*

connective

a word that connects sentences or phrases, such as *hitherto*

consonant

a letter of the alphabet that is not a vowel, such as *b*, *c* or *d*

contraction

a shortened form of a word, as in *aren't* for *are not*

derive

to come or be formed from something, as when one word is formed from another one: *likeable* is derived from *like*

dictionary

a book giving the words of a language in alphabetical order, together with their meanings

digraph

two letters expressing a single sound, such as *ph* in the word *digraph*

disyllabic

used to describe a word which has only two syllables, such as *butter*

homonym

a word which has the same spelling as another but a different meaning, such as *lead* (a metal) and *lead* (to show the way by going first)

homophone

a word which sounds the same as another but is different in spelling and meaning, such as *pair* and *pear*

hyphen

a short stroke (-) used to link or separate parts of a word or phrase, as in *self-confident*

inflection

a change in the form of a word to show tense, number, etc, and also the new form of a word which has been changed in this way, such as *houses* or *talked*

irregular

used to describe a word which is not inflected in the usual way and does not follow the usual spelling pattern or rules, such as the verb *swim*

letter pattern or **letter string**

an arrangement of letters, often one which is common to many words, such as *-ough* or *-ight*

mnemonic

a rhyme or other guide which helps you to remember something, such as *an almond has an oval shape*

monosyllabic

used to describe a word which has only one syllable, such as *cheese*

morpheme
a simple linguistic unit that has meaning, and cannot be divided into smaller units, such as *out*, *go* and *-ing* in *outgoing*

morphology
the study of the forms of words

noun
the word used as the name of someone or something. **A common noun** is a name for any one of a class of things, such as *dog* and *idea*, and a **proper noun** is a name for a particular person, place or thing, such as *Shakespeare* and *Mount Fuji*

phoneme
the smallest significant unit of sound in a word, such as *m*, *ou* and *se* in *mouse*

phrase
a small group of words expressing a single idea, such as *after dinner*

plural
the form of a word which indicates more than one person or thing: *mice* is the plural of *mouse*

pluralize
to make a word into a plural, for example by adding *-s* to *dog* to make *dogs*

polysyllabic
used to describe a word which has three or more syllables, such as *margarine*

positive
the form of an adjective that is neither comparative nor superlative, such as *big*, *happy*

possessive
used to describe an adjective or pronoun which shows possession, such as *my*, *your*, *their*

prefix
a syllable or word which can be added to the beginning of a word to make another word, such as *dis-*

preposition
a word placed before a noun or pronoun to show its relation to another word, such as *through* in *through the door*

proofread
to read and correct, reading carefully through your writing to spot any mistakes you have made

quartile
one of the four parts that a sequence can be divided into, such as *a-d*, *e-l*, *m-r* and *s-z* in a dictionary

regular
used to describe a word which is inflected in the usual way, following the usual spelling pattern or rules, such as *talk*

root word
a word from which other words have developed or been formed, eg *help* is the root word of *helpful* and *helpless*

sentence
a number of words which together make a complete statement or question

shape
the way a word looks on the page, its visual pattern

silent letter
a letter which is not pronounced, such as the *g* in *gnat*

singular
the opposite of plural, the form of a noun or verb that indicates one person or thing, such as *mouse*

spellchecker or spellcheck
a program in a word-processor or computer that automatically checks the accuracy of the spelling in an electronic document

strategy
a plan or technique used to improve your spelling permanently

stress
an extra weight laid on a part of a word when it is pronounced, such as *but*-ter

suffix
a syllable or word which can be added to the end of a word to make another word, such as *-tion*

superlative
the form of an adjective which shows the highest degree of something, such as *biggest*, *happiest*

syllable
a word or part of a word spoken with one breath, such as *mar*, *gar* and *ine* in the word *margarine*

synonym
a word which has the same, or nearly the same, meaning as another: *erase* is a synonym of *delete*

thesaurus
a reference book listing words and their synonyms

unsounded consonant
a consonant which is not pronounced, a silent letter such as the *k* in *knight*

unstressed vowel
a vowel which is not clearly pronounced when a word is said aloud, such as the *i* in *family*

variant or **variant spelling**

a different way of spelling a word, an alternative spelling: *judgment* is a variant of *judgement*

verb

the word that tells you what someone or something does in a sentence, such as *talk* or *think*

vocabulary

the range of words used by an individual or group, or the words of a particular language

vowel

the letters *a, e, i, o, u*, and sometimes *y*, which represent sounds made by the voice that do not require the use of the tongue, teeth or lips

word

a written or spoken sign representing a thing or an idea

word family

several words which share common features, or the same root word, such as *signal, significant, signature*

word web

a diagram showing the links between words

Spelling Rules

Here are some simple rules, most of them to do with forming words from others in English. This is not a complete list, and there are often exceptions to these rules. However, knowing these basic rules can help you to spell many words. Remember that there may be more exceptions to a rule than those examples shown here.

1. Adding -ing, -ed, -er, -s

a. The base form (infinitive) of most verbs does not change and **-ing**, **-ed**, or **-er** is simply added to the end:

> **stay:** staying, stayed
> **walk:** walking, walked, walker

-s is added to the end of most verbs to make the present tense. This rule is unaffected by most of the following points.

b. If the base form of the verb is very short and ends in a single vowel letter followed by a single consonant letter, then the last letter has to be doubled before **-ing**, **-ed**, or **-er** is added:

> **run:** running
> **pot:** potting, potted
> **stir:** stirrer

c. If the base form of the verb is longer and ends in a single vowel letter followed by a single consonant letter, whether or not you double the final letter depends on how you say it. If you pronounce the last part of the word more definitely than the previous parts (that is, you put *stress* on the final part), then you have to double the final letter before you add **-ing**, **-ed**, or **-er**:

> **regret:** regretting, regretted
> **prefer:** preferring, preferred
> **distil:** distiller

But if the stress is not on the final part, the final letter is not doubled:

> **enter:** entering, entered
> **gossip:** gossiping, gossiped

If the last syllable has a short vowel and ends in **-l** you have to double the **l**, regardless of where the stress comes:

> **equal:** equalling, equalled
> **repel:** repelling, repelled

d. If a verb ends in **-c**, then a **k** is added before **-ing**, **-ed**, or **-er**:

> **panic:** panicking, panicked
> **picnic:** picnicking, picnicked, picnicker

e. If a word ends in a consonant followed by **-e** ('silent e'), the final **-e** is dropped before adding **-ing**, **-ed**, or **-er**:

> **hope:** hoping, hoped
> **love:** loving, loved, lover
> **mine:** mining, mined, miner

But notice that words ending in **-oe**, **-ee** and **-ye** are exceptions to this rule when adding **-ing**:

> **hoe:** hoeing, hoed, hoer
> **agree:** agreeing, agreed
> **dye:** dyeing, dyed, dyer

f. If a verb ends in **-ie**, the **-ie** is changed to **-y** before the ending **-ing** is added:

> **die:** dying
> **lie:** lying

This does not happen when the ending **-ed** is added. This time, the **-e** is dropped before **-ed** is added:

> **die:** died
> **lie:** lied

g. With verbs that end in a consonant followed by **-y**, the opposite happens. The **-y** ending is kept when **-ing** is added, to avoid having an awkward double **i** which would look unusual and be tricky to say. But **-y** is changed to **-i** when **-ed** or **-er** is added:

> **cry:** crying, cried, crier
> **try:** trying, tried, trier
> **marry:** marrying, married

This also happens when the ending **-s** is added to make some present tense forms:

> **cry:** cries
> **try:** tries
> **marry:** marries

But if a verb has a vowel before the **-y**, keep the **-y** ending when you add **-s** and **-ed**:

> **stay:** stays, stayed
> **play:** plays, played

But watch out for exceptions:
>**lay:** lays, laying, laid
>**pay:** pays, paying, paid
>**say:** says, saying, said

h. The present tense of verbs ending in **-ch**, **-sh**, **-s**, **-x** and **-z** is formed by adding **-es**:
>**touch:** touches
>**wash:** washes
>**hiss:** hisses
>**fix:** fixes
>**waltz:** waltzes

2. Plurals

a. Often plurals can be formed simply by adding **-s**:
>**horse:** horses
>**banana:** bananas

b. Plurals of nouns ending in **-ch**, **-sh**, **-s**, **-x** and **-z** are formed by adding **-es**:
>**church:** churches
>**flash:** flashes
>**loss:** losses
>**box:** boxes
>**waltz:** waltzes

This makes them easier to say. But be careful if the noun ends in a **-ch** that is pronounced **k**, as then you only add **-s** to form the plural:
>**stomach:** stomachs
>**monarch:** monarchs

And watch out for other exceptions:
>**fez:** fezzes
>**quiz:** quizzes

c. Plurals of nouns ending in **-f** and **-fe** are sometimes formed by changing the **-f** or **-fe** to **-ve** before adding **-s**:
>**life:** lives
>**thief:** thieves
>**knife:** knives

But not always:
>**roof:** roofs
>**belief:** beliefs
>**chief:** chiefs
>**proof:** proofs

    safe: safes
    sniff: sniffs

And some can do either:
    scarf: scarfs or scarves
    hoof: hoofs or hooves
    dwarf: dwarfs or dwarves

d. Plurals of nouns ending in a consonant followed by **-y** are formed by changing the **-y** to **-ie** and adding **-s**:
    berry: berries
    hanky: hankies
    fly: flies

The plurals of nouns that have a vowel before the **-y** are simply formed with **-s**:
    boy: boys
    day: days

e. Plurals of nouns ending in **-o** are often formed by just adding **-s**:
    piano: pianos
    radio: radios
    zoo: zoos

But some add **-es** instead:
    potato: potatoes
    tomato: tomatoes
    hero: heroes
    echo: echoes

And some can add either **-s** or **-es**:
    banjo: banjos or banjoes
    domino: dominos or dominoes
    manifesto: manifestos or manifestoes

f. Some nouns change their vowels to form the plural:
    foot: feet
    goose: geese
    tooth: teeth
    man: men

g. There is also a plural formed by adding **-en**:
    child: children
    ox: oxen

h. And some do not change at all:
> **sheep:** sheep
> **deer:** deer

i. Words which have come into English from other languages often have plurals which do not follow these rules. This is because the plural form is also taken from the source language, which is unlikely to form plurals in the same way as English words do:
> **analysis:** analyses
> **stimulus:** stimuli
> **oasis:** oases

Some have more than one plural form:
> **appendix:** appendixes or appendices
> **stadium:** stadiums or stadia
> **antenna:** antennas or antennae

The plural of words which end in **-eau** can be formed by adding either **-s** or **-x**:
> **gateau:** gateaus or gateaux
> **plateau:** plateaus or plateaux

3. Adding -ish and -y

a. Adjectives can often be spelt simply by adding **-ish** or **-y** to a noun:
> **tiger:** tigerish
> **dream:** dreamy

b. However, if the noun is very short and ends in a single vowel letter followed by a single consonant letter, then the last letter has to be doubled before **-ish** or **-y** is added:
> **fad:** faddish
> **grit:** gritty

c. If a word ends in a consonant followed by **-e** ('silent e'), the final **-e** is dropped before adding **-ish** or **-y**:
> **style:** stylish
> **grease:** greasy

However, there are a lot of exceptions to this rule:
> **price:** pricey
> **same:** samey
> **mate:** matey

4. Adding -er and -est

a. Comparatives and superlatives can often be spelt simply by adding **-er** or **-est** to an adjective:

> **hard:** harder, hardest
> **loud:** louder, loudest

b. However, if the noun is very short and ends in a single vowel letter followed by a single consonant letter, then the last letter has to be doubled before **-er** or **-est** is added:

> **red:** redder, reddest
> **big:** bigger, biggest

c. If an adjective ends in **-e**, the final **-e** is dropped before adding **-er** or **-est**:

> **white:** whiter, whitest
> **simple:** simpler, simplest
> **free:** freer, freest

d. If an adjective has two syllables and ends in **-y**, you have to change the **-y** to **-i** before adding **-er** or **-est**:

> **angry:** angrier, angriest
> **funny:** funnier, funniest

But look at these one-syllable adjectives ending in **-y**:

> **dry:** drier, driest
> **sly:** slyer, slyest
> **shy:** shier or shyer, shiest or shyest

e. Remember that there are some exceptions:

> **good:** better, best
> **bad:** worse, worst
> **far:** further, furthest or farther, farthest

5. Adding -ly

a. **-ly** is often simply added to the end of adjectives to make adverbs:

> **foolish:** foolishly
> **strange:** strangely
> **surprising:** surprisingly

b. If an adjective ends in a consonant followed by **-le**, the final **-e** is dropped before adding **-ly**:

> **simple:** simply
> **double:** doubly

The adjectives *true*, *due*, *whole* and *eerie* also drop the final **-e** before **-ly** is added:

> **true:** truly
> **due:** duly
> **whole:** wholly
> **eerie:** eerily

c. If an adjective ends in **-y**, the **-y** ending is changed to **-i** when **-ly** is added:
> **happy:** happily
> **weary:** wearily

But again there are some exceptions:
> **dry:** drily or dryly
> **shy:** shily or shyly

d. If an adjective ends in **-ic**, the ending **-ally** (rather than just **-ly**) is added:
> **basic:** basically
> **economic:** economically

But an exception to this rule is:
> **public:** publicly

6. Adding -able and -ible

a. **-able** is often simply added to the end of other words to make adjectives:
> **remark:** remarkable
> **respect:** respectable

b. If a word ends in a consonant followed by **-e** ('silent e'), the final **-e** is dropped before adding **-able**:
> **advise:** advisable
> **debate:** debatable

However, if the word ends in **-ce** or **-ge**, the **-e** is kept when adding **-able**:
> **notice:** noticeable
> **change:** changeable

There are also a few other exceptions to this rule, when the **-able** ending is added to short words ending in **-e**:
> **like:** likeable
> **size:** sizeable

c. If the word is very short and ends in a single vowel letter followed by a single consonant letter, then the last letter has to be doubled before **-able** is added:
> **get:** gettable

d. If the word is longer and ends in a single vowel letter followed by a single consonant letter, whether or not you double the final letter depends on how you say it. If when you say it you pronounce the last part of the word more definitely than the previous parts (that is, you put *stress* on the final part), then you have to double the final letter before you add **-able**:

> **regret:** regrettable
> **forget:** forgettable

An exception to this rule happens with words ending in **-fer**. The final letter is not doubled:

> **prefer:** preferable
> **transfer:** transferable

e. With verbs that end in a consonant followed by **-y**, the **-y** ending is changed to **-i** when **-able** is added:

> **justify:** justifiable

f. **-able** is a more common suffix than **-ible**, and is used to make new words with this ending, but it is worth remembering some of the common adjectives that end in **-ible**:

audible	incredible
comprehensible	legible
credible	negligible
edible	permissible
eligible	reversible
flexible	sensible
illegible	visible

g. Words with the suffix **-ible** often have a root verb that has changed in some other way:

> **defend:** defensible
> **permit:** permissible
> **neglect:** negligible

Many **-ible** words don't seem to be related to a verb at all:

credible	ostensible
fallible	possible

7. Adding -ful, al- and -til

a. Remember that when the word **full** becomes the suffix **-ful** it drops the final **l**:

> **hope:** hopeful
> **faith:** faithful
> **colour:** colourful

The same rule applies to the words **all** and **till** which drop the final **l** when used as a prefix or suffix:

>**all:** already, altogether
>**till:** until

b. If the root word ends in **-y**, the **-y** ending is changed to **-i** when **-ful** is added:

>**beauty:** beautiful
>**pity:** pitiful
>**fancy:** fanciful

c. The ending **-ful** can be added to a word for a container of some sort, forming a word meaning the amount that the container can hold, for example *bagful*, *cupful*, *pocketful*, *spoonful*. The quantity does not have to be in the container – a *spoonful* of sugar is still a *spoonful* when it is in the cup.

Full is used as a separate word. Phrases like *three bags full of sand* and *a glass full of milk* tell us about the container rather than the quantity – they tell us that the containers are full.

If you are not sure, remember that the ending **-ful** makes a word that means a *quantity*, the word **full** is to do with *containers*.

8. Adding -ize or -ise

Nowadays it is acceptable to use either **-ize** or **-ise** for most words ending in this sound:

>**characterize** or **characterise**
>**realize** or **realise**
>**apologize** or **apologise**

It is worth learning some of the common words that can only be spelt with **-ise** at the end:

advertise	exercise
advise	improvise
arise	revise
comprise	rise
compromise	supervise
despise	surprise
devise	televise

There are also a few that are always spelt with **-ize**:

capsize	size

And remember that a few words are spelt **-yse**:

analyse	electrolyse
breathalyse	paralyse
catalyse	psychoanalyse

9. i before e except after c

You will probably have heard the rule 'i before e except after c'. This works when the word has an 'ee' sound, like *deep*.

i before **e**:	**e** before **i** after **c**:
believe	ceiling
chief	receipt
siege	perceive
niece	receive

However, there are some very common exceptions to this rule that are worth learning:

weird	either
seize	neither
caffeine	species
protein	

If the word has a long 'a' sound, like *hay*, then it is usually written **ei**:

weigh	vein
eight	veil

There are also some other words to be careful with as the rule does not apply to them:

height	ancient
their	glacier
heir	society
science	

The most common pattern in this kind of words is **ie**. It might also help to remember that if these letters come at the beginning of a word, they are spelt **ei** and if they come at the end of a word, they are almost always spelt **ie**.

10. Adding endings to -our words

a. When you add certain endings to words that end in **-our**, such as *armour*, you take the **u** out of the **-our**. The endings where you have to do this are **-ant**, **-ary**, **-ation**, **-iferous**, **-fic**, **-ise** or **-ize**, and **-ous**:

glamour: glamorize
humour: humorous
honour: honorary

b. You leave the **u** in if you are adding the endings **-able**, **-er**, **-ism**, **-ist**, **-ite**:
> **honour:** honourable
> **favour:** favourite

11. -ous and -us

-ous is an adjective ending:

famous	**enormous**
anonymous	**poisonous**

and **-us** is a noun ending:

cactus	**octopus**
circus	**thesaurus**

Some words which originally came into English from Latin, such as *emeritus*, are exceptions to this rule, because many Latin adjectives end in **-us**.

12. -se and -ce

-se is a verb ending:

practise	**devise**
advise	**license**

and **-ce** is a noun ending:

practice	**device**
advice	**licence**

It may help if you remember that 'ice' is a noun.

13. -ceed, -cede and -sede

There are three words which end in **-ceed**:
> **proceed**
> **succeed**
> **exceed**

And only one which ends in **-sede**:
> **supersede**

All the others with the same final sound end with the letter pattern **-cede**:
> **precede**
> **concede**
> **recede**

American Spelling

If you have seen any pieces of writing from the United States you will probably have noticed that some words are spelt differently. There are a number of minor differences between British English and American English spelling. These are some of the most important ones.

1. When the endings **-ing**, **-ed**, and **-er** are added to verbs ending in **l** and **p** in British English, the **l** and **p** are doubled:

> **travel:** travelling
> **kidnap:** kidnapped

In American English, they are not doubled:

> **travel:** traveling
> **kidnap:** kidnaped

It is worth noting that the British English examples are exceptions to Spelling Rule number 1c. The American spellings agree with this rule.

2. For verbs that end in **-ize** or **-ise**, Americans prefer the spelling **-ize**.

3. Most words that end **-our** in British English end **-or** in American English, for example *color*, *humor*. *Saviour* and *glamour* are exceptions to this and are spelt the same way in both Britain and the United States.

4. Many words which end **-re** in British English end **-er** in American English, for example *center*, *theater*, *fiber*. Exceptions to this are words that end **-cre** or **-gre**: *acre*, *massacre* and *ogre* are spelt the same way.

5. In the United States they tend to replace the **oe** and **ae** with a single **e** in words which come from Latin and Greek, much more than they do in Britain. For example, where British English tends to have the spellings *foetus* and *diarrhoea*, American English usually has the spellings *fetus* and *diarrhea*.

6. Here is a short list of words spelt differently in American English:

British	*American*
axe	ax
catalogue	catalog
cheque	check
plough	plow
sceptic	skeptic
tyre	tire

You might also come across American spellings if you read science books. Scientists commonly use American spellings, regardless of their own nationality. This makes it easier for them to communicate discoveries and theories internationally. In your science lessons at school you will probably use the British spellings, but you might also see American spellings such as *sulfur* instead of *sulphur* and *cesium* instead of *caesium*.

One Word or Two?

This section deals with single words you might sometimes write as two words, and two-word phrases you might sometimes write as one word. Sometimes a single word can sound similar to a phrase of two or more words, but mean something different. These are also listed here.

all right, alright
It is best to spell this as two words **all right**. Some people consider the spelling **alright** to be incorrect.

already, all ready
Already is an adverb expressing things to do with time:
Are you leaving *already*?

All ready is a phrase made up of words with two separate meanings:
If you are *all ready* now, then we'll go.

altogether, all together
Altogether means 'completely' or 'in total':
Altogether we've collected £50.
I'm not *altogether* happy with your essay.

All together means 'all in a group':
I'll put these books *all together* on the shelf.

If you are not sure, try this test. **All together** can be separated by other words, **altogether** cannot:
I'll put *all these books together* on the shelf.

anyone, any one
Anyone means 'any person at all':
Anyone could tell you that.

Any one means 'any single one'. It can refer to people or things:
Choose *any one* of these cards.

If you are not sure, try this test. **Anyone** can be replaced by the word *anybody*, **any one** cannot:
Anybody could tell you that.

can not, cannot
Cannot must be used unless the word **not** is linked to the following words and needs to be emphasized. Compare these two sentences:
He *cannot* sing.
He *can not* only sing but he can dance as well.

ever, -ever
If **ever** is being used to give extra emphasis to words like *why, how* or *where* it is written as a separate word:
What ever shall we do?
How ever did you manage that?

If **ever** means 'any (thing, place, way etc) at all', it is joined to the word it is modifying to form a single word:
Do *whatever* you please.
Go *wherever* he tells you.

A single word such as **whenever** is usually part of a statement, whereas separate words like **when ever** are usually part of a question.

everyone, every one
Every one means 'each individual one' and can refer to people or things:
I looked at all the cups, and *every one* had a chip in it.

Everyone means 'every person, all people':
Everyone thinks I'm crazy.
In this street, *everyone* has a car.

If you are not sure, try this test. **Everyone** can be replaced by the word *everybody*, **every one** cannot.
Everybody thinks I'm crazy.

forever, for ever
For ever is more often written as two words, but **forever** is also correct. Some people think that **forever** should mean 'continually' (*I'm forever getting this wrong*), and **for ever** should mean 'for all time' (*I'll love you for ever*), but it is not necessary to use the words this way.

inasmuch as, in as much as
Both are correct, but **inasmuch as** is more common.

in fact
This is always written as two words.

insofar as, in so far as
Both are correct, but **in so far as** is more common.

in spite of
This is always written as three words.

instead of
This is always written as two words – **instead** is one word.

into, in to
It is a bit tricky to make the distinction between these two.
Into is a preposition. It tells you that there is movement from outside something to a position inside:
He walked *into* the room.

Or movement against something:
He bumped *into* the door.

It also indicates a change of state or condition:
The wizard turned them *into* frogs.

In to is the adverb *in* along with the preposition *to*, and is different from **into**.
Compare these two sentences:
He came *into* the room.
He came *in to* tell us the news.

In the second sentence *to* relates to the verb *tell* rather than the room. You cannot go *into tell*, because tell is a verb, not a noun.

maybe, may be
Maybe means 'perhaps':
Maybe **he will come this afternoon.**

May be is a phrase made up of the verb *may* and the verb *be*:
He *may be* coming this afternoon.

no-one, no one
The difference between **no-one** and **no one** is like the difference between *anyone* and *any one*, *everyone* and *every one*.
No-one means 'no person':
There's *no-one* there.

No one means no single individual, either a person or a thing:
No one **person could possibly eat all that.**

As a test, **no-one** can be replaced by the word *nobody*, **no one** cannot.
There's *nobody* there.

It has to be said that nowadays the hyphenated form **no-one** is often not
used, and **no one** is often used to mean 'nobody'. It is, however, more clear
what you are trying to say if you use the hyphenated form **no-one** to mean
'nobody'.

onto, on to

Onto is a single preposition:
The book fell *onto* the table.

On to is the adverb *on* along with the preposition *to*:
He went *on to* talk about his schooldays.

Unlike **into**, not everyone uses the word **onto**. Many people prefer to use **on
to** no matter what the meaning is.

sometime, some time

Sometime means 'at some point in time':
I'll do it *sometime*.

Some time means 'a little time':
I'll need *some time* to do this.

thank you

Thank you is usually written as two words:
Thank you for the book.

It is sometimes written **thank-you** if you are not saying it directly to
someone:
I'd like to say *thank-you* for the book.

Other Chambers School Titles

Chambers School Dictionary
£6.99
0550 10009 1
608pp

Chambers School Thesaurus
£6.99
0550 15004 8
608pp

Chambers School Grammar
£6.99
0550 14011 5
288pp

Chambers School Science Dictionary
£9.99
0550 10070 9
416pp

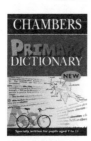

Chambers Primary Dictionary
£7.99
0550 10046 6
640pp

Chambers Primary Thesaurus
£7.99
0550 10047 4
352pp

Chambers Study Dictionary
£9.99
0550 10044 X
968pp

Chambers Study Thesaurus
£9.99
0550 10045 8
768pp